GOVERNMENTAL SECRECY AND THE FOUNDING FATHERS

Contributions in Legal Studies
Series Editor: *Paul L. Murphy*

GOVERNMENTAL SECRECY AND THE FOUNDING FATHERS

A Study in Constitutional Controls

DANIEL N. HOFFMAN

Contributions in Legal Studies, Number 17

GREENWOOD PRESS
WESTPORT, CONNECTICUT • LONDON, ENGLAND

Library of Congress Cataloging in Publication Data

Hoffman, Daniel N. 1942-
  Governmental secrecy and the founding fathers.

  (Contributions in legal studies ; no. 17 ISSN 0147-
1074)
  Bibliography: p.
  Includes index.
  1. Executive privilege (Government information)—
United States—History. 2. Government information—
United States—History. 3. Official secrets—United
States—History. I. Title. II. Series.
KF4570.H63   342.73'06   80-24554
ISBN 0-313-22166-9 (lib. bdg.)

Library of Congress Catalog Card Number: 80-24554
ISBN: 0-313-22166-9
ISSN: 0147-1074

First published in 1981

Greenwood Press
A division of Congressional Information Service, Inc.
88 Post Road West, Westport, Connecticut 06881

Printed in the United States of America

10 9 8 7 6 5 4 3 2 1

To my father and my mother

CONTENTS

ACKNOWLEDGMENTS————————

Profound thanks are due to all who read and commented on portions of this study in its many stages of development. Their thoughtful reactions added immeasurably to the substance and style of the final work.

Special appreciation for assistance beyond the call of duty, or even reason, must be extended to Hayward R. Alker, Jr., Gar Alperovitz, Britta J. Anderson, Walter Dean Burnham, Morton H. Halperin, Chad Hansen, Carlton Iddings, Duncan Kennedy, H.G. McCann, Christine M. Marwick, Beth Mintz, Jeffrey L. Pressman, and David H. Rosenbloom.

The research was partly supported by a grant from the Ford Foundation, and invaluable facilities were provided by the Center for National Security Studies.

GOVERNMENTAL SECRECY AND THE FOUNDING FATHERS

INTRODUCTION _____ 1

Almost two hundred years ago a group of talented and eminent Americans gathered in Philadelphia to write a new Constitution for the United States. On many questions there was great disagreement among them; but, whether from personal commitment or from motives of sheer expediency, all were agreed that the new government must be explicitly founded on the principles of popular sovereignty and the rule of law. Popular sovereignty meant that officials must be accountable to the people for their conduct; the rule of law meant that governmental actions would be legitimized, in significant part, not by their substance but by the constitutional regularity of the procedures whereby decisions were made.

These considerations would seem to have direct and clearcut implications for the practice of secrecy in government: secrecy is on its face antithetical to the concepts of official accountability and the rule of law, for it prevents an accurate public assessment of what has been done or what is about to be done and of the fairness of the decisionmaking procedures that are employed.

We are taught to believe that the Founding Fathers took these basic principles seriously, and, what is far more important, that the system they designed was capable of ensuring that leaders would respect these principles even if they did not personally have a strong commitment to republican values.

If this is so, it ought to be demonstrable that the Constitution provides effective checks on governmental secrecy. Otherwise we would have to conclude that the framers failed, intentionally or not, to realize the objectives we have traditionally attributed to them. Such a finding would have important implications not only for our historical understanding but also for our situation today, for we continue to place substantial reliance on constitutional safeguards for the protection of our liberties.

Even the most cursory history shows that secrecy has been a persistent phenomenon and a continuing bone of contention for our government. This study undertakes to explain this and to do so from a constitutionalist perspective: that is, I shall regard the control of secrecy as a challenge to the intentional regulatory capacity of our political system, as formalized through the norms and procedures of public law.

In the modern debates on governmental secrecy, several versions of the intent of the Founding Fathers have been offered. There is broad agreement on the definition of the problem, but diverse interpretations of the solution, if any, that the founders reached. The problem, it is commonly held, was to strike a balance between the values of broad participation and official accountability, on the one hand, and those of national security and efficient decisionmaking, on the other. Participation and accountability were inherent in the function of the legislative branch of government, while security and energetic leadership were the province of the executive. The secrecy issue, as the founders saw it, was thus framed in terms of the respective powers of Congress and the president to control information.

According to modern spokesmen for the executive branch, the founders wisely resolved this issue by vesting in the president an uncontrolled discretion to withhold information from Congress and the country, whenever he deemed it prudent to do so. This doctrine of discretion, or "executive privilege" as it is called today, is said to have been securely established in the time of George Washington.[1]

One alternative reading of the early history is that the founders failed to reach agreement on the way presidential and congressional powers were to be reconciled. According to Raoul Berger, for example, the spokesmen for congressional prerogatives to demand information were just as clear and consistent in their posture as were executive spokesmen, if not more so; because the Supreme Court was not called upon to arbitrate between them, the law in fact remained unsettled.[2]

A third view holds that the founders did not regard the secrecy issue as one of constitutional law, strictly speaking. Instead, recognizing that it would be useless and inappropriate to impose hard and fast rules on this delicate subject, the founders wisely committed the issue to the fluctuating, pragmatic restraints of the political process. When circumstances produced a confrontation between the branches of government over access to information, it was ultimately up to the people to decide between them.[3]

Unfortunately, each of these perspectives has rested on relatively fragmentary evidence; each provides at best a partial and misleading account of what the founders were attempting to accomplish and what they actually achieved. Surely, little faith can be placed in any account of the origins of executive privilege that ignores both the first occasion on which such a privilege was asserted and the first occasion on which papers supplied to Congress were actually censored.[4] Moreover, the very obscurity in which these episodes have languished casts doubt upon the assumption that the Founding Fathers were attempting to develop a principled and consistent approach to the problem of secrecy. Yet the quantity and quality of the founders' discussions of the law of secrecy belie the simplistic conclusion that secrecy was never regarded as a legal issue. Even if recent expositions of the framers' intent have partaken more of invention than of discovery, this does not mean that the effort to derive coherent lessons from the early historical experience is futile.

A review of the debate on executive privilege prompted J.R. Wiggins to write a somber essay on the shortcomings of "Lawyers as Judges of History."[5] Wiggins began by remarking that lawyers' readings of history tend to be "somewhat subjective"; he implied that the remedy would come from more careful and dispassionate research. Wiggins himself took the view that "executive privilege" is a myth, but he failed to address himself to the more disturbing question, whether the concept of the "intent of the framers" is not a myth as well. Indeed, given the elusiveness of the distinction between principled behavior and sheer expediency, between action in compliance with rules and rationalizations concocted after the fact by the protagonists or their defenders, one is prompted to wonder how much substance there is to the ideal of the rule of law itself.

Insofar as this is an empirical question, it goes to the integrity of the legal system as a realm of normative discourse. This issue has been confronted in different ways by official participants and outside observers.

The model of the legal process implicit and sometimes explicit in the opinions of the Supreme Court, in the work of legal advocates, and in the belief systems of many ordinary citizens is one based on the concept of dispassionate and precedent-biased reflection. In the paradigm case, judges are asked to dispose of a conflict between two parties in a principled manner. They seek a viable rule linking this case with others, aided by advocates who call their attention to relevant texts, precedents, facts, and policy arguments. Constrained by these presentations, the judges determine and apply a rule which does justice to the parties and to the whole society. The integrity of this process is seen as residing in the institutional independence of the judiciary; the constraints of the adversarial process; the discipline imposed by public and professional comment on the fairness, consistency, and subtlety of the courts' work; and finally by the personal morality of law officers.[6]

Empirical social scientists and "realistic" jurisprudents have criticized this model of adjudication as naive. Recognizing the role of political and often frankly result-oriented thinking in many cases, some analysts have discerned systematic social biases in the judicial performance, and some have concluded that the "rule of law" is little more than an elaborate cloak for exploitation and injustice.[7]

Whatever may be said of the objectivity of judges in a given time and place, the judicial paradigm clearly does not apply to the work of, say, the First Congress. No one seriously contends that legislatures actually behave that way; few would claim that they ought to. Rather, pragmatic bargaining is basic to their function. Yet the intent of the Founding Fathers, both as framers of the Constitution and throughout their later careers, is often expounded as if the objectivity and rational consistency of their pronouncements could be taken for granted.

A notion of the rule of law more suitable to an evaluation of the founders' intent would recognize frankly that there was intense political disagreement among them on some points; while on others, they shared prejudices that most Americans would find unwarranted today. That their decisions did not always meet the highest possible standards of fairness and rationality cannot come as a total surprise. Without a doubt the imperatives of nationbuilding, of domestic and international political conflict, often relegated concerns for the rule of law to the background. Yet this fact is not necessarily fatal for a more sophisticated model of the legal order: one which holds that there is a genius built into the very structure of government, which helps to rationalize and balance the flow of decisionmaking even though participants may have selfish, conflicting, or irrational ends in view.

To measure the integrity of the overall policymaking process would be a difficult scholarly undertaking, but the outputs of the system with respect to the "law of secrecy" can be more meaningfully assessed. Secrecy is a procedural issue. To some extent in procedural matters, having a stable rule is a value in itself, apart from the assessment of the rule's specific content. Or at least, we are prepared to recognize instability in the rules or a high incidence of apparent violation of established procedures as a sign that the system is undergoing heavy stress. Where the pattern is persistent, the claim that the rule of law prevails is not easy to maintain. Evidence of persistent efforts to rationalize and justify the flow of behavior in terms of a flexible and evolving rule system can still help distinguish such a case, however, from one of open disregard of established norms. The two cases are different at least with respect to impact on the appearance of legitimacy, and a heavy investment in maintaining appearances of law-abiding conduct might be thought to bode well for more substantive measures of justice as well.[8]

In 1974, when I began this study, these questions seemed especially relevant, for there were those who claimed that the executive was above the law. In his brief to the Supreme Court defending his right to withhold his tapes from the special prosecutor, Richard M. Nixon had ventured a curious little jest:

Lest the President's position be misunderstood, it must be stressed we do not suggest that the President has the attributes of a king. *Inter alia,* a king rules by inheritance and for life.[9]

The argument seemed to be, in effect, that a president, once duly elected, has all the powers of an absolute monarch, at least where the control of government information is concerned. If scholarship had discredited the government's most impressive efforts to show that this was what the founders actually intended, no one had really demonstrated that the founders held a contrary intent, or that the Constitution in fact supplied any effective check on presidential power in this sphere. The question might be clouded by ideological prejudice and conceptual confusion, but there seemed to be a testable empirical dimension to it as well.

This study set out to lay the problem finally to rest, at least as far as the events of the Federalist period (1787–1800) were in question. While a case might have been made for extending the full-dress treatment beyond 1800, two countervailing concerns proved decisive: the sheer bulk of material that turned up for the pre-1800 period and the fact that 1800 marked the start of a new era in party politics and, with the advent of judicial review, in constitutional law as well. Nevertheless, it will be argued, the findings of this study have relevance for the understanding of secrecy practices in later periods, including the present.

If legal analysts have slighted the complexity of secrecy as a political phenomenon, social scientists have seldom viewed it as a potential object of intentional regulation. Secrecy appears in the empirical literature as endemic to social and organizational behavior because it is functional in a wide variety of ways;[10] yet in more policy-oriented studies the standard normative-ideological and rational-balancing formulations tend to prevail.[11] The question is seldom asked, how such a simplistic norm system can deal effectively with behavior so varied in its causes and consequences from one situation to another. How, for instance, can the law of executive privilege take account of the fact that Congress is sometimes controlled by the president's allies, sometimes by his opponents, and sometimes by neither? And if this difficulty is deemed to justify refraining from making hard and fast rules on the subject, what are the costs of this omission likely to be?

The history of secrecy in the Federalist period is a case study that promised to shed a good deal of light on these questions. The first task was to set the factual record straight, insofar as available documents would permit. In light of an exhaustive survey of a wide range of primary and secondary sources,[12] it became clear that the legal legacy of the founders was substantially more complex than previous studies had suggested. If the founders were not agreed on the doctrine of executive privilege as expounded by recent official spokesmen, neither were they divided into two clear-cut schools of thought, espousing liberal and conservative views, or presidential and congressional prerogatives respectively. Rather, the course of legal development is to be understood in the context of the overall functioning of the political process.

The legal precedents of the Federalist period developed in a tortuous and sporadic manner that is certainly not adequately described in terms of a quasi-judicial lawmaking model. There was, by the end of the period, a general consensus on some basic doctrinal points, including the president's right to censor documents requested by Congress, at least where the protection of individual safety required it. This and other rules about political communication and secrecy emerged neither from a process of careful, collective deliberation about the costs and benefits for the nation of adopting one rule or another, nor from a sensible, stable compromise between the institutional claims of the several governmental bodies, but from a series of piecemeal decisions, each of which was strongly affected if not entirely dominated by the short-run partisan and policy concerns of those participating. Nevertheless, the energy and skill invested in constitutional analysis and disputation, much of it strictly for official and not for public consumption, went far beyond the minimum required for keeping up appearances. The gaps and inconsistencies in the course of doctrinal development arose not from sheer indifference or incompetence but from the fact that legalization had to compete with other objectives of equal or greater priority. There was, in overview, an earnest but only partially successful effort to bring secrecy behavior under the control of constitutional norms and mechanisms.

The most promising basis for constitutional regulation lay not in explicit textual norms but in the built-in difference between congressional and executive perspectives and incentives. (In the Federalist period, the courts played only a peripheral role.) The structure of separated powers was designed, if not to generate stable and efficient procedures for governmental communications, at least to prevent abuses of power, such as arbitrary and excessive secrecy. The actual working of this system was pervasively affected by the unforeseen growth of political parties, which imposed a new, crosscutting pattern of loyalties upon the formal structure of interbranch relations. At the same time, the nation experienced a protracted and intense crisis in foreign relations, creating tremendous pressures for unity and decisive leadership. These phenomena strongly discouraged Congress from exercising a steady and vigorous check on executive power and disrupted the maturation of procedures for generating legal consensus among the branches of government.

The emergent alternative to a stable system of legal controls on secrecy developed less by choice than by default; it consisted essentially of the transformation of secrecy into an electoral campaign issue. Leaders were subject to repudiation at the polls if they failed to mobilize public support for their policies, or if they acted in an excessively high-handed and arbitrary manner. The old politics of status deference was giving way to a more open, participatory style; even those leaders most frightened and repelled by this process of social, ideological, and political change were forced to adapt and even to assist its development. Party competition and public opinion were increasingly effective forces for publicity over time.

Nevertheless, this kind of normative control system was not functionally equivalent to legal regulation in the strict sense. The defective regulation of official discretion was revealed by the end of the Federalist period to have significant costs, when a dominant party took electoral success as vindicating both its proclaimed policies and its haughty style. Secrecy was used by high officials to promote warlike policies, and harsh repression of political opponents was triggered by leaks of sensitive official information. While the Federalists' "reign of terror" was terminated by the elections of 1800, not all of their "precedents" were repudiated by the victorious Republicans; the system remained vulnerable to similar cycles of abuse in future times of crisis.[13] And so it remains today.

The Framing

of the

Constitution————————2

Intellectual and Political Background

The classical literature of statecraft, advising rulers on the proper conduct of their affairs, took an ambivalent attitude toward secrecy, as writers struggled to reconcile conflicting pragmatic and moral perspectives. In private life, Christian morality tended to regard secrecy as suspect—the mark of one who had something sinful to conceal. But many churchmen invoked a distinction between private and public spheres of morality: the control of information particular to the sovereign was seen as a natural prerogative of secular authority. Indeed, secrets of state were viewed as symbolizing and safeguarding the dignity of the ruler and the integrity of his function. The secular garden too had its forbidden fruit. Not only was specific political knowledge to be carefully kept from public view, because the *arcana imperii* were hard for laymen to understand and accept. The entire workings of government were to be surrounded by an air of mystery, to maintain the awe in which the ruler was held by the ruled.

This doctrine, validating secrecy as more or less a good in itself, was a natural concomitant of the prevailing view that governing was a function bestowed by divine authority on a select few, and that those not of noble blood had no right to participate in the business of government.[1] It was supported also by the psychological insight that people tend to fear what they do not understand, whereas familiarity has a propensity to breed contempt. Thus Francis Bacon counselled princes to be reticent even with their closest advisers, lest their schemes be betrayed and their weaknesses be exposed to hostile view.[2]

Machiavelli, a keen student of elite as well as mass psychology, treated secrecy as basically a matter of prudence. Remarking on the special difficulties faced by republics in practicing secrecy and deception, he recounted how the Athenian assembly had once appointed a representative to entertain a secret proposal by Themistocles. It proved to involve betrayal of an ally. When the representative reported that the plan was advantageous but dishonest, the assembly declined to pursue it.[3]

A secrecy doctrine reflecting the ideology of one-man rule had to be qualified in light of pragmatic concerns as monarchs grew more and more dependent on numerous officials and financiers, often drawn from relatively humble ranks, for the effective conduct of government. Bacon's counsel to the ruler was unsuited for plans that could only be carried out with the cooperation of a bureaucracy or of a parliament. In this context, the norm of secrecy was also increasingly subject to moral attack.

The rise of a counter-ideology was closely linked to the claims of an economically and socially ascendant bourgeoisie to a share in political power. Backed by commercial wealth, emboldened by spreading literacy and anticlerical religious doctrines, the new class asserted a right to participate in key decisions, such as taxation, and sought to exercise this right through control of parliamentary institutions and enhancement of the prerogatives of those bodies. Bourgeois politicians and theoreticians clearly perceived that meaningful participation depended on timely access to critical information. The anti-monarchical movements of the seventeenth and eighteenth centuries thus tended to brand governmental secrecy as an outmoded relic of absolutist, aristocratical regimes. Just as the churchman must talk directly with God, rather than repose his trust in a bishop who alone is consecrated to perform the sacred rites and mysteries, so also the citizen must personally participate in public affairs, and not simply trust his betters to derive sound policy from secret facts and esoteric principles. The more radical republicans, with Bentham, maintained that even an elected representative assembly was no more justified than a monarch in resorting to secrecy. Governmental secrecy was intrinsically wrong, seeming to belie the average man's capacity to understand and judge the issues of the day. Were men enlightened and rational, surely secrets would be unnecessary. The dissemination of information would uplift the public mind and help bring about the enlightenment needed to make self-government work.[4]

Of course, the advent of republican theories and forms of government did not entirely suppress the old prudential arguments for secrecy, nor could it have without somehow eliminating the sources of political conflict themselves. Moderates were obliged to recognize that international disputes, rivalries between kings and parliaments, and exigencies of class struggle made secrecy essential from time to time. In fact, the idea that effective government was a rather esoteric business best left to the discretion of propertied elites was very much alive.

What republican theory did accomplish, though, was to reverse the old presumption in favor of secrecy, based on the divine right of kings and nobles, and replace it with a presumption in favor of publicity, based on the doctrine of popular sovereignty. Defenders of secrecy were now obliged to develop new, more limited rationales for the practice; increasingly, too, they were compelled to reach out actively for public support for their policies. As citizens learned they could influence policy by withholding taxes and moral support, or by using the ever-widening franchise to choose among competing elites, publicity became more and more advantageous to both incumbents and challengers.

In eighteenth-century England and America, these ideological and social developments were reflected in changes in formal governmental practice. The Tudor system of press licensing was abandoned in England in 1695, and the law of libel evolved in a permissive direction; newspapers flourished. Parliamentary proceedings, once kept strictly secret from public and crown alike, began to be legally reported in the reign of George III. Of equal significance, Parliament repeatedly asserted its power as "grand inquest of the nation" to inquire into the doings and wrongdoings of the king's ministers, to demand documents, call witnesses, and take such remedial actions, up to and including impeachment, as it deemed necessary. In all these respects, the American colonies either followed suit or surged ahead.[5]

American legislatures typically kept journals of their proceedings, and sometimes public meetings were held. Of the constitutions adopted by the states during the Revolution, two (those of New York and Pennsylvania) required that legislative sessions be generally public. Eight states specifically empowered their legislatures to call for the records of executive bodies; none contained a contrary or even a qualifying proposition. In addition, America had a relatively liberal concept of freedom of the press reaching back to the *Zenger* trial of 1735.[6]

The Revolution, whatever the motives of its various leaders may have been, put a premium on the doctrine of popular sovereignty as a legitimizing force, and over the years the base of political participation substantially broadened. Yet for obvious defensive reasons, the Continental Congress swore its members to secrecy, and initially none of its proceedings was officially published. These consisted largely of military plans, diplomatic feelers to European powers, and desperate efforts to raise funds. Even under wartime conditions, though, the trend was toward greater publicity. With democratic sentiment raised to new heights by the rhetoric invoked to justify the war, and with pressures to regularize and streamline the structures of government, the goals of efficiency and of legitimation seemed to coincide. Periodic publication of congressional proceedings was inaugurated in 1777, and weekly publication became the rule in 1779.[7] After 1781, ostensibly due to lack of public interest, the Articles of Confederation required only a monthly publication. In principle, any information laid before Congress was a matter of public record unless placed under specific injunction of secrecy; and the votes and official acts of Congress were likewise, unless entered in a separate secret journal reserved for matters of delicate nature.[8]

The new government of the United States did not emulate New York and Pennsylvania in holding regular public sessions; Congress viewed itself more as a grand council of the states than as a popular representative body, and its correspondence with the state governments was deemed, in principle, an adequate publicity system. In 1783, however, Alexander Hamilton of New York and James Wilson of Pennsylvania spearheaded an effort to open the doors of Congress to a public audience for a debate on the national debt. The effort, branded by southerners as a move to subject Congress to the local merchants' influence, was rebuffed. It was soon renewed as a broader proposition, to open the doors for all business, "unless otherwise ordered by a vote or by the rules of the house" and was again defeated.[9]

Secrecy, though deemed essential for effective military and diplomatic action, created serious irritants in domestic politics. Toward the war's end, conflict surfaced in Congress over the financial problems of the government. Finance Minister Robert Morris of Pennsylvania was assailed by Rhode Islanders over his support for a national impost. In 1782, he was charged with deliberately understating the credit and assets of the United States in order to concoct a case for the tax, whose real purpose was to create an oppressive government establishment like that of King George.[10]

Efforts by Rhode Island delegates to Congress to expose Morris's maneuvers and defeat the impost produced moves in Congress to silence and discredit the offending members. When David Howell admitted that he had leaked to the newspapers certain extracts from the official correspondence of American representatives abroad, most delegates, including Hamilton and Virginia's James Madison, felt that a sharp rebuke was in order. Howell had given a wildly optimistic view of the situation, falsely claiming total American success in its borrowing campaign—a claim the government could hardly disavow, however, without severe embarrassment. Moreover, he had leaked word of a pending treaty with Sweden not yet known to third countries. These matters were delicate; yet the fact that the specific documents in question had not been placed under injunction of secrecy, according to rule, supplied a partial defense for Howell, as did his claim that his constituency, the government of Rhode Island, had a perfect right to know the proceedings of the national government. After much wrangling, Congress resolved to send a report to the governor of Rhode Island, pointedly suggesting this might be needed to clear up the misconceptions created by Howell's distorted account. Howell was obliged to resign as a delegate; a move to adopt a rule imposing a secrecy oath on all members of Congress failed of passage.[11]

A better reception was accorded to proposals to strengthen the administrative bureaus of the government. By early 1782 the financial and diplomatic affairs of the government had been taken from committees and confided to the care of full-time secretaries, not themselves members of Congress. Yet both Congress as a body and individual members thereof had free access to the records of said offices, with public disclosure subject to majority vote. At first secrecy was decided on a case-by-case basis; later, in 1784, Congress resolved that all correspondence from agents abroad should be treated as secret until declassified by vote.[12]

The system of relatively centralized decisionmaking was still weak in key respects: the states could not be obliged to defray essential expenses, honor the terms of the peace with Great Britain, or support the diplomatic efforts of the national government. Bitter conflict erupted when Foreign Secretary John Jay, in his negotiations with Spain, sought approval to abandon certain terms that had been insisted upon by southern states. Jay's opponents, who felt that he not only placed northern over southern interests, but sometimes favored English over American views, wanted to go public with their charges. Congress refused to lift its injunction of secrecy; the episode's aftertaste lingered for a solid decade.[13]

One final secrecy episode from this period was the congressional response to Shay's Rebellion. A secret committee report advocated using force against the rebels and proposed overcoming the resistance of the state of Massachusetts to the introduction of outside troops by falsely claiming that Indians rather than Shaysites were the designated target. This plan, however, was not implemented.[14]

Now, there were several distinct points of view to be heard on the significance of these episodes. Each involved political controversy, and not surprisingly the various antagonists drew diverse conclusions. To some, the salient point was the difficulty of protecting sensitive diplomatic, financial, or military information in a system where every member of Congress was entitled to such information as a matter of course. To others, the salient point was the danger of abuses inherent in even such a modest delegation of executive authority as had been made to Morris and Jay under the Articles of Confederation. The power to act in secret was a power to serve partial interests. Thus those who endorsed the need for secrecy could be, and were, painted variously as prudent statesmen or would-be tyrants. In the 1780s a rift had progressively developed between advocates and opponents of constitutional reform, aiming at a stronger national government. The advocates tended to support both an augmentation of national authority—to tax, regulate commerce, and so forth—at the expense of the states, and a reshaping of the national government so that its powers could be more effectively exercised. They felt the existing government had conspicuously failed to achieve the goals of national unity and fiscal and military strength; and they labelled the situation of the country as critical.

Indeed, it was true that there was rivalry and suspicion between the commercial centers of the North and the agricultural interests of the South. Inhabitants of the seaboard had economic and political perspectives sharply different from those of the frontier. Reconciliation and integration of the regions was inhibited by formidable physical barriers to communication and trade[15] as well as by religious and cultural cleavages that seemed very substantial to Americans trying to work together with their compatriots.

Cooperation might have been easier in good times, but the economy had not entirely recovered from the Revolution. The unpaid foreign and domestic debt was substantial; poverty was rampant, and conspicuously so among veterans of the war. The clamor for relief was rising, and bitter class conflict had erupted in several states. Violent episodes between frontiersmen and Indian tribes were another cause of incessant suffering and anxiety for the future.

The powers of Europe, and especially Great Britain, were vigorously engaged in overt and covert schemes to exploit these tensions. Offers of commercial preference were extended to various states or territories in hopes of weaning their loyalties away from the Union; diplomatic and military support was tendered to warlike Indians; full implementation of the peace accord of 1783 was repeatedly postponed.[16]

Nationalists were agreed that the future of the Union was in doubt. Not only might the states drift further apart, but ultimately the restoration of foreign rule might present itself as the only alternative to utter chaos. The answer, they believed, was a strong government that could stand up to the powers of Europe, to the Indians, and to radical dissidents at home, putting an end to the reign of vacillation, parochialism, and anarchy. At the same time, this proposal was hampered by a tremendous public aversion to any system that smacked of the monarchy so recently overthrown. Indeed, for all the problems facing the country there was widespread opposition to strengthening the general government, and this was based on libertarian and democratic sentiments as well as the mutual jealousies of regional elites. Structurally, moreover, change was almost ruled out by the fact that the Articles of Confederation required the unanimous consent of member states to amend its terms.

Unanimity could not be obtained while many influentials were decrying proposals for a stronger government as unnecessary in fact and pernicious in principle. Not all were persuaded that a genuine crisis existed or that the national interest, as opposed to factional ones, demanded constitutional change. Rhode Island, for one, continued to be dominated by forces unalterably opposed to the nationalist drive. In many states, constitutional issues were intertwined with disputes over specific policies and the right of various social groups or political factions to participate in or to control the governmental process.

From the beginning, then, there has been a split among observers of the constitutional movement, between those who presented the men of 1787 and their political heirs as farsighted statesmen acting on behalf of the national interest, and those who told the same story in terms of a reactionary coup by a clique of merchants, bankers, and large landowners animated largely by immediate profit motives.[17] This split persists today and seems to point to mutually inconsistent interpretations of attitudes toward and decisions about secrecy. For the purposes of this study, however, no choice between these views is really necessary. The framers may not have represented the total range of social classes and interests that existed, but they did pretty well encompass the range of things that could be said about governmental secrecy—then or, for that matter, even now. A substantial opening of the political process had already occurred, in some cases at the initiative of "conservatives," such as Hamilton. By the same token, libertarians like Madison had supported moves to clamp down on communications, such as Howell's leak, that seemed to threaten national security. Very few whose voices counted politically were prepared to endorse a radical call for absolute publicity. To the extent that the nationalists and their opponents did have distinctive views on the issue, the minority voice was able to be heard during and after the Constitutional Convention.

The interpretation of the framing advanced by Charles Beard and his followers might be thought to imply that, since the Constitution was really a work of class oppression rather than of nation-building, its language has neither normative force nor, probably, causal effect, but can be dismissed as essentially window dressing. Yet it is a *non sequitur* in terms of constitutional theory itself to suppose that the putative cynicism of the framers could suffice to deprive their work of deeper interest. The purpose of this study is to show how the constitutional control system has worked, and this does not necessarily depend on how any given person intended it to work. What the skeptical account contributes is the point that the Constitution, whatever its wording and whatever the hopes that inspired its adoption, would have to be used in a context marked by significant levels of class, regional, and other conflict. Yet there were also significant elements of common interest and ideological consensus. It remains to be seen which elements predominated in the specific ways the framers dealt with problems of secrecy.

There was, in fact, a characteristic bias to the pronouncements of nationalist leaders when confronted with issues of secrecy. It was by no means a bias toward secrecy as such. Publicity was never opposed in principle; rather it was seen as unworkable in certain contexts or spheres of activity. As a result, the values of effective government and accountable government had to be balanced and reconciled. The favored device for accomplishing this was institutional pluralism.

The notions of a mixed constitution, separation of powers, and checks and balances had been elaborated by various British and French theorists over the years. A key claim of all these thinkers was that efficiency, liberty, and social harmony could be advanced in tandem by a division of institutional responsibilities.[18] American nationalists, in particular, looked to the scheme of a strong, independent executive and an open, responsive legislature. Of course, this broad formula was compatible with a great variety of working systems. In practice, the legislature might be a rubber stamp, or it might prevent the pursuit of any effective policy. The executive might be a figurehead, or a caesar. There was disagreement as to which hazard—tyranny or impotence—was the greater in the America of the Confederation period. Yet observers of all stripes tended to share a belief in the efficacy of constitutional arrangements, if properly drawn, to achieve desired results. In the 1780s both proponents and opponents of a stronger government appealed to the national interest, both sides purporting to believe that constitutional choices were relevant, important, and rationally decidable by the citizenry. To a degree, this posture tended to become a self-fulfilling one.

The Constitutional Convention was the culmination of a protracted nationalist drive to secure amendments to the Articles of Confederation. A convention called at Annapolis in 1786 was poorly attended; disappointed delegates worked for a new meeting the following year and proposed that the delegates' mandate should be broadened beyond the original project of enhancing the government's tax and commerce powers, "to devise such further provisions as shall appear to them necessary to render the constitution of the Federal Government adequate to the exigencies of the Union."[19]

The men who gathered in Philadelphia in May 1787 were a decidedly elite group in terms of wealth and background, as well as in talent. Yet they differed widely in doctrinal predilection as well as in economic and political interest. Sectional, cultural, and personal rivalries stood in the way of consensus. True, most shared the assumption that a stronger government was needed, and that people of their class would prosper if one could be established. Some may have hoped to profit in a more immediate sense from appreciation in the value of property they held. Yet if they stood to benefit from the changes on which they could agree, this was not sufficient to bring such changes about. Their power was only to recommend, not to dictate. They would have to persuade the states that reform would benefit all, and that a stronger national government could enhance, not destroy, the liberties for which the people had shed their blood.

The Secrecy of the Convention

At the very outset the framers agreed to reveal nothing of their doings while the convention was in progress. The chamber would

be guarded by sentries, and the debates would not be officially recorded. The official journal would show only formal motions and
roll call votes tabulated by state.[20] Only the delegates themselves
were to have access to the journal.

One delegate's carelessness actually prompted the presiding officer, General Washington, to issue a stiff reprimand.

> "I am sorry to find that some one Member of this Body, has been so
> neglectful of the secrets of the Convention as to drop in the State
> House a copy of their proceedings. . . . I must entreat Gentlemen to
> be more careful, least our transactions get into the News Papers, and
> disturb the public repose by premature speculations. . . ." At the
> same time, he bowed, picked up his hat, and quitted the room with a
> dignity so severe that every person seemed alarmed.[21]

This secrecy encouraged a torrent of wild speculation about what
was afoot, until rumors that a foreign prince was to be offered the
crown had to be countered by denials leaked to the press. In the
face of criticism from friends and colleagues who had hoped to be
kept closely informed, delegates argued that secrecy was needed to
protect the convention from outside pressure until a complete plan
could be developed. Madison said bluntly that "No Constitution
would ever have been adopted by the Convention if the debates had
been public."[22]

At the time of final adjournment the question of publicity arose
once again. Some delegates thought the journals should be de-
stroyed; but the convention voted to deposit them in Washington's
care, "subject to the order of Congress, if ever formed under the
Constitution."[23] Continued secrecy was now deemed essential to
the prospects for ratification. Hamilton wrote:

> Had the deliberations been open while going on, the clamours of fac-
> tion would have prevented any satisfactory result. Had they been
> afterwards disclosed, much food would have been afforded to inflam-
> matory declamation. Propositions, made without due reflection, would
> have been handles for a profusion of ill-natured accusation.[24]

It was certainly true that the convention had entertained some
very controversial ideas. Thus, in introducing the Virginia plan,
Governor Edmund Randolph had advised the convention that:

> Our chief danger arises from the democratic parts of our constitu-
> tions. . . . None of the [state] constitutions have provided sufficient
> checks against the democracy.[25]

Yet the major conflicts among the framers involved state and sectional interests. The elitist tendency of the convention's work was apparent from the Constitution itself; the crucial secret was the process whereby the document had evolved. In the ratification debates the Constitution was effectively promoted as a grand design, rather than a patchwork of compromises. This could scarcely have been done if each provision were identified with the demands of a particular faction; the debate would then have tended to focus on the concessions made by each side, rather than the merits of the plan as a whole.

Still, the usefulness of secrecy was not enough to banish ideological misgivings. The point was forcefully made by Jefferson, observing events from his diplomatic station in Paris:

> I am sorry that they began their deliberations by so abominable a
> precedent as that of tying up the tongues of their members. Nothing
> can justify this example but the innocence of their intentions, & igno-
> rance of the value of public discussions. I have no doubt that all their
> other measures will be good & wise. It is really an assembly of demi-
> gods.[26]

If Jefferson overspoke in suggesting that secrecy could never be justified, he also did so in calling the convention's secrecy a "precedent." In a strict legal sense it was nothing of the kind, for the convention was in essence an extralegal act. The framers held themselves answerable not to the written law or the existing governmental structures but to a higher law, to the people, and to the judgment of history. Thus the Constitution could declare that the ratification of nine states would give it force, even though the Articles of Confederation provided for amendments by unanimous consent. The delegates' refusal to consult with the authorities that had appointed them and the failure of some delegations to abide by instructions limiting their powers[27] were not merely tactical maneuvers. They also dramatized the impotence and irrelevance of the existing order and underlined the emphatic break with the past that the new Constitution entailed. In a sense the convention was a symbolic rite of passage for the nation, and secrecy enhanced the magical power of the event.

The point is not simply that the convention was a special case. It was, indeed, unique, and therefore of little force as a precedent, but beyond this, the reticence of the framers can be viewed in light of their hope to design a system that would win acceptance and function properly in spite of the shortcomings of those who created it and those who would succeed them. Despite Jefferson's talk of "demigods," the Founding Fathers were eminently realistic about the temptations to which political man is subject, and they claimed no personal immunity. The genius of constitutionalism lay in its honest confrontation of such realities and its attempt to contain them by the resort to checks and balances, fair procedures, and public accountability. The merit of the framers' design deserves to be judged without reference to the impurities of personal motives or the vicissitudes of the negotiating process. Moreover, even if the secrecy of the convention reflected an antidemocratic bias on the framers' part, they did not offer the convention itself as a model for the new government. On the contrary, one principle they tried to build into the constitutional design was the very one to which Jefferson had appealed: government not by mystique but by laws made with the informed consent of the governed.

Of course this was not the only important principle involved. Few thoughtful observers, in fact, would have endorsed the radical claim that secrecy is an unqualified evil.[28] Where national security was involved, in particular, most public men were ready to grant that secrecy was often necessary. Predictably, the most ardent devotees of popular sovereignty accepted this fact reluctantly and wished to minimize its impact on the cardinal rule of publicity. Those more devoted to energy in government were apt to take an expansive view of the degree to which secrecy was essential. Thus men could differ sharply in their assessments of the recent American experience. In John Jay's view,

So often and so essentially have we heretofore suffered from the want of secrecy and despatch, that the Constitution would have been inexcusably defective, if no attention had been paid to those objects.[29]

To Jefferson, the very same want of secrecy was a source of pride.

> [T]he old Congress set an example to the world. . . . The first misfortune of the Revolutionary war, induced a motion to suppress or garble the account of it. It was rejected with indignation. The whole truth was given in all its details, and there never was another attempt in that body to disguise it.[30]

Neither of these men attended the Constitutional Convention, but both points of view were ably represented. Since the work of the convention was focused on institutional design, however, abstract philosophical questions about secrecy were bypassed. The balance between energy and responsibility in government was to be regulated by the device of separated powers. Thus the "intent of the framers" regarding secrecy was manifest primarily in the duties or incentives to release information and the privileges or capabilities to withhold it, which they vested in the several branches of government, and in the procedures they provided for resolving difficulties that might develop in regulating the flow of governmental information.

Congressional Publicity and Secrecy

Under the Articles of Confederation the national government consisted simply of the Congress, a body in which each state delegation had one vote and important decisions required the concurrence of at least nine states.[31] The Articles provided for reporting most congressional proceedings promptly to the states, with a significant exception:

> The Congress . . . shall publish a Journal of their proceedings monthly, except such parts thereof relating to treaties, alliances or military operations, as in their judgment require secrecy; and the yeas and nays of the delegates of each state on any question shall be entered on the Journal, when it is desired by any delegate; and the delegates of a state, or any of them, at his or their request shall be furnished

with a transcript of the said Journal, except such parts as are above
excepted, to lay before the legislatures of the several states.[32]

It was quite clear that this provision could not be retained without change in the new Constitution. Whether or not it provided for
the right "amount" of secrecy, the clause was not geared to the
new institutional structure being developed. First of all, it pointed
too emphatically to the states as the audience for congressional proceedings. Second, it presupposed a single governing body in which
both legislative and executive powers were vested.

Under the new federal scheme, the role of the states was to be
downgraded. Members of Congress would be not just emissaries of
the state governments but also representatives of the people in a
more direct sense. Thus far the framers were agreed, but not all of
them wished to have the state governments totally subordinated to
the national, or the people of the smaller states to those of the
larger. The smaller states fought to preserve the principle of equal
representation for each state, regardless of population. This issue,
of course, was finally resolved by the compromise of a bicameral
legislature, in which one house would follow each of the contending plans.

The Senate, it was contemplated, would resemble the old Congress in representing the special interests of the states. The House
of Representatives was to be a more "popular" body, both in its
mode of selecting members and in its lines of communication. It
was essential for members of the House, therefore, to operate with
high visibility, whereas senators could perform their quasi-diplo-
matic functions in a less formal and public manner.

The bicameral plan developed to deal with the rival views of
federalism was also useful in resolving the tension between the
principles of energetic leadership and popular participation. The
old government lacked a powerful executive, and the framers were
determined to repair the defect. Yet there was much concern that a
strong executive would promote the special interests of his own
state and region at the expense of the rest. Ultimately the framers
took advantage of bicameralism by giving the Senate a share in the
executive power. The Senate was envisaged as a handpicked council
of elder statesmen, like those in most of the states, which might sit

with the president and deliberate on "executive" matters, especially those of foreign policy. This council would control the president's freedom of action, while avoiding the instability or paralysis that might flow from giving an executive role to such an unwieldy and heterogeneous body as the lower house. Such ideas could well have supported an expectation that the Senate, unlike the House, would not necessarily conduct its affairs in public.

Yet the allocation of executive functions was a wide open question when the convention first came to consider the matter of congressional publicity. The intricate history of Article 1, section 5 shows how unresolved questions about the division of powers bedeviled the framers in their attempt to deal with the secrecy issue.[33]

The Committee of Detail, instructed to draft a detailed constitutional plan, turned naturally to the Articles of Confederation as a starting point. Working from the provision quoted earlier, James Wilson adapted its language to the new institutional scheme, while broadening the provision for secrecy by dropping the former limitation to diplomatic and military matters.

> Each House shall keep a Journal of its Proceedings, and shall from Time to Time publish them, except such parts as in their Judgment require Secrecy; and the Yeas and Nays of the Members of each House on any Question shall at the Desire of any Member be entered on the Journal.[34]

John Rutledge, another member of the committee, and, like Wilson, a future Supreme Court justice, suggested significant changes, which were incorporated into the committee's report to the floor.

> The House of Representatives and the Senate when it shall be acting in a legislative Capacity shall keep a Journal of its Proceedings, and shall from Time to Time publish them, and the Yeas and Nays of the Members of each House on any Question shall at the Desire of one-fifth of the Members be entered on the Journal.[35]

While Wilson's version would have given both houses unlimited discretion to impose secrecy, the committee report reduced discretion to a minimum. It gave the House no power of secrecy and divided the Senate's functions, as it were, mechanically into entirely public "legislative" functions and entirely secret "executive" ones.

The matter came before the full convention on August 10. At the very close of the session, Elbridge Gerry of Massachusetts offered an amendment to the secrecy provision drafted by the committee. Gerry, who was to prove an unusually stubborn and consistent advocate of publicity, moved to strike the words, "when acting in a legislative capacity." The clause would then read simply, "The House of Representatives and the Senate shall keep a Journal of [their] Proceedings, and shall from Time to Time publish them." It would contain no provision whatever for secrecy. Gerry's amendment passed by a vote of seven states to three, but on the morning of August 11 the matter was quickly reopened.[36] Madison and Rutledge now offered a new amendment, restoring a secrecy option for "such non-legislative activity of the Senate" as that body judged to require secrecy. This proposal was similar to the committee draft, but more flexible in that it made publication of the Senate's executive[37] business a discretionary matter. This amendment the convention rejected by a resounding vote of ten states to one.

On the face of it this vote, with that on Gerry's amendment, suggests that the convention was opposed to any form of congressional secrecy. Another impression emerges from John Mercer's remark in opposition to the Madison-Rutledge amendment: "This implies that other powers than legislative will be given to the Senate which he hoped would not be given."[38] Both the committee report and the new amendment presupposed that executive power would be divided between the president and the Senate—an idea unacceptable to those who wished all executive power to lie with the president, but also repugnant to those who wished both the House and Senate to share in it. By now all sides had focused on the secrecy clause as a test case, anticipatory to the main debate on Article 2.

Gerry and Roger Sherman tried to bypass the collateral issues by returning to the formula of the Articles. They offered an amendment providing simply that each house should publish the journals of its proceedings, "except such as relate to treaties and military operations." This was seen as another partisan stratagem, for, as Madison noted, "Their object was to give each House a discretion in such cases." This amendment was defeated by a nine to two vote. Again, the result signified neither a wholesale rejection of secrecy nor a determination to extend it to matters beyond the diplomatic and military spheres.

Oliver Ellsworth now proposed that the entire clause be abandoned. The legislature, he urged, would not fail to publish, for the people would not permit this.[39] This proposal met with unanimous disapproval, and, as Madison recorded:

> Mr. Wilson thought the expunging of the clause would be very improper. The people have a right to know what their Agents are doing or have done, and it should not be in the option of the Legislature to conceal their proceedings. Besides as this is a clause in the existing Confederation, the not retaining it would furnish the adversaries of the reform with a pretext by which weak and suspicious minds may be easily misled.[40]

The problem of making some provision for secrecy remained, and the convention finally resorted to a proviso that had the virtue of being utterly noncommittal as to the substantive powers of either house. By a vote of six to four, with one state abstaining, they approved a formula essentially identical to Wilson's original draft in committee.

> The House of Representatives, and the Senate, shall keep a journal of their proceedings, and shall, from time to time, publish them, except such parts thereof as in their judgment require secrecy.[41]

The extreme flexibility of this language enabled it to gain majority support, but it also seemed to some to invite abuses. As late as September 14, a move was made to restore a stricter formulation.

> Col. Mason & Mr. Gerry moved to insert after the word "parts" the words "of the proceedings of the Senate" so as to require publication of all the proceedings of the House of Representatives. It was intimated on the other side that cases might arise where secrecy might be necessary in both Houses—Measures preparatory to a declaration of

war in which the House of Representatives was to concur, were instanced.[42]

The motion failed, by a vote of seven to three, with one abstention, and a move to reconsider was rebuffed, seven states to four. The convention, rapidly nearing completion of its work, was disinclined to reopen the vexing search for a formula that would perfectly satisfy everyone.

Mason, however, was determined to narrow the loophole in at least one crucial respect, and so he moved to add to Article 1, section 9 a requirement "that an account of the public expenditures should be annually published." After replacing the term "annually" with the more flexible "from time to time," the convention agreed unanimously to this amendment.[43] Certainly the failure to insert a secrecy proviso in this clause was no oversight. While the framers accepted the need for secrecy in international affairs, they saw no need to compromise on the fundamental principle of legislative accountability in the disposition of public funds.

Gerry and Mason, at least, remained dissatisfied. Both refused to sign the completed Constitution, and Gerry gave the secrecy of the House's journals a prominent place among his stated reasons.[44] As we shall see, the ratification debates occasioned further criticism of the loose language of Article 1, section 5. Yet this ambiguity was trivial in comparison to the vagueness of the Constitution concerning the powers of the president.

Executive Secrecy and Publicity

The framers agreed that the new government of the United States ought to possess a strong, independent executive body. Yet so powerful was sectional rivalry that substantial support existed for the idea of a regionally balanced three-man executive or a Council of Revision to control the president.

Various objections were offered to these plans. Among the many advantages of a single executive, delegates repeatedly mentioned the greater secrecy with which one man could conduct the nation's foreign affairs. Yet the framers realized that this capability posed a threat to the democratic concept of accountability.[45] On June 4, for example, George Mason said:

> The chief advantages which have been urged in favor of unity in the Executive, are the secrecy, the dispatch, the vigor and energy which the government will derive from it, especially in time of war. That these are great advantages I shall most readily allow. . . . Yet perhaps a little reflection may incline us to doubt whether these advantages are not greater in theory than in practice, or lead us to enquire whether there is not some pervading principle in republican government which sets at naught & tramples upon that boasted superiority.[46]

If the plan of a one-man executive finally prevailed, it was not because the framers did not care about accountability. Rather they were unwilling to achieve it by giving the states a power to paralyze the executive branch. They wished the president to be accountable not to the states but to all the people, and even those most concerned for accountability were unpersuaded that a multiple executive would help to achieve this. Thus John Dickinson declared on June 6:

> Secrecy, vigor & despatch are not the principal properties required in the Executive. Important as these are, that of responsibility is more so, which can only be preserved, by leaving it singly to discharge its functions.[47]

William Davie made the point more explicitly in the North Carolina ratification debate.

> With respect to the unity of the Executive, the superior energy and secrecy wherewith one person can act, was one of the principles on which the Convention went. But a more predominant principle was, the more obvious responsibility of one person. It was observed that, if there were a plurality of persons, and a crime should be committed, when their conduct was to be examined, it would be impossible to fix the fact on any one of them, but that the public were never at a loss when there was but one man.[48]

What, then, was to be the mode of presidential accountability to the people; and how was it to be reconciled with the desiderata of "vigor, secrecy, and despatch?" The answer lay in the president's relationship with Congress—in the crucial device of separation of powers.

The president, as the framers conceived him, was to be a remote and awe-inspiring figure rather than a politician with the common touch. His ties with the people would be indirect; they had no immediate role in his election, in guiding his conduct of office, or in his impeachment for grave misconduct. Indeed, aside from foreign ambassadors and the heads of executive departments, the two houses of Congress were the president's only necessary links with the outside world.

The primary safeguard against tyranny was that the president's power to take independent initiatives was carefully circumscribed. His main duty was to execute the laws passed by Congress, and his discretion was further limited by congressional control of the purse strings. In fact, for the most part the framers were less concerned with restraining the president than with making it possible for him to provide a modicum of leadership. They feared that a Congress jealous of its prerogatives would not respond favorably to legislative proposals coming from the executive branch. It was the desire to legitimize such proposals that called forth an explicit statement of the president's right and duty to keep Congress informed.

The idea seems to have originated with the constitutional plan submitted by Charles Pinckney, which said of the president,

> It shall be his Duty to inform the Legislature of the Condition of the United States so far as may respect his Department—to recommend Matters to their Consideration. . . .[49]

The Committee of Detail incorporated a similar provision into its report.

> He shall from Time to Time give Information to the Legislature of the State of the Union; he may recommend to their Consideration such measures as he shall judge necessary & expedient.[50]

The only substantive change made by the convention was to strengthen the provision that the president "may" recommend measures, providing instead that he "shall" do so. It occasioned no discussion that the duty to inform Congress, thus inserted in Article 2, section 3, was couched in mandatory language. It must have seemed obvious that legislative proposals offered without supporting information could not be countenanced. The framers wished the president to make such proposals and to document them. They did not address the prospect of calls for information initiated by Congress, and there is no indication that they foresaw the possibility of presidential attempts to withhold from Congress any information it might need to perform its constitutional functions. While eight state constitutions gave their legislatures power to call for the journal of their executive council, the need for such a clause was not so obvious in the new federal scheme, where the Senate itself was to serve as an executive council.

The only rationale for secrecy that anyone had articulated pertained to the need to keep some information from foreign enemies. The framers recognized that to deal effectively with rapidly developing crises presidents might need more freedom of action in international affairs than elsewhere. Because such power could pose a special threat to liberty at home, they devoted careful attention to devising a sophisticated system of checks and balances among the president and the two houses of Congress.

One very important presidential responsibility was delineated by the first paragraph of Article 2, section 2, which designated him commander-in-chief of the armed forces. This role implied certain prerogatives in connection with military emergencies and ongoing warfare; but the powers to declare war, to provide for calling up the militia, and to make laws regulating the armed forces were reserved to Congress.

The president was also designated as the officer who would receive representatives from other governments. The conduct of negotiations would be primarily his responsibility, but the power to make treaties was to be shared with the Senate. The compact size of that body made its participation in such business seem practicable; a different view prevailed as to the lower house. As General C.C. Pinckney told the South Carolina ratifying convention, "[T]he secrecy and despatch which are so frequently necessary in negotiations evinced the impropriety of vesting it [in the legislature]."[51] Nevertheless, the House of Representatives too was given an important role in national security affairs. Its participation was explicitly necessary to any decision to declare war, to appropriate funds for defense, to enact laws regulating the armed forces and the militia, and to regulate foreign commerce.

This allocation of powers represented the framers' attempt to accommodate the needs of national security with the policymaking structures of a free society. The principles involved are not difficult to infer: the president should be able to take swift, effective action to meet a crisis and should exercise leadership in the day-to-day conduct of foreign affairs, but the broad outlines of policy should be set with the participation of Congress and implemented with its informed consent, so that the interests of the states and the people will not be flouted or misconstrued.[52]

A system that requires the sharing of power necessarily requires the sharing of information as well. The framers attended to the need for secrecy in national security affairs by giving the leading role to the president, whose activities would not in the ordinary course be made public. To the extent that the Senate and the House had roles to play, it went without saying that they were entitled to the information on which a sound judgment would depend.[53] Because Congress was subject to a general requirement of publicity, it and it alone required an explicit power of secrecy in connection with its special "executive" functions. Hence the provision of Article 1, section 5, authorizing Congress to exercise its judgment to protect national security secrets.

By the same token, the framers attended to the need for accountability primarily through limitations on the powers granted to the several governing bodies. Most such powers were carefully enumerated, and checked by other powers located elsewhere. Moreover, because the Senate and House were accountable to the states and to the people, provision was made for publicizing their decisions so that these could be carefully evaluated by the electorate. The accountability of the president ran primarily to Congress, between elections at least. Thus it was made his duty to inform Congress of matters requiring its attention; and Congress was given control of the purse strings, plus the ultimate sanction of impeachment.[54]

Ambiguities and Demands for Change

Secrecy issues received relatively little attention in the debates over ratification of the Constitution. Thus little insight is gained on the subject from the *Federalist Papers,* written by Madison, Hamilton, and Jay to support the struggle for ratification in New York.

In Number 64, Jay expounded on the need for secrecy in diplomatic affairs.

> It seldom happens in the negotiation of treaties, of whatever nature, but that perfect *secrecy* and immediate despatch are sometimes requisite. . . . Those matters which in negotiations usually require the most secrecy and the most despatch, are those preparatory and auxiliary measures which are not otherwise important in a national view, than as they tend to facilitate the attainment of the objects of the negotiation. For these, the President will find no difficulty to provide; and should any circumstance occur which requires the advice and consent of the Senate, he may at any time convene them.[55]

In Number 84, Hamilton broached the issue of accountability in structural terms.

> The executive and legislative bodies of each state will be so many sentinels over the persons employed in every department of the national administration; and as it will be in their power to adopt and pursue a regular and effectual system of intelligence, they can never be at a loss to know the behaviour of those who represent their constituents in the national councils, and can readily communicate the same knowledge to the people. Their disposition to apprise the community of whatever may prejudice its interests from another quarter, may be relied upon, if it were only from the rivalship of power.[56]

Thus Hamilton and Jay made it clear that the Constitution had a place for secrecy, specifically with respect to the national security functions of the executive branch. No suggestion was made that secrecy would or should be practiced in other spheres, or that it would be absolute even as to these. As a safeguard against abuses, they could point to the vigilance of the states, the checking powers of Congress, and the free press; but they did not grapple with the question of whether executive secrecy might not prevent Congress, the states, and the people from discovering abuses in time. What, for example, if a president refused to convene the Senate and ask their advice and consent?[57]

This problem received little attention, but the ratification debates did see renewed criticism of the loose language of Article 1, section 5. In Virginia, Mason and Patrick Henry led an attack on the clause. Mason cautioned:

> In matters relative to military operations, and foreign negotiations, secrecy was necessary sometimes. But he did not conceive that the receipts and expenditures of the public money ought ever to be concealed. . . . Under this veil they may conceal any thing and every thing. Why not insert words that would exclude ambiguity and danger? The words of the Confederation, that defective system, are, in this respect, more eligible.[58]

Madison defended the clause by insisting that the convention had not intended to expand the practice of secrecy beyond the domain of military and diplomatic affairs. The clause should be given a restrictive reading.

> That part which authorizes the government to withhold from the public knowledge what in their judgment may require secrecy, is imitated from the confederation—that very system which the gentleman advocates.[59]

Patrick Henry forcefully expressed his fear that the convention had gone too far.

> Give us at least a plausible apology why Congress should keep their proceedings in secret. . . . The liberties of a people never were, nor ever will be, secure when the transactions of their rulers may be concealed from them. . . . I am not an advocate for divulging indiscriminately all the operations of government, though the practice of our ancestors, in some degree, justifies it. Such transactions as relate to military operations or affairs of great consequence, the immediate promulgation of which might defeat the interests of the community, I would not wish to be published, till the end which required their secrecy should have been effected. But to cover with the veil of secrecy

the common routine of business, is an abomination in the eyes of every intelligent man, and every friend to his country.[60]

To which John Marshall replied,

In this plan, secrecy is only used when it would be fatal and pernicious to publish the schemes of government.[61]

Madison's and Marshall's reassurances were not enough to quell all misgivings. The Virginia convention, impressed by Henry's warning, proposed a constitutional amendment to make the offending clause read as follows:

That the journals of the proceedings of the Senate and House of Representatives shall be published at least once in every year, except such parts thereof, relating to treaties, alliances, or military operations, as, in their judgment, require secrecy.[62]

Identical justifications, reassurances, and reform proposals were heard in North Carolina; indeed, that state declined to ratify until Congress took action on its demand for a list of constitutional amendments, including that just quoted.[63]

In New York a different series of proposals was advanced. At one point an amendment was offered to Article 1, section 9.

Provided, That the words from time to time shall be so construed, as that the receipts and expenditures of public money shall be published at least once in every year, and be transmitted to the executives of the several states, to be laid before the legislatures thereof.[64]

This proposal was dropped after Hamilton argued that it would be "improper in a war, or on the eve of a war, to publish a state of accounts &ct to all the world."[65] Yet it was he who proposed an amendment, similar to the Virginia-North Carolina proposal, to strengthen Article 1, section 5.

That the journals of Congress shall be published at least once a year with the exception of such parts relating to treaties or military operations as in the judgment of either house shall require secrecy.[66]

The amendment ultimately endorsed by the New York convention contained this language, and added,

> [T]hat both Houses of Congress shall always keep their Doors open during their Sessions, unless the Business may in their Opinion require Secrecy.[67]

This was modeled, of course, on the New York Constitution and on Hamilton's 1783 proposal to the old Congress.

Neither the New York nor the Virginia-North Carolina proposal made any headway; for, in light of what appeared to be a general consensus on the intent of the existing constitutional language, there was little urgency to the demand for change. Without exception, both supporters and opponents of the proposed amendments maintained that the justification for secrecy was limited to the most highly sensitive military and diplomatic affairs; they differed only as to whether the Constitution made this sufficiently clear. The reassurances offered by supporters of the Constitution, including men who had played important roles in the convention, form a useful gloss upon the text. These reassurances were politically essential in the context of the ratification debates, and also fully consistent with what the framers had said at the convention.

The First Congress was confronted with nearly one hundred different constitutional amendments that had been proposed by the ratifying conventions. Most pressing was the demand for adoption of a Bill of Rights. James Madison, whose abilities, experiences, and close ties to the president gave him great influence in the House, quickly took charge of the business. He wished to avert the calling of another convention, and he calculated that this could be done by having Congress quickly adopt a Bill of Rights, based on those few amendments that had been recommended by many states and ignoring other proposals. Among those he left out were the proposed changes to Article 1, section 5. When the battle was over, he wrote to Edmund Randolph that "It has been absolutely necessary in order to effect anything, to abbreviate debate, and exclude every proposition of a doubtful and unimportant nature."[68]

The Constitution would not have been ratified in key states if not for explicit guarantees that a Bill of Rights would be added. As in the case of Article 1, section 5, here again it was charged that the framers had carried their passion for flexibility to extremes. Yet in this instance, explicit amendments were insisted upon, while as to secrecy informal assurances were found sufficient. The proposed amendments to Article 1, section 5 seemed relatively unimportant even to those most suspicious of the new Constitution's penchant for strong government. Although there were several attempts by anti-federalists in Congress to reinstate some of the discarded amendments, those concerning congressional publicity were not among those pressed. Even Elbridge Gerry preferred to concentrate his efforts on matters of greater interest to his constituents.[69]

It is not surprising that the First Congress deemed it unnecessary to limit its own discretion as far as secrecy was concerned. Yet it would be wrong to conclude that it placed a low value on public debate. The House of Representatives had already begun holding public sessions and permitted stenographers to record its debates for daily publication. If the doors were occasionally shut, it was only for debate on matters relating to "treaties, alliances, or military operations." Thus, the proposed amendments would only have formalized what the lower house, at least, was already doing.[70]

Moreover, it was the First Congress that drafted and approved the First Amendment, in which are solemnized the rights of free speech, free press, the freedom to assemble, and the freedom to petition for redress of grievances. In the long run, this proved a greater contribution to the free circulation of information than the stillborn amendments to Article 1 could plausibly have made. By helping to legitimize mounting demands for broad and meaningful participation, the First Amendment weakened the case for secrecy and ultimately went far toward redressing whatever antidemocratic biases the original Constitution showed.[71]

This is not to say that the Constitution, even as supplemented by the Bill of Rights, was a fully perfected system for regulating political communications. As we shall see, history had many surprises to offer, and really, this was inherent in the ambiguity of the constitutional plan with respect to many important specifics. The functions of the several branches would intersect at numerous points; clearly cooperation would be essential, but mechanisms and guidelines frequently were lacking. For example, the mode and timing of the

Senate's participation in treatymaking were not detailed. Moreover, although the House was given no explicit role in this process, many treaties would in fact require the appropriation of funds, and hence the House's assent, for their implementation. Another important ambiguity pertained to the relationship between Congress and subordinate officials of the executive branch. In view of the congressional powers to establish offices, appropriate funds, and approve presidential nominees—not to mention the impeachment power—the executive departments could by no means be termed an exclusive presidential preserve. Yet the implicit congressional powers to regulate, to investigate,[72] and to communicate directly with subordinate executive officers were not detailed. Certainly reasonable men could differ as to how these powers should best be exercised; ambitious men were apt to differ violently.

The framers knew that a struggle for power was inherent in the constitutional system. This was not simply a product of human nature or of fortuitous compromises negotiated at the convention. Rather the system of checks and balances represented a conscious effort to tame the force of ambition and harness it to the cause of liberty. To accomplish this without depriving government of the power to act with "vigor, secrecy and despatch," the system had to be endowed with a generous measure of flexibility.

The very idea of a written constitution was a daring attempt to impose the restraints of positive law upon governmental power. This aspiration was realistic within limits; pushed too far, it would prove absurd and self-defeating. Ambition, inequality, and social conflict could not be abolished by fiat. No written law could supersede the need for judgment, discretion, and leadership if the nation were to survive and prosper. Nor could a written constitution long endure if it lacked the flexibility to adapt to historical change.

If struggles for power among the branches of government were inevitable, and indeed designed into the system, it might have been foreseen that access to information would become a bone of contention from time to time. If the framers contemplated this prospect, however, there is no record of it in the Constitution or in the convention's journals. They did seek to regulate the flow of information from Congress to the public, though only in very general terms. They left unaddressed the problems of communication between the coequal branches, save for the "State of the Union" clause, which empowered the president to speak but did not make clear the extent of his right, if any, to be silent.

This reticence or oversight meant that interbranch relations would have to be structured, and conflicts resolved, largely through negotiations among the leadership. And what if they could not agree? In extraordinary cases impeachment might provide a solution of sorts, but normally this device would not pertain. Ultimately the voters might be asked to judge, but this is not an efficient, stable, or particularly principled method of resolving interbranch disputes.

Nowadays we place much trust in another mode of conflict resolution, in which an "impartial" arbiter or limited jurisdiction is called upon by the parties to propose or impose a solution. It is of interest, however, that the Constitution did not expressly identify the Supreme Court as a potential arbiter of executive-legislative disputes. Indeed, the convention's records are silent on the whole subject of judicial review—the Court's power to determine the meaning of the Constitution authoritatively. The intent of the framers in this regard is, of course, a topic of scholarly dispute;[73] but even after the Supreme Court established its power in 1803 to invalidate federal laws,[74] it was not called upon to referee direct clashes between Congress and the president, such as might arise over the allocation of national security powers, over access to secret information, or over the right to publish it. Whether or not the Court had power to decide such cases in theory,[75] as a practical matter rival institutions would not invoke the Court's assistance unless it appeared both necessary and potentially useful to do so. In the period of this study neither Congress nor the president was so inclined; the judicial role in matters of interest here was largely confined to criminal cases brought by the government against political dissidents. In such cases, the Sixth Amendment entitled the accused to a public trial. Moreover, Article 3, section 3, pertaining to trials for treason, prohibited the use of confessions not made in open court. Mindful of the gruesome history of British Star Chamber trials, the framers inserted this provision despite the risk that a public trial might bring state secrets to light.

In sum, the Constitution can be said to have subjected governmental secrecy to the rule of law in a subtle, partial, but meaningful sense. While the spirit of the document bespoke a broad presumption in favor of publicity, it did not contain unambiguous guidelines, backed by impartial arbiters and formal sanctions, to secure that result. It did, however, structure the process whereby information would be disclosed or withheld, identifying the actors who would make the key decisions, the prerogatives and rationales they might plausibly invoke, the official antagonists they might encounter, the procedures lawfully available for conflict resolution, and the constituents from whom all authority was ultimately derived. These provisions did not purport to ensure a rigidly determinate set of outcomes; rather the Constitution was advertised as flexible and open to adaptation. The integrity, stability, and fairness of the system were to be safeguarded not by the virtue of the rulers or their fear of legal punishment but by their conflicting ambitions. Competing institutions and factions would be constrained by the imperatives of institutional cooperation and constituent support and by what could plausibly be justified within the context of legitimate norms and recognized practices. So long as political actors took constitutional norms and processes seriously—or even troubled to pretend to do so—the game of politics would be a distinctively constitutional game.

INSTITUTION BUILDING AND EXECUTIVE LEADERSHIP___3

When the new government assembled in New York in the spring of 1789, many fundamental structural decisions had to be faced. The executive departments and the lower judiciary remained to be organized; the president and the two houses of Congress had to establish procedures for their internal operations and for communicating with each other. The Constitution offered no specific guidance for most of these decisions; it did, however, structure the manner in which they were to be made. True to the scheme of separated powers, each body took responsibility for organizing its own operations, free from external control if not always immune to criticism.

The decisions of each institution were shaped by its position in the constitutional structure. The resulting differences in perspective affected matters of substance as well as those of style. The arrangements adopted at the outset were not controlled by purely practical concerns, such as efficiency or information security, which had yet to take on concrete meaning in the light of actual experience. At this stage issues about communication arose in the context of establishing regular and direct lines of access between one institution or role and another. Initially, each body separately determined how it would prefer to communicate with the others; in case of disagreement, negotiation was necessary. These decisions did not, in general, attract much attention or occasion lengthy dispute. Yet they are important in that they set the context for future struggles over access to information by providing or failing to provide the formal channels through which specific information might be transmitted or demanded.

A review of these early decisions calls attention to some typical features of rulemaking when procedural questions arise in abstract form, detached from the immediate substantive interests of organized political forces. Often a rather casually adopted rule becomes a bone of contention later when its effects on competing interests become more salient. In an alternative scenario, formal rulemaking may be deferred entirely until conflict makes stable procedures seem necessary. At that stage, however, it may be far more difficult to arrive at a consensus on the proper procedures.

The Executive Branch

From its inception the office of the presidency was exalted by an awe-inspiring array of symbols, rituals, and regalia. Though the Constitution did not prescribe this, it accorded perfectly with Washington's personal style and, in the view of his advisers, with the needs of the country. They felt that the standing of the new government at home and abroad would suffer greatly if the chief magistrate could not project a very respectable, indeed an almost regal, authority. One aspect of this was the necessity to treat access to the president's person as a very special privilege. For all but the most eminent characters, it would be confined to purely ceremonial occasions. Besides his rare public appearances, the president held audiences and dinners for members of official society; yet these were extremely formal affairs, and the president's conversations with guests were apparently confined to innocuous, nonpolitical subjects.[1]

Of course, Washington's responsibilities did not permit him to be totally isolated. He carried on a very extensive and significant correspondence with leading figures and friends in all branches of government and around the country at large, and sometimes ordinary citizens wrote to him spontaneously on issues of concern to them. Washington personally read not only all of his own mail but the official correspondence of his department heads as well.[2]

In the beginning outside contacts seem to have been very helpful to the president; men like Madison and Jay (now chief justice of the

Supreme Court) had a good deal of influence on his early decisions. Over time, however, the preferential access of the department heads made him more and more dependent on their information and advice. Very often the executive decisionmaking process consisted of confidential discussions between the president and a single department head. Needless to say, these meetings were private.

The policymaking level of the executive branch was restricted to the president, three department heads, and the attorney general. This circumstance, together with the autonomy of the executive branch in the formal communication system established by the Constitution and the First Congress, minimized the need for formal and systematic regulations of executive communication practices.[3] The president's private secretary carried messages to Congress, and occasional proclamations were published in the press. The executive had no constitutional or political obligation to publicize its internal deliberations, beyond what was conveyed through face-to-face contacts of the leadership group.

The executive was highly differentiated according to functional specialty. Even at the secretarial level there was little need for direct interdepartmental contact. Thus the integration of the executive function depended vitally on presidential attitudes and skills. Washington chose to meet with his department heads primarily on a one-to-one basis rather than as a group, even before signs of friction among them appeared. Most business fell within the exclusive province of one department, and it seemed improper to consult those not having official responsibility for a matter. In the weightiest affairs of state, however, or where legal technicalities were involved, Washington tended to consult more broadly, through the constitutional mechanism of requesting written opinions from the several department heads and the attorney general.[4] He then weighed the several opinions and, where there was substantial disagreement, almost invariably adopted that of the majority. There were also occasional cabinet meetings, but these were not frequent or important in Washington's first term.

A crucial feature of the communications of the executive branch arose less from a constitutional necessity than from the purposes motivating its members—especially Treasury Secretary Alexander Hamilton and Foreign Affairs Secretary Thomas Jefferson. In theory the executive might have been content to execute the laws passed by Congress on Congress's initiative or simply to recommend measures and wait upon the congressional judgment. This appears, indeed, to have been the president's personal inclination. His advisers, however, were disinclined to function so passively. Hamilton, in particular, was bent on leadership—on displaying that energy of which so much had been spoken. This made it essential to engage in close and continual contacts with congressional figures whose influence might determine the fate of proposed legislation. The president, while standing aloof from these activities, permitted them to continue. These developments, however, were obnoxious to Jefferson, both on policy grounds and because some of Hamilton's proposals invaded his own sphere of responsibility. Hamilton's efforts also alarmed those in Congress who felt strongly about legislative prerogative and feared the executive power as a threat to the liberties of the people and the rights of the states. The resulting conflicts led directly to the development of political factions oriented toward support or opposition for Hamilton's measures.

The prominence in this story of a few individuals poses a constant temptation to overlook the role of structural factors in shaping political developments. Yet it is absolutely clear that secrecy behavior was not a product of individual personality traits, but rather a function of the formal role an actor held and of his political goals of the moment. The facts belie any attempt to identify one character as consistently prone to secrecy and another as consistently hostile to it by virtue of emotional makeup. Despite occasional doctrinaire pronouncements, all the protagonists were highly flexible in their communication practices, responding to the opportunities and risks they perceived in concrete situations. The situations in which they found themselves, moreover, were defined in part by their constitutional responsibilities and prerogatives.

George Washington was less committed than his department heads to particular policy goals and also less confident of his judgment on questions of constitutional interpretation. While confessing his lack of political experience and legal expertise, Washington was determined to lay down sound precedents for the future, and not disposed to rely on his personal popularity as a substitute for lawfulness in administrative procedure and public policy. The legal opinions he obtained from his advisers were carefully studied. They were not designed as window dressing and indeed were not normally circulated outside the executive branch.[5] The result, however, was scarcely a model of formal administrative regularity. Though Washington has been described as disinclined to delegate important responsibilities, his age, infirmity, and lack of experience placed limits on his personal command of the situation. It is unclear to what extent he was aware of the full scope of his subordinates' activities at any given time.[6]

The program Hamilton proposed in 1790–91 included funding of the national debt, assumption of state debts, imposition of excise taxes, and establishment of a national bank. It is not necessary to analyze here the details of this ambitious system and the arguments advanced for and against it. The important fact is that the program aroused persistent and increasingly powerful opposition. It was widely perceived as discriminating in favor of northern, urban, financial, and commercial interests, and against those of southerners, frontiersmen, farmers, and laborers. Moreover, the pro-British tendency of Hamilton's system infuriated many for whom the Revolution was a recent, even an uncompleted struggle. Like Jefferson, Madison and others in Congress were out of sympathy with Hamilton's ideas and offended by his efforts to manipulate the legislative process. There ensued a split in the ranks of the erstwhile nationalist movement and a completely new alignment in American politics.[7]

From the beginning Hamilton did not shrink from taking a hand in affairs outside the Treasury's jurisdiction. Henry Knox, the secretary of war, submitted readily enough to Hamilton's overwhelming assistance. Jefferson's late arrival on the scene in March 1790 obliged him to acquiesce in what had already been done respecting his own official preserve.[8]

The United States had no formal diplomatic ties with Great Britain. In 1789, however, Hamilton had carried on extensive talks with one George Beckwith, an unofficial agent of the crown. These contacts were designed to forge closer ties, although neither government had openly endorsed such an effort. Moreover, the contacts continued even after Jefferson assumed his post. It is doubtful that the president was fully aware of what was happening, and it seems certain Jefferson was not. In fact, Hamilton's dealings with Beckwith have been described by one historian as an attempt "to commit the government of the United States to a policy toward Great Britain at variance with that officially agreed upon. . . . There can be no doubt that [Hamilton's] misrepresentation and fabrication were deliberate and calculated."[9]

Despite the president's commitment to procedural regularity, policy differences and personal rivalries were engendering an incredible profusion of irregular communication channels in diplomacy and in governmental affairs. Hamilton worked to isolate Jefferson within the administration, conduct diplomacy behind his back, and undercut his influence with Congress. Jefferson, for his part, had the discreet assistance of John Beckley, clerk of the House of Representatives, in monitoring the activities of Hamilton's congressional allies; and he apparently had ears within the Treasury as well.[10] Certainly he became at least partly aware of Hamilton's intrigues, for in 1792 he wrote to the president denouncing Hamilton's "cabals" with legislators and unauthorized "conferences" with foreign ambassadors.[11] Yet Jefferson's own communications were hardly restricted to official messages that had the president's approval. Indeed, one writer observes that "Jefferson's letters to James Madison were at times so charged with state secrets that he dared not trust them to the mails."[12]

By early 1792 the president could no longer ignore the rift in his administration. His response consisted of a futile effort to mediate between the rival secretaries, accompanied by quiet measures, such as the establishment of his own secret channel to Ambassador Gouverneur Morris at Paris, which only exacerbated the growing web of intrigue.[13] It was too late to restore policy consensus and personal trust by open and reasoned discussion and too late to return to the simplicity of the framers' governmental plan. George Washington, who abhorred the very mention of political parties, had presided over their creation.

The House of Representatives

The early House's way of doing business emphasized consensus and persuasion more than formal procedures and authority structures. The modest size of the House (sixty-five members in the First

Congress) made it possible to do a large part of the House's work in committee of the whole. Matters of technical detail or special political difficulty were often referred to ad hoc select committees for report, but this device was not used as a means of stifling dissent. The composition of committees was determined by concerns of regional and doctrinal balance as well as by individual competence and interest in the subject at hand.

An easygoing manner was encouraged by other factors besides the size of the House. Most important was the essentially nonpartisan structure of national politics at first.[14] The First Congress did contain a small group of six to ten who had opposed the ratification of the Constitution and who tended to vote as a bloc on questions of national versus state power. Yet neither their ideas nor their numbers served to make them an effective opposition force. Though differences were beginning to surface among the erstwhile nationalists, they united firmly behind James Madison in rebuffing all challenges from the anti-Federalist side.

Absent a pattern of stable and coherent factional activity, the House was not pressed to formalize its decisionmaking procedures. As a result there was a tendency toward interminable debate on every question that arose. As may be imagined, this mode of proceeding was not at all efficient. Yet few items were on the agenda at first, and the advantages of more streamlined procedures were not yet compelling enough to force the abandonment of unrestricted and spontaneous participation. It was the inexorable rise of partisan conflict that would lead to changes in due course. Partly because of its openness, the House was the most conducive forum for the growth of parties, and it was partisanship that soon enough engendered controversy about the publicity of House proceedings.

The Constitution identified the House of Representatives as the institution chiefly responsible for disseminating information to the people. The official journal kept by the clerk was of the traditional sort: it reported only the formal resolutions offered and votes taken in the House, together with the individual yeas and nays when called for by the requisite one-fifth of those present. These limitations quickly proved of little significance, however, for the House at the outset adopted a far more meaningful publicity posture by choosing to admit the public to most of its debates.[15]

This step, historically unprecedented, was clearly not mandated by the Constitution;[16] yet it was well attuned to the constitutional role of the House. Admitting the public brought the national government close to the people in a dramatic way. Unlike the occasional publication of a journal, the visitors' gallery offered a spectacle capable of attracting broad interest and conveying valuable information.

There is no record of the discussion that preceded the adoption of this policy. We know only that when the city of New York remodelled the hall destined for the House's use, a visitors' gallery was provided. The House began admitting visitors on April 8, 1789, only two days after the first assembling of a quorum.

The House debates came to be well attended, and visitors relayed to others their direct experience with the workings of representative government. More important than visitors' accounts, however, were the efforts of the journalistic profession. Even before the opening of Congress, at least one journalist appeared in New York with the object of securing a position as official reporter of the House. The House declined to make such an appointment, but the government encouraged the dissemination of national news and helped make the publishing of the debates a viable economic venture. The reports published at the capital by enterprising stenographers were widely reprinted in local papers throughout the country, and the national papers themselves were widely distributed by congressmen under their franking privilege.[17]

The activities of the press aroused controversy when some members complained of bias and error in the published reports. On September 21, 1789, Aedanus Burke of South Carolina introduced resolutions condemning misrepresentations and omissions in the newspapers, and declaring that the House should no longer "give sanction" to the stenographers. In the ensuing debate—which, it must be noted, is available only through the work of the same stenographers—it quickly appeared that the House was unwilling to shut off press coverage, and ultimately Burke withdrew his motion. Chastened, the stenographers withdrew from the House floor to the gallery; but this was found to increase the incidence of error, and the House soon induced them to return to the foot of the speaker's chair.[18]

This episode shows the House's appreciation for the value of publicity and also points to the role of factionalism in this sphere. Representative Burke was an anti-Federalist and so were four of the other five members who spoke in this debate.[19] These men felt that their views were not receiving adequate coverage, yet further to reduce publicity could scarcely serve their cause. Thus several of Burke's allies spoke against his resolution and induced him to withdraw it. The House's support for publicity was at once an affirmation of press freedom and a rebuke for the anti-Federalists' display of pique.

The House's commitment to publicity was strongly reaffirmed in December 1791 in its response to proposals to curtail the franking privilege. This move may well have been prompted by the recent advent of an antiadministration newspaper, which some congressmen were zealously distributing to their constituents. The main argument offered in support, however, was a simple desire to save money. Representative William Vans Murray of Maryland argued that because the House's proceedings were public, members did not require an additional, subsidized communication channel, as did executive officers whose business might require secrecy and dispatch. For the House majority, however, the cost of the frank was far outweighed by its success in aiding the diffusion of information. The importance of this function was stressed in the debate.

> It is treading on dangerous ground, to take any measures that may stop the channels of public information. . . . The motives for adopting certain measures, ought always to be explained to influential characters in the different parts of the Union. . . . Wherever the newspapers had extended, or even the correspondence of the members, no opposition had been made to the laws; whereas the contrary was experienced in those parts to which the information had not penetrated.[20]

As Murray had suggested, the publicizing of executive proceedings was viewed by the House in a very different light from that of its own debates. The question arose, albeit indirectly, when they turned to basic legislation on the duties of executive departments. In the debate on the president's power to remove department heads, two different concepts of interbranch communications came to the fore. Both sides referred to executive secrecy as a relevant consideration. The nationalists looked favorably on executive power as the locus of governmental energy and leaned toward the view that department heads would be subordinates of the president, privy to his confidence and under his control. In this view the relationship between Congress and the departments would necessarily be indirect and attenuated. Congress would be in no position to second-guess a president's judgment that his subordinate should be removed, a judgment which might rest on "suspicions of a very delicate nature" that could not properly be shared with others.[21]

The anti-Federalist position emphasized the constitutional principle that the president and the department heads were separately accountable, through impeachment, for their individual conduct. Should department heads become mere "creatures" of the president, they would cease to provide a check on his conduct. He could then prevent them from revealing his misdeeds and might even use them to obtrude upon the legislature and "govern and direct" its measures. In any case the president ought to be responsible for his exercise of the removal power, which could be ensured by giving the Senate a right to demand his reasons.[22]

The nationalist side was strengthened by the circumstance that the removal power debate arose in connection with the law establishing the Department of Foreign Affairs.[23] For in this area the values of "vigor, secrecy and despatch" were especially important, and the role of the legislature relatively modest. When it turned to the Treasury Department, the House felt it necessary to make further provision for a working relationship between the secretary and Congress. While the secretary would be removable by the president without Senate consent, in this case the House imposed comprehensive reporting responsibilities, namely a duty

> to make report, and give information to either branch of the legislature, in person or in writing (as he may be required), respecting all matters referred to him by the Senate or House of Representatives, or which shall appertain to his office;[24]

as well as further duties to report on receipts and expenditures from time to time.

Each department head was given custodial authority over the records of his department; the House supplied no guidelines to regulate outside access to official records, and the War and Foreign Affairs Department bills contained no specific reporting mandates.[25] Yet the record does not bespeak a conscious decision on the House's part to deny itself or others useful information. Secrecy was alluded to in the removal power debate as a potential obstacle to the discovery of grave misconduct; there was little sign of recognition that it might have adverse effects on the normal policymaking process. In 1789 the government was operating in a relatively harmonious, nonpartisan atmosphere that made such questions remote, abstract, and unpleasant to discuss.

As the details and tendency of Hamilton's grand design became apparent, the situation changed markedly. Madison and other House influentials moved into more and more emphatic opposition, while men like William Smith, Fisher Ames, and Theodore Sedgwick became leaders of the pro-Hamilton forces. The House debates over Hamilton's measures aroused great public interest and excitement. The press not only reported the debates but carried extensive editorial comment and reader response, the latter often written pseudonymously by prominent figures. Sometimes provocative leaks occurred, ranging from shocking remarks allegedly made in the Senate to the text of Jefferson's cabinet opinion opposing a national bank.[26]

By 1791 Madison and Jefferson decided that Fenno's *Gazette of the United States,* the leading national newspaper, was too biased in Hamilton's favor to be a forum for their views. This paper had been set up under Hamilton's aegis to serve as a mouthpiece for the United States government. It was paid to publish the laws of the land and other official materials, and its editor maintained close ties with Hamilton's group. Madison and Jefferson now arranged for the establishment of a new paper, Freneau's *National Gazette,* to disseminate the opposition viewpoint. Thus began a new phase in American journalism. Though many editors continued to claim nonpartisan status, as time went on there were few who deserved that title. Not many received direct high-level patronage and support as did Fenno and Freneau, but few remained aloof from the increasingly acrimonious debate that raged about them.[27]

While the debate was primarily concerned with the impact of

Hamilton's financial measures, the Second Congress was also impelled to reexamine its constitutional role in light of the new realities of partisan conflict. In this the House was discreetly encouraged by the secretary of state.[28] In his diary Jefferson noted a dinner meeting in June 1792 with several members of the House, at which the subject of secretarial reports to the legislature was discussed. According to Jefferson, the congressmen agreed with him that the constant references of legislative business to department heads were a great source of "mischief." Just a few days later one of these men raised the issue on the House floor, objecting to a motion then before the House to refer a certain question to Hamilton for report. A protracted quarrel ensued, and though the motion was carried by a narrow margin, Jefferson recorded with evident glee that the episode left Hamilton "deeply wounded."[29]

Members realized that by attacking Hamilton's influence channels they jeopardized their access to needed information. Thus the opposition tried to distinguish sharply between calls for information on the one hand and plans or opinions on the other. They insisted that the House wanted and needed information from the secretary, but they wanted no part of his legislative proposals. The other side retorted that the distinction was unworkable. The House could not afford to dispense with Hamilton's expert assistance, and it was better to receive it openly than otherwise.[30]

The opposition was unconvinced, for, while continuing to resist the policy leadership of the secretary, they mounted a spate of vexatious demands for information to assist their own deliberations. This information was so useful to the House that Hamilton's friends could not oppose the requests, though the secretary resented this duty nearly as much as he wished to perform the other. One of his friends grumbled, "Taking advantage of Congressional prerogative, a fool can ask more questions in a day than a wise man can answer in a month. . . . I would almost as soon be a Virginia negro as a public officer under such a master."[31] Yet outright refusals to supply information did not occur. Instead, Hamilton and Jefferson each sought to keep Congress supplied with information and analysis favorable to their policy views.

It was in the field of foreign commerce that the management of information was marked by the most complex and significant maneuvers. It was a function of the legislature to make laws for the regulation of foreign commerce. Yet by virtue of their official responsibilities both Hamilton and Jefferson were deeply involved in attempts to influence the exercise of congressional judgment. Hamilton viewed foreign commerce as the prime source of revenue, and the excise tax enacted by the First Congress was his brainchild.[32] For Jefferson, trade was America's main bargaining chip in her relations with the powers of Europe.

As early as 1789 the question arose whether France, as America's treaty ally, was entitled to preferential treatment vis-à-vis Great Britain. Not only was British trade policy highly protectionist, but British-American relations were troubled on many other fronts.[33] In view of the heavy British reliance on American raw materials and agricultural products, Madison believed that commercial policy could be used to extract concessions from Britain on some of the outstanding issues. In 1789 Madison proposed a protectionist system that not only favored American over foreign goods and shipping, but discriminated in favor of treaty allies (i.e., France) and against other foreign powers (i.e., primarily Britain). Hamilton was horrified. In his view these measures not only imperiled the major source of American trade and excise revenue, but ran counter to the political imperative of conciliating and forging friendly ties with the British government. He took the issue to the president, who determined that it would be American policy to negotiate rather than to engage in trade warfare. Before the Senate could complete action on Madison's trade bill, the president dispatched Gouverneur Morris to London. The Senate, although it had not been consulted on Morris's mission,[34] now acquiesced in the president's decision to negotiate and erased the discriminatory portions of the House's trade bill.

Morris's pessimistic reports soon persuaded Jefferson that no settlement was in prospect and that Madison's approach was therefore superior. In December 1790 he reported to Washington that Morris's mission had failed. This report, reluctantly submitted by the president to Congress in February 1791, spurred the revival in the House of Madison's proposals. But, after Beckwith warned Hamilton that the British would retaliate in kind, Hamilton induced the House not only to postpone action on the Navigation Act but to return Jefferson's report pending further developments.

Hamilton had secret assurances from Beckwith that progress would be made in the talks before the next congressional session. Jefferson, confident that Hamilton's optimism was unfounded, acquiesced in the delay; but, at Hamilton's urging, Britain finally agreed to send a fully accredited ambassador to America, thus indefinitely forestalling action on Madison's bill. Jefferson's report was pigeonholed for over two years while talks with George Hammond, the new British minister, ground on.[35] The negotiations, of course, were Jefferson's responsibility; yet Hammond wrote to his superior that he preferred to negotiate with Hamilton rather than the secretary of state and employed the former channel as much as possible.[36]

If the bypassing of the State Department was a blatant impropriety, the subtle preemption of congressional prerogative by resort to endless negotiations was of greater constitutional significance. So long as its actual legislative function was thus held in abeyance, the House had no occasion to make an issue of the adequacy or timeliness of the information made available by the executive branch.

The Senate

There were only twenty senators at first,[37] and they were a highly elite group in socioeconomic terms. From the start they consciously adopted a tone quite different from that of the House, dramatizing their claim to special powers and higher status.

On May 19, 1789, the Senate arranged for the keeping of its journals, one for legislative and one for executive business. The legislative journal was to be published monthly;[38] the executive journal not at all. These arrangements barely met the minimal publicity requirement of Article 1, section 5. With respect to executive business, they did not oblige the Senate to exercise case-by-case discretion in imposing secrecy. Senators were free to communicate privately with constituents concerning legislative business, save where the Senate voted to impose an injunction of secrecy.[39] Executive proceedings, however, were not supposed to be discussed out-of-doors, and copying of extracts from the executive journal was strictly forbidden.[40]

The situation was not ameliorated by the non-admission of visitors to the Senate. Indeed, the Senate's chamber did not have a gallery.

Where the House spontaneously opened its doors to the public, the Senate with equal rapidity committed itself to the opposite course. There is no indication that the subject was even discussed at the outset, and the Senate's initial set of standing rules said nothing about it. The Senate was closed not only to ordinary citizens but to members of the House and other officials as well.[41]

It was not long before murmurs of protest began to appear in the press and elsewhere, for invidious comparison of the Senate's attitude to that of the House was inevitable. "Condorcet" stated,

> This Patrician stile, this concealment, this affectation of preeminence but illy accords with the spirit of republican government. . . . It is a strange maxim in republican policy, that the agents of the people should keep their deliberations concealed from those from whom they derive their political existence. . . . Upright intentions, and upright conduct are not afraid or ashamed of publicity.[42]

Though senators must have smarted under such criticism, they were not disposed to yield to it. Indeed, they viewed their constitutional position as deliberately insulated from the direct force of public opinion, so that it became a matter of principle to ignore such criticism. As one senator put it, "I do not desire that the private conduct or public proceedings of this body should be exposed to the daily inspection of a populace." Or, as another said a few years later, "he would consider himself unqualified for the Senate if he could be swayed by popular influence."[43] Content to rely upon face-to-face contacts and private correspondence, most senators felt that publicity could only detract from their status and damage their character as the upper house, representing the special interests of the states and of propertied men, and designated as the president's advisory council on executive matters.

A moving force behind this lofty posture was John Adams, vice-president of the United States and president of the Senate. Adams was an admirer of the British constitution and a great believer in protocol. His repeated agonizing over questions like the proper title for addressing the president—Abigail Adams called Washington "His Majesty"[44]—gave rise to rumors of monarchical plotting behind the Senate's closed doors.

The truth was that the Senate had nothing of great moment to hide; it was simply determined to remain aloof from the people and from the other bodies of government. Secrecy was an important attribute of the lofty image that Adams and his allies wished the Senate to project. It was also necessary to realize the operating advantages that, in theory at least, accrued to the Senate by virtue of its small and relatively homogeneous membership. Instead of proceeding on an informal basis, striving for rational persuasion and generating consensus, an open Senate would no doubt become much like the House, which to the senators seemed more like a theater or a circus than a deliberative body.[45] Though Senator William Maclay of Pennsylvania and a few others had misgivings about secrecy and about Adams's aristocratic predilections in general, the pressures for conformity and solidarity were very strong. In the absence of effective outside support or internal factional organization, individuals challenging the Senate's posture would simply reap ostracism as their reward.

Moreover, secrecy made it harder for dissident senators to assert themselves. Maclay alleged not only that the journals were full of mistakes, but that there were deliberate attempts to conceal the existence of dissent.[46] The Senate repeatedly refused to allow the entry of dissenting views in the journals; where a minority could not command a one-fifth vote, even the yeas and nays might not be recorded.[47]

Much of the early dissidence within the Senate was inspired by states' rights sentiment and linked to remnants of the old anti-Federalist movement. Thus one of the salient justifications for secrecy was that it would reduce the influence of state-bound loyalties and issues, strengthen solidarity in the Senate, and thereby bolster the authority of the national government. Now, it is true, the consolidation of national unity and governmental authority was a serious and relevant concern. The anti-Federalist doctrine that senators were subject to binding instructions from their states did pose a danger to national power.[48] Yet, in light of the anger and scorn its policy aroused, it must have been clear to the Senate that secrecy was ill-designed to serve the purpose of nationbuilding. If the framers had intended the secrecy of the Senate, they had seriously misjudged the extent to which the old politics of status deference remained viable.[49] The aloofness and pomp which Adams thought essential to respectable government were instead the object of mockery. If the Senate's elite constituents were more appreciative of this policy than most citizens, they did not see fit to say so in public. The Senate's friends had to admit that its secrecy was a political embarrassment, and even the president was cautiously disapproving.[50]

At first the Senate's special constitutional relationship to the states helped to justify the failure to provide for general publicity. However, the secrecy issue was soon placed on the Senate's agenda by the states' rights faction in that body. The legislatures of Virginia and North Carolina regarded their senators as subject to binding instructions. The first exercise of this prerogative took place on December 16, 1789, when Virginia instructed her senators to exert "their utmost endeavors" to open the Senate's doors. A resolution to this effect was accordingly introduced on April 29, 1790. According to Maclay's diary, no one spoke in opposition; yet the resolution garnered only three votes: two from Virginia and Maclay's own.[51]

Over the next few years at least six state governments, most of them in the South, associated themselves with the demand for open doors.[52] They might have been content to instruct their senators to keep them better informed through private channels; yet public access seemed both symbolically and practically important to those who feared the Senate as an engine of consolidation of national power at the expense of the states and the people. The legislature of North Carolina resolved:

> Whereas, the secrecy of the Senate of the United States, the alarming measures of the late session of Congress, and the silence observed by the Senators from this state, in not corresponding with the legislature or executive thereof, strongly impress this general assembly with the necessity of declaring their sentiments thereon.

> Resolved, that the Senators representing this state in Congress of the United States be, and they hereby are directed, to use their constant and unremitted exertions to have the doors of the Senate of the United States kept open, that the public may have access to hear the debates of the Senate, when in its legislative or judicial capacity.

Resolved, that when in Congress they may be directed to correspond regularly and constantly with the Legislature, but during recess thereof with the executive.

Resolved, that they use their endeavours to have such of the journals as are not of a secret nature printed, and transmitted by post or otherwise to the executive, regularly, during each session of Congress.[53]

A new formal resolution for opening the doors was introduced in the Senate on February 24, 1791, by Virginia's James Monroe. This resolution was carefully qualified; it would have opened the Senate's doors only "whilst the Senate shall be sitting in a legislative capacity, except on such occasions as, in their judgment, may require secrecy."[54] Yet it aroused violent opposition on two grounds: that senators would only "make speeches for the gallery and for the public papers" instead of joining in serious discussion and because of the sanction it lent to the pernicious doctrine of the states' power to instruct. Thus Robert Morris of Pennsylvania declared that "We were Senators of the United States, and had nothing to do with one state more than another."[55] Ultimately four senators deliberately violated their instructions by voting to continue secrecy. The resolution was defeated by a decisive seventeen to nine margin. On March 26, 1792, the issue was once more brought to a vote. Secrecy was upheld by seventeen to eight, in a nearly exact rerun of the 1791 contest. The drive for open doors appeared to have bogged down.[56]

While the intervention of the states had mustered a few votes in support of publicity, it also set limits to the support that drive could muster, for the Senate was dominated by men of strong nationalist persuasion. Yet it would be an error to overemphasize the linkage between the secrecy issue and that of states' rights. Publicity was consistently supported by at least a few senators of impeccable nationalist credentials. Moreover, the Senate adhered to secrecy by similar margins in a context that had very little to do with states' rights. This is shown clearly by the fate of a proposal advanced in April 1792 by the senators from Georgia. Both men had voted against opening the doors in March; now, however, they moved the admission to Senate debates of members of the House of Representatives. This modest proposal, far from gaining support by virtue of its divorce from the states' rights issue, was able to garner only six affirmative votes.[57]

An episode in January and February 1793 witnessed a further doctrinal elaboration. Like its forebears, this latest open-doors resolution was circumspect in scope: it did not apply to executive business and left ample discretion even as to legislative business.

> Resolved . . . that it be a standing rule that the doors of the Senate Chamber remain open whilst the Senate shall be sitting in a Legislative and Judicative capacity, except on such occasions as, in their judgment, may require secrecy.[58]

In a lengthy preamble, the resolution stoutly affirmed the individual responsibility of senators to their constituents, yet it discreetly failed to specify who those constituents were—the states or the people. Considering that senators were not popularly elected, the preamble went remarkably far in implying that senators were responsible to the people as well as to the states. Against the background of the issue's history, this may be taken as an effort to dissociate the drive for open doors from the states' rights movement. If this was a new theory of the Senate's role, it proved no more persuasive with the Senate than the states' rights theory had been. In fact, the preamble was rejected by twenty-one votes to seven, while the operative part was defeated by only eighteen to ten.[59] This tally reflected little net shift in sentiment since 1792. Though three Senators did switch sides on the issue in 1793, the net gain of two votes for opening the doors is accounted for simply by the absence of Kentucky's senators in 1792. The overall alignment in both years conformed, with interesting exceptions, to partisan cleavages.[60] Thus any hope of change seemed dependent on the fortunes of the opposition at the polls.

It seems clear that the Senate's obstinacy placed it at a political disadvantage vis-à-vis the House, for it made the latter the sole forum for open policy debate within the government. Yet it took some time before the significance of this was felt in the upper house. Thus in setting protocols for communication with the House, the Senate sought to obtain symbolic recognition of its superiority, but the House in joint committee negotiations successfully resisted most of the Senate's demands. It was this attitude that led the House to reject Senate proposals for a joint committee to plan the calendar of legislative business. As practice developed, the two houses did not often find it desirable or necessary to work directly together. However, in reconciling disagreements over legislation enacted by the two houses a joint committee procedure proved quite successful. It is of interest that these conference committees did not meet secretly, but were open to members of both houses. This ground rule was doubtless adopted at the House's insistence, in view of the senators' penchant for secrecy.[61]

The Senate's arrogance where the House was concerned stood in sharp contrast to its attitude toward the executive branch. Thus the foreign affairs bill showed no trace of any Senate concern to secure access to diplomatic information for the exercise of its executive business. Presumably senators felt the matter should be resolved in bilateral Senate-executive negotiations, rather than in legislation enacted with House concurrence.

Negotiations began in June 1789 when the president submitted his first ambassadorial nomination to the Senate. The submission was by written message, to the surprise of some who had expected the president to appear in person before his council. The Senate did order the acting foreign secretary[62] to appear and inform the Senate on the nominee's qualifications, but later the question arose of whether the Senate should vote on the nomination by voice vote or by secret ballot. Since voting would take place in executive session, the yeas and nays would in neither event be made public. At the same time, Maclay argued that a secret vote was necessary to preserve senatorial prerogative: few members would dare defy the president before their colleagues. At first the Senate opted for the ballot procedure, yet this display of independence was shortlived. In August the question was brought up for reconsideration, and a committee was chosen to meet with the president and discuss the procedures to be followed. The committee respectfully assured the president that the Senate would be content to abide by his own preference.[63] After consulting with Madison, the president requested that the Senate make provision for receiving either oral or written communications from the president and for giving its advice and consent in either the presence or the absence of the president, as his judgment might dictate from case to case. However, Washington came out strongly for open balloting by the Senate in either event, stating that "nothing would sooner induce him to relinquish nominations by written message than to accomplish this end." On August 21, 1789, the Senate compliantly adopted a resolution providing for either oral or written communications in the president's discretion and providing further that voting on nominations would be *viva voce* (oral).[64] Any lingering ambiguity about the thrust of this policy was dispelled by a pair of resolutions adopted January 27, 1792.

> Ordered, That the President of the United States be furnished with an authenticated transcript of the Executive records of the Senate, from time to time.

> Ordered, That no executive business, in future, be published by the Secretary of the Senate.[65]

Even these gestures of submission to the executive do not tell the whole story, for in addition the president was able to fill certain posts without obtaining the consent of the Senate at all. A law of 1790 authorized him to employ secret intelligence agents, who reported to the president and/or the foreign secretary only. Their emolument was drawn from the president's contingency fund and accounted for by presidential voucher.[66] Most such agents were strictly observers. Of greater constitutional and practical significance was the president's use of special, unaccredited agents to conduct exploratory talks with foreign governments. Before 1792 the United States had no regular, full-time ambassadors stationed abroad. Such special missions as that of Gouverneur Morris to London were not submitted to the Senate for approval. Morris was dispatched in October 1789 while Congress was in recess, and his mission was not formally announced to the Senate until Jefferson's report of February 1791 declared its failure. Whether or not individual senators knew unofficially of the negotiations, clearly the Senate as a body was suffering a substantial erosion of its advice and consent prerogative.

The informality of Morris's mission was partly justified by the

British refusal to accredit a minister to the United States, but considerations of domestic politics were also involved.[67] When Washington finally, in December 1791, nominated Morris as permanent minister to Paris, he encountered substantial Senate opposition. Hamilton had been disappointed with Morris's performance at London, and Jefferson had misgivings because of Morris's equivocal attitude toward the French Revolution.[68] Though Morris had the president's personal confidence and support to a unique degree, the Senate confirmed his nomination by the narrow margin of sixteen to eleven.[69]

This episode did not enhance the president's desire to work closely with the Senate; in fact, it was not only the Senate that had slipped a notch in the president's esteem. An extraordinary exchange took place between Washington and Morris shortly after the latter assumed his new post. Morris wrote to the president out of discomfiture at working under a man who had opposed his appointment.

> I have hitherto in my letters communicated to you many things which I should not willingly entrust to others, and in the course of events I may again possess information which it might be well that you were acquainted with. At the same time it is I presume expected that the public servants will correspond fully and freely with the Office of Foreign Affairs. It might therefore be deemed improper, not to say *all,* in my letters to the office. I wish therefore you would give me your candid opinion on this subject.[70]

The president replied,

> There can be but few things of a public nature (likely to fall in your line, requiring to be acted upon by this government) that may not be freely communicated to the Department to which it belongs; because, in proceedings thereon, the head of the department will, necessarily be made acquainted therewith. But there may nevertheless be other matters, more remote in their consequences, of the utmost importance to be known that not more than one intermediate person would be entrusted with; *here,* necessity as well as propriety, will confine you to a point. Cases, *not altogether* under the control of necessity, may also arise to render it advisable to do this and your own good judgment will be the best direction in these.[71]

Here Washington was tacitly authorizing Morris to use his "good judgment" along lines that Jefferson would never have sanctioned. Morris proceeded to engage in secret contacts with the French royal family and to relay their "merely personal" sentiments to Washington from time to time. In fact, Morris was active in attempting to save the lives of the royal family and may have been involved in plots to restore their authority as well.[72] If these activities were known to the president, they could not be revealed to Thomas Jefferson and certainly not to the full Senate. The range of opinion in that body precluded its effective use as an advisory council.

Of course the Constitution did not require the president to disclose all of Morris's activities to the Senate. Once confirmed, the Senate's role in supervising his conduct was left unspecified by the framers. Neither the president nor the foreign secretary desired an expansive interpretation of that role. In 1790 Jefferson had advised the President that

> The transaction of business with foreign nations is Executive altogether. . . . The Senate is not supposed by the constitution to be acquainted with the concerns of the Executive department. It was not intended that these should be communicated to them; nor can they therefore be qualified to judge of the necessity which calls for a mission to any particular place, or of the particular grade . . . which special and secret circumstances may call for. . . . They are only to see that no unfit person be employed.[73]

Thus the Senate would not have a substantive foreign policy role to play unless a treaty were to be negotiated. Yet the treaty power too was subject to progressive erosion in this period.

One question settled quite early was whether the Senate should have its own direct, official communications with foreign powers. When the French National Assembly addressed certain messages of a ceremonial nature to the president and Congress jointly, Washington at first transmitted them unopened to the Senate. Adams, however, returned them to the president, no doubt on the theory that the nation should speak with one voice in international affairs.[74] This principle was soon well settled as doctrine, even if there were substantial lapses in implementation.

The question of the extent, timing, and manner of senatorial participation in treatymaking was not so smoothly resolved. On August 22, 1789, George Washington came in person to the Senate to discuss a proposed negotiation with the Creek nation. The unhappy result is well known. When some senators wished to refer the president's proposal to a committee, rather than vote upon it point by point under his very eyes, Washington "started up in a violent fret." Later he declared that "he would be damned if he ever went there again."[75]

The abrupt abandonment of face-to-face discussions did not signify a total retreat from advance consultation.[76] On the contrary, the president continued to keep the Senate intimately informed, by periodic written messages, of the slow progress of the negotiations. It was about a year later that he transmitted this interesting message:

> In consequence of the general principles agreed to by the Senate in August 1789, the adjustment of the terms of a treaty is far advanced between the United States and the . . . Creek nation. . . .
>
> Hence it becomes an object of real importance to form new channels for the commerce of the Creeks through the United States. But this operation will require time, as the present arrangements cannot suddenly be broken without the greatest violation of faith and morals.
>
> It therefore appears to be important to form a secret article of a treaty, similar to the one which accompanies this message. If the Senate should require any further explanation, the Secretary of War will attend them for this purpose. . . .

Secret Article

> The commerce necessary for the Creek nation shall be carried on through the ports, and by the citizens of the United States, if substantial and effectual arrangements shall be made for that purpose by the United States on or before August 1, 1792.
>
> In the mean time, the said commerce may be carried on through its present channels, and according to its present regulations.[77]

The Senate approved the secret article that same day and the final treaty soon thereafter. The record does not reveal that anyone was troubled by the precedent of a secret treaty, ostensibly dignified by the Constitution as part of the "supreme law of the land" and capable in principle of embroiling the nation in international hostilities.

A further departure from constitutional purity came in early 1793, when General Putnam concluded an Indian treaty on which there had been no advance consultation whatever. This treaty was not ratified, but the record does not show that the failure to consult had any part in the Senate's objections. Still, the president could no longer argue that, because the treaty was consistent with the envoy's instructions, the Senate was bound to consent to it.[78]

Both branches gained freedom of action from the new procedure, and this may explain why, in a context of increasing partisanship, it was so casually adopted. One factor in the new executive attitude was increasing concern about the confidentiality of American negotiating postures. The cabinet unanimously advised the president against advance consultation; in Jefferson's words,

> We all thought if the Senate should be consulted, and apprised of our line, it would become known to [George] Hammond, and we would lose all chance of saving anything more than our ultimatum.[79]

Thus it was a perceived need for secrecy that supplied a rationale for sharply reducing the Senate's role in treatymaking. The formal secrecy of Senate proceedings had not induced the president to take it into his confidence. As Jefferson wrote, Washington had "no opinion of the secrecy of the Senate" and could see no use in withholding information from the House if it had to be given to the Senate anyway. Jefferson illustrated his point with a minor indiscretion committed by a senator at an official dinner; one wonders what he, and the president, would have thought of Senator William Samuel Johnson's extremely extensive and open discussions with the British agent George Beckwith.[80]

Given the burgeoning intrigues within the cabinet, to withhold information from Congress was not an effective way to keep the powers of Europe in the dark about American intentions. Nevertheless, this provided a strong rationale for keeping foreign policy information within a narrow circle. With respect to European affairs, the Senate, and the House as well, were in general favored only with belated and partial briefings. These briefings, often accompanied by carefully selected extracts of diplomatic correspondence, were designed to serve the interests of administration (or secretarial) policy; their timing and content were a matter of executive discretion.[81]

Constitutionally the House and Senate occupied distinct positions respecting the conduct of foreign affairs; yet in practice there was a striking convergence. It was soon clear that the Senate would not serve as a true advisory council, that its role in treatymaking and diplomacy was to be essentially passive and after the fact. When its formal powers did come into play, the Senate might grumble over policy or call for fuller information;[82] yet the president had little reason to apprehend outright defiance from within a body that sat behind closed doors, kept no record of its debates, and expected dissenting members to keep silent.[83]

From the outset, moreover, there were important negotiations that never came before the Senate in pursuance of its constitutional duties, because no formal nomination or treaty was involved. While there may have been ample justification in some instances for the decision to proceed informally, the record suggests that the more controversial a measure was, the greater was the tendency to bypass or minimize formal consultation with the Senate.

Meanwhile, the House's formal cooperation was sought in connection with certain diplomatic matters. One of these involved relations with the Barbary powers of Algiers, Tunis, and Tripoli. In 1791 Congress was consulted on the policy to be pursued toward these powers. Though the president and Senate could conclude a treaty, in this case the very commencement of negotiations would require substantial cash payments. Ultimately it might be necessary to pay huge sums in tribute and ransom in order to end the depredations on American shipping in the Mediterranean and free the sailors taken hostage. If the House were unwilling to spend these sums, the talks would be futile. Over the Senate's strong objection, the president proceeded to ask the House for advance appropriations. A Senate committee had met with him to complain that this step was in derogation of the Senate's prerogative and that it compromised the necessary secrecy as to the amount the United States was willing to pay. According to Jefferson, the president was unpersuaded by these conceptual arguments to risk a very real embarrassment in opening talks without assurance of legislative support; he had, moreover, "no confidence in the secrecy of the Senate."[84]

In general the president made no great distinction at this time between the respective rights of the Senate and the House to receive information and be consulted. Though the Senate received a few special briefings in connection with its treaty function, more often the president sent identical messages to both houses, reporting on diplomatic events and extracting portions of official dispatches. In the Barbary case, for three years he adhered to this policy, "in accord with the opinion of Jefferson, that when negotiating a treaty which would require subsequent legislation, it was good policy for the executive to keep in close touch with both branches of the legislature."[85] The political situation did not encourage the observance of legal niceties in some respects; yet by means of scrupulous deference to the executive in both substantive and procedural matters, each house assured itself of a degree of consultation and participation in foreign affairs. For both houses, exclusion of the public was part of the quid pro quo. Nevertheless, the most sensitive aspects of foreign policy were closely held by the executive, and the increasingly convoluted struggle between Hamilton and Jefferson on relations with Britain and France was not submitted to Congress for arbitration. Congress and the country were content to leave these matters in executive hands so long as their confidence in the competence and good faith of the administration remained substantially intact.

The Senate would have stood on firm constitutional ground in demanding for itself a greater role in executive business. However, the framers had not foreseen that instead of fighting for its institutional prerogative, the Senate leadership might find it prudent to defer to the president. In practice both their procedural and their substantive decisions were generally favorable to the presidency. Initially, secrecy in the Senate had seemed to serve the purposes of that body; but by 1792 it should have been clear that this was not the case. The secrecy of the Senate was beneficial primarily to the executive branch; it also, more or less incidentally, enhanced the importance of the House as the sole forum for public policy debate within the government.

Confidentiality and Executive Privilege: The St. Clair Precedent

Until now there has been much talk of secrecy *behavior* and relatively little of secrecy *law*. That is because none of the institutions of government had relied heavily on formal rules to govern its communications, and interbranch relations had been handled in a manner so informal as to verge on anarchy. Nevertheless, a number of important customary practices were well established during Washington's first term. The secrecy of the Senate was one example; it remains to consider how the House handled such sensitive information as was entrusted to it by the executive from time to time.

On August 8, 1789, the House received its first presidential message bearing on sensitive diplomatic or military matters. In this case advance appropriations were wanted for certain Indian negotiations; a separate request pertained to measures for the regulation of the militia. The president did not ask the House to keep his message secret, but at once

> a desultory conversation arose respecting the propriety of shutting the gallery doors, inasmuch as it was probable the statements and papers referred to in the Message might contain matters requiring to be kept secret. After the question had been agitated some time, the gallery doors were shut.[86]

One could wish for a fuller account of the discussion on this occasion, but it is safe to say that the House was eager to establish its character as responsible, prudent, and worthy of the president's confidence. Thus it imitated the Senate in closing its doors for delicate business, and recording the secret proceedings in a separate, secret journal.[87] The practice followed on this occasion was scrupulously adhered to throughout Washington's first term. In time the president began to guide the House's judgment by specifically designating particular communications as confidential. The first instance of this occurred on January 12, 1790, when the president addressed both houses in the following terms:

> I conceive, that an unreserved but confidential communication of all the papers relative to the recent negotiations with some of the Southern tribes of Indians is indispensably requisite for the information of Congress. I am persuaded, that they will effectively prevent either transcripts or publications of all such circumstances as might be injurious to the public interests.[88]

The practice of designating current military and diplomatic information as "confidential" quickly became routine, except where the executive chose to publicize a situation in order to prepare public opinion for unpleasant, potentially dangerous, or expensive undertakings.[89] In no case did the House defy the president's judgment by publishing confidential information, yet its responsible posture did not necessarily ensure it access to full information from the executive, any more than that of the Senate had done. Instead, as the political rift widened between the adherents of Hamilton and those of Madison and Jefferson, the regulation of interbranch communications became ever more delicate and problematic.

In December 1791 the president ruefully notified Congress that an entire division of the United States Army had been decimated in a surprise Indian attack. Serious questions soon were raised about the government's responsibility for the disaster. The American troops were said to have been undone by inadequate provisions, unusable ammunition, and nondelivery of their pay. Officials close to Hamilton and Secretary of War Henry Knox were accused of incompetence and corruption. The military situation on the frontier was now highly precarious. Clearly, a firm presidential response was needed to restore confidence and meet the threat.

In January 1792 the president asked Knox to prepare a public statement on Indian policy, recounting the government's failed peace efforts and the reasons why a military buildup was now considered essential. This unprecedented appeal by the president on behalf of administration policy was designed to defuse the substantial opposition in Congress to the expense of a major arms buildup. One supporting item submitted by Washington on a "confidential" basis was a message from a friendly Indian chief known as the "Cornplanter." When the customary motion was made to clear the galleries for the reading of this document, someone objected that the statement had already appeared in the newspapers. This unprecedented challenge to a presidential request was brushed aside on the theory that "although it might be very proper that the speech itself should be read, yet, as it had been confidentially received from the Executive, there would be a manifest trespass on propriety and decorum in having it read with open galleries."[90]

The defense appropriation was approved on January 30, 1792,[91] but there were still grave questions outstanding about the massacre of General St. Clair's expedition. On February 2 it was moved in the House that a committee be established to inquire into the causes of St. Clair's defeat.[92] This too was unprecedented and presented new questions about the control of information. In light of the recent fuss over keeping the Cornplanter's speech secret and in light of the explicitly informative purpose of the proposed investigation, there was reason to doubt whether the president's requests for confidentiality would be treated as deferentially as in the past. Thus it is probably no coincidence that on February 17, 1792, the House for the first time adopted a formal rule to govern the handling of confidential messages.

> Resolved, That it be a Standing Order of this House that whenever confidential communications are received from the President of the United States, the House shall be cleared of all persons except the members and the Clerk, and so continue during the reading of such communications, and during all debates and proceedings to be had thereon.
>
> And that, when the Speaker, or any other member shall inform the House that he has communications to make, which he conceives ought to be secret, the House shall, in like manner, be cleared till the communication be made; the House shall then determine whether the matter requires secrecy or not, and take order accordingly.[93]

This order, whether adopted spontaneously or by interbranch negotiations, was probably intended to smooth the way for the projected investigation. If so, it did not succeed in quelling all misgivings, for on March 27, a motion was brought forward to request the president to conduct an in-house investigation instead. However, this was defeated by a vote of thirty-five to twenty-one, and the House then voted forty-four to ten to go forward with its own investigation.[94]

The official report of the debate on this occasion makes for confusing reading. From the bewildering variety of questions raised one would hardly guess that the inquiry proposal had been before the House for two months and that members had had ample time to consider what course the House should follow. A clearer perspective on the episode is gained by examining the alignment on the two roll calls that capped the debate. Twenty-eight representatives voted against a presidential investigation and for an investigation conducted by the House. This was Madison's position, but he carried only about half of his usual supporters with him and this time was joined by at least nine staunch friends of the administration, such as Theodore Sedgwick of Massachusetts. Meanwhile, there were fourteen members who first supported a presidential inquiry but then voted for a congressional investigation when the former proposal was defeated. More than half of these men were oppositionists, including such close Madison allies as William Branch Giles and William Findley. In fact it was Giles, Madison's veritable second in command, who had moved for a presidential inquiry in the first place. Just six members, including Hamilton's champions Fisher Ames and William Smith, voted against both forms of investigation, while four men supported a presidential inquiry but opposed one conducted by the House. Curiously, two of these last four, John Page and Thomas Sumter, had been anti-Federalists and foes of executive power in the First Congress and had voted with Madison on most issues in the present, Second Congress.[95]

The defection of so many from their usual voting blocs is intriguing. Although party division had not yet reached the level of cohesion and discipline it would attain in the Third Congress, it was unusual for men like Giles and Page to split from Madison on a major issue. When that did occur, it was usually because Madison had decided to support the administration and could not persuade his allies to go along. The present roll calls show an extraordinary departure from the normal pattern on the opposition side; and the normally pro-administration members show a similar fragmentation. Ames, Sedgwick, and Artemis Ward of Massachusetts voted together in most cases. On this occasion Ames opposed both motions, Ward supported both, and Sedgwick voted with Madison to support a congressional inquiry only.

It is possible that there were secret deals or subtle maneuvers involved here, but the most straightforward explanation would point to the divergent pressure of partisan and institutional allegiances in a transitional period when these were struggling for control of members' hearts and minds. Those opposing any investigation may be identified as committed to the partisan cause of Hamilton and his friends. Many of those supporting an investigation regardless of who might conduct it may also have had partisan motives, though perhaps some of them simply wished to resolve the doubts about St. Clair's expedition, let the chips fall where they might. While these two groups, totalling twenty members in all, downplayed the separation of powers question, thirty-two members treated that question as decisive—twenty-eight supported a congressional investigation only, while four favored a presidential inquiry but opposed one conducted by the House. One-third to one-half of these men were deserting their normal allies in so voting.

Thus it was a bipartisan majority that consciously set the precedent for congressional investigations of executive malfeasance. The committee they appointed to inquire into St. Clair's debacle was bipartisan in composition, and it was "empowered to call for such persons, papers, and records as may be necessary to assist their inquiries."[96] On March 30, the committee directed to the secretary of war a call for certain documents; Knox promptly wrote to Washington for guidance.[97] Washington, declaring his concern to set a proper precedent on the occasion, convened a cabinet meeting. This was an unusual step, as the president's custom was simply to call for written opinions from the department heads.[98] Unfortunately no official record of the cabinet's deliberations was preserved. Our information of what transpired in this case comes from Jefferson's diary.

At the March 31 meeting, it was decided that the novel questions presented required further thought. The president revealed his concern that "there might be papers of so secret a nature that they ought not to be given up." A second meeting was held on April 1, when, according to Jefferson, four points were agreed upon.

1. that the house was an inquest, therefore might institute inquiries
2. that they might call for papers generally

3. that the Executive ought to communicate such papers as the public good would permit & ought to refuse those the disclosure of which would injure the public. Consequently were to exercise a discretion.

4. that neither the committee nor House had a right to call on the head of a department, who & whose papers were under the President alone, but that the committee should instruct their chairman to move the house to address the President. . . . Finally agreed to speak separately to the members of the committee and bring them by persuasion into the right channel. It was agreed in this case that there was not a paper which might not be properly produced.[99]

This memorandum, commonly cited as the earliest legal precedent on the president's constitutional power to withhold information, deserves careful attention.[100] Properly speaking, of course, this diary entry is not an official document. Jefferson was writing not as an official spokesman for the executive branch but as an interested participant in an ongoing political struggle that cut across institutional boundaries. His memorandum, not published until years after the event, calls for analysis sensitive to the political as well as the legal issues that were involved.

President Washington was concerned about establishing a proper balance between executive and legislative prerogatives; at the same time he had to contend with the immediate crisis of confidence affecting the Treasury and War departments and the army. He desired no confrontation with the legislature, but sought ways to preserve the dignity of his office and the integrity of his own administration. For the cabinet, too, momentous questions of state were interwoven with personal political risk and opportunity. With Hamilton in a vulnerable position, it must have been Jefferson who seized the chance to drive home a point that had concerned him for so long: it was dangerous for the president to permit direct communications between Congress and department heads that were not subject to his control. In the context of this investigation it was difficult for Hamilton and Knox to argue the contrary. To avail themselves of the president's protection, they had to accept the principle of presidential control over their communications with Congress. The secrecy issue proved a face-saving method to establish this. According to Jefferson, Hamilton made some resistance to the fourth point of decision, thinking himself "subject to Congress in some points"; he was ready to admit, however, that he thought himself, "not so far subject as to be obliged to produce all papers they might call for. They might demand secrets of a very mischievous nature." Such a determination, however, was best left to the president and not to a department head.

Thus a subtle confluence of interests led all concerned to agree on a position that maximized presidential power at the expense of department heads and at the expense of Congress as well. The need to protect state secrets supplied a crucial doctrinal prop for this bargain, even though no actual secrets were jeopardized in the present case and even though the House had just adopted a standing order to formalize its commitment to honor presidential requests for confidentiality.

There is in fact no evidence that the standing order played any role in the cabinet's deliberations. Perhaps the cabinet members simply had no confidence in the secrecy of the House and feared that confidential information would leak out despite the official policy. Perhaps they even felt it would be inappropriate for the president to ask the House to conceal evidence in the case of a formal investigation. Even so, the separation of powers and the public interest might require some leeway for the president in the event of irresponsible probes. Hence, as Jefferson put it, they were to "exercise a discretion."

The decisive point is that no participant in the cabinet discussion had an interest in speaking out for congressional prerogative or in suggesting that the concern for secrecy might be exaggerated or beside the point. Moreover, the House itself never had occasion to protest the principles ostensibly decided by the cabinet, for these were never formally announced and no information was actually withheld.

On April 4 the president ordered Knox to give the House all the papers it had requested;[101] thereafter, the secrecy issue disappeared entirely from view until the House issued its final report in February 1793. This report was too mild and complacent to give general satisfaction; and when Ensign John Morgan went to the press with charges of a coverup, General St. Clair had Morgan arrested for mutiny. Eventually Morgan was convicted of the lesser offense of insubordination and let off with a reprimand.[102]

The opposition press raised a storm of protest over Morgan's harassment, but they had no occasion to protest the president's position on the sharing of information with Congress. Indeed, it is unclear that the opposition really knew what his position was. No formal claim of privilege had at any rate been made.

In the aftermath of the St. Clair episode the House reverted to its preoccupation with resisting Hamilton's policy guidance. Emboldened by their success in the 1792 elections in which they had won control of the House and a near deadlock in the Senate, opposition forces in the lame-duck Second Congress redoubled their efforts. In November 1792 the opposition made another of its perennial attempts to defeat a call upon Hamilton for a legislative proposal. One opposition spokesman, John Mercer of Maryland, argued that only the president might properly submit plans and went on to intimate that the president might also have a power to withhold information. This is the earliest trace of that idea in the *Annals* of Congress. Unfortunately the text is hopelessly garbled at the key point; one can only conjecture that Mercer was aware of the St. Clair "precedent."[103] Whether or not he and his colleagues knew of the cabinet's discussions, the formulations adopted there were far from the last word on the subject.

Conclusions

The communication practices of the American government as of early 1793 were a far cry from anything the framers of the Constitution could have anticipated. Many of them, indeed, seemed to run counter to the spirit, if not the letter, of the framers' plan. That these developments occurred so soon and under the auspices of the founding generation itself could lead one to simplistic and cynical conclusions: that politics is always lawless; that there was nothing the framers could have done to change this; and perhaps that they never really expected, or sincerely tried, to establish the rule of law. This charge would be hasty, for lawlessness comes in significantly different varieties. It scarcely advances understanding to attribute all secrecy behavior to some one general characteristic of human nature or political life. Rather it appears that most secrecy behavior is complexly determined. Private motives of personal, class, or factional advantage are often inextricably bound up with public considerations of institutional integrity or national security. This fact vastly complicates both the task of moral evaluation and, more important, that of regulating such behavior in lawlike ways.

The men of 1789 were not always the paragons of wisdom and virtue described in patriotic mythology; yet neither were they especially cynical, corrupt, incompetent, or naive. Many of the specific problems they encountered were traceable to the boldness of their experiment in constitutional government. In particular, they were obliged by the novelty of their institutions to operate without the constraints of law and custom that usually define a system of set routines and vested interests.

The Constitution was quite deliberately framed in abstract terms, and it had little to say about governmental communication in general or secrecy in particular. There were many gaps in the design, and extensive adaptations were found necessary. Some of these were accomplished through open, formal procedures; some were informal, flexible, and based on tacit consensus; some were adversarial and covert. What was done reflected the ingenuity and energy of a handful of men. Yet they were men publicly committed to establishing and preserving the rule of law; and their activity was profoundly shaped by the structures that were constitutionally laid down for gathering information, weighing alternatives, and exercising authority. Thus each separate institution rapidly evolved a characteristic style of communication to deal with its own distinctive responsibilities, problems, and internal makeup.

The communication practices of the executive were both informal and highly fragmented. Neither the Constitution nor basic legislation imposed many constraints on the situation, and the president saw no reason to issue formal orders to deal with problems that arose. The principle of executive discretion was ideally adapted to the requirements of the major figures involved. It strengthened the presidential office and permitted the president to bypass formal consultations in favor of informal, vicarious contacts in which his personal prestige was not at risk. George Washington was not a lax or an insensitive administrator, but he faced a formidable problem in trying to hold his administration together. He valued the diversity of opinion among his talented aides and was willing to tolerate substantial ambiguity in both procedures and substantive policies in order to keep his and the country's options open. Though he deplored the feud between Hamilton and Jefferson, he could not intervene too aggressively without risking the probable resignation of one or both. Thus he was obliged to tolerate whatever unorthodox maneuvers came to his attention and even engaged in one or two of his own. Historians are unable to determine whether certain legislative contacts and diplomatic leaks by cabinet officers were or were not in violation of Washington's wishes; yet he cannot have been wholly unaware of them all.[104]

It would not have been wholly irrational to cultivate knowingly a modicum of unauthorized communication. The multiplicity of channels certainly enhanced the flow of useful information into and within the government. It may have profited the United States if foreign governments could not always be certain who spoke for the president and what his policy really was, but domestic imperatives were doubtless more important.

Hamilton thrived under this informal system, which left him free to pursue his policy goals under the president's mantle, to develop substantial influence in Congress, and to dabble in diplomacy, while sidestepping the constitutional questions implicit in these activities. Jefferson's position was perhaps the most difficult. Insofar as he represented a minority view in administration councils, he might have sought not only to align himself with sympathetic elements in Congress but to advocate congressional prerogative within the administration. As it happened, however, Jefferson's potential allies were powerful only within the lower house. He had nothing to gain by espousing the prerogatives of the Senate; in fact, he was delighted to avoid consulting them and never hesitated to remind the president that anything the Senate learned would soon be known in London. Even in the House, Hamilton's friends could usually command a majority. The House, moreover, had fewer responsibilities in the area of concern to Jefferson, and so he acquiesced in that body's disposition to leave the initiative with the administration respecting foreign affairs. Jefferson's political situation led him to join with Washington and Hamilton in supporting the doctrine of presidential discretion, while both secretaries sought to influence the president and Congress to support their respective policy views.

The result of this interplay was that a great deal of information flowed to Congress on an informal basis, but that formal consultations, especially in the realm of foreign affairs, tended to be restricted to very safe or absolutely necessary occasions. The need to protect state secrets provided the rationale, but the imperative of containing and masking the increasing tensions within the government was perhaps the more urgent cause.

The development of this system was attended with surprisingly little controversy. In particular, the president at no time in these years found it necessary to exercise, or even formally to assert, a power to withhold information from Congress. For the time being Congress was content with what it received and the conditions under which it was supplied. Secrecy practices were not subject to formalization except where controversy arose in a proper, authoritative forum and resisted consensual solution. This would seldom occur so long as a small group of elite policymakers shrank from drawing outsiders into the decisionmaking process.[105] Yet the early years of the Republic witnessed a rapid development of forces favorable to popular participation and to the formation of factions spanning institutional boundaries. As the logic of democratic ideology was reinforced by the imperatives of partisan struggle, secrecy became more and more difficult to justify.

The House, for its part, had no difficulty in establishing a basic posture of openness in its decisionmaking procedures. Publicity was seen as natural for that relatively "popular" body and helped to bring the government closer to the people and assure higher levels of support. Publicity did not appear to prejudice seriously the functions of the House or the interests of any potent group within it. The House's commitment to publicity went well beyond what was strictly required by the Constitution, yet it was qualified by a recognition that competing values might sometimes dictate exceptions to the general rule. Rather than attempting to codify these exceptions, however, the House preferred to treat the occasional need for secrecy as a matter entirely within the discretion of appropriate officials.

The First Congress did attempt by legislation to regulate certain aspects of its communications with the executive. In this it sought to strike a careful balance between the logic of the separation of powers and the practical need of Congress for expert advice and technical information from the executive. The early arrangement, based largely on abstract constitutional analysis, was soon subjected to intense reexamination in the context of Hamilton's concrete policy initiatives. His activities and the reactions against them built close working relationships between like-minded leaders in the several branches and led fairly directly to the beginnings of party formation in Congress. The public followed these events with interest, but the constitutional issues were purely for the several branches to decide. The House opposition was sensitive to the defense of legislative prerogative, yet it did not go to extremes either in demanding information from the executive or in trying to press for changes in the House's way of doing business. One reason was a sheer lack of votes; another was the absence of a clear-cut constitutional mandate, especially in the crucial realm of foreign affairs. In general, access to information was not yet a conspicuous issue; if questions arose, they were settled by quiet negotiations.

Only at the very end of this period did the House find it necessary to formalize, by standing order, its practice of deferring to the executive in handling "confidential" information. This step followed hard upon the first open protest against such deference; and it immediately preceded the House's first venture into the business of investigating the executive branch. In this instance, therefore, formalization appears not as a recognition of matured consensus, but as an effort to avert or contain incipient conflict. The rule adopted did not reflect the actual balance of power and was not destined to endure.

In the House, partisan conflict induced a move away from the early relaxed and open attitude. The situation in the Senate evolved quite differently. The senators were not popularly elected, and there was some justification for the view that their constituents were the state governments and not the people. Moreover the Senate had special executive functions and was expected to sit with the president as his advisory council. Thus it was natural that the Senate initially placed less value on publicity than did the House. Nevertheless, it carried the practice of secrecy to surprising lengths and continued to do so long after it had become clear that both its special relationship with the state governments and its conciliar function were stillborn. As of spring 1793 the secrecy policy of the Senate appeared unwavering, having been repeatedly approved by majorities of at least two to one. It mattered little whether access was demanded on behalf of the people, the states, or members of the House, or even what exceptions were provided for. Yet the benefits that accrued to the Senate from its policy were intangible to say the least. The crucial payoff of secrecy, it seemed at first, pertained to the institutional integrity of the Senate itself. The private format was claimed to be more efficient and more conducive to reaching consensus. The House's audience not only led members into oratorical excess, but interrupted the proceedings with captious displays of popular sentiment.

Secrecy may indeed have helped somewhat to expedite business and reconcile differences of opinion; yet the Senate had not freed itself of longwinded speeches or wrangling over trivia, much less of sectional rivalries. Besides, much of the Senate's important work was done by carefully selected ad hoc committees;[106] though dissidents may have been aware of what was going on, they lacked the votes to do much about it. Publicity surely would not have affected the character of the Senate's deliberations as much as was feared, for when the doors finally did open, the actual impact on the Senate's way of doing business was minimal.[107]

In any event, the real impact of secrecy on the Senate's institutional integrity was predominantly negative. With the passage of time it became clear that the Senate's secret deliberations were not really under its autonomous control but at the service of a policy-oriented alliance between leading senators and the Adams-Hamilton-Knox wing of the executive branch. Secrecy was one of the conditions that permitted this alliance to flourish.

It is true that the Senate's posture was consistent with its envisaged role as council to the president. Had the practice of face-to-face meetings with the president taken hold, no one would have suggested that they be held in public. Yet the Senate's secrecy from the outset applied to legislative as well as executive business, and the policy was continued long after the abandonment of the conciliar idea. Blanket secrecy was not designed for the protection of specific types of sensitive information. Virtually all the information provided to the Senate in this period was also shared with the House, where measures far less drastic were found adequate to protect the national interest. This policy also did not ensure the Senate's access to executive information. In fact, where secrecy was truly vital to the executive, the Senate, despite its policy, tended to be left in the dark.

Even granting that a strong presidency was widely perceived as essential to the authority and credibility of the new government at home and abroad, the Senate's steady acquiescence in the erosion of its prerogatives is difficult to understand. When the Senate accepted the principle that the president might consult with them in the manner and at the time of his own choosing, when it agreed, for its part, to keep no secrets from the president and to reveal none of his to the country, when it made no protest to the president's opening sensitive negotiations without submitting his envoy's name or instructions for its approval, when it so readily agreed to the inclusion of a secret article in the first treaty to which it gave its assent, and when senators who opposed the treaty on other grounds were not allowed to enter their protest in the journal, no doubt the reasons pertained in large part to domestic politics. The Senate majority saw no reason to insist on a greater formal role, since it supported the executive policies in force and was friendly to those in charge. From a partisan perspective, it would not be a constructive step to enact procedures facilitating greater participation by dissident members of the Senate.

Secrecy did preclude the opposition from bringing external pressures to bear on the Senate majority, but it also prevented the Senate leadership from having any persuasive impact on public opinion and was itself something of an irritant and a handle for criticism. Thus even from a partisan viewpoint, secrecy was a mixed blessing at best.[108] Ideologically anachronistic and institutionally dysfunctional, the policy was based to a large extent on reflexive status anxiety rather than on more tangible benefits. Yet neither democratic ideology nor institutional self-interest was potent enough to change the early Senate's attitude. Once again, partisan struggle would be the transforming factor.

The Senate's blanket rule of secrecy was not the only early

"precedent" marked for extinction. The House's standing order on confidentiality and the president's inchoate idea of his power to withhold information from Congress were to prove equally unstable in the face of the raging political strife of Washington's second term. As conditions changed, it did not seem appropriate to adhere mechanically to these early procedural ground rules; they came to be altered, reinterpreted, or sometimes ignored. These discontinuities cannot but complicate the effort to depict governmental secrecy behavior as subject to the rule of law, for procedural regularity is a crucial dimension of that concept. Yet a norm of regularity need not exclude all change; in general, it sanctions change that is effected through lawful channels and accompanied by reasoned justification. For a time, the founders succeeded rather well in living up to these conditions.

Party Conflict and Congressional Rebellion_____4

In 1792 Washington and Adams won easy reelection. At the same time, in a congressional election marked by an unprecedented focus on national, as opposed to local issues, the Madison-Jefferson faction won control of the House and became a force to be reckoned with in the Senate as well. This election, along with Jefferson's resignation from the cabinet, set the branches of government on ever diverging paths. Increasingly self-conscious, cohesive political parties now sought to use their strongholds in the separate branches to struggle for control of policy outputs. This struggle was more open and legitimate, as well as more intense, than what had gone before. Its openness and its congruity with formal institutional boundaries encouraged the elaboration of legal doctrine, giving incentive and opportunity for new efforts to develop or modify the rules and procedures applicable to policymaking. Though the rising intensity of conflict and the salience of foreign policy issues made agreement on the rules more difficult, substantial progress initially was made in formalizing and refining the early, consensual norms of publicity and secrecy.

The Opening of the Senate's Doors

In the first five years of its existence neither public ridicule nor formal protests by state legislatures had swayed the Senate from its closed-doors policy. Annual proposals to open the doors were defeated by comfortable margins with little sign of prospects for early change. The elections of 1792, however, had significant impact on the complexion of the Senate that convened in December 1793. All ten of those who had supported open doors in February 1793 were still present, while only eleven of the eighteen who voted against it had returned.[1] Opposition ranks were augmented by several new faces; in addition, the voting behavior of the independents shifted significantly toward the opposition pattern. Many questions now were decided by one- and two-vote margins. Moreover, even the loyal administration supporters among the new men had no established record or commitment on the secrecy issue.

The open-doors resolutions of January 16, 1794, were introduced by Alexander Martin of North Carolina. Martin's preamble and resolutions resembled closely those of 1793; though he did give a more explicit nod to the concept of popular sovereignty, at the same time he shrewdly appealed to the institutional prestige of the Senate itself and the government's need for public support.[2]

While the resolutions were pending, an unprecedented situation developed: dispute over the credentials of Albert Gallatin, newly elected senator from Pennsylvania. The technical issue was whether the foreign-born electee had been a citizen for the constitutionally requisite nine years; the political significance of the controversy was immense. Gallatin was a talented and influential oppositionist and very popular in Philadelphia, the seat of government. Both senators and local citizens were keenly interested in the outcome of the credentials dispute.

On February 10, a motion was made that the doors be opened for a public debate on this particular occasion. The next day, without reported debate or record vote, the motion was carried. Regrettably, no firsthand account of this unexpected decision has come to light; one is reduced, accordingly, to speculation.[3]

Gallatin's political allies must have stood solidly in support of a public hearing. For them ideology and party interest clearly coincided. However, the motion could not have carried without some nonpartisan support. Perhaps some were swayed by the consideration that, in agreeing to open the doors for this debate, they would not necessarily set a precedent applicable to ordinary legislative business. Indeed, though he was not charged with any offense, the debate was generally referred to as Gallatin's "trial." The quasi-judicial character of the proceeding may have made publicity seem unusually appropriate.[4] Or perhaps it was simply that senators appreciated the political imperative to appear scrupulously fair in handling this particular matter.

Martin's resolutions for a permanent opening of the doors came up for debate on February 19, the second day of Gallatin's "trial." The first day had apparently been nontraumatic,[5] but this did not convince the Senate majority that Martin's proposal deserved their support. Indeed, preliminary shows of hands indicated that the old attitudes were entirely unchanged. First the Senate summarily rejected Martin's preamble; then it voted to postpone the main question until the next session of Congress. Of the twenty-seven senators voting on this motion, nineteen had participated in the 1793 vote. Ten of them had voted for open doors and nine for secrecy, and not one altered his position now. Of the eight new senators now voting, the five Federalists voted to postpone; the three Republicans supported open doors. The open-doors contingent thus rose to thirteen, while, due to the absence of three senators who had voted for secrecy in 1793,[6] the pro-secrecy forces numbered only fourteen this day.

It was thus an accident of poor attendance that brought the open-doors movement within one vote of success. This accident, however, permitted the latent weakness of the pro-secrecy position to become manifest.

It could not escape the senators that public opinion was growing increasingly organized, intense, and potent. So far the Republican opposition had reaped the lion's share of benefit at the polls. The role of Senate Federalists would be more crucial than ever; only public exposure could allow them to exert an influence proportionate to their talents. For the younger generation, a more popular and democratic style held fewer terrors than for men who reached political maturity under an aloof, aristocratic regime. Moreover, the ideological case for blanket secrecy was incoherent. Unlike supporters of open doors, defenders of secrecy did not thereby win points with their constituents.[7] In short, the benefits of secrecy were meager; if only partisans were willing to defy tradition in a losing cause, many others were apparently only superficially committed to it.

Stephen Bradley of Vermont had voted for secrecy both in 1792 and in 1793, though he did support the 1792 effort to admit members of the House to the Senate chamber. However, in the present session he voted with the opposition on many important issues, and, despite his record on the secrecy issue, he cannot have been a true believer. When he observed that Martin's resolutions had come within a single vote of passage, Bradley moved that the question be reconsidered, signaling his intention to change his vote. At this point three other New Englanders joined him in defecting from the secrecy camp, and the motion to reconsider was carried by a margin of seventeen to ten.[8]

The vote was apparently preceded by a vigorous debate of which unfortunately no detailed account has been found.[9] The official record reveals only that the old guard managed to secure two modifications of Martin's proposal: implementation was postponed until the next session, and the resolution was narrowed to cover legislative proceedings only and not, as had been proposed, the judicial functions of the Senate. The amended open-doors resolution was adopted on February 20, 1794, by an overwhelming margin of nineteen to eight.[10]

It is most peculiar that the sequence of events by which the Senate reversed its policy began with its opening the doors for Gallatin's "trial" and ended with its decision to exempt future judicial proceedings from publicity. Even if Gallatin's trial was not a "judicial" proceeding in the strictest sense—the main reference was surely to impeachment trials—the logic of this sequence of decisions remains obscure.

Gallatin's trial, at any rate, had apparently been an edifying spectacle to watch, and the Senate's new publicity posture was hailed as a welcome change of heart.[11] Ironically, it was the trial that had the more tangible political impact, for Gallatin's expulsion at once deprived Senate Republicans of an able voice and a crucial vote. There was no comparable change in the Senate's performance when the doors finally opened for regular business on December 9, 1795.[12] The opening of the doors was a symbolic watershed, signaling a major change in the Senate's self-image and a partial repudiation of its old leadership. The direct effects on decisionmaking, however, were attenuated by other barriers to democratization, including the indirect election of Senators, the length of their terms, the continuing power of the old guard, and what proved a very limited public interest in attending the Senate or reading the stenographers' incomplete reports of its debates.

That the opening of the Senate had only a modest direct impact is hardly surprising in retrospect; yet it does not follow that the issue was an unimportant one. The long and bitter struggle to open the doors reflected the intellectual and political difficulties involved in adapting the constitutional structure to the changing imperatives of partisan contention. The implications of conflict for secrecy and publicity policy were dialectically reversed as the political context changed. For years, some senators had voted for secrecy because the open-doors movement was part of an attack upon their whole political philosophy, and entailed a condemnation of the style and substance of their careers. Their instinctive response to conflict was literally to close ranks. The catalyst for change was the election of 1792, but a partisan head count cannot explain the difference between a pro-secrecy vote of eighteen to ten in 1793 and a pro-publicity vote of nineteen to eight on the final tally of 1794. Although the Republican faction in the latter year certainly numbered no more than fourteen,[13] it was clear that the old, elitist style in politics was obsolescent, and publicity was now the more effective instrument of struggle. The New England Federalists who crossed over must have recognized that opening the doors would enhance the Senate's image and their own careers, and it might also yield benefits in the form of increased policy support. As things stood, the Senate had risked becoming a body without a real constituency. Both the House and the executive branch were increasingly taking their cases aggressively to the people; it was fitting that the Senate should position itself to do likewise.

Foreign Crisis and the Politics of Executive Publicity

The international crisis triggered by the French Revolution had tremendous impact on American politics. It set an agenda dominated to an unusual degree by military and diplomatic issues, while widening ideological rifts polarized both the governing class and an increasingly opinionated public. Some Americans applauded the victories of republicanism over monarchism, while others deplored the weakening of the traditional social order and associated forms of political authority. By 1793 the issues were no longer abstract: events in Europe were forcing increasingly difficult choices upon the American government.

Congress was in recess when news of war between France and Britain reached America in April 1793. The president quickly convened the cabinet and submitted for their consideration an elaborate list of questions about the options open to the government.[14]

All were agreed that neutrality would be preferable to involvement in the war. The weakness of the American military posture, especially at sea, was an obvious and sufficient reason for this conclusion. Hamilton, in fact, already had promised the British minister that neutrality would be the policy of the United States.[15] However, awkward questions were posed by the French-American Treaty of Alliance dating back to 1778 and supported by strong pro-French sentiment in the country. Hamilton saw it as essential for the executive to take a firm stand in order to make neutrality work. Jefferson, however, feared that Hamilton and his friends would manage to implement neutrality in a highly pro-British manner unless Congress were to formulate the guidelines. Moreover, there was a powerful constitutional argument that if the president could not declare a state of war without the assent of Congress, he ought not to impose neutrality unilaterally either.

It was Jefferson who placed the question of convening an emergency session of Congress on the cabinet's agenda, and he felt so strongly on the issue that later he induced Madison to write an essay attacking the administration for usurping the legislative power.[16] Yet the cabinet's April decision that Congress should not be convened and that the president should immediately issue a proclamation of neutrality was unanimous. Not only did Jefferson go along, but he agreed to conceal the fact that the idea of convening Congress had even been considered, and later he helped to head off a debate in Congress on the constitutionality of the proclamation.[17]

This ambivalent, not to say devious, course of action was accompanied by a significant change in Jefferson's constitutional thinking, one he could not openly espouse and act upon without placing himself in a most awkward position. Jefferson had formerly been a warm supporter of executive discretion in foreign affairs. Now, as the sharing of power with the Senate and the House had more to offer in terms of his own policy goals, he grew increasingly sensitive to the dangers implicit in Hamilton's sweeping concept of executive power. Yet his freedom to speak out against that doctrine was limited by his official cabinet status and probably also by a real fear that Congress might rashly involve the country in war with Britain. Indeed, to have come out openly for congressional prerogative would have played directly into the hands of a foreign power. For this was the period when France's minister to America, Citizen Edmond Genêt, sought to make common cause with Congress against the president and to rally the American people against neutrality.

Though he continued to urge the president to convene Congress as soon as possible, Jefferson was obliged to lecture Genêt on the impropriety of Genêt's identical demand and of his plan to lobby in Congress for a policy change.[18] Clearly the situation was not conducive to doctrinal or behavioral consistency. In fact, Jefferson's position was so uncomfortable that he soon notified the president of his intention to resign at the end of 1793.[19] The issues before the country could no longer be resolved or contained within the confines of the executive branch, and his isolated position in the cabinet had largely depleted his usefulness there. At this point the causes in which he believed could better be served from outside the government. The congressional opposition was stronger than ever, and the role of public opinion in shaping executive decisions seemed destined to grow. By now even Hamilton was insisting that the president counter Genêt's activities with a publicity campaign of his own.[20] What began as a policy dispute within a tiny governing elite would fast become a partisan conflict mobilizing a substantial part of the citizenry. This development was realized as a by-product of tactical elite decisions, induced by the fact that a policy like neutrality could not be implemented without broad public understanding and support. The democratic ideals of the American Revolution, amplified and extended by French revolutionary thinkers and politicians, were bearing fruit in American politics in ways that the framers could not have anticipated.

In autumn the president set to work on his opening message to the Third Congress. It was essential to persuade Congress and the country that the administration had acted properly in issuing the Proclamation of Neutrality and that supporting legislation, including large military appropriations, should be promptly enacted. To this end Jefferson proposed a very extensive briefing on the international situation and the issues outstanding between the United States and the several European powers.[21] At a cabinet meeting of November 28, conflict erupted over the selection of documents to be placed before Congress and the option of designating some or all as "confidential." Hamilton, who was loath to supply Anglophobes with ammunition, urged that the entire message on British relations be placed on a confidential basis since it referred to matters still under negotiation, while Attorney General Edmund Randolph took the view that certain of the documents should not be given to Congress at all. Jefferson argued, though, that talks with Britain on both sides of the ocean were hopelessly stalled.

> I began to tremble now for the whole, lest all should be kept secret. I urged, especially, the duty now incumbent on the President, to lay before the legislature and the public what had passed on the inexecution of the treaty . . . that . . . it could no longer be considered as a negotiation pending. . . . The President took up the subject with more vehemence than I have seen him show, and decided without reserve, that [all the British documents] should go in as public. . . . This was the first instance I had seen of his deciding on the opinion of one against that of three others, which proved his own to have been very strong.[22]

With far less difficulty the cabinet agreed that negotiations with Spain and the Barbary powers were in fact pending and that the relevant messages would be confidential. The message on French relations posed a different problem. Though no negotiations were pending, it was decided not to include certain documents respecting Genêt's controversy with the administration and the bitter internal wrangles he had provoked. Apparently, where the safety and honor of individuals were at stake, the security of "confidential" communications was not to be relied upon.[23]

After the meeting Hamilton continued to press for confidential treatment of the message on British relations.[24] On December 2,

1793, Jefferson penned a memorandum to the president, opposing this suggestion in urgent and sweeping terms. This document, written in the final month of his tenure as secretary of state, reflected the full extent to which his thinking on executive publicity had changed. It made the following points: that Congress would certainly publish the message anyway; that all the information was already known to Great Britain, and no harm could be done by its publication; that negotiations had collapsed; that the effect on public opinion would be beneficial to the government; that it would be wrong to publish American grievances against France and conceal those against Britain; that

> no ground of support for the Executive will ever be so sure as a complete knowledge of their proceedings by the people, and it is only in cases where the public good could be injured, and *because* it would be injured, that proceedings should be secret.—in such cases it is the duty of the Executive to sacrifice their personal interest (which would be promoted by publicity) to the public interest;

and, finally, that the president had the same "duty" to inform his constituents as did the legislature.[25]

Now this was a strong performance. It recognized the value of publicity both as a means and as an end, speaking the language of duty as well as assessing the pragmatic interests involved. The distinction between the public good and the political needs of the administration was an important conceptual refinement not previously explicit in cabinet deliberations on secrecy. Though Jefferson argued that in this case both factors favored publicity, he stated clearly that in case of conflict the public good ought to prevail. Jefferson's arguments must have impressed Washington favorably, for he made no attempt to restrain Congress from publishing the diplomatic correspondence with Britain that Jefferson selected for inclusion in his message of December 5.

Promptly, as Jefferson had predicted, the House resolved to print up five hundred copies for public distribution.[26] British Minister George Hammond was doubly distressed—by the publication of the message and by its one-sidedness. At this point, the best he could do was try to set the record straight. His informal protest that two important documents had been omitted led directly to a House resolution of January 20, 1794, calling on the president to supply one of the missing letters, "or such parts as he may think proper."[27] This was the first instance of a congressional call for information that explicitly recognized the executive discretion to censor which the cabinet had discussed at the time of the St. Clair investigation. It may be that the principle was already generally accepted, for there is no evidence that members were conscious now of setting an important precedent. At any rate, this innovation was easy for all to swallow under the circumstances. Hammond, who alerted the House to the "chasm" in Washington's message, thought Jefferson guilty of willful duplicity.[28] The Republicans, by being unusually deferential in calling for the letter, could repudiate Hammond and underscore their belief that Jefferson must have had sufficient reason for withholding it. The Federalist minority had no interest in leaving Jefferson with an escape hatch in this case, but the polite form of the resolution was in keeping with their generally supportive stand on executive discretion. Then again, the resolution did not really make clear whether Congress was *granting* permission to withhold part of the letter or *recognizing* a presidential power that was beyond its ability to restrict.

Whatever the House intended, Washington did not exercise his option, but supplied a complete copy of the letter, which the House duly published.[29] More important, the House did not thereafter make it a consistent practice to qualify its calls for information; indeed, most of the calls issued in the next two years were unqualified. The episode was perhaps more significant as a portent of congressional assertiveness than as a precedent for deference.

It is ironic that this assertiveness was instigated by the British minister. In principle Hammond looked with great disfavor on the publication of diplomatic correspondence, but he could not restrain the United States government from publishing its grievances against his own and so was driven to seek an even more extensive publication in order to bring the British side before the public. For similar reasons, the political interplay between Hamilton and Jefferson had led both of them to support a greater measure of publicity than either individual might have preferred. For their respective congressional allies, access to executive information was at a premium, and this imperative was more than enough to outweigh the diplomat's traditional scruples. Hammond, though, had great difficulty overcoming his distaste for the new public style. Never would he emulate Citizen Genêt in organizing mass meetings or writing for the American press. Instead he became involved in a bitter running battle with Edmund Randolph, Jefferson's successor as secretary of state, over the "injudicious," "partial," and "uncandid" American publicity practices.[30]

An interesting contretemps arose in connection with the president's message to Congress of February 24, transmitting a fresh exchange of notes between Hammond and Randolph in which Hammond acknowledged that he had not yet been authorized by his government to resume the suspended negotiations. These papers were not specifically designated confidential by the president, but were sent together with other papers that were so designated, leaving the executive's intention, perhaps intentionally, somewhat unclear. The House initially placed the Randolph/Hammond notes under injunction of secrecy, but two days later, in a secret session, the injunction was lifted, and the notes were promptly published in the newspapers.[31] Hammond, unaware of the House's resolution, penned a strong protest to Randolph, demanding to know by what authority the notes had been published.[32] Randolph's reply only increased Hammond's pique. After admonishing Hammond that he really had no right to inquire into the matter, Randolph informed him

> that the publication was not made by an executive authority; that nothing more was done by that authority than to send copies of the two letters to each House of Congress.
>
> From this explanation, no inference will, I am persuaded, be drawn of an admission that there was impropriety in the publication, howsoever made.[33]

In thus affirming the power of Congress to publish diplomatic papers on its own authority, the executive was adhering to constitutional orthodoxy while keeping its tactical options open. The separation of powers made it hard for outsiders to fix the blame when information was published, yet the timing and scope of publicity remained substantially under executive control, since Congress could not publish what it did not have. The president had not yet refused the House any information specifically called for, but he continued to exercise a discretion in what he selected for submission, and his power to withhold especially sensitive items had been noticed in a resolution of the House. In addition, he could always ask the House to treat his messages as confidential, though, as will appear, he could no longer count on the House's automatic compliance. It testifies to the gravity of the situation and the level of public concern that there were very few instances where documents on British relations were so designated;[34] and, in general, the flow of information to Congress and the public on this subject was very complete.

The president's message of December 5, 1793, defending his Proclamation of Neutrality, naturally covered French as well as British relations. In particular the dismissal of Genêt required justification, and the message included copious extracts from the Jefferson/Genêt correspondence, documenting Genêt's disrespectful attitude toward the government and the efforts to subvert American neutrality that led to his being declared persona non grata. Yet part of the story was carefully omitted.[35] Though he had acquiesced in Genêt's dismissal, Jefferson had protested vehemently when Hamilton wished to issue a special proclamation detailing Genêt's misconduct. When Jefferson persuaded the president that the step was unnecessary, Hamilton, acting through Senator Rufus King and Chief Justice John Jay, had leaked an account of Genêt's doings to the press.[36] Genêt's demand that Jay and King be prosecuted for libel had produced conflicting statements from Hamilton, Jefferson, Jay, King, and others as to what Genêt had actually said on certain occasions. The Federalists claimed that Genêt had threatened seriously to overthrow the government by an "appeal to the people" and that Jefferson had so understood Genêt at the time. Genêt, with Jefferson's support, insisted that it had been merely a passionate attempt to convince the government to alter its policy. The administration had refused to press Genêt's libel suit,[37] and the "appeal to the people" episode was omitted from the president's message—not because it was secret but because the cabinet wished to let the matter drop.[38]

In marked contrast to the president's openness respecting the correspondence of Hammond and Genêt with the State Department was his reticence about the conduct of Gouverneur Morris as American minister to France. Nothing had become public to arouse special interest in his doings, and no spontaneous communication was made save for a single, carefully edited dispatch relating Morris's efforts on behalf of distressed American shipowners.[39] On one occasion Madison informally approached Randolph for information on another Morris dispatch, of which rumors had apparently leaked out. As Randolph reported it to the president, "upon my answering that there were some things interwoven with the main subject, which ought not to be promulged, he admitted, that the discretion of the President was always to be the guide."[40] Yet many in Congress were no longer so willing to trust the president's discretion.

Congress was able, with Hammond's aid, to discover minor gaps in a presidential message and to obtain a missing document, but the more significant challenge to executive discretion involved the congressional handling of "confidential" messages, which were resorted to in cases where secret negotiations were in progress.

Early in 1792 President Washington had nominated two envoys to Madrid, whose announced mission was to conclude a treaty adjusting the western boundaries of the United States and opening the Mississippi River to navigation. When he decided to extend the talks to cover commercial relations as well, Jefferson insisted that this expansion of the envoys' powers be submitted to the Senate for approval.[41] The new negotiations made no perceptible progress, and the government's continuing failure to open the Mississippi as well as its inability to protect the settlers against Spanish-supported Indian incursions were potent sources of western disaffection.[42] Energetic steps were needed to persuade the western settlers—or their representatives—that the government could and would protect their interests. As part of this effort a copious history of the Spanish negotiations was laid before Congress on December 16, 1793. Because the talks were still in progress, the message was designated confidential.[43]

The information in the president's message to Congress could not relieve the House's anxiety about the volatile state of public opinion along the frontier, but it felt unable to take the initiative in publicizing the facts. Instead it moved, together with the Senate, to persuade the president himself to do so. Both houses had been favored with resolutions from the Kentucky legislature calling for information on the state of the Spanish negotiations. The House's official records do not document its response,[44] but on May 15, 1794, a Senate committee, to which the Kentucky resolution had been referred, reported back.

> That, in the present state of the business, it would be improper for Congress to interfere. But the committee recommend, that, in order to satisfy the citizens of the United States more immediately interested in the event of this negotiation, that the United States have uniformly asserted their right to the free use of the navigation of the river Mississippi, and have employed, and will continue to pursue, such measures as are best adapted to obtain the enjoyment of this important territorial right, it be

> Resolved by the Senate, that the President of the United States be, and he hereby is, requested to cause to be communicated to the Executive of the State of Kentucky, such part of the existing negotiation between the United States and Spain, relative to this subject, as he may deem advisable and consistent with the course of negotiations.[45]

The committee's report was accepted, and there is reason to believe that the House in fact passed a similar resolution. In a memorandum of July 15, 1794, Randolph called Washington's attention to the continuing unrest in Kentucky, to the resolves of that state's legislature, and to those of Congress. Though he suggested that the president was under no duty to comply with such resolutions, Randolph observed that it would be prudent to do as the "two Houses" had recommended:

> Although individuals of whatsoever number, great or small, have a right to petition, memorialize or remonstrate for a redress of grievances; there is a respect, which every government ought to exact for itself. To charge the general government with design in not adopting effectual measures for attaining the navigation—to intimate, that its measures have been uniformly concealed from the people of Kentucky, and veiled [in] mysterious secrecy, and that civil liberty is

prostituted, when the servants of the people are suffered to tell them, that communications which they may judge important ought not to be entrusted to them; as if the Executive was bound to promulge, what it might deem injurious to the public interest to be known; to demand that Spain be compelled to acknowledge their right, or that an end be put to all negotiations on that subject; to censure the President for tame submission and to exclaim against the want of protection, after all that has been done;—these things have no claim upon a formal answer; many of them being unfounded, and all intolerable upon principle. . . .

It is impossible to satisfy the expectations expressed . . . without establishing a precedent for throwing open the archives of the Executive to the whole world on all occasions. As much has already been communicated to the Governor of Kentucky in the letter of the 29th of March last as can be with propriety; except what may be added in consequence of the recommendation of the two Houses of Congress. . . .

The Secretary of State is therefore of opinion, that a letter be written to the Governor of Kentucky in pursuance of the resolution of the Senate and House of Representatives; and if in the course of writing it, any matter can be interwoven, which may obviate the complaints, which have been uttered, without appearing to be intended as answers to the resolutions, and without violating the degree of secrecy, due to negotiations existing, or the respect due to the Government, that it ought to be attended to.[46]

In due course Colonel James Innes of Virginia was selected to carry out the mission of briefing Kentucky leaders on the Spanish negotiations.[47] Randolph instructed him as follows:

It has been a maxim in the administration of the President of the United States, to satisfy all persons, that their interests have not been neglected, when adequate communications can be made without violating any rule of propriety. . . .

From the manifestation of the temper, prevailing in Kentucky, the Senate were induced to recommend to the President, to cause certain explanations to be made to the government. . . .

The combination of these various causes determined the President to send thither some character, qualified to fulfill the wishes of the Senate and himself, by full, but discreet and temperate representations, without losing sight of the existing position of the negociation, which being incomplete, requires delicacy in the mention of it, both from respect to the Court of Madrid, and the danger of precipitating the people into some heedless, or injurious speeches or conduct. . . .

The real object of your errand being to disabuse the minds of the people, it will be best to obtain the most public hearing. If therefore the Assembly should have risen, you will follow your discretion in pursuing this object. . . .

When you are about to speak of the state of things at this moment, say, that . . . the President . . . has . . . resolved to dispatch an Envoy extraordinary to Madrid, who shall be charged to bring the negociation to a conclusion, without any unnecessary delay. . . .

[Y]ou will communicate the information, which you have collected, with the utmost discretion, fulfilling at the same time the design of your errand. You will comment upon the resolutions of the two Houses of Congress . . . and your agency as demonstrations of the confidence which the people ought to repose in government.[48]

The administration was now prepared to go to the length of discussing the proposed sending of a special envoy and the tenor of his instructions before this proposal was even laid before the Senate. This was a highly untraditional gesture and one the Senate in the old days would surely have found insulting to its dignity. Now the early disclosure had been brought about by its own resolution.

The mission apparently did help to mobilize support in Kentucky for administration policy.[49] In many ways the episode exemplified the best potentials inherent in a flexible, informal, and cooperative approach to interbranch and public communications. Yet one essential condition for its success would seem to have been the existence of broad, bipartisan support within the official community for the administration's Spanish policy. In other cases, where strong disagreement prevailed about what could and should be done, it was becoming increasingly necessary for the separate branches to interact in a more formalistic and independent manner. In fact, the Innes mission proved almost the last gasp of the informal system based on policy consensus and mutual trust. By this time, for example, the House had already asserted a right to disclose on its own initiative secrets supplied it by the president on a confidential basis.

The Amendment of the House's Standing Order

Negotiations with the Barbary powers had been in progress since 1791, and periodic reports had been submitted to the two houses, mostly on a confidential basis.[50] The presidential message of December 16, 1793, contained a reasoned request for secrecy as to two particulars: the identity of a confidential source and the total amount the United States was prepared to pay in tribute and ransom.[51] The House began, as was customary, to consider the message behind closed doors, but, unexpectedly, several Republican members questioned the need for secrecy. When Federalists replied that, because the message was "confidential," the standing order of February 1792 left the House no choice in the matter, the standing order itself came under sharp attack. Madison declared that it ought to be rescinded; it had been adopted, he said, "for sundry reasons" and on a "particular occasion" and, in short, was no longer appropriate to the realities of interbranch relations. A Federalist spokesman replied that "the rule had been adopted after mature consideration, and he did not have any doubt that, when the reasons on which it was founded were fully known, it would appear to be a wise regulation."[52]

On December 30, Representative John Nicholas formally moved that the rule be reconsidered. The House, he urged, ought to retain a discretion to determine the need for secrecy in each given case. Most of the foreign policy questions pending were of a commercial nature; "communications relative thereto ought to be made as public as possible, for the people at large are generally and immediately concerned." In rebuttal, Federalists insisted that secrecy was necessary in many cases; "the government may be deprived of the most essential information from their foreign agents, should all security be removed from the safekeeping of confidential communications."[53] Benjamin Franklin Bache's *General Advertiser* carried a pair of letters signed "Gracchus," adding detail to the official report and taking the Federalist viewpoint severely to task.

> This day, Sir, my curiosity led me to hear the debates in Congress, they turned on the propriety of opening the doors during certain discussions. Many strange remarks were made, but I was struck dumb with astonishment at the sentiments . . . [t]hat the executive alone shall have the right of judging what shall be kept secret, and what shall be made public, and that the representatives of a free people, are incompetent to determine on the interests of those who delegated them. . . . The practice of shutting the doors of Congress which has obtained lately begins to create suspicion; it has been so frequent that the people begin to fear it will grow into a habit. It looks a little strange that a servant should shut the door against his master. . . .
>
> If the executive has the right to keep Congress ignorant of its transactions, if Congress have not the authority to act upon communications from the executive as they think proper, the President is paramount to the people, and Congress the mere creatures of executive authority. This is a change of sovereignty.[54]

The Republicans' argument had a great deal of merit, for certainly, the need for secrecy in some cases did not prove that the House should have no discretion. And so the House approved an amendment to its standing order, to provide that when confidential messages were received, the House was to inspect the papers and "determine whether the matter communicated requires secrecy, or not, and take order accordingly."[55] The members thereby officially espoused the view that, as Jefferson had intimated in his final memorandum to the president, and as Randolph had suggested in his rebuke to the British minister, George Hammond, the House could not lawfully be restrained from communicating to their constituents as they saw fit.

Behind the constitutional message, of course, was the fact that foreign policy could no longer be considered a nonpartisan affair. Still, the House proceeded to exercise its newly claimed discretion in an extremely cautious way. When a motion was made under the new standing order to open the doors for the remainder of the debate on Algerine affairs, it was defeated by a one-vote margin.[56]

On January 2 the House adopted secret resolutions to appropriate additional sums for the negotiations, to establish a naval force, and to refer the details to a committee.[57]

These were important decisions in fiscal terms alone. On January 7 a motion was made to publish them. It carried, and the House further ordered:

> That a committee be appointed to select such parts of the President's communications, respecting the Regency of Algiers, as his letter, accompanying said communications, suggests it would be proper to keep secret, and that they report the same to the House.[58]

Then, on February 6, the House resolved:

> That the communications made by the President to this House, respecting the Regencies of Algiers, Tripoli, and Tunis, be hereafter considered as public, except such parts as were marked by the committee, to whom the same were referred to be kept secret.[59]

The language of these resolves suggests that the House effectively deferred to the president's judgment here, as it did also with respect to the confidential message on Spanish relations, and the few British or French documents that the president designated confidential. In each case, selection of the parts to be published was either left directly to the executive, or performed by an ad hoc House committee pursuant to fairly clear guidelines.[60]

At the same time, the House attempted to exert a measure of institutional control over its members' communications. In providing for a determination by the House itself, the new rule implicitly rejected the idea that it should lie with individual members to decide what should be made public.

Under the old rule there had been quite a bit of leakage.[61] Thus the papers carried an open letter from Representative William Branch Giles on one aspect of the Algerine business as early as December 31, a week before the House voted to hold public debate on it.[62] As one editorial put it, the new rule only bowed to the inevitable: if disclosure could not be prevented, it had better be done by order of the House than by the illicit act of an individual.[63] Yet not all members admitted the House's authority to gag their communications with constituents. Thus, when members were asked by the ad hoc committee not to refer in the public debate to the secret portions of the president's message,

> Mr. Hunter said he would treat the committee as he would wish them to treat him. He had no design of condemning the committee; but he could not think of attempting to discuss a question where he was not at liberty to call for and examine the very materials requisite for deciding his opinion.[64]

Whereupon the House apparently dropped the idea of formally gagging the public debate and instead went into committee of the whole, thus moving the discussion behind closed doors.

This episode sheds light on both the significance and the limitations of formal regulations in shaping the course of events. The House was no longer bound to honor presidential requests for secrecy; yet members arguably were no more bound to honor its own. As a practical matter, even closing the doors could not guarantee that there would be no leaks. Federalist members had warned the House that its rule change might affect the president's exercise of his discretion in informing them; ultimately, the people might be more in the dark than ever. The Republicans were unmoved, because the old pattern of deference seemed unsuited both to their constitutional philosophy and to their political needs. In the event, despite the House's moderation in implementing the new rule, the Federalist warning was to prove amply justified.

The executive had for a time embarked upon a course of broad disclosure in order to win public support for its policies, and so far the partisan dynamics of the situation had led to even fuller disclosure than was initially contemplated. The results, however, were not what the president had hoped for. Though Congress agreeably passed a Neutrality Act ratifying and providing for enforcement of the president's Proclamation,[65] its overall policy thrust proved quite inconsistent with his conciliatory posture toward Great Britain. In March 1794 a temporary embargo on trade with Britain and her possessions was enacted. Proposals even more warlike, ranging from a permanent nonintercourse bill to the sequestration of debts owed to British citizens, were under serious consideration in both houses, jeopardizing the policy of neutrality and the peace as well. Contrary to Jefferson's somewhat pious assertion that publicity would always increase support for the government, in those days the news seemed to play into the hands of the administration's critics. More and more, Congress seemed to find the president's leadership inept, lacking in firmness, and faithless toward republican ideals. The administration's publicity effort was clouded severely by the fact that there were so many provocations and virtually no meaningful conciliatory gestures from Britain or Spain to report. The administration, however, was deeply committed to its conciliatory policy. Despite recent increases in defense spending, the United States remained without a navy and only modestly equipped for war on land. Jefferson had retired, and Hamilton was convinced that Britain would never back down in the face of economic pressures. There was no effective counter-voice in the cabinet. The warlike measures afoot in Congress, Federalists believed, could only serve a French interest and not that of the United States. Though amply informed of the facts, the opposition would not listen to reason. Their new assertiveness in pressing for and publishing sensitive documents was simply a direct threat to efficient management and substantive wisdom in policymaking. Inevitably, doubts began to arise about the continuing value of openness and even about the opposition's true intentions.

The Gouverneur Morris Investigation

One of the major milestones in this narrative was the Senate's launching in early 1794 of an inquiry into the conduct of Gouverneur Morris, the American minister to France. This episode is not included in most of the well-known accounts of the development of executive privilege, and they stand in need of modification in light of what happened and what did not happen in this case.[66]

Morris's political views were repugnant to the opposition, and his brashness offended proper New England Federalists as well. Only the president's personal influence had secured his appointment in 1792. Throughout his tenure charges had circulated that he did not accept the French Revolution as established fact or favor the further spread of republican institutions and ideas in Europe. By late 1793 the French government had in fact decided to request Morris's recall; it may have been leaks or rumors to this effect that prompted a proposal in the Senate on January 17, 1794, to call upon the secretary of state for Morris's official correspondence with the French and the American governments.[67] The resolution was unqualified in scope.

On January 23, the Federalists offered an amendment to address the call directly to the president himself. Next day, the amended resolution carried by a vote of thirteen to eleven. Allowing for absences, the division was virtually identical to the votes on Gallatin's expulsion and on the open-doors proposal. It was, in short, a partisan measure.[68] Fisher Ames, a leading House Federalist, wrote to a friend that he hoped the president would not comply. He feared for Morris's safety if his papers were made public while he remained in France. He also thought the call was constitutionally improper: "these fellows claim a share in diplomatic business, which is intended to unpresident the chief magistrate."[69]

Washington himself treated the call as raising new and difficult questions and took his cabinet's advice on what his response should be. It was Randolph who thoroughly explored the legal dimensions of the case in a very interesting series of memoranda.[70]

There is some doubt as to the sequence of events by which the executive branch reached its decision. Several of Randolph's memoranda are of uncertain date, raising a question whether the decisionmaking process was in fact a legally scrupulous one or whether the outcome was essentially predetermined before the constitutional issues had been analyzed.

In the earliest memorandum, dated Saturday, January 25, Randolph simply reported that he was in the process of going through the Morris correspondence, pursuant to earlier communications with Hamilton and the president. The second item, dated January 26, is a direct follow-up.

> I have examined all Mr. Morris's ministerial correspondence; and after the impression, which I had received from others, whom I supposed to be conversant with it, I am really astonished to find as little of what is exceptionable, and so much of what the most violent

would call patriotic. The parts to be ~~suppressed~~ withheld, will probably be of three denominations: 1. What relates to Mr. G[enê]t; 2. some harsh expressions on the conduct of the rulers in France, which, if returned to that country, might expose him to danger; 3. the authors of some interesting information who, if known, would be infallibly denounced. He speaks indeed of his *court;* a phrase, which he might as well have let alone.[71]

The phrase, "parts to be withheld," seems to presuppose a decision to censor the correspondence—a decision which, so far as the record shows, had not yet been taken. Logic thus argues for assigning the earliest possible date, January 26, to a separate memorandum, dated only "Sunday evening," in which Randolph took up the constitutional aspects of the case. Already, it would seem, the options under consideration had narrowed to two, and a full compliance was not one of them:

Mr. Randolph has just had the honor of receiving the President's letter. . . .[72]

If the resolution was made in the executive character of the Senate, then a resistance *in toto* seems at present the true path; because they are *executive,* only on *nominations* or *treaties;* and can call for papers relative to these subjects, only when the one or the other is propounded to them by the President.

On the other hand, as a branch of the *legislature,* the Senate have a greater latitude of power. They may call for papers, although they do not relate to a business, actually depending before them. They may call for them, with a view to originate business. But then, the President interposes his discretion, so as to give them no more, than, in his judgment, is fit to be given.

So that a very important question seems to be, whether the vote be a legislative or executive vote. It now stands on the legislative journal.[73]

For the sake of clarity a closely related memorandum will now be presented, although it is dated Sunday evening, February 2.

The President will be pleased to recollect, that a distinction was taken at the first interview, between the resolution as an executive and a legislative act. At least it was not meant by E.R. that if the papers were asked for in a legislative capacity, although without qualification, what was proper for the public eye should not be sent. The only idea, which he contemplated was, that what was required without qualification, should not be granted without qualification; but that what was improper should be withheld.

E. R. had asked himself, how the President was to know, whether the resolution was a legislative or executive act? For it is very probable, that it will not be specified. To this the answer appears to be, that if the President choose to understand it, without more accurate information, to be executive, he may then oppose in toto. If he choose to understand it as a legislative act, for the sake of avoiding unnecessary contest, he may do so, without injury to the executive rights, and discriminate such parts of the correspondence, as are unfit to be communicated. Or if he should be of opinion that he ought to observe a different line of conduct, according as the resolution may be executive or legislative, and will not undertake to decide, whether it be of an executive or legislative nature, he may, it is presumed, call for an explanation, as to the source, from which it proceeds.[74]

Randolph cited no authority or precedent for his executive/legislative distinction, nor, indeed, for his assumption that if the request was in a legislative capacity, the president might withhold such parts as he thought proper. The lack of overt memory is puzzling in that Randolph had been attorney general in 1792, at the time of the St. Clair investigation. Now, Randolph's analysis was strikingly new. Note, for example, his disavowal of the proposition that, if the Senate improperly omitted to qualify its request, the president ought to slap its hand by refusing the call in toto. No one had charged in 1792 that it was effrontery on the House's part to issue an unqualified call for papers, much less that the call should therefore be defied. Indeed, I have uncovered only one instance prior to the present case in which a call for papers had been expressly qualified. That was the House's call for Jefferson's letter, instigated by Hammond on January 20 and complied with on January 22, 1794, a few days before the present memoranda were written. The Senate, so far as is known, had never qualified a call for papers or been asked to do so.[75]

Whatever precedent had been set in the House, moreover, arguably did not apply to the right of the Senate to call for papers. Randolph's view apparently was that the Senate's right would be absolute when acting in an executive capacity, but, because it could not initiate executive business, the right applied only when the president laid a nomination or a treaty before it. Otherwise, the president could censor the papers for purposes such as those listed in the January 26 memorandum.[76]

This theory, plausible or not, was certainly novel. A contemporary observer linked the president's tightening attitude to the Senate's decision to open its doors.[77] This is an interesting speculation, but since the events were so closely timed, it makes little difference to an effort to reconstruct the cabinet's thought process.

The formal record of the cabinet's deliberations is unenlightening, and makes no reference to Randolph's analysis set forth in his letters to the president. Because of the uncertain date of the latter, we cannot be sure that Randolph's theory was before the cabinet when it met on January 28.[78] The minute simply states that:

> General Knox is of opinion, that ~~all~~ no part of the correspondence should be sent to the Senate.

> Colo. Hamilton, that the correct mode of proceeding is to do, what General Knox advises; but that the principle is safe, by ~~selecting~~ excepting such parts as the President may choose to withhold:

> Mr. Randolph, that all the correspondence, proper from its nature to be communicated to the Senate, should be sent; but that what the President thinks improper, should not be sent.[79]

Neither is it clear whether Attorney General William Bradford had the benefit of Randolph's ideas in preparing his separate, also undated opinion.[80] Bradford advised the president that:

> Every call of this nature, where the correspondence is secret and no specific object pointed at, must be presumed to proceed upon the

idea, that the papers requested are proper to be communicated. And it could scarcely be supposed, even if the words were stronger, that the Senate intended to include any letters, the disclosure of which might endanger national honour or individual safety.

The Attorney General is therefore of opinion, that it will be advise-able for the President to communicate to the Senate such parts of the said correspondence as upon examination he shall deem safe and proper to disclose: withholding all such, as any circumstances, may render improper to be communicated.[81]

One may seize upon Bradford's phrase, "and no specific object pointed at," to support an inference that, like Randolph, he would have taken a different view had the Senate expressly acted in its executive capacity, but this is not a necessary inference. The attorney general was focusing on the fact that the call for papers was unqualified, not on its basis or motive. Like the secretary of state, Bradford concluded that the president had a discretion all the same. He broadened this discretion beyond what Randolph had made explicit in his January 26 memorandum, appending the criterion of "national honour" to those of individual safety.[82]

Not only was doctrine evolving with impressive speed, but an overt effort was made to nail down interbranch agreement on the principles involved. Randolph was detailed for these consultations; in another undated memorandum, he informed Washington of the results.

E. Randolph has the honor of informing the President, that he saw Judge Wilson yesterday, and Mr. Madison last evening.

The former, to whom E. R. took an occasion of bringing up the subject of the resolution of the Senate in a general shape, said, that what they might have, he thought, ought to be sent; and what they ought not to have, ought not to be sent.

The latter expressed himself thus: "I told Colo. [James] Monroe, as far as delicacy would permit, that there must be many things, which the President cannot communicate with propriety: that if he was to select such as he thought proper, and transmit them, and the Senate were to make an opposition, the people would go with the President against the Senate.''

Mr. Madison then dilated upon the other view of the case; the withholding of papers altogether. This he conceived to be utterly inadmissible; whether the principle, or the particular suspicion, which some persons entertain of the diplomatic character, be considered. The consequence, he did suppose, would be, as has been already suggested to the President, that instead of a dispute with the Senate, the house of representatives would make common cause.[83]

Now James Wilson was a justice of the Supreme Court and a legal scholar of great reputation, who had played an influential role at the Constitutional Convention. Yet he could not speak for the entire Court, and the Court itself, unable or unwilling to provide the executive with advisory opinions, was necessarily mute.[84] Wilson's terse opinion added little authority to what others had said; that of Madison, however, was another matter entirely.

In view of Madison's role as leader of the House opposition, his conversation with Randolph was no dispassionate legal speculation. It was, rather, a delicate political negotiation, and Madison, instead of supporting Monroe, his Senate ally, to the hilt, was promising to support the president if he should withhold parts of the Morris papers from the Senate.

Insofar as both his institutional and his partisan interests would have encouraged Madison to take a more intransigent stand, Madison's conduct tended to disconfirm the theory of checks and balances he himself had worked out.[85] Perhaps it bespoke a deep constitutional conviction on his part that the president did have power to withhold information, though certainly the existing body of precedent was hardly overwhelming. Or perhaps Madison's response reflected a more pragmatic reading of public opinion and a personal distaste for sharp confrontations. At any rate, the apparent consensus that now emerged could be described, provisionally, as a workable and principled rule to regulate the transfer of sensitive information, consistent with the independence and integrity of each branch. Only the future could show how far this characterization was really valid.

The president accepted the virtually unanimous advice he had received, whether or not he appreciated the legal subtleties of Randolph's arguments. The documentary record breaks after Randolph's February 2 memorandum, resuming with the president's message to the Senate of February 26. In the interim, the president had finally decided to withhold "those particulars, which in my judgment, for public considerations, ought not be communicated."[86] He had also decided to designate the entire correspondence as confidential—a matter nowhere discussed in any of the memoranda of record and another innovation, insofar as no ongoing negotiations were existent that could be prejudiced by disclosure.

It is not known just when and by whom the Morris correspondence was actually sanitized, though Randolph had identified some sensitive passages a month earlier. Though the deleted passages were not extensive, their import can only be grasped in context of what was allowed to remain.[87] The criteria Randolph had mentioned on January 26 form our most explicit guide to divining the censor's intent, though not necessarily a definitive one. A careful comparison of the original and the censored versions indicates that many of the deleted sentences and phrases[88] did fall into the three categories listed by Randolph; yet perhaps four additional categories of deletion can also be identified. Randolph's categories all pertained to personal safety: items related to Genêt, harsh expressions on the conduct of French leaders, and identity of confidential informants.

The delicacy of Genêt's case lay in the fact that the American protests to France over his conduct had placed his life in danger. Ultimately, Genêt was spared only through Washington's good offices. Morris's report of a French offer to conciliate the United States by having the troublemaker arrested was excised, along with his other mentions of the case.[89]

Morris's letters often took individual French politicians to task for alleged corruption or incompetence, and the censor was thorough in excising specific names, or, where context made identity obvious, entire passages of this character.[90]

Finally, while there are no obvious instances of deletion of an informant's name, there are cases where accounts of intrigues afoot were omitted. Perhaps the sources of Morris's information would have been obvious to French insiders.[91]

The four additional categories of deleted matter were comments on the French national character, predictions on the likely course of French politics, remarks about the royal family and its plight, and policy advice to the American government. Publication of these passages would not have endangered any identifiable person, save perhaps Morris himself.

Morris's opinion of the public and private morals prevailing in France was extremely low, and he had a deeply pessimistic view of the prospects for early establishment of stable government there. He also had a tactless way of putting things. The censor deleted many of Morris's more offensive or flippant remarks and forebodings without really concealing the fact that, as Morris saw it, there was a great deal of corruption and violence being perpetrated in the name of democracy. Some examples of what was deleted include:

> The best picture I can give of the French nation is that of cattle before a thunder storm.[92]

> [I]t furnishes a new instance of the instability of human affairs, especially of those which depend on the opinion of an ignorant populace.[93]

> [T]he populace of the large towns, who, having some chance to gain by turning all things topsy turvy, and who, being happily secure against the possibility of loss, because they have nothing to lose, are always the ready instruments of mischief to those who can bring themselves to use them for destructive purposes.[94]

> It is the old story of King Log, and how long it may be before Jupiter sends them a crane to destroy the frogs and froglings, is a matter of uncertainty.[95]

> [A]nd, certainly, the most intelligent must be convinced that the republican virtues are not yet of Gallic growth.[96]

> [I]n the present situation of this country, the laws are but little respected; and it would seem as if pompous declarations of the rights

of man were reiterated only to render the daily violation of them more shocking.[97]

To balance the picture, here are some observations which the censor suffered to remain:

> The expense of the last month exceeded the income by about ten millions of dollars. . . . The dilapidation in every department is unexampled, and they have, to crown all, an increasing paper money, which already amounts to above three hundred million of dollars. From such facts it is impossible not to draw the most sinister presages.[98]

> As to the Government, every member of it is engaged in the defence of himself, or the attack of his neighbor.[99]

> Thank God we have no populace in America, and I hope the education and manners will long prevent that evil.[100]

> If, under these circumstances, the foreign force were out of question, I should have no doubt that the republican form would take place quietly enough, and continue as long as the morals of the country would permit. You know the state of morals here, and can, of course, (if it be necessary) form the calculation for yourself.[101]

> There seems to be more of treason in this country than was imagined, and every day increases suspicion, which, whether well or ill founded, has always the effect of distracting the public councils.[102]

If the censor was selective in suppressing Morris's unfavorable and pessimistic remarks about French politics in general, he was equally selective—or careless—in concealing where Morris's particular sympathies lay. In several passages Morris betrayed not only a strong affection for the king and the Marquis de Lafayette, but a substantial measure of support for their political aspirations and a decided familiarity with their secret plans and maneuvers. While not proving that Morris was actively involved in French right-wing politics, these statements were potentially embarrassing to his informants; thus, their removal can be explained by reference to Randolph's third category. Not so for expressions of sentiment like these:

> He [the king] died in a manner becoming his dignity.[103]

> [S]o that, if one were to judge by what passes in that quarter, France would be nearly unanimous in the re-establishment of royalty, should they come in force to Paris.[104]

> I own to you that I am not sanguine as to the success [of a planned move by Lafayette against the Jacobins].[105]

On the other hand, these remarks survived the censor's scrutiny:

> The present intention of the King is to secure the liberty of France; but whether he will preserve the steady purpose through those varying events, which must soon take place, to me appears uncertain.[106]

> [I]t would seem strange that the mildest monarch who ever graced the French throne . . . a man whom none can charge with a criminal or cruel act . . . should be prosecuted even to the death. Yet such is the fact. I think it highly probable that he may suffer, and for the following causes: The majority of the Assembly found it necessary to raise, against this unhappy Prince, the national odium, in order to justify the dethroning him . . . and to induce the ready adoption of a republican form of Government. . . . If he is saved it will be by the justice of his cause, which will have some little effect, and by the pity which is universally felt (though none dare express it openly) for the very harsh treatment which he has endured.[107]

> Here, they hang people for giving an opinion in favor of royalty, (that is, they cut off their heads) but yet I am told that such opinion is openly avowed and supported in the streets.[108]

The final category of deleted matter consisted of explicit policy recommendations by Morris. Some of these were less friendly toward France than was existing policy; others, however, would have pleased the opposition, for Morris was hardly more benign in his judgments on Britain than in those on France. Morris suggested, among other things, that the United States build a fleet on Lake Erie and fortify the western frontier; that she attempt to turn the Indians against British Canada; that she refrain from making a commercial treaty with France; that she attempt to terminate the existing treaty of alliance with that country; and that she cooperate with the French government in punishing Genêt.[109]

Finally, the censor did not disturb the self-serving passages in which Morris begged for more detailed instructions on how he should conduct himself and disclaimed any intent to interfere in internal French affairs.[110] Indeed, Morris had instructed the American consul at Marseilles to the same effect.

> [Y]ou should take part as little as possible in revolutions or counter revolutions; but especially in the latter, because, if we had any right to interfere in the politics of this country, we should undoubtedly take part with those who wish to establish a free government.[111]

All the same, the censor did not feel justified in deleting the passages, noted with annoyance by Randolph, in which Morris told how he had repeatedly taunted the French by stating that he could not accommodate their wishes before receiving "the orders of my court."[112]

It is difficult to reach a confident generalization from these facts about the intent behind the censor's work. Randolph's three narrow categories would seem to account for fewer than half of the deletions made,[113] though it is arguable that many other deletions were directed to a similar, personal safety-related end—to protect Morris against reprisals while in France. Even without the disclosure of his official correspondence, there had in fact been calls by French radicals for his execution.[114] Still, one is powerfully tempted to conclude that the potential international and domestic repercussions of a full disclosure were also very much on the censor's mind.

No doubt the domestic and the foreign, the private and the public, dangers of the situation were inextricably interwoven. The censorship of the papers tended to blunt their inflammatory impact on both sides of the ocean. Even if the primary concern was to reduce international discord, the censor inevitably furthered a partisan interest in deflecting the charges that Morris, the president's handpicked representative, did not support the publicly acknowledged official policy of the United States.

The avoidance of gratuitous disruption in American-French relations would surely be a legitimate concern; indeed, one wonders why Randolph had failed to mention it. Perhaps the reason is that heretofore, such concerns had been invoked to justify designating information as confidential, not to justify withholding it from Congress altogether. Yet Attorney General Bradford did suggest that information might be withheld from the Senate in this case to protect the national honor. Just as Hammond had felt doubly injured when Randolph's sharp rebukes to him were published, so France might feel that disclosure of Morris's insults would compound the injury his whole line of conduct had offered to national pride.

The new, self-assertive Senate could no longer be trusted to keep the secret. Some senators would have been infuriated by Morris's gibes; leaks were only to be expected. Moreover, if Morris's impeachment were to be demanded, the evidence against him could hardly remain secret, whether or not the Senate's rule required it to open its "judicial" proceedings to the public.

Yet if a secret was preserved by the censor, it was not the fact of Morris's antirevolutionary bias but only that of his flippant and indiscreet style. Ironically, the censor himself was probably not privy to the darkest of Morris's secrets. For Morris's official correspondence gave no hint that he had been deeply involved in a plot to smuggle Louis XVI out of France and had used his diplomatic immunity to shelter several nobles from arrest.[115] The senators who called for Morris's papers may have suspected him of some such intrigues, but Morris's verbal indiscretion had not extended to the folly of reporting such activities to Thomas Jefferson.[116] The censor therefore had no occasion to conceal any crimes; he merely made the papers more sober in tone and kinder to individual reputations. Whether the national honor, as opposed to Morris's—or Washington's—own was thereby protected is a moot point.

The Senate's reaction to the Morris papers, as sanitized, was all that the censor could have wished. In fact, after a few sessions spent in reading the papers, they let the whole matter drop. As Monroe told the story,

Two days past he laid before us a voluminous correspondence, stating "that he had omitted such parts as in his judgment ought not to be communicated." It has not yet been taken up. The opinion however of many is that his discretion should extend to time only, but this assumes the control over the whole subject & in all respects. The removal of Mr. G[allatin], if it would have been proper in any event to discuss this point (considering the Senate a branch of the legislature) will I presume prevent it.[117]

With Gallatin's expulsion the Senate opposition had lost a crucial vote. The call for papers had originally passed by only thirteen to eleven, with Gallatin participating. The situation was no longer conducive to head-on confrontations, especially when Madison had warned Monroe that support from the House would not be forthcoming. Moreover, the Senate apparently concluded from what it had seen that Morris was guilty of no grave misconduct, and it must have known by now of his impending recall.[118] Thus there was little incentive to press the investigation.[119]

From Monroe's language, indeed, it seems that the opposition was unsure of its legal as well as its political ground. The expression, "considering the Senate a branch of the legislature," indicates that Monroe was familiar with Randolph's legal theory. By acquiescing in the president's censorship of the papers, the Senate implicitly joined the emerging consensus on a rule which recognized the president's discretion to withhold information from Congress "for public considerations." Yet the legal regularization of interbranch communications was far from complete. The president did not volunteer, and the Senate failed to insist upon, the articulation of more definite standards to determine when withholding would be appropriate or the types of information that might be withheld. Nor, of course, did the Senate articulate any limits to its own discretion in releasing such information as might be confided to it. The potential for controversy remained great.[120]

A writer for the opposition press discerned most clearly the opportunities for abuse of power and decried the evils of secrecy with irony and passion. "Secrecy," he wrote,

is a weapon . . . of wonderful efficacy; it prevents many disquietudes among the people; . . . it gives permanency to men and measures. . . .

It throws a splendour around the Executive. . . . What a pity that even the Senate is so far depreciated, as not to merit a knowledge of the whole proceedings of the Executive. . . . The people are still more fortunate; . . . for although the Senate are *permitted* to have a squint, the people ought to be kept in profound ignorance. . . . Happy people, that are saved from the drudgery of thinking for themselves!![121]

A rebuttal, printed the next day, reminded readers that certain secrets must be kept from foreigners and declared that Americans "have too much confidence in the Executive to suppose any information proper to be divulged will be reserved."[122] Perhaps this was wishful thinking, yet to support its policies the administration was coming to rely less on the force of persuasion and more on appeals to the people's confidence in the president as a man. The opposition, for its part, was not yet prepared to attack the president directly, but felt no such inhibition with respect to his Federalist advisers. The Morris investigation was one line of attack; another was the prolonged investigation of Hamilton's conduct as secretary of the treasury. These moves were capable of affecting policy in important if indirect ways. For example, Morris's successor as minister to France turned out to be none other than Monroe, who had spearheaded the Senate's attack on Morris. While there is no suggestion that a deal was involved—Monroe was not offered the post until long after the investigation was dropped, and he was not the first candidate approached—there is a lesson in the outcome. In some ways, the interests of party were assuming clear priority over those of insitutions, and it was a more attractive prospect to enter the executive branch by election or appointment than to attempt to control it from without.

The Hamilton Investigations

The Third Congress's investigation of Hamilton was actually a sequel to an inconclusive confrontation that took place in the second session of the Second Congress late in 1792. Hamilton's critics in this lame-duck Congress were emboldened by their party's success in the 1792 elections, and Hamilton was vulnerable to attack for the way he had handled certain loans negotiated abroad and for failure to inform Congress of what he had done. The House's power to conduct a probe rested on a firm constitutional footing. There was no doubt, after the St. Clair investigation, of its authority to control and investigate the disposition of public funds; and the charges, though somewhat technical, could be framed in terms of the alleged violation of specific laws and duties. Hamilton's defense, in turn, raised a broad question of constitutional principle, for he invoked an unwritten law of administrative necessity and convenience to justify departures from the strict letter of the law. To the opposition, the case had overtones of corruption and covert foreign policy maneuver that raised the charges against Hamilton well above the level of procedural hairsplitting. His defense, moreover, struck at the very heart of their political and legal leverage within government.

In response to a resolution of December 27, 1792,[123] Hamilton submitted a report to the House on his loan transactions. William Branch Giles, a chief opposition spokesman, branded this report obscure and evasive. Whether it was intentionally so or not, many members admitted to being thoroughly confused. It began to dawn on some how little the activities of the Treasury had been understood by Congress in the past. As if to compensate for its lax record, the House now demanded a full accounting of the handling of the foreign and domestic debt since 1790.[124]

Working at a furious pace, Hamilton assembled a more copious, detailed report on the pertinent transactions. Accompanying his statement of accounts was an aggressive, sometimes condescending, rebuttal of the opposition's charges and insinuations.[125] To the charge that he had been remiss in informing Congress of the measures taken over the years, Hamilton replied that the information had never been called for.[126] He did not deny the House's right to demand full information, but he did warn that, in the president's view, a publication of some of the information would be "not without inconvenience."[127] At the same time, as if to underscore his insistence that he had nothing to hide, Hamilton went so far as to have the bulk of his report printed and disseminated nationwide through private channels.[128]

Hamilton's report did not put an end to the controversy. It did appear, after all, that moneys borrowed abroad and supposed to be allocated to the foreign debt had been drawn into the United States and deposited in the Bank of the United States. Why had these funds not been held in Europe to meet installments on the debt to France as these came due? Jefferson, for one, insisted that Hamilton had acted from highly improper motives, and there is reason to believe that he was the author of the resolutions of censure introduced by Giles on February 28, 1793, only three days before the Second Congress was to adjourn.[129] Of the specific charges against Hamilton, two are of special interest here.

> [He had] omitted to discharge an essential duty of his office, in failing to give Congress official information in due time, of the moneys drawn by him from Europe into the United States. . . . [and was] guilty of an indecorum to this House, in undertaking to judge of its motives in calling for information which was demandable of him, from the constitution of his office; and in failing to give all the necessary information within his knowledge, relatively to the subjects of the reference made to him.[130]

A vigorous debate was held upon the charges. One question that could not be settled with the information then available was whether the president had specifically authorized Hamilton's dubious transactions. The Federalists asserted that Hamilton had acted with Washington's approval, so that any violation of the law (supposing the president's sanction did not dispel all doubt) was not the secretary's fault. The opposition took the president's silence as indicating that he had not approved; but, if the transactions were authorized by the president, the opposition charged, Hamilton was remiss in failing to report his action to Congress. Federalists argued that the House had in fact been adequately informed; moreover, additional information beyond what appeared in the periodic reports was always available to members on an individual basis. Finally, some contended that the informing function was under the president's control rather than the secretary's, so that any failure to give information could not, in any event, be charged against Hamilton.[131]

The vote on the censure resolutions was a solid victory for Hamilton, as each charge was defeated by a majority of at least two to one. The charge of failure to inform Congress received the greatest support, but even this garnered only fifteen votes.[132] There is a temptation to dismiss the episode as little more than an abortive partisan effort to force Hamilton's resignation. Yet it clearly had a broader, constitutional significance. The climate created by the investigation did place new constraints on executive policymaking, for Hamilton was obliged to abandon his proposal for a new loan; the suspension of payments to France was lifted; and the French request for an advance on payments due was approved. This represented a sharp reversal of the administration's earlier posture, which had hinged on doubts about the stability of the French government.[133]

Moreover this was, after all, the first occasion on which Congress formally entertained charges of improper withholding of information by the executive branch. Legally speaking, Hamilton's acquittal established no right to withhold, in that no such right was formally asserted by the executive or ruled upon by the House. The pronouncements of congressmen were so diverse as to deprive the vote of clear doctrinal thrust. It could be taken to mean either that adequate information had, in fact, been supplied; or that, if not, the fault was not Hamilton's; or that the House's failure to demand the specific information in question provided an excuse; or simply that the censure proceeding was improper in timing and wanting in procedural safeguards. What was clear, at all events, was that the old permissiveness in oversight was a thing of the past.

Opposition spokesmen continued to circulate charges against Hamilton during the congressional recess. Determined to win an unequivocal vindication, Hamilton boldly asked the Third Congress to reopen the investigation. In February 1794, a bipartisan committee was established and empowered to call for persons, papers, and records.[134] Several specific points of inquiry were mandated by the House, including the question of Hamilton's specific legal authority for the drawing of funds into the United States. To the committee's written interrogatory on this point, Hamilton responded with a question and a challenge. Did the committee expect the secretary to produce specific instructions given him by the president? If so, he declared, he felt constrained to object. As far as the

House was concerned, the only relevant question was whether the appropriation laws had been complied with. A purported defect in his authority from the president was "immaterial and irrelevant" to the legislature if its mandate had been carried out; while, on the other hand, even an explicit presidential order could not make lawful what Congress had forbidden. On no assumption, therefore, did the House have a proper basis for inquiring into Hamilton's relationship with the president.

> That question must, then, be a matter purely between the President and the agent, not examinable by the Legislature, without interfering with the province of the Chief Magistrate, with whom alone the responsibility is.[135]

Now this raised the controversy to a new level of constitutional significance. This was the most far-reaching, formal claim of privilege yet submitted to Congress by an official of the executive branch, and by a subordinate official at that.

Under the circumstances, the claim was not one calculated to win the committee's approval. It was obvious that Hamilton's acts were neither expressly authorized nor expressly prohibited by the laws. Nevertheless, it did not follow that the matter was outside the legislature's investigative competence. Hamilton's appeal to the separation of powers ignored the legally and politically relevant distinction between a sphere of presidential discretion in executing the law and the exercise of uncontrolled discretion by a department head. Under the Constitution, presidents and department heads were separately responsible and liable to impeachment for their misconduct. If the House had an investigative power, surely it covered the Treasury's handling of public funds. Under the Constitution and the Treasury Act fiscal matters were uniquely within its sphere of discretion. Congress had power either to impose specific duties directly upon the secretary or to have the laws executed according to presidential instructions. Here Congress had chosen the latter course, and it wished now to determine how its policy had been implemented.[136] Even if the president might have some constitutional privilege to object, the committee was not obliged to let Hamilton vicariously assert it. The St. Clair precedent, indeed, suggested otherwise.

In the event, the committee did not expressly refute Hamilton's argument but responded by simply renewing its request that he specify under what authority he had acted.[117] Hamilton could not resist further without active presidential support, and that evidently was lacking. Abandoning the claim of privilege, he now submitted to the committee an extensive reply, alluding to various oral consultations with the president and appending two letters from his files in which, he claimed, the president had authorized the transactions in question. In fact the letters were quite general in terms, implying that the president had scarcely supervised Hamilton in these matters and may not have had an adequate grasp of the legal or political implications.[138] The committee, after some hesitation, decided to press its inquiry one step further and asked Hamilton to present his case to the president and to "obtain from him such declaration concerning the same, as the President may think proper to make."[139] This request, tantamount if not identical to a call for testimony, placed Washington in a delicate position, legally as well as politically. For advice he turned to Randolph, a former attorney general who often worried over legal technicalities that other advisers ignored. Yet Randolph apparently saw no constitutional issue at stake in the present case. His answering memorandum, dated April 1, 1794, made no mention of the St. Clair investigation or of the recent Gouverneur Morris episode and addressed itself purely to the politics of the situation, stressing the need for the president to maintain a neutral, nonpartisan stance.[140] Ultimately the president addressed to Hamilton, for submission to the committee, a letter in which he stated that, to the best of his recollection, Hamilton's account was "substantially" accurate. There was no hint of support for Hamilton's claim of executive privilege and not much for Hamilton himself, to that gentleman's dismay.

Though the effort to claim a broad privilege for cabinet communications thus ended in tacit executive surrender, the significance of the precedent was once again open to conflicting interpretations. Though there had been no overt withholding of information, the committee's procedure had been deferential and indirect. It is unclear what they might have thought it proper to do had the president's reply been less satisfactory. As matters went, the committee was content to let the issue rest.[141]

The committee's report made no findings of misconduct on Hamilton's part. Though he had not volunteered detailed information on the loan transactions, it did not appear that he had had any obvious occasion to do so.[142] Despite the augmented strength of the opposition, no further action was taken by the House. Though he had reason to feel exonerated, however, Hamilton's policy influence was clearly on the wane. In March the House had refused to receive a revenue plan he had drawn up, voting to have its own committee develop a proposal instead. That Hamilton was suffered to testify before this committee did not sweeten the pill; the secretary, it was said, was "cursedly mortified" by the rebuff, and the episode confirmed him in his determination to resign.[143]

Left for the future was the development of more effective mechanisms for ongoing oversight. Hamilton himself had remarked, in the course of these investigations, on the desirability of more predictable reporting routines to protect his department from disruption by "unexpected, desultory and distressing calls for lengthy and complicated statements."[144] Yet no legislative proposals were developed by the investigating committee, whether because their real interest was confined to the political attack on Hamilton, or because their failure to discover any flagrant wrongdoing removed the impetus for structural reform. Even from the perspective of exposure pure and simple, the House made no effort to clarify the exact extent of its powers; nor had the executive undertaken to rationalize and reconcile the various actions taken and doctrines announced in recent months. To assess the consistency and the import of the "precedents" of this period, therefore, is an analytical task that, so far as the record shows, the founders themselves never carried out.

Conclusions

The years 1793–94 were marked by rapid changes in governmental secrecy doctrine, initially brought on by developments external to the institutions of government. The outbreak of war and revolution in Europe and the increasing polarization of American sentiment on issues of foreign and domestic policy were reflected, after the 1792 elections, in a new pattern of interbranch relations. Though the initial steps toward party formation had originated within the government and were taken with a view toward coordinating the work of the executive and legislative branches, the Congress that convened in late 1793 was in fact far more independent-minded than its predecessors had been. The small and initially cohesive nationalist elite that had brought the new government into being found itself now at loggerheads over fundamentals; moreover, the proponents of different viewpoints were entrenched in different institutions, each of which might use its constitutional powers to initiate action or block action initiated elsewhere. The effective employment of such powers, however, depended upon public support and therefore upon publicity as to the facts and the options open to America. The relatively closed, informal and consensual governmental process of the early years had to be adapted to the new political environment. In January-February 1794 each of the major rules that had been developed respecting governmental communications was reassessed accordingly.

1. The House of Representatives, despite its generally open publicity posture, had compromised its independence in 1792 by agreeing to a standing rule that barred the publication of papers transmitted by the president on a "confidential" basis. Now, in December 1793, the opposition-controlled Third Congress amended the rule, declaring its authority to disclose such material if it deemed this appropriate. Soon thereafter the House embarked on a far-reaching investigation of the Treasury department and launched a bold legislative program respecting foreign commerce. These measures entailed an unprecedented series of calls for sensitive information.

2. The secrecy posture of the early Senate had presupposed an internal homogeneity, an aloofness from public opinion, and a meek subservience to the executive that were no longer realistic premises. The opposition's electoral gains produced new votes for their perennial demand that the doors be opened; in addition, a number of Federalist senators were persuaded to support this demand so that they could better counter the public influence of the opposition-controlled House. Thus, in February 1794 a bipartisan majority voted to open the doors for ordinary legislative business. Though executive business was exempt from the new dispensation, the Senate also showed a new assertiveness in the diplomatic sphere by calling on the president to publicize his confidential negotiations with

Spain and to submit to them the official correspondence of his minister to France. The latter move, at least, was clearly partisan in sponsorship and intent.

3. These developments were ominous to an administration that had hoped to persuade a majority in Congress to support its legislative program and to acquiesce in its diplomatic initiatives. The unprecedented communication effort that began with the president's opening message to Congress had by no means silenced the opposition; on the contrary, it had whetted their appetite for information and their assertiveness both in legislative policy and in seeking to influence executive action. The "confidential" label had so far been applied only to documents pertaining to pending negotiations; yet even here Congress had moved to disclose parts of certain documents and pressured the executive to release still more information.

The president's reactions were informed by considerations of constitutional principle as well as of political expediency. The administration recognized the constitutional orthodoxy of the House's new standing order; it not only failed to protest its adoption, but sternly rebuffed the British protest when the House on its own authority published a diplomatic paper. In addition, the president made no objection to the House's calls for further information, such as Hammond's letter to Jefferson or his own instructions to Hamilton concerning foreign loans. Likewise, the president made no effort to dissuade the Senate from opening its doors, and he complied with its request that he brief Kentuckians on the status of the Spanish negotiations.

All this was consistent with a straightforward view of the separation of powers under which the president and Congress had equal power to decide what information the conduct of their own business required and what part of it could safely be published. Yet these principles did not resolve latent issues about who should prevail in a struggle to control the conduct of department heads, ambassadors, or soldiers in the field or to control information relevant to the same. These questions, when brought to a head by direct policy clashes between the parties dominant in the several branches, proved increasingly difficult to submit to legalistic solutions.

The president did take pains to elicit congressional recognition that in responding to calls for information he was, after all, vested with a certain discretion—that the St. Clair doctrine, in effect, was operative. The House was induced to qualify its call for Hammond's letter to Jefferson by excepting "such parts as he may think proper," and it called only for "such declaration as he may think proper" concerning Washington's dealings with Hamilton. The Senate's resolution that prompted the Innes mission to Kentucky was, in form, simply a request that the president communicate "such parts of the existing negotiation, as he may deem advisable." None of these calls elicited any overt resistance.

Only in the Gouverneur Morris episode, when the call for papers was unqualified, did the executive directly resist. Randolph contemplated a total refusal to teach the Senate a lesson, and he questioned the Senate's purpose in making the call, since the president had laid no relevant executive business before it. These ideas went far beyond a doctrine that the president was the best judge of the need for secrecy to protect individual safety or national honor. For the moment, however, the president contented himself with censoring the papers given to the Senate, ostensibly "for public considerations," and marking them confidential even though they did not pertain to existing negotiations. These were important innovations and they need explaining.

Politically, the call for Morris's papers struck directly at the president, and on a vulnerable point, for Morris was his handpicked choice and had conducted himself in a highly controversial manner. Constitutionally, the call was arguably objectionable in that, first, it was unqualified, and second, it was not directly related either to any business initiated by the president, to any legislation or impeachment trial pending before the Senate, or even to any matter placed on the agenda by obvious constituent pressures. Morris's correspondence was not of a nature that would have led to spontaneous executive disclosure, even on a confidential basis, and there was no notorious event like the St. Clair debacle to justify an open-ended investigation. With Morris's recall already in the works, the only purpose the investigation could serve would be to embarrass the president.

By his partial compliance with the Senate's resolution, the president admitted the Senate under the umbrella of the St. Clair doctrine, which gave the House a general power to investigate and to call for papers. By making no protest to the censorship and taking no further action on the president's message, the Senate in turn tacitly acquiesced in the principle of a presidential discretion to censor—though not necessarily in a discretion unlimited as to situation or subject matter.

The final point of the St. Clair doctrine, according to Jefferson, was that department heads were subject to presidential control in responding to calls for information. The Senate recognized this principle by amending its resolution so as to call upon the president, and not the secretary of state, for Morris's papers. Yet the Hamilton investigations followed a very different pattern, suggesting that, at this period, accommodation between the branches was a two-way street. This probe presented the president with an opportunity to reaffirm his power of secrecy and apply it in a politically sensitive case involving not diplomatic correspondence but the internal operations of the cabinet. Why did Randolph not refer to the president's discretion, if only by way of comfort, in advising the president how to respond, as he did when urging Washington to accommodate the Senate in the Kentucky matter? Why did the president say nothing to admonish the House on the limits of its investigative power?

The president's failure to raise any objection to the Hamilton probe could conceivably be interpreted in modern terms as a concession that the secrecy power did not extend to an "advice" privilege but only to "state secrets." However, this would be a highly anachronistic interpretation. Without question the constitutional rationale and historical practice of executive secrecy was best developed in the realm of foreign affairs. Yet the argument for secrecy rested squarely on the axiom of separated powers, and it was after all the St. Clair investigation, which targeted the Treasury and War departments, that had prompted the first cabinet discussion of a censorship power. Moreover, Randolph's analysis of the Morris case did not rest on the special nature of foreign affairs but seemed to imply that all congressional calls for information, if issued in a legislative capacity, were subject to presidential discretion.

The likeliest explanation of the president's conduct appears to be that, whatever his advisers may have thought, Congress had made clear that it perceived a clear distinction between the several departments as far as oversight was concerned. Ever since 1789, legislation had placed special reporting requirements on the Treasury, and though calls for information were generally addressed directly to department heads, in the case of foreign affairs it was the usual practice to address them instead to the president himself. In short, the notion that department heads were subject to the president's control in informing Congress had clearly been accepted by Congress with regard to the secretary of state. As to the other departments, however, Congress persisted in claiming a power of direct supervision and was not accustomed to qualifying in any way its calls upon them for information. The president's response to the Hamilton probe went far toward acquiescing in this congressional stance, though, once again, ample room was left for future doctrinal innovation.[145]

It is worth stressing that, in keeping with the whole constitutional approach of checks and balances, the distinction between the Morris and the Hamilton cases was drawn along structural rather than functional lines. Both episodes actually involved considerations of foreign as well as domestic politics, but the evolving doctrine of interbranch relations was geared more to the prerogatives and formal communication practices of specific institutions than to the particular issues and interests implicated in a given fact situation. For constitutional purposes the key question seemed to be which formal power was being exercised by which branch or department of government. This sort of formalistic analysis seemed to promise relatively determinate outcomes; indeed, if rigidly applied there was a risk of seriously dysfunctional results, such as indiscriminate secrecy in matters committed to the State Department or abuses of the investigative power in matters committed to the Treasury.

Yet for all that, the system of separated but overlapping powers placed certain limitations on executive autonomy even in the foreign realm and on effective congressional oversight even in fiscal matters. In a situation of mutual distrust and anxiety there was in fact a risk of governmental paralysis that formalism could not cure. Indeed, the limits of formalism were reflected in the very lack of specificity in the prescribed procedures for conducting investigations, the enunciated standards for withholding or releasing information, and the sanctions available should the investigative power or the secrecy power be abused. Formal criteria often functioned as triggers not for automatic responses but for the exercise of discretion. In the prevailing political climate decisionmakers were reluctant to tie their hands by accepting severe limitations on their discretion. They had to deal with the fact that their adversaries, too, were keeping their options open. The effort to cope with these uncertainties was soon to produce strange departures in official behavior—departures that were structured, however, by previous doctrinal commitments as well as by pressing political imperatives.

CONSTITUTIONAL IMPASSE AND THE FAILURE OF LEGALIZATION 5

The moment in spring 1794 when the Senate called for Morris's papers and the House investigated Hamilton was also marked, as it happened, by a new crisis in British-American relations. The government's patient diplomacy had so far failed to wrest from Great Britain any relaxation of her harsh policies in restraint of American commerce, capture of American ships, impressment of seamen, and so forth. Britain had never surrendered the fortified posts on the frontier, as the peace of 1783 required her to do, and recently had gone so far as to establish a new fortification inside American territory near Detroit. In March the public learned that Lord Dorchester, his majesty's governor in Canada, had told the Indians that war between the United States and Britain was inevitable and that Indian demands could best be met by armed struggle rather than by making a treaty with the Americans. The public response of the administration was merely to call for resumption of the suspended negotiations.[1]

In Congress measures far more aggressive were afoot. In March a thirty-day embargo was laid on all shipping in American ports. Bills were introduced to sequester all debts owed to British subjects and to suspend all trade indefinitely. An expensive defense buildup was also in the works. Though the tenor of this legislative program was warlike, Republican leaders argued that Britain would agree, in the face of such firmness, to a negotiated solution of the outstanding issues. After all, Britain was embroiled in war with France and could ill afford to open a second front.

To the administration this calculation seemed wildly irresponsible. The president had taken Congress into his confidence and asked for its support of his policy of neutrality and peace; yet it seemed bent on propelling the nation into a disastrous conflict. The costs of war, both economic and political, loomed very large. The public and congressional antipathy toward Britain was the greatest threat to peace, and Federalists were struck by the apparent connection between this political sentiment and a radical, disorganizing, antigovernment movement they saw springing up about them. To many Federalists—and now they had almost exclusive access to the president himself—the issue was not simply one of avoiding war but also one of maintaining the very integrity of government and social order.

Genêt's tenure as French ambassador had been marked by a series of demagogic public appearances around the country in which he sought to promote pressure on, if not outright opposition to, administration policy. Federalist anxieties mounted as they witnessed the appearance of Democratic Societies—local political discussion clubs on the Jacobin model—in many cities, organized with Genêt's enthusiastic support if not at his instigation.[2] Conservatives were deeply afraid that a spread of French-style politics would ultimately spell the ruin of their political power, their private property, and even their physical safety. The unpleasant prospect of making concessions to Britain was less distasteful than the prospect of surrendering control of national policy to "the swinish multitude."

Jay's Mission

On March 10, 1794, four Federalist senators—George Cabot, Oliver Ellsworth, Rufus King, and Caleb Strong—met privately at King's residence to discuss the situation. They agreed that rapid action was necessary to "calm the public mind, as well as the public councils." To seize the initiative, they decided, a special envoy must be sent to England to demand a redress of grievances and to settle the issues outstanding. The envoy they had in mind was Alexander Hamilton.[3]

Now this was not an orthodox proceeding, in light of the doctrine, ostensibly well established by this date, that the Senate was not empowered to initiate diplomatic business but only to pass upon nominations and treaties submitted to it by the president. The gentlemen involved were not even a committee appointed by the Senate; in truth they were acting not as senators but as leaders of the Federalist party. The institution whose prerogatives they needed to employ was the presidency.

Ellsworth approached Washington and found that the president had serious reservations. In particular, he felt that Hamilton would be a far too controversial nominee.[4] The Federalists caucused and designated Chief Justice Jay as their preferred substitute and enlisted Hamilton's aid in persuading Washington to undertake the mission.

Hamilton's argument was based candidly on the threat posed by the warlike measures afoot in Congress. Jay's mission would provide a basis for averting enactment of this legislation, just as in 1791 the exchange of ministers and the opening of talks had induced Congress to defer action on Madison's tariff and tonnage bills.[5] Hamilton's arguments had weight with the president, and on April 14 he decided to adopt the Federalists' plan.[6] And now a question arose: in laying Jay's nomination before the Senate, how much should the Senate be told, and what role should it play in setting guidelines for the proposed negotiations?

Until now it had been the usual, though not invariable practice to lay an envoy's proposed instructions before the Senate in connection with his nomination. In the present case a more reticent line was adopted; Washington decided simply to inform the Senate that Jay would attempt to secure a redress of grievances in order to forestall a resort to arms.[7] Rufus King recorded in a letter the reasons why Jay's instructions were not to be laid before the Senate: the opposition, he predicted, would resist the nomination, and "if likely to be carried, attempts will be made to embarrass it with unreasonable instructions."[8]

The nomination was submitted on April 16,[9] and the next day the opposition offered a motion to call upon the president "to inform [the] Senate of the whole business with which the proposed envoy is to be charged." Gallatin's ouster, however, had cost the opposition more than his single vote, and, on crucial issues, moderates like

Stephen Bradley and Jonathan Langdon were no longer prepared to challenge the administration as they had in backing the call for Morris's papers. The motion was defeated. Thereupon Republicans moved to call for Jay's 1786 report to the old Congress in which, it was said, Jay had declared himself convinced that several of America's longstanding grievances against Britain lacked merit and should be abandoned. To the opposition, this report seemed highly relevant to the question before the Senate, i.e., Jay's qualifications to undertake the mission of demanding a redress of American grievances. The motion was defeated by a pro-administration majority.[10]

The opposition, it appears, now resorted to other means of informing itself, for a memorandum from the secretary of state to the president, dated April 19, reported that Senator James Monroe had obtained a certain document "without my privity and against the rule of the office." Randolph, obviously embarrassed, denied that his department had lent itself to partisan machinations, and pointed out that Rufus King of the Federalist side, "was employed in the examination of the same books, at the same time."[11] Loose housekeeping procedures had let the cat out of the bag,[12] and, since effective secrecy could not be maintained, the Federalists predictably fell back on the object of assuring that a full and balanced record was made. On April 18 a new resolution, calling on the president for all of Jay's reports as foreign secretary, was introduced by King and passed by the Senate.[13] The information was promptly given; the following day the nomination was approved by a margin of eighteen to eight.[14]

The Senate's proceedings were soon reported in the press, and a vigorous discussion on the propriety of the mission ensued. For the most part, objections centered on Jay's political record and on the impropriety of his holding judicial and executive posts at the same time. This last innovation raised the spectre of a judiciary corrupted by executive patronage, and the proposed mission defied the system of checks and balances in other ways, too. At least one observer perceived a violation of the Senate's constitutional right to participate in framing an envoy's instructions.[15] Even more significant, perhaps, was the effective suppression of the legislative process. In nominating Jay, the president had asked both houses of Congress to refrain, pending the outcome of Jay's negotiations, from adopting the anti-British measures then nearing final passage. Hamilton's strategy proved highly successful, for Congress took no further action hostile toward Great Britain prior to its adjournment in June 1794.[16]

In theory, now, the peace initiative was entirely under presidential control. Yet the real planning unit was a group not readily nameable in constitutional terms. With members drawn from all three branches of the government, it was, in fact, something like the central committee of the Federalist party. It was Hamilton, Ellsworth, King, Cabot, and Jay who on April 21 held a conference to determine the broad outlines of the mandate Jay would carry.[17]

The president had asked Randolph, in consultation with the cabinet, to draft the guidelines for an honorable peace. The secretary of state, however, was not Hamilton's equal in intellect, personal force, or tactical shrewdness. Moreover, his personal feud with Hammond had put his ability to deal with Britain in doubt. Thus Hamilton was able to take a major role in planning Jay's mission without suffering rebuke by Randolph for a breach of departmental etiquette. Ultimately the major part of Jay's instructions was Hamilton's creation.[18]

Hamilton's overriding aim was to preserve maximum flexibility for Jay, since rigid guidelines might impede a settlement and would be difficult to modify once Jay left the country.[19] Randolph went along with this flexible approach with little protest, until it was proposed to authorize Jay not just to settle outstanding claims, but to conclude a treaty of amity and commerce as well. Randolph insisted that this expansion of Jay's powers should not be effected without submitting the matter to the Senate.[20] His argument stood on firm constitutional ground, for only two years earlier Jefferson had persuaded Washington that an identical expansion of the powers of his envoys to Spain required the Senate's express approval.[21] There is no record of any legal rebuttal to Randolph's written protest, but the protest was ignored. The Federalists had persuaded Washington that everything depended on the early success of Jay's mission, and Randolph could not effect a delay. Like Jefferson, he was unwilling to associate himself with an open challenge to the president in the name of congressional prerogative.[22] Like Jefferson too, he failed in quiet efforts to dissuade the president from heeding Hamilton's counsel. It was Hamilton's mission as much as Jay's, and it was Hamilton who, before and after Jay's departure, undertook to give Hammond a private briefing on the administration's expectations from the mission. In so doing, he extended to Hammond assurances that significantly and gratuitously weakened the American bargaining position.[23]

Otherwise the flexibility of Jay's instructions and his geographic isolation left him with essentially unfettered discretion. The talks were shrouded, moreover, in nearly absolute secrecy. Jay's official reports to Randolph and his letters to Washington, public and private, were brief and general in terms, though his private letters to Hamilton and King were a bit more informative.[24] Very little of what Jay wrote was made officially public, and there were no messages to Congress on the progress of the negotiations.

The doctrinal justification advanced on behalf of secrecy was, at best, an imperfect reflection of the real interests at work. It was true, as Jay warned his superiors, that premature publicity might anger the British; Jay even found it prudent to apologize to Lord Grenville for the earlier disclosures of diplomatic correspondence that had prompted Hammond's bitter complaints.[25] Yet both sides had long ceased to practice an inflexible secrecy, for British as well as American newspapers carried some information on the progress of the negotiations. The most important official disclosure on the American side was of Grenville's promise to Jay to afford some relief to merchants whose vessels had been seized.[26] On the whole, then, the secrecy usual with ongoing negotiations was maintained; yet disclosures occurred when useful for quieting the fears of powerful constituencies.

In one case the president quashed Randolph's plan to publish a certain Jay dispatch; his reasons were:

1. That the substance of it has already been published. . . .
2. that we shall be immediately charged with preparing the public mind for yieldings and sacrifices;
3. because nothing being said of [the demand that Britain surrender] the posts . . . unpleasant impressions may be uselessly left in the minds of many;

4. because I have read the letter to those here who are alone interested . . . and

5. because it not being absolutely necessary to be posted in a newspaper, both you [Jay] and ourselves will be more the masters of the whole matter at its winding up.[27]

A different technique was used in an effort to allay French misgivings about Jay's mission without appearing to violate diplomatic norms. Monroe, in Paris, could not induce Jay to give him a copy of the draft treaty,[28] but Randolph sent a reassuring message to the French government. When Jay reproached him, Randolph replied that he was only carrying out the mandate of the House of Representatives.[29]

Keeping affirmative publicity efforts to a minimum avoided giving offense to the British, yet little was successfully kept secret from the British themselves. Not only were they in possession of the key to Jay's cipher,[30] but Hamilton had given away the American bargaining strategy in his talks with Hammond. In fact, government secrets—and not only those of the American government—were constantly being compromised by indiscreet or corrupt officials, secret agents, and seizures of vessels carrying diplomatic pouches.[31] As the administration knew full well, reticence toward Congress and the public could not avoid these embarrassments. Whatever the subjective motives of Washington and others in keeping Jay's instructions secret and failing to inform the nation of his progress, the main effect was to exclude from participation those Americans who were most uneasy about the very existence of the mission and would have preferred that any talks be conducted by a different person and under far more stringent guidelines. This mode of proceeding could be constitutionally justified only by an interpretation of the separation of powers that, while recognizing the independent role of Congress in making foreign policy, increasingly identified that role as one to be played out only after the executive branch had completed its largely outcome-determining work. Meanwhile, under the cloak of Washington's constitutional and personal authority, the Federalist party had in fact seized control of the policymaking process; the eventual congressional and public review of its policy would occur at a time and in a manner of its own choosing.

That the prevailing concept of executive power was quite flexible was clear to all concerned, and it was seen by most as properly so. Perhaps it requires hindsight to see that the system was not simply flexible but dangerously unstable. Yet telltale signals could already be observed. One was the way in which each particular controversy about secrecy and publicity called forth a very particularistic discussion without much reference to previous cases and without the public articulation of a consistent set of guidelines that could be referred to in subsequent cases.

Thus, in the Gouverneur Morris episode, Randolph had argued for the president's power to withhold information from the Senate when acting in its *legislative* capacity. On this analysis the opposition's call for information in connection with Jay's nomination, an *executive* proceeding, was entirely proper and should have met with no resistance. Yet the Senate Federalists voted it down without announcing any principle to justify their act. Later, in direct defiance of precedent, the president decided not to disclose to the Senate a fundamental change in Jay's instructions. This, too, was done with no attempt at principled justification. The available records leave little doubt that these acts were known to be at variance with precedent and that their mainspring was political expediency.[32] Given the political situation that now obtained, the Federalists felt immune from effective attack and free to postpone the effort of articulating legal rationalizations for their conduct. Considering Washington's oft-expressed concern for legal regularity, the apparent shift in attitude is surprising. At the same time, the president's health was failing and his advisers were increasingly hostage to the view that emergency knows no law. Unfortunately the emergency with which they were confronted proved an enduring one, involving questions of domestic security as well as foreign dangers. The temptations to abuse of power were formidable and relentless.

Domestic Turmoil and Executive Power

During the second half of 1794, with Congress in recess and Jay quietly at work in London, the political spotlight fell on events taking place outside government. Congressional elections were due in November, but in the summer months the coming elections received far less press coverage than did the growing resistance in western Pennsylvania to the authority of the national government.

The whiskey tax, an integral part of Hamilton's fiscal system, fell most heavily on frontiersmen for whom whiskey was a prime source of cash income. Resentment over their heavy tax load was compounded by the government's failure to suppress the Indians and open the Mississippi to navigation. These discontents, fueled by intrigues of foreign agents,[33] had grown stronger over the years. Unsuccessful efforts to obtain repeal of the excise were followed by sporadic outbursts of unlawful resistance to collection of the tax. In July 1794 the issue reached flash point with an episode of mob violence in which one life was lost.

The unrest in Pennsylvania was not an isolated problem, for Kentuckians were at the same moment demanding action on the Spanish front, and the opposition press was increasingly strident in its criticism of the administration, emboldened by the ideas circulating in the urban Democratic Societies. Confronted with all this unruly opposition, the president decided that the government must assert its authority strongly before all authority was lost. As the Federalists saw it, an impressive show of force in western Pennsylvania would not only stabilize the situation there, but hopefully would have a sobering effect elsewhere in America and abroad.

In August an army of 15,000 was drawn from four states, including Pennsylvania, and set out for Pittsburgh with Washington and Colonel Alexander Hamilton at its head. Though no armed resistance was encountered, the army stayed in the field until it was judged that the political objectives of the expedition had been attained. Some twenty dissidents were arrested, but only two were actually convicted of any offense, and these Washington eventually pardoned. He returned to Philadelphia late in October and quickly set to work on his opening message to the new congressional session. His remarks in this message on the Whiskey Rebellion laid blame on the Democratic Societies, inaugurating a new era in partisan politics.

Neither the opposition press nor the Democratic Societies had condoned the resistance to the laws in Pennsylvania; in fact, they had publicly denounced the rebellion. Yet they had at the same time pronounced the injustice of Hamilton's fiscal system as the root cause of the troubles and had questioned the motives behind the timing and magnitude of the government's show of force. The Federalists were more convinced than ever that the Democratic Societies were the seed, planted by Genêt, of violent revolution in America. Further, they believed that even if the societies had not actively instigated the Whiskey Rebellion, their rhetoric and conduct were helping to mobilize a stratum of the populace whose participation and whose interests could not be assimilated within the existing political and legal framework. Washington had viewed the Democratic Societies with distaste for some time, but the rebellion convinced him now that they were a direct menace to law and order.[34] His personal intervention against them might nip revolution in the bud.

It seems clear that the president did not appreciate the full significance of this decision, because he viewed the societies as an alien and extremist element. However, while men like Jefferson and Madison had not joined the local clubs or involved themselves directly in the democratic movement, there was substantial ideological and policy convergence between the Democratic Societies and the Republican opposition. In fact, the societies were the most active grass-roots force behind candidates of the Republican persuasion in the 1794 elections. The president may have viewed his message strictly as an affirmation of governmental authority, but it was in fact a keenly felt partisan stroke as well. This decision, taken on Randolph's advice,[35] placed the president for the first time unequivocally in the Federalist camp and subjected him to partisan attacks previously reserved for Hamilton and other party leaders. Madison termed the message Washington's greatest political mistake.[36] Certainly the gesture came too late to swing the 1794 elections. In the House, Republicans swept the frontier country and major cities, emerging with an enhanced majority.[37] In the Senate, however, the Federalists scored major gains, so that the opposition could look forward, in the Fourth Congress, to no more than eleven out of thirty seats.[38]

In the campaign, critics of the administration denounced appeasement of Britain and Spain, and Hamilton's fiscal system; they gave relatively little weight to the constitutional issues raised by Jay's secret mission and by the president's zealous use of police power.[39] Yet the specific question of secrecy did surface from time to time. There were pleas for information on Jay's progress, and defenders of the peoples' right to assemble and petition castigated those who would "envelop the proceedings of government in impenetrable and mysterious secrecy."[40] Yet the climate produced by the Whiskey Rebellion and the president's message was not favorable to expansive statements of populist doctrine. Instead, it revived the old distrust of "faction" in politics and cast a pall on the drive for broader participation. At least as Federalists understood it, Washington's message was a denunciation of opposition to the administration as such, and they induced the House to reply to his message in rather extravagantly approving terms.

> And we learn with greatest concern that any misrepresentations whatever of the Government and its proceedings, either by individuals or combinations of men, should have been made and so far credited as to foment the flagrant outrage which has been committed on the laws.[41]

This declaration was scarcely marked by any solicitude for freedom of speech or the concept of individual, as opposed to collective, responsibility for wrongdoing. In fact, it was in the immediate aftermath of Washington's message that mere verbal criticism of the government came, for the first time, to be branded with the stigma of criminal disloyalty. Opposition editors came under increasingly severe attack, including strong pressures to reveal confidential sources,[42] until, in April 1795, Thomas Greenleaf of New York was actually indicted, on the explicit orders of the administration, for publishing in his paper a libel against British Minister Hammond. The fact that Randolph was also attacked in the same diatribe may have influenced this decision, though Randolph denied it.[43] While the prosecution was not carried through to completion, it was an ominous forewarning of things to come.[44] Greenleaf's colleagues noted wryly the contrast between the government's position in this case and its earlier refusal to prosecute Jay and King for their alleged libel of French Minister Genêt.[45] There was little, save self-restraint, that the editors could do to protect themselves, nor was a chastened Congress moved to act in their behalf. It may be that the congressional opposition consciously chose to sacrifice the pure principles of legislative prerogative and limited government for the sake of future electoral success.[46] The time, however, was soon approaching when the legislature could no longer afford to temporize, if its own powers and the liberties of the people were to be preserved.

Meanwhile, as the country awaited news from Europe, Hamilton made public his decision to resign as of January 31, 1795. Henry Knox chose to resign as secretary of war in the same month. Of the original inner circle only Randolph now remained. Hamilton's replacement was Oliver Wolcott of Connecticut; Knox's was Timothy Pickering of Massachusetts. Both were stalwart Federalists who, like their colleagues in the legislature and like Washington himself, were accustomed to turn constantly to Hamilton for advice. Though he no longer held any official post, Hamilton thus continued to exercise an unrivaled influence in governmental councils, through a mixture of direct and indirect, open and secret, channels. It was, nevertheless, the end of an era.

From the special perspective of this study the legacy of Hamilton's official career is a fascinating paradox. His personal contribution to the evolving law and practice of publicity was by no means so illiberal as one might suppose. In 1788 in the New York ratifying convention he advocated a constitutional amendment to require greater publicity in legislative proceedings. In 1789 he helped to formulate the act requiring the secretary of the treasury to keep Congress informed of the state of the nation's finances. When Congress moved to assert its investigative powers, Hamilton complied fully, if sometimes grudgingly, with its demands for information. When the cabinet deliberated on the extent to which Congress and the people should be informed of developments in foreign affairs, Hamilton's attitude, like Jefferson's, was guided by considerations of expediency. On more than one occasion he advocated appeals to the people to marshal support for executive policy. He was also not above leaking information not only to the press, but to British agents such as Beckwith and Hammond, when he felt that official communications were insufficient or misleading. In fact, it is not Hamilton but Jefferson in whom biographers have discerned a penchant for secrecy as a strong personality trait.[47]

While we recognize Hamilton's contributions to publicity, both in specific episodes and on the structural level, it must be emphasized that he was above all a man of action, often impatient with procedural niceties that hindered him in getting things done. A firm believer in energetic government, he worked steadily to establish a strong executive—one that could pursue its policies even in the face of substantial opposition. His quest for public support was never an end in itself. Though prudence might often dictate the sharing of information, especially with mercantile and financial elites, the idea of clear-cut legal limits on governmental secrecy and executive power would have to find another champion.

In theory such a champion ought to have emerged in the ranks of the congressional opposition, where partisan and institutional incentives alike seemed to call for limits on executive power. Yet the president's censorship of the Morris dispatches and his use of Jay's mission to circumvent the legislative power did not elicit any coherent congressional protest, nor did his subsequent use of military force against citizens protesting an unjust tax, and his denunciation of peaceful political association and discussion as inimical to law and order. But Jay's Treaty proved a greater incitement to resistance than all that had gone before.

Jay's Treaty

In November 1794 the administration learned that Jay was about to conclude his negotiations. After months of painfully slow progress the negotiations had suddenly speeded up, and completion of a treaty was imminent. The reason for the sudden acceleration of the business was that Jay, despairing of reaching any agreement if he adhered to his previous demands, had decided to back down on a number of significant points. According to certain papers that Jay never transmitted to the president, his haste apparently reflected a desire to forestall objections from his superiors.[48]

Jay's message caused much disquiet in Philadelphia. If the proposed treaty arguably was not flatly inconsistent with his instructions, it utterly failed to redress many of the grievances most deeply felt by Americans. Granting that the normalization of ties was a great achievement, the concrete benefits obtained by Jay were very modest. Knowing how hard-pressed the British were in their European war, the administration had expected Jay to exact substantially better terms, but the British position had hardened after Foreign Secretary Lord William Grenville learned from Hammond how desperately Hamilton and his party feared the threat of war.[49]

Randolph wrote promptly to Jay, warning him of the objectionable features of the proposed treaty, but the messages did not arrive in time.[50] Jay signed the treaty on November 19, and it reached the United States on March 7, 1795. Washington and Randolph were now faced with a dilemma. The president felt little enthusiasm for the treaty and shrunk from signing it without first testing the climate of opinion. Indeed, demands for disclosure of the treaty had surfaced even before the president had the text in hand.[51] Yet an immediate publication would violate established procedures and might suggest a want of firmness in the government. Ratification was the duty of the president and Senate, not a decision to be accomplished by referendum. The administration decided to temporize. A special session of the Senate was called for June; until then the treaty would be kept secret.[52]

A separate question arose concerning the supporting papers to be given the Senate along with the treaty. There were matters in Jay's instructions and in his correspondence with Randolph which might increase opposition to the treaty in the Senate. In particular Randolph's belated warnings to Jay would surely have a divisive effect. Now, there was no precedent for a decision to censor these papers. The Senate's proceeding would be executive in nature; Randolph's analysis in the Morris episode indicated that its right to the information was unrestricted. However, a new argument now suggested itself: any documents that had no impact on the course of the negotiations or the shape of the final agreement were, strictly speaking, irrelevant to the Senate's deliberations. Therefore, as Randolph wrote to Jay, it would be "just" to withhold such papers from the Senate.[53] Washington sent the treaty to the Senate on June 8, 1795, without a word of comment on its merits or demerits. Attached were Jay's instructions and so much of his official correspondence as transpired before Jay signed the treaty. This communication was governed, according to Randolph, by the administration's guiding principle of "unvaried candour."[54]

Despite the administration's candor, the leading provisions of the treaty were by now known to the public in their broad outlines, probably because the British government, having more reason to be proud of the treaty, had been less fastidious in keeping its contents secret. A vigorous public debate ensued, undeterred by Federalist objections that it was improper for private citizens to attempt to influence the president and Senate in exercising their discretion.[55]

The opposition assailed not only the provisions of the treaty itself but also the procedures by which it had been made. The constitutional objections to the conduct of the executive were numerous and far from trivial.[56] In particular, the opposition press was now full of protests on the point of secrecy.

> The English prints have already announced the prominent characters of the Treaty, and yet the people of the United States are kept in as profound ignorance of it by their administration, as if they were Hottentots or Orangutans! . . .
>
> If . . . the people are the sovereign, how extraordinary that they should be kept in profound ignorance.[57]

Federalist spokesmen took very high ground in attempting to rebut these charges, asserting the impropriety of interference by the public with governmental decisionmaking.

> To publish the Treaty before ratification, would render them liable to be swayed, not by the general voice of their country, but by the mere opinions prevailing at the seat of government. If the Senate act for the whole United States . . . it behooves them to . . . admit of no other guide for forming their decision, than what their own knowledge of the nation's interest presents.[58]

As the opposition pointed out, this argument proved entirely too much. It might even seem to follow that:

> it would be sedition to express an opinion in our public prints, throwing any degree of blame on a public measure, because it would have a tendency to give strength to an opposition to government. . . . If ex-

ternal influence destroys responsibility, why is the President, or any other officer of government, suffered to read a newspaper?[59]

This warning of the tyranny implicit in the Federalist position may have seemed hysterical at the time, yet it proved a most accurate prophecy.

The Senate convened on June 8 in a tense and partisan mood to deliberate on the still secret treaty. Federalist leaders calculated that the needed two-thirds majority was barely attainable, but not so, perhaps, in the face of adverse publicity. At once, therefore, the Senate's proceedings were placed under a strict injunction of secrecy.[60] On June 12 the opposition moved to lift the injunction but were defeated by a margin of twenty to nine. This was a bellweather vote. All the Federalists voted for secrecy, as did Alexander Martin, who had sponsored the open-doors resolution of 1794.[61]

The debate over ratification continued until June 24, but we know little of what was said. The Senate did call for and receive certain additional documents, but these related to the earlier history of British-American diplomacy, not to the recent negotiations.[62] The executive journal also records the defeat of a motion declaring that the treaty should be rejected because of seven key defects. Four of these were purely political, but three were constitutional: one treaty article invaded the powers of the states, and two others infringed the power of the legislature to enact future measures regulating foreign commerce.[63] On June 24 the Senate voted approval of the treaty by a bare two-thirds margin of twenty to ten, on condition that one article be renegotiated. The outcome might have been different, if not for secrecy and if not for some highly questionable techniques employed to gain the support of fence-sitting senators.[64]

Before adjourning, the Senate had once more to confront the secrecy issue: should the treaty now be published by the Senate, or should this step be left to the president? On June 25, Senator Aaron Burr of New York moved to rescind the injunction on all discussion, while maintaining a ban on publication of the actual text. Ellsworth objected that the matter should be left entirely to the president, but his counter motion was voted down, and Burr's, after some vacillation, was adopted.[65] The Senate thus recognized its power to make the treaty's contents public by indirect means, though it left the timing of official publication to the president.[66]

Even while the Senate debated, Senator Pierce Butler of South Carolina had leaked a copy of the treaty to Madison. After adjournment, discussion was free on all sides. King admitted showing Hammond the text, though he denied having let him retain a copy, and Secretary Wolcott divulged it to his father.[67] With Hamilton and King now urging formal publication,[68] the president soon agreed and authorized Randolph to release a copy to the *Philadelphia Gazette,* the usual outlet for official proclamations. Before the arrangements were complete, the treaty was printed by *Aurora* editor Benjamin Franklin Bache, with Senator Stevens T. Mason of Virginia taking responsibility for the act.[69]

Because the president's prior decision to publish was not at once made known, Mason's act was accorded more importance than it perhaps deserved. For a time he became the great hero of one party and the arch villain of the other. Mason defended his breach of the Senate's resolution as obedient to a higher duty, since the secrecy of the treaty had been clearly improper. The opposition press, of course, agreed.[70] The Federalist press found Mason's act heinous; yet the Federalist-dominated Senate, when it reconvened, made no move to censure Mason for the infraction. The reasons cannot be documented, but it may be presumed that a mix of legal and political considerations was involved.

The Senate, still disposed toward informality in its internal procedures, had no rule applicable to Mason's act. Moreover, there was no precedent for punishing any national officeholder, under the present Constitution, for leaking information. If not strictly immune from punishment for such conduct,[71] Mason surely had tradition on his side.[72] To innovate in this case and punish him might simply elevate Mason to martyrdom.[73] Besides, it was probably known to all that he had not been the only one to leak the treaty's contents. Mason had made a plausible principled defense of his conduct, and facts casting doubt on the purity of his motives were unknown to his contemporaries.[74] Thus the Senate had more reason to let the matter drop than to pursue it further.

Once the treaty was published, the consuming question was whether the president would sign it. Washington was deluged with memorials and petitions against the treaty; large, tumultuous public demonstrations took place from Boston to Charleston. Jay and his treaty were repeatedly burned in effigy. Some of this activity was spontaneous, but much of it was secretly orchestrated. This effort marked a new phase in the development of mass participation politics.[75]

While Federalists were alarmed by these activities and denounced those who would bypass the system of indirect representation mandated by the Constitution,[76] they did not see how their own efforts to bypass the legislative process and insulate the Senate from the people had contributed to the situation. In the end they had little choice but to enter the fray with essays, petitions, and mass meetings of their own.[77]

The president was in a quandary. His advisers had studied the treaty carefully and, for all its frankly acknowledged defects, concluded that it ought to be ratified. But Washington was chagrined by the extent and vehemence of public opposition. In July he removed to Mt. Vernon, and for seven weeks he kept his reflections secret not only from the public but even, for a time, from most of his cabinet.[78] To the petitions he received, he returned a brusque, uniform reply: "While I feel the most lively gratitude for the many instances of approbation from my country, I can not otherwise deserve it, than by obeying the dictates of my conscience."[79]

Despite this aloof posture Washington cannot have been entirely deaf to the debate that raged around him.[80] For a time he weighed the option of a ratification with certain conditions; then, in mid-August, he suddenly decided to sign the treaty unconditionally.[81] This reversal was precipitated by a most extraordinary development.

For a long time Edmund Randolph had been the only cabinet officer not fully committed to Jay's Treaty and the entire Federalist program. Though he did not directly oppose ratification, his advice had been partly responsible for the delay.[82] The British had detested Randolph since his unfriendly exchanges with Hammond and suspected him of covert Republican sympathies. Grenville had even told Jay that the secretary of state was an obstacle to the improvement of American-British relations.[83] Now, fortune provided them with the means of Randolph's undoing.

The lethal weapon was a dispatch from the French minister

Joseph Fauchet to his government, written in October 1794. The ship carrying this dispatch was captured by a British vessel in March 1795, and on July 28 Hammond turned it over to Secretary of the Treasury Oliver Wolcott.[84] Genêt's successor had strange things to tell of Randolph: the American had favored Fauchet with "precious confessions"; he had avowed himself France's friend; he had accused his colleagues of "hastening" the Whiskey Rebellion to justify raising an army in a drive bent on "absolute power"; and, most damaging of all, he had approached Fauchet for money, saying it was needed to avert a civil war in America. It appeared that Randolph was chargeable at least with indiscretion and duplicity, possibly also with soliciting bribes and conceivably with treason.

Wolcott's shock quickly gave way to glee. No doubt the president's delay in signing the treaty was another piece of Randolph's evil work; his exposure was precisely what the Federalists needed. Wolcott and Secretary of War Timothy Pickering secretly summoned the president to Philadelphia. He arrived on August 11 and met with the two secretaries that night. The next day, he informed an astonished Randolph of his decision to sign the treaty without delay. A week later he abruptly confronted Randolph with Fauchet's incriminating dispatch. Randolph, protesting his innocence but realizing he had irretrievably lost the president's confidence, resigned.

These events did not at once become public. When the resignation and signing were known, a torrent of denunciation erupted upon the president's head. At first Randolph's resignation was seen as a protest against the signing or as the fruit of some Federalist plot. When the gravity of Randolph's apparent misdeeds emerged, the Republicans abandoned his cause, but they continued to insist that the president had overreacted: to sign the treaty had been hasty and irrational.[85]

Randolph in due course published a lengthy "Vindication," revealing a number of cabinet secrets in the process. He argued that his downfall was a plot fomented by Hammond and the Federalists to induce Washington to sign the treaty. He claimed, with Fauchet's sworn support, that his "precious confessions"[86] had not betrayed governmental secrets, but simply reassured Fauchet of his own and the president's good feelings toward France.

In all likelihood, Randolph had been no more free with cabinet secrets than had Hamilton and the others. His frequent requests for Washington's permission to disclose particular documents are a matter of record, bespeaking a high degree of prudence in this respect.[87] The business of Randolph's request for French money during the Whiskey Rebellion was harder to explain. Randolph's and Fauchet's versions of the incident did not quite gibe; and, in fact, neither version made perfect sense. Randolph's ostensible purpose was to enlist Fauchet's aid in exposing and neutralizing certain British intrigues designed to wreck the Republican party and to exacerbate tensions between the government and western settlers. Yet Randolph could not recollect the details of plot and counterplot, nor could he show the propriety of turning to a foreign ambassador for counterintelligence funding. Though he insisted that Washington had been briefed on the meeting with Fauchet, the president evinced no recollection of it and obviously did not believe that the truth was favorable to Randolph.[88]

Randolph's "Vindication" did not remove the cloud from his name, though no criminal charges were ever brought against him. The historians' verdict as to what really occurred is equivocal, and the whole story will probably never be known.[89] In any case, the incident hardened the president's and the Federalists' suspicions that the Republican party was a conscious or unconscious tool of the French government and that its adherents could not be trusted with sensitive information.

Though the treaty now was legally ratified, the Republicans continued to denounce it with undiminished vigor and redoubled their attacks on the once untouchable Washington himself. The concluding paragraphs of a manifesto known as "The Political Creed of 1795" stated:

11. I believe that honest government requires no secrets. . . .
12. I believe that all honest men in a government wish their conduct and principles made known to the governed.
13. I believe it is the duty of every freeman to watch over the conduct of every man who is entrusted with his freedom.
14. I believe that a blind confidence in any men who have been of service to their country, has enslaved, and will ever enslave all the nations of the earth.

15. I believe . . . that a good general may be a most miserable politician.[90]

More than one writer specifically pointed to secrecy in the treaty-making process as a ground for impeachment,[91] but there was no prospect that the Senate would go along with an impeachment of Washington or of Jay. As a practical matter, aside from certain of the state governments,[92] the House of Representatives was the only forum in which the opposition could bring its power to bear. Its strategy, therefore, now focused on the effort to block the treaty in the House by withholding the appropriations needed to give it effect.[93] The House was deluged with petitions opposing the treaty and calling upon that body to block it. The lower houses of two state legislatures formally pronounced the treaty unconstitutional, and attempts were made in some states to instruct representatives to vote against the appropriations.[94] Vehement constitutional objections were raised, and many of these pertained to the House's own prerogatives, past and future.

At the outset of Jay's mission the House had dropped its program of commercial warfare against Britain in deference to the president's desire to seek a negotiated solution. Now it was clear that Jay had failed to obtain adequate redress; even worse, the treaty purported to sign away the House's power to impose discriminatory tariffs or to sequester debts owed to British citizens.[95] Jay's Treaty was an insult to the House from start to finish.

Now, the possibility of clashes between the treaty power and the legislative power was inherent in the constitutional system; no neutral principled solution was obvious. The ambiguity of the Constitution on the House's power to block the treaty prompted a few spontaneous judicial pronouncements, and even a few grand juries got into the act,[96] but no question ripe for adjudication had yet arisen. Nor did party leaders show any disposition to seek a solution through the judicial process. The Supreme Court had not yet laid claim to a role as final arbiter of constitutional disputes. It lacked prestige and visibility, and, for the Republicans, it lacked the crucial qualification of even a superficial nonpartisanship. Jay had remained chief justice throughout his stay abroad, resigning only after his election as governor of New York. His colleagues were unlikely to interfere with his achievement, but the Federalists, for their part, did not require judicial assistance.

Several proposals were circulated for amending the Constitution, including one relating directly to our subject: a group of New Jerseyites resolved that the Constitution should be amended to require that "the Senate doors be always open to the public except during war or other extraordinary occasions."[97] Constitutional amendment, like adjudication, however, was simply not a viable way of dealing with the pressing and highly partisan issues before the country. The decision, it appeared, would lie with the House of Representatives.

Livingston's Resolution

Washington submitted his appropriations request to the House on March 1, 1796. Madison announced his determination to block it and believed he had the votes.[98] Efforts were made to organize the Republican members of the House into a unified and disciplined majority bloc. The attempt was not a complete success, as many members felt free to follow their own inclinations rather than the dictates of party leaders.

It was not Madison but Edward Livingston of New York who on March 2 submitted a resolution, requesting the president to provide the House with a copy of Jay's instructions and his correspondence relative to the treaty. Madison was apparently surprised and dismayed, but Livingston would not withdraw his motion. Instead, he agreed to a softening amendment: "excepting such of said papers as any existing negotiation may render improper to be disclosed."[99] Madison still felt that Livingston's resolution was a tactical mistake— if not, indeed, a constitutional one. As a tactic, it diverted energy from the attack on the treaty's merits to a side issue of executive secrecy. Moreover, the only known precedent for a qualified call for papers had simply allowed Washington to withhold "such parts as he might think proper." Indeed, during the Morris affair Madison had admitted to Randolph that "the discretion of the President was always to be the guide."[100] In neither of these cases had any relevant negotiation been pending. Thus Livingston's resolution, as amended, bore the aspect of an effort to limit the scope of the president's hitherto undefined discretion to withhold information.[101]

Always more comfortable with the role of nationalist statesman than that of opposition party leader, Madison remained convinced that a strong presidency was an essential unifying force for the new nation and its government. This concern apparently made him more solicitous than Livingston for the powers of the executive—an ironical stance for the advocate of separated powers who had argued so persuasively in *The Federalist* that the ambition of officeholders to expand the prerogatives of their own institutions would guarantee a mutual checking action.

The House did not share Madison's view, for it rebuffed, without recorded debate, his effort to substitute a resolution that would have granted the president a broader discretion—to withhold "so much of said papers as, in his judgment, it may not be consistent with the interest of the United States, at this time, to disclose."[102]

The stage was now set for a great debate on Livingston's resolution, which occupied the House for an entire month. In the process the legal aspects of the House's right to information were ventilated with unprecedented thoroughness. As soon became apparent, the constitutional text could not be decisive as to the propriety of the call for papers. Several members did assert that the president's duty to "inform Congress from time to time of the State of the Union" implied a corresponding right of Congress to demand information, but the point was not approved by many speakers. The clause was generally understood as referring to spontaneous presidential communications; it appeared to leave the time and manner of informing Congress up to the president. If it could not be read to obligate him to comply with any and all demands for information, neither did the Federalists look to this provision as the basis of any presidential power to refuse such demands.

The Federalists' first line of attack on the resolution was to question its purpose. The call for papers was totally improper, they said, unless the papers were required by the House in order to perform a function conferred upon it by the Constitution.

Livingston replied that the House ought to determine whether Jay had violated the president's instructions. Having inspected some of the papers while they were at the Senate,[103] Livingston professed to believe that more careful study might suggest an impeachment. But the primary purpose of his resolution was to help the House decide whether to grant the requested appropriations. "The House," Livingston concluded, "had a right to call for the information: if the president had any reasons of State that would make the information improper, he would say so."[104]

As the Federalists were quick to point out, there was no proposal before the House to impeach Jay or anyone else. Although the opposition press had broached the idea, it was plain that public opinion was not ready for such a step, and that in any case, the Senate would not vote to convict. The Republicans claimed, however, that a declared impeachment was not necessary to support the call for papers. Instead they relied, in part, on their derived or implied power of "superintendence over the officers of Government," as the "grand inquest of the nation."[105] This approach had the advantage of not requiring senatorial cooperation. Its aim was not removal of the officeholder but informing the nation; yet, like the impeachment power, this broad oversight power was now claimed to imply "the right to inspect every paper and transaction in any department."[106]

Although there was no explicit reference in the debate to the St. Clair and the Hamilton investigations, the Federalists did not and could not deny, after those episodes, that the House possessed a broad oversight power. Instead they claimed that this power applied only to offices created by statute, whereas Livingston's resolution was directed to the president himself. Even if the inquest function could reach the president insofar as his duty to execute the laws was concerned, it would not apply, they insisted, to his exercise of the treaty power. The House was pointedly excluded by the Constitution from a role in treatymaking and surely had no right to compel the president to make public his executive business. True, Livingston's resolution did not commit the House to making the requested papers public, but there was little doubt that without publicity no meaningful use could be made of them.[107]

Some members replied that publicity would be all to the good. Abraham Baldwin of Georgia, a veteran of the Constitutional Convention and chairman of the committee that investigated Hamilton, made a speech to this effect which aroused heated controversy.

He thought the importance of having many Governmental secrets was diminishing. The doctrine of publicity, he said, had been daily gaining ground in public transactions in general . . . and what experience he had had in public matters confirmed him in the opinion that the greater the publicity measures the greater the success.[108]

Later Baldwin elaborated on his argument and admonished one of his critics.

Let that gentleman look at the secret Journal of the old Congress and see how it continually diminished till it was become almost nothing; let him look over the United States, and see how many public bodies which used to deliberate in secret now have their doors open; let him look over the communications, of mere Executive business, from the President of the United States, for these two or three years past; let him read the rule of their own House, as it now stands, on the subject of clearing the gallery, and see how much it is narrowed from the rule which was in force for the first two or three years—and then let him declare whether there is not some foundation for the assertions which he had attempted to combat.[109]

Federalist spokesmen retorted that sometimes secrecy was necessary and proper. The House's rules recognized this; Baldwin himself had recently supported a motion to clear the galleries.[110] Moreover, to establish the value of publicity did not dispose of the separation of powers issue. Thus Representative Joshua Coit of Connecticut, for one, replied that:

he fully agreed with the gentleman from Georgia that the more public Governmental proceedings could with propriety be made, the better; but that House had not the right to direct the President on that head . . . for, if they considered the President as attentive at all times to the duties of his office, it would be arrogancy in that House to attempt to influence him in that particular.[111]

Many Federalists echoed this position; one, Representative Nathaniel Smith of Connecticut, contributed a more original idea. He first argued "that each department of Government ought to be the sole judge when to make any part of its proceedings public"; but immediately added, "Besides, if the object is to publish them, in that case there ought to be an act passed regularly, directing them to be published."[112] Given the Senate's attitude this was not a serious proposal, and no one else took it up.

Now, the Federalists' claim that the president had sole responsibility for publicizing executive matters was not a straightforward account of the precedents. Congress had, without rebuke, requested the president to publicize executive affairs on more than one occasion; moreover, both its right to call for papers and its right to declassify and release them, if transmitted, were well established.[113] Livingston's resolution was a request, not an order, and the opposition conceded that the president had a certain discretion in replying to a call for papers. It was hardly "arrogancy" for the House to make such a call.

Nevertheless the Federalists could make a strong case that calls for papers were normally in aid of legislation, and the Republicans did not rely on the oversight or informing function of the House as the sole basis for Livingston's resolution. Instead they invoked the House's right to deliberate upon the pending appropriation measure. Many argued that the case was no different from any other act of legislation: the House had full discretion and, in order to exercise it wisely, full information was needed. In rebuttal it was said that the House had no right to disapprove a treaty ratified by president and Senate and therefore lacked discretion in this case. The nation's faith was pledged; there was nothing to deliberate.

Most members, it seemed, were inclined to favor an intermediate position. The embarrassment involved in repudiating the treaty at this stage would indeed be great; yet few denied that at least in extreme cases, it would be proper for the House to block a treaty by withholding funds. This would be true, in particular, where a treaty offended against the Constitution.[114]

The opposition had in fact identified a long list of constitutional infirmities in Jay's Treaty. Did these allegations, however sound, support the call for papers? The Federalists argued persuasively in the negative. If the treaty's provisions were unconstitutional, this would be apparent from its text. As for the procedures of treaty-making, if Jay had violated his instructions, the defect was cured by the ratification of the president and Senate. Thus the papers called for were irrelevant to any constitutional question before the House.

The force of these arguments threw the Republicans back to their central point: the treaty was improvident, injurious to the national interest, and contrary to the will of the people. Thus it was the House's right and duty to oppose it—or at least not to approve it without a full and independent investigation. In light of the history of Jay's mission, the Federalist cries that the House was usurping treatymaking power were disingenuous. The House was entitled to exercise the legislative discretion which had been so long postponed and circumvented by the machinations of the administration and its congressional allies.

To demonstrate the propriety of the call for papers, Livingston reviewed certain precedents on communication between the president and the House concerning diplomatic activities. From the outset of the American government, Livingston showed, Washington had always recognized that Congress had independent discretion as to appropriations for the conduct of foreign affairs, and had always supplied the information needed for its deliberations. In 1789 he had sought advance appropriations before commencing negotiations with the Indians. In 1791 and 1793 he had done the same before negotiating with Algiers. In recent years he had provided the House with copious information on foreign affairs, including his instructions to the envoys to Spain. All this information had been deemed relevant to the House's legitimate business, and until now its right to such information had never been controverted.[115]

Unaccountably, neither Livingston nor his opponents referred to the precedent of the Morris episode. The principle ostensibly established in that case was that the Senate, acting as a branch of the legislature, did have a right to call for papers—without, it would seem, being required to specify the purposes for which they were wanted. Now the Federalists were taking an entirely new stance: that the House had no right to inquire, because it had no right to deliberate. It is hard to see how this view could be squared with the Morris precedent, but no one tried. The Federalists admitted that Washington had often graciously shared information with the House. This, they asserted, could not impair his right to withhold information whenever his judgment so dictated. In the present case he had already exercised his judgment by not including the additional documents with his appropriations request, and that, for party stalwarts, was the end of the matter.[116]

This argument cut so deeply into the House's prerogatives that a number of treaty supporters proved willing to support Livingston's resolution out of institutional esprit de corps. No doubt they hoped too that the papers called for might help to justify some of the treaty's unpalatable features.[117] On March 24, 1796, Livingston's resolution was passed by a resounding majority of sixty-two to thirty-seven.[118] This was not a typical partisan division by any means. As one writer has observed, Livingston's resolution "received the greatest support of any anti-administration measure in the entire decade," reflecting in part "the House's frustration over its declining influence, especially on foreign policy matters."[119]

Defiance and Legal Impasse

The president, as was his custom, promptly consulted his cabinet on the options legally and politically open to him in responding to the resolution. He also consulted a private citizen, Alexander Hamilton. Between March 26 and March 31 he received a series of elaborate opinions from his advisers.[120]

Charles Lee, the attorney general,[121] was of the opinion that the president had a legal right to refuse the papers. Despite the House's general right to call for information for proper legislative purposes, in the present case a total refusal might be warranted, since the House had not set forth any proper constitutional basis for the call. In particular the House had no right to reject the treaty, which was already the law of the land, and Lee cited the still-secret records of the Constitutional Convention to show that the framers had explicitly rejected a proposal to require legislative sanction for treaties. In any case, under the State of the Union clause, the president was to exercise discretion as to the time and manner of informing Congress. His discretion surely included the power to withhold confidential communications pertaining to a "treaty either pending or finally concluded." Nevertheless, Lee opined, it might be prudent in this case for the president to give the House what he had given the Senate, provided he made clear to the House that it could not demand the papers as a matter of right.[122]

In a separate memorandum Lee tried to distinguish the precedents adduced by Livingston, which showed that the president had often spontaneously shared diplomatic information with the House

and had never controverted its deliberative role in the foreign policy sphere. Lee quickly dismissed these episodes, noting that, for
example, the president's application in 1789 for advance appropriations for an Indian treaty "was before any fund existed for foreign
intercourse"; his recent communications respecting foreign affairs
"were voluntary and to show whether offensive measures ought to
be resorted to." Lee's central point was that Washington had
never, in so many words, admitted an obligation to comply with
congressional calls for information about pending or finished negotiations, but he did not deal with the Morris investigation or any
other precedents besides those cited by Livingston. It was, in sum, a
rather superficial performance.[123]

James McHenry, the secretary of war, agreed with Lee. Absent a
declared purpose to impeach, the House had no right to compel the
president to surrender the papers; yet perhaps the president should
not stand rigidly on his rights.

> It is worthy too of consideration, whether in a government like ours
> a freer communication in such cases, than is usual in a country where
> the Executive and one branch of government are hereditary, is not a
> matter of policy as well as of necessity if not of propriety.[124]

Like Lee, McHenry thought it expedient that the president should
comply with the request, at least in part, while reserving his right to
do otherwise in the future.[125]

Oliver Wolcott, secretary of the treasury, took a similar constitutional line. The treaty power, he argued, had been given to the president and Senate precisely to preserve the "secrecy and despatch"
often necessary in diplomacy. The resolution thus exceeded the
House's power in principle; moreover, it was insufficiently qualified in scope.

> Except when an Impeachment is proposed and a formal inquiry insti-
> tuted, I am of opinion that the House of Representatives has no right
> to demand papers relating to foreign negociations either pending or
> compleated.[126]

Was there nevertheless a prudential argument for complying with
the resolution? On this point Wolcott differed with Lee and

McHenry: he thought a refusal by the president would bolster public confidence in the government.

> That the public jealousy can be excited to any considerable degree is not probable.—It is known to the world that Mr. Randolph was acquainted with the whole course of negociation and that his malignity would prompt him to disclose any measures which could embarrass the Executive will not be doubted.—All the correspondence was submitted to the Senate and is admitted to have been seen; the knowledge of what the papers contain has therefore become too general to admit of the propagation of an opinion, that the President or negociator would be affected by a more full disclosure. The public would therefore in my opinion attribute a refusal on the part of the President to its proper motive, a determination to support the Constitution.[127]

Wolcott's recommendation, therefore, was that the president should withhold the papers entirely.

Timothy Pickering, who had moved from the War to the State Department upon Randolph's resignation, agreed with Wolcott's advice, and it was Pickering's draft of a reply to the House that Washington, with some alterations, ultimately adopted as his own. Like the other secretaries, Pickering stated that in the event of a declared purpose to impeach, it would be "the duty of the President to furnish all the evidence which could be derived from the papers in his possession." In the actual state of the case, however, no satisfactory foundation for the resolution had been laid; and besides, "all the papers ~~called for~~ relating to the treaty with Great Britain were laid before the Senate."[128]

Pickering, like Lee, submitted a separate memorandum on Livingston's precedents. Pickering's analysis was fuller than Lee's but still dealt only with those few cases Livingston had cited. Pickering argued first, and paradoxically, that "All the instances cited relate to communications *prior to the making of the treaties:* whereas the object now contended for is, a right to *sanction* or *reject* treaties *after they are made.*"[129] One might have thought that a right of the House to participate in advance would imply, *a fortiori,* a right to subsequent knowledge. But Pickering argued that Livingston's Indian and Algerine precedents were not in point, since these savages and pirates would only negotiate with cash on the table. As for Washington's messages on the Spanish negotiations, Livingston had claimed that these were sent to the House because commercial relations were subject to the legislative power. Pickering retorted that the president had negotiated with Spain for two years before taking the House into his confidence. He did so not in deference to the House's power to regulate commerce, but only because the deadlock of the negotiations and the disorders in Kentucky had raised alarms of war. The Senate, in contrast, had been shown the envoys' instructions before the talks began. "Thus," Pickering concluded, "it appears that the cases cited by Mr. Livingston do not yield a shadow of support to his resolution: and indeed his speech is made up of contemptible sophistry and florid declamation."[130]

With all respect due the secretary, perhaps the most contemptible sophistries in this instance were Pickering's own. In particular, his account of the president's handling of the Spanish negotiations made out a strong indictment of the handling of Jay's mission. Jay's instructions, unlike those of the Spanish envoys, had not been shown to the Senate in advance, although it was in session and the business was of the greatest importance. Moreover, if public unrest and a possibility of war made it proper to inform the House in the Spanish case, the same considerations applied now with even greater force.[131] Thus, even if Livingston had misstated the reasons for Washington's earlier openness, Pickering's argument only enhanced the relevance of Livingston's precedents, nor did Pickering have a word to say about the Gouverneur Morris episode and the reasoning espoused by the executive in that case.

It was Alexander Hamilton who supplied the most thorough and sophisticated analysis of the respective powers of Congress and the president. Hamilton had been in touch with Washington and the Federalists on this matter throughout the House debates. On March 7, he wrote to Washington that "those who think" would support a defiance of such an indefinite, unexplained demand as the House was contemplating.

> It will be fatal to the negotiating power of the government if it is to be a matter of course for a call of either House of Congress to bring forth all the communications, however confidential.[132]

It deserves attention that Hamilton in this letter denied a right in *either* house to demand diplomatic papers, for his subsequent argument rested largely on the constitutional exclusion of the House of Representatives from the treaty power. In distinguishing the houses, Hamilton could cite the framers' belief that only the Senate could be safely entrusted with executive secrets, but clearly Hamilton himself had no such belief. His advice to Washington in the Morris episode showed that he was not, in fact, prepared to grant the Senate a right to see such papers "as a matter of course." Because it was only the House with which the administration was currently embroiled, however, it proved advantageous to lay emphasis on the differences between the powers of the two houses.

Apparently Washington next asked Hamilton to evaluate Lee and McHenry's proposal for a partial compliance; for on March 24 and 26 Hamilton wrote to him that, "considering the matter *externally* as well as *internally,*" his review of the papers had convinced him that a total refusal would be more expedient. Even individual inspections by members visiting the State Department (with copying not permitted) could "do harm to the President and to the government."[133] Thus Hamilton, though not holding any official post, had access to the papers in question—a right he felt could not safely be accorded to congressmen even on an informal basis. His idea that internal political concerns were an appropriate ground for withholding information from Congress was never openly avowed in official pronouncements on the subject. In a letter of March 28, Hamilton gave a frank and detailed review of the faults in Jay's instructions—passing over in silence his personal role in drafting them. They were "in general a crude mass—which will do no credit to the administration."[134]

Finally, on March 29 he submitted to Washington his draft of a proposed message to the House. This letter arrived too late for Washington to use; all the same, it was perhaps as powerful and as principled a defense as could be made of the president's right to withhold the papers. It did not, of course, enter into a discussion of the questions of expediency that Hamilton had pursued in his earlier letters to the president.

For Hamilton, the constitutional questions presented by Livingston's resolution were just two: had the president a duty to protect state secrets and had the House a right to disapprove a treaty? His argument upon the former point was unusually lengthy and complex. In essence, Hamilton's propositions were as follows:

> It is contrary to the general practice of Governments to promulge the intermediate transactions of a foreign negotiation without weighty and special reasons. . . . [P]articular occurences *of a negotiation* . . . if immediately disclosed, might tend to embarrassment and mischief in the interior affairs of the Country. . . . Moreover, it is not uncommon for the instructions to negotiating Agents . . . to . . . manifest views, which, if disclosed, might renew sources of jealousy and ill will which a treaty had extinguished—might exhibit eventual plans of proceeding which had better remain unknown for future emergencies, and might even furnish occasion for suspicion, and pretext for discontent to other powers.[135]

If after-the-fact publicity was apt to cause internal political embarrassment or disrupt relations with the treaty partner and third countries, even the fear of publicity tended to distort and inhibit the negotiating process. Where a government could not guarantee secrecy, the other side's envoys would shrink from making concessions.

> The disposition to a liberal and perhaps for that very reason to a wise policy in them might be checked by the reflection that it might afterwards appear from the disclosures of the other side that they had not made as good bargains as they might have made.

[Meanwhile,]

> the Agents of such a nation, themselves, would have strong inducements to extreme reserve in their communications with their own government, lest parts of their conduct might subject them in other quarters to unfriendly and uncandid constructions. . . . And thus in different ways the channels of information to a Government might be materially obstructed.[136]

Although many of these conditions did not apply directly to the case at hand, Hamilton urged that full disclosure would create a dangerous precedent. Even a partial compliance should not be considered unless the call for papers was supported by some purpose which the House was constitutionally entitled to pursue.

Since Hamilton, like the cabinet, did not recognize publicity for its own sake as a legislative function, the question of the House's role in treatymaking now became crucial. And on this question, at least, the intent of the framers seemed very clear.

> The frequent absolute necessity of secrecy not only in the conduct of a foreign negotiation, but at certain conjunctions as to the very articles of a treaty is a natural reason why a part and that the least numerous part of the legislative body was united with the Executive in the making of treaties in exclusion of the other and the more numerous. . . .

> If the House of Representatives, called upon to act in aid of a Treaty made by the President and Senate believe it to be unwarranted by the Constitution which they are sworn to support, it is not to be denied that they may pause in the execution; until a decision of the point of constitutionality in the Supreme Court of the United States shall have settled the question. But this is the only discretion in that House, as to the obligation to carry a Treaty . . . into effect.[137]

Hamilton's reference to the possibility of adjudicating the treaty's constitutionality was unique. No one in Congress or the cabinet had suggested it, and the president did not take up the idea.

Even if he had understated the House's power to make constitutional judgments, Hamilton insisted, it would not follow that the call for papers was proper.

> Nothing extrinsic to the Treaty, or in the manner of the negotiation, can make it constitutional or unconstitutional, good or bad, salutary or pernicious—the internal evidence it affords is the only proper standard of its merits. . . .

> Even with reference to an animadversion on the conduct of the Agents who made the Treaty—the presumption of a criminal mismanagement of the interests of the United States ought first it is conceived to be deduced from the intrinsic nature of the Treaty and ought to be pronounced to exist previous to a further inquiry to ascertain the guilt or the guilty.[138]

Thus, in the absence of a declared impeachment proceeding, all of the president's advisers agreed that he was not legally obliged to comply with the House's request. Even if the call for papers had an adequate constitutional basis, he would have a discretion to withhold particular information in the public interest. In this case, they argued, the resolution of the House was entirely unwarranted, though Lee and McHenry thought it would be prudent to volunteer some of the papers anyway.

The president ultimately rejected the idea of even a partial compliance with Livingston's resolution. His message of March 30 was based on Pickering's draft but followed the contours of Hamilton's analysis.

> The nature of foreign negotiations requires caution and their success must often depend on secrecy; and even when brought to a conclusion, a full disclosure of all the measures, demands, or eventual concessions which may have been proposed or contemplated would be extremely impolitic. . . . The necessity of such caution and secrecy was one cogent reason for vesting the power of making Treaties in the President with the advice and consent of the Senate; the principle on which that body was formed confining it to a small number of members. To admit, then, a right in the House of Representatives to demand, and to have, as a matter of course, all the papers respecting a negotiation with a foreign Power, would be to establish a dangerous precedent.

> It does not occur that the inspection of the papers asked for can be relative to any purpose under the cognizance of the House of Representatives, except that of an impeachment; which the resolution has not expressed. I repeat, that I have no disposition to withhold any information which the duty of my station will permit, or the public good shall require, to be disclosed; and, in fact, all the papers affecting the negotiation were laid before the Senate, when the Treaty itself was communicated for their consideration and advice. . . .

> Having been a member of the General Convention . . . I have ever entertained but one opinion on this subject . . . that the power of making Treaties is exclusively vested in the President, by and with the advice and consent of the Senate . . . and that every Treaty so made, and promulgated, thenceforward becomes the law of the land. . . .

In this construction of the Constitution every House of Representatives has heretofore acquiesced. . . .

If other proofs than these, and the plain letter of the Constitution itself, be necessary to ascertain the point under consideration, they may be found in the Journals of the General Convention, which I have deposited in the office of the Department of State. In those Journals it will appear, that a proposition was made, "that no treaty shall be binding on the United States which was not ratified by a law," and that the proposition was explicitly rejected.

As therefore, it is perfectly clear to my understanding, that the assent of the House of Representatives is not necessary to the validity of a Treaty; as the Treaty with Great Britain exhibits in itself all the objects requiring legislative provision, and on these the papers called for can throw no light; and as it is essential to the due administration of the Government, that the boundaries fixed by the Constitution between the different departments should be preserved—a just regard to the Constitution and to the duty of my office, under all the circumstances of this case, forbid a compliance with your request.[139]

Now, the president took high and novel ground in not only affirming his power to withhold specific sensitive information from Congress, but also denying the right of the legislature to call for papers without specifying a purpose persuasive to himself. This argument had been toyed with and dropped in the Morris episode, although the Senate's purpose in calling for those papers had been far from obvious. At that time, the censorship of the papers was deemed adequate to protect the interests confided to the executive by the Constitution. A new reading of the precedents had led Pickering, for one, to the verge of a bizarre theory that the House's right to information on Jay's conduct was actually diminished to nothing when the treaty was laid before that body. Until that moment the case would have exactly paralleled the Morris investigation, and an argument for total refusal could not plausibly have been framed as a rebuff to usurpation of the prerogatives of president and Senate. Had the executive still wished to defy the call, it would have been necessary to confront squarely the applicability of the House's grand inquest power—an issue the president's message wholly failed to address. The issue of the House's want of treaty power served as a red herring, obscuring the extent to which the executive was not just innovating but actually departing from precedent. The obfuscation, moreover, was not entirely inadvertent.

If the president's message was less than thorough in its analysis of the powers of the House, it was less than candid in its treatment of those of the Senate; for the president implied that the right of the Senate in its executive capacity to inspect diplomatic papers was secure and, apparently, unlimited, whereas, in fact, the information given to the Senate had been belated and incomplete in important respects. Advance consultation had been far less than precedent dictated, and in submitting the completed treaty the president had silently exercised a discretion to withhold papers from the Senate. If it was technically true that all papers "affecting the negotiation" had been given, it was also true that important papers had been withheld—ostensibly because their dating made them irrelevant, but actually because their contents were potentially embarrassing.

The president was no more forthcoming as to the criteria he employed for deciding what to keep secret when a proper call for papers was made. He did remark on the frequent need for secrecy even as to completed negotiations—implying that the secrecy proviso in Livingston's resolution was too narrow, as Madison for one had been prepared to concede. In the end, though, he did not commit himself to any criterion more specific than the "public good"; he did not state that he viewed it as a proper ground for withholding papers that their disclosure might, in Hamilton's words, "do no credit to the administration." He did not even say whether any of the papers called for in this case were such as could not safely be made public. His argument came ultimately to this: a right in Congress to demand papers as a matter of course would be dangerous; therefore the president must have absolute discretion to withhold; therefore it was his duty to withhold even innocuous information if releasing it might be thought to establish a dangerous precedent. The only safeguard against abuse of discretion to which the message could point was Washington's own character and regard for his oath of office. Neither Hamilton's suggestion of an adjudicated solution nor Representative Nathaniel Smith's of a legislated one commended itself to the chief executive.

In a final move that aptly illustrated the true state of affairs, the president boldly violated the injunction of secrecy imposed by the framers and quoted the journal of the Constitutional Convention, to which his congressional challengers had no access. Though in executive custody, this journal was to be published only pursuant to order of Congress—an order which was still many years in the future.[140]

The president probably did not realize how unorthodox a performance his message really was. Persuaded that Livingston's resolution was a usurpation, he saw his own position as a defense of the constitutional status quo. His advisers, of course, said nothing to suggest otherwise. Unlike the situation in Congress, where the executive branch always had vigorous spokesmen to defend its prerogatives, the executive branch was politically homogeneous. There was no one in the president's circle with a legal duty or a political interest in advocating, or even reciting, the congressional viewpoint. What Washington got from those on whom he relied for accurate memory and disinterested advice was in fact a highly unorthodox partisan perspective.

Yet it would not do to suggest that the aging president was simply tricked by his advisers into betraying his natural inclinations toward candor and openness. For the pressures of foreign crisis and domestic rebellion, the shock of Randolph's apparent betrayal, and the personal attacks to which the president had lately been subject in the newspapers had led him by stages to willing participation in a siege mentality.

A letter the president wrote to Hamilton shortly after sending his message to the House leaves an impression that Washington had decided upon a total refusal even prior to receiving the opinions of his cabinet.[141] Even if that is so, it is possible that strong contrary advice might have altered his determination, especially if backed by a cogent legal argument. No such argument was forthcoming.

Yet not even Federalists were unanimous in approving the president's stand when it became known. Hamilton, it is true, was overjoyed,[142] but John Adams wrote to Abigail, "I cannot deny the right of the House to ask for papers, nor to express their opinions upon the merits of a treaty. My ideas are very high of the rights and powers of the House of Representatives."[143] Other Federalists like

Justice James Iredell of the Supreme Court and Governor Samuel Johnston of North Carolina also wrote privately that the president would have done better to comply.[144] Now the next move was up to the House itself.

After the impressive margin by which the resolution had passed, a total refusal was the last thing the House expected. As Madison wrote to Monroe, the president's stand was quite extreme, bearing the earmarks of a partisan stratagem designed to provoke a showdown.

> The prevailing belief was, that he would send a part, if not the whole, of the papers applied for. . . . You will find by his Message, in answer, that he not only ran into the extreme of an absolute refusal, but assigned reasons worse than the refusal itself. I have no doubt that the advice, and even the Message itself, were contrived in New York [by Hamilton].[145]

At this juncture the House Republicans held the first formal party caucus in American history. They agreed on the need to reaffirm the House's rights and powers, though they were divided on the proper means of doing so. Madison's view reflected his usual approach: "it is necessary to avoid, as much as possible, an overt rencontre with the Executive."[146]

Resolutions of protest were subsequently introduced by Thomas Blount of North Carolina, announcing the sense of the House that, first, though it claimed no agency in ratifying treaties, it did insist on its right to deliberate on the expediency of granting appropriations; and second, that it deemed it unnecessary to state any purpose in calling for information "desired by [it], and which may relate to any Constitutional functions of the House."[147]

Madison made a major speech in support of these resolutions, attempting to articulate and defend the principles that, in his view at least, had been recognized prior to Jay's mission and now stood repudiated by the president's message. While the existing impasse could be finally resolved only through further negotiations, through the electoral process, or through constitutional amendment, at least the House should go on record as rejecting the president's novel and unwarranted propositions.

He thought it clear that the House must have a right, in all cases, to ask for information which might assist their deliberations on the subjects submitted to them by the Constitution: being responsible nevertheless, for the propriety of the measure. He was as ready to admit that the Executive had a right, under a due responsibility, also, to withhold information, when of a nature that did not permit the disclosure of it at the time. And if the refusal of the President had been founded simply on a representation, that the state of the business within his department, and the contents of the papers asked for, required it, although he might have regretted the refusal, he should have been little disposed to criticize it. But the message had contested what appeared to him a clear and important right of the House; and stated reasons for refusing the papers, which, with all the respect he could feel for the executive, he could not regard as satisfactory or proper.

One of the reasons was, that it did not occur to the Executive that the papers could be relative to any purpose under the cognizance, and in the contemplation of the House. The other was, that the purpose for which they were wanted was not expressed in the resolution of the House.

With respect to the first, it implied that the Executive was not only to judge of the proper objects and functions of the Executive department, but, also, of the objects and functions of the House. He was not only to decide how far the Executive trust would permit a disclosure of information, but how far the Legislative trust could derive advantage from it. It belonged, he said, for each department to judge for itself. . . .

As far as he could recollect, no precedent could be found in the records of the House, or elsewhere, in which the particular object in calling for information was expressed in the call. It was not only contrary to right to require this, but it would often be improper in the House to express the object. In the particular case of an impeachment . . . it would involve the preposterous idea of first determining to impeach, and then inquiring whether an impeachment ought to take place.[148]

Madison took the president to task for improperly disclosing an extract from the journal of the Constitutional Convention, and he strongly urged the House to adopt Blount's protest resolutions. He did not, however, declare that the president's conduct would warrant a rejection of the treaty appropriations, much less an impeachment.

To Madison's surprise, the Federalists raised little resistance to Blount's resolutions, which were quickly passed by a vote of fifty-seven to thirteen. Apparently the president's message had won no converts among supporters of Livingston's resolution, whatever its effect outside the House.[149] Nevertheless, the Federalists were fairly united in support of Jay's Treaty itself. When the president ignored the House's protest, some Republicans urged that the appropriations be refused in retaliation. On April 14, Representative William Maclay introduced a resolution to the effect that,

> With such information as the House possesses, it is not expedient at this time to concur in passing the laws necessary for carrying the said Treaty into effect.[150]

The Federalists insisted that the faith of the nation was pledged to honor the ratified treaty, and that, even if the House had a legal right to deny the funds, the consequences would be disastrous for the nation. To refuse the funds out of institutional pique would be the height of irresponsibility. After some parliamentary skirmishing it was agreed that Maclay's resolution would not be brought to a vote unless the appropriations were first defeated. Madison had calculated that the Republican majority would hold firm in the vote on the appropriations.[151] The Federalists, however, mounted an extremely vigorous and skillful campaign to muster votes for the treaty. In the country at large, an effort was made to present the issue as a vote of confidence in the president. Rhetoric failing, bankers, it was said, threatened to deny credit to those who would not sign petitions in favor of the treaty.[152] In the floor debate the Federalists relied heavily on the threat of war if the treaty were blocked. Private correspondence reveals that a diverse set of tactics was used to exert direct and indirect pressure on vulnerable members.[153] Hamilton proposed that the Senate should block adjournment until the funds were granted; others apparently were prepared to bring the entire legislative process to a standstill.[154] Jefferson even claimed that Senators Rufus King and George Cabot had threatened to break up the Union itself.[155]

The Republicans countered with publicity campaigns of their own and with special pressures on key representatives, but this time they were outmaneuvered politically. Madison wrote:

> The people were everywhere called on to chuse between peace and war. . . . This stratagem produced in many places a fever, and in New England a delirium for the Treaty, which soon covered the table with petitions. The counter petitions . . . did not keep pace. Indeed, there was not time for distant parts, where the Treaty was odious, to express their sentiments before the occurrence was over.[156]

On April 28, a test vote in committee of the whole resulted in a forty-nine to forty-nine tie, which the speaker, nominally a Republican, broke by voting in favor of the appropriation. Two days later the full House took up the question. The Republicans, now fearing that the bill would pass, tried to salvage a moral victory by attaching a preamble that declared the treaty "highly objectionable." This too was defeated by the speaker's tie-breaking vote. Finally the appropriation passed by a margin of fifty-one to forty-eight.[157]

Madison's postmortem blamed his party's defeat on "the unsteadiness, the follies, the perverseness, and the defections among our friends."[158] It was no idle perversity, however, that led some who had voted for Livingston's resolution to support the appropriations bill. It was one thing to take a firm stand on the constitutional powers of the House, as they had done, and another thing to force the nation into an international and domestic crisis of the first magnitude. Without an absolutely clear mandate from their constituents, it is no wonder some members shrunk from this responsibility.[159]

Federalists, ancient and modern, have sometimes claimed that the passage of the appropriations signified acquiescence by the House in the president's position on his right to withhold information. This claim is patently false. The constitutional questions were expressly dealt with by the House in the Blount resolutions and were not at issue in the vote on the appropriations. Of course, the president adhered to his position just as firmly as the House did to its own. The House was unprepared to use its power of the purse to compel surrender of the papers, but the result, in doctrinal terms, was a standoff.

The debate on Livingston's resolutions had not been a waste of time. Even if it did not settle the meaning of the Constitution to the satisfaction of all concerned, the debate had important educational functions. Press coverage and public comment had been spirited; indeed, a number of novel arguments surfaced in the press.[160]

Opposition writers made much of the inconsistency of the Federalists' arguments. The president had wished the treaty published after the Senate's recess, so that public opinion could be made known; later he refused to be influenced by that opinion. Federalists had denied the people's right to petition against the treaty, insisting that it was a matter for Congress to decide upon; yet later they both denied the right of Congress to deliberate and deluged that body with petitions. They insisted that the withheld papers were of a secret nature and could not safely be communicated; yet they also argued that the papers' contents were already well enough known, since individual members had seen them while in the Senate's custody. In short, the Federalists were not arguing from principle but from a cynical desire to have their treaty at any cost.[161]

Federalist writers tended to represent the Republicans simply as reckless and unprincipled usurpers, whose constitutional protests against the treaty were neither logical nor sincere. To forestall peace with Britain, they seemed prepared to wreck the government. Randolph's ruin showed how far the secret friends of France were willing to go.[162] Federalists looked to the 1796 election for a mandate to deal with such disloyal creatures—if necessary, according to law. If the constitutional situation was equivocal, the balance of political power was swinging decisively in their favor. Further constitutional argumentation began to seem at best a time-consuming luxury.

Conclusions

Prior to Jay's mission there appeared to be broad agreement, in general terms, on the right of Congress to call for information, its right to disclose information in its possession, and the president's right to withhold specific information for good and sufficient reason. Any of these powers might be subject to abuse; in such an event the remedies would lie in the political modes of accountability established by the Constitution.

These principles, though they stood in need of more precise criteria to govern their application to particular cases, had seemed consistent in spirit with the framers' plan and with the practical needs of the government as well. Experience, however, was to prove otherwise.

In April 1794 Hamilton and the Senate Federalist leaders decided that the continued participation of Congress in foreign policymaking and the rising pressures of public opinion on the government could not be tolerated. Through the ensuing maneuvers the Federalists succeeded in drastically altering both the substance of American foreign policy and the procedures by which it was made—from a posture of neutrality implemented by interbranch cooperation to a pro-British policy implemented by secret and frankly unilateral executive action. What passed for "executive" power, moreover, was in fact the dominance of a partisan grouping that spanned all the branches of government and was headed by a private citizen, Alexander Hamilton.

After the foreign policy crisis in the spring of 1794 and the Whiskey Rebellion, negotiation and compromise with the opposition appeared to Federalist leaders to be neither possible nor necessary. Jay's mission was in essence a negation of the sharing of power, and the president's response to Livingston's resolution reflected this development. The president had not withheld specific information to prevent harm to the country; he had openly declared that foreign policy was his exclusive preserve and that it was effrontery for the House to request information on the subject.

The role of secrets and secrecy issues in this rapid transformation of the political process was pervasive. Secrecy was a crucial technique in the seizure of power that the Federalists accomplished in the president's name. It provided them with a public-spirited rationale for resorting to unilateral "executive" action and taking an ever narrower view of the prerogatives of Congress. And though the Republicans became increasingly alarmed about the right of Congress and the people to know what the administration was doing, neither press criticism of secrecy nor formal resolutions of the House were effective in arresting the trend toward tighter restraints on the flow of information.

Thus the effort to establish a stable and broadly acceptable communication policy for the government at large seemed to have ended in failure. That effort had not, after all, been either party's primary concern; and in any case, the structures of government were not designed to generate stable solutions—or so it now appeared. Crisis seemed to place a premium on the enhancement of executive power, on flexible, discretionary forms of authority rather than formal, legalistic ones. Given the existing partisan alignments there were few forums in which an effective counter might be raised and a potentially meaningful constitutional discourse held. All but two were under Federalist control. To argue for limits on secrecy was, in effect, to use the House of Representatives and the opposition press as vehicles for partisan attack on the president's foreign policy and his way of making decisions; but the press could only discuss and not decide, while the House could decide only for itself. This was not, constitutionally or politically, an especially promising state of affairs, but a decision not to press the issue was, in effect, a decision to tolerate further accretions of uncontrolled discretion to those acting under the presidential aegis. In fact, by the time Jay's Treaty gave the Republicans a politically viable issue on which to stand, the Federalists had won the president firmly to their side and committed the nation to a course that could not be altered without very great embarrassment.

While the outcome may reflect questionable strategic and tactical judgments on the part of Madison and his party, we should not underestimate the constraints placed upon them by the felt needs of national unity and security. The presidency was the key symbol of national strength, and Washington's personal popularity stood in telling contrast to the Republicans' numerical weakness in Congress. With the exception of that brief but fertile period in early 1794, they never were able to command a majority in both houses at once. Neither legislation nor impeachment could pass the Senate against Federalist opposition, nor, incidentally, were the courts at all sympathetic to opposition politics.

Until the debate on Livingston's resolution, secrecy issues were ventilated primarily in the newspapers, not in any forum with rulemaking power. These debates did mobilize public interest and instruct the people on republican ideology; moreover, press criticism probably did affect the opening of the Senate, the decline of the Democratic Societies, Washington's decision to publish Jay's Treaty, and other concrete decisions or events. These influences, however, were episodic rather than systemic and not typically oriented toward the adjustment of policymaking procedures. Abstract issues of communication technique had their heyday in Washington's first term, when procedures had to be developed from scratch and political vested interests seldom had bearing. In later periods secrecy issues were typically attached to, and dominated by, other concerns.

Even in the great House debate on Livingston's resolution, the secrecy issue was confusingly bound up with that of the treaty's merits and the House's right to judge its merits. From the viewpoint of partisan tactics, perhaps this was a wise choice. Certainly the vote on the resolution did not bear out Madison's worry that the call for papers was a counterproductive way of attacking the treaty, but this approach did make the secrecy issue, to some extent, hostage to the treaty itself. The people were in no position to fine-tune the decisionmaking process or adjudicate questions of constitutional law. What was asked of them was their signature on petitions for or against the treaty, their attendance at mass meetings, and their votes. Ultimately the Republicans failed to stop Jay's Treaty, failed to force the president to surrender the papers, and failed to carry the election of 1796. This outcome did not by any means reflect a dispassionate judgment on the secrecy issue or on the long-run advantages of a balanced and stable communication system; yet it inevitably had consequences in those areas.

The net result was that in Washington's second term the constitutional system offered no effective, built-in controls on escalating governmental secrecy and executive power. To some extent, especially in the early part of the period, the development of the system can be described as an adaptive response, not inconsistent with the framers' expectations, to the problems facing the country. The Constitution was not, after all, meant to preclude the effective conduct of foreign affairs, nor was public policy necessarily intended to be made always in a totally open and democratic manner. It can also be argued that the administration's foreign policy was beneficial to the country and reflected the will not only of wealthy elites but of a legitimate electoral majority.

Nevertheless, to say that the system was working as the framers intended is to yield to a monumental cynicism, for however conservative their politics may have been, surely their aim was not to provide a disguise for lawless authoritarianism. Yet many of the maneuvers recounted in this chapter were too casual, unilateral, and inconsistent with precedent to be called lawful. The apparent success of these maneuvers gave rise to a sense that the executive power was effectively above the law. Many Federalists were now prepared to go to appalling lengths to silence opposition. The constitutional control system, as it had evolved in Washington's years, did not prevent these burgeoning abuses; instead, Federalists were able at each stage to appeal to the doctrine of discretion as warrant for their acts. Secrecy was to play an intimate role in stimulating and facilitating the abuses of the Adams years. The great issue by then, however, was not the right to know; it was the right to dissent.

One-Party Rule
and Legal Repression_____6

The Federalists Clean House

The climactic episode of Washington's presidency was the confrontation over Jay's Treaty, ending in a dramatic failure of the president and the House of Representatives to agree on the norms of interbranch communication. In the aftermath both parties appealed to the people for vindication. A presidential election was in the offing, and Washington, tired and failing in health, could not be dissuaded from retiring. His decision was, however, kept secret until September 1796, hampering the Republicans in planning and organizing their campaign.[1]

The Federalists, after some hesitation and with some misgivings, chose Vice-President John Adams as their candidate to succeed Washington. Meanwhile, the Jay Treaty struggle had lured Jefferson out of political retirement, and he permitted the Republicans to promote him as their candidate. The Republicans' key issue was the treaty, though they also appealed to the electorate as defenders of true republican principles in domestic affairs.[2] The Federalists defended the treaty and charged that their opponents were tools of the French government. Jefferson suffered the embarrassment, indeed, of French Minister Pierre Adet's open support, yet he came within three electoral votes of victory and thus succeeded to the vice-presidency.[3]

In the congressional elections the Republicans did not fare so well. Despite the unpopularity of Jay's Treaty, the Federalists retained a powerful electoral base founded in class and sectional interests. They were bolstered by Washington's tacit support and by the fact that, after all, he had kept the country out of war. Indeed, the Federalists' depiction of the opposition to the treaty as irresponsible and purely partisan in motivation may have had a certain persuasive effect.[4]

The campaign witnessed great innovations in party organization and led to massive personnel changes in the government. If the elections could not and did not, in themselves, accomplish any clarification in the norms governing policymaking procedure and the control of official information, they did leave the Federalists in a position to introduce changes in procedure without effective resistance. For four years they would enjoy complete control in every branch of the government, though at first their House majority was precarious.[5] This development permitted certain improvements in the flow of information within government, but at the same time the nonrepresentation of opposition viewpoints led to serious difficulties in the relations between the government and the people.

With the Federalists firmly in control, the Republicans were unable to raise effective challenges to secrecy. In fact, the Federalists often preferred to exploit their advantage by means of carefully orchestrated publicity campaigns. Congressional calls for information now were gratefully complied with, confidential messages freely disclosed—and the Federalists profited.[6] It was as if the Jay Treaty debate had never taken place. Counterinformation was difficult to obtain through authorized channels, however, and the use of leaks to bring such information before the public proved a dangerous tactic, playing into Federalist charges that the Republicans were a disloyal faction controlled by foreign agents.

New developments in French-American relations provided an ominous warning of the Federalists' intentions and the techniques they were disposed to employ, even before Washington's departure. The Jay negotiations had aroused deep misgivings in France, and the announcement that a treaty had been concluded placed the American minister at Paris, James Monroe, in an unenviable position. He had to explain how this treaty could have come about, when repeated French overtures for a commercial treaty had been ignored. When details became known, it appeared that, even if Jay's Treaty was not strictly inconsistent with the terms of the French-American Treaty of Alliance of 1778, its provisions were in numerous respects helpful to the British war effort and burdensome to the French. Monroe, though obviously personally friendly toward France, had allowed himself to serve as bearer of false and deceptive assurances; he could not now arrest the deterioration of French-American relations that Jay's Treaty set in motion.[7]

On June 24, 1796, a concerned president asked his cabinet whether he had power, in the recess of the Senate, to send a special envoy to France to try to improve the situation.[8] It is strange that Washington had doubts on this score after all that had happened. He had dispatched Morris to London on a similar mission in 1789, while the Senate was in recess. He had issued the Proclamation of Neutrality in 1793 to preserve peace until Congress should convene. There had, of course, been attacks on the propriety of Jay's mission, but those did not pertain to the issue of presidential power to deal with exigencies during the recess of Congress. Nor had Washington previously given signs that he found any of the criticisms persuasive. If it was proper to send Jay's nomination to the Senate without disclosing his purpose to conclude a treaty, the mission now in contemplation could have been easily justified as well.

The cabinet, having previously shown not the slightest disposition to discern constitutional limits on executive discretion in foreign affairs, now suddenly revealed an unexpected passion for strict construction. Its reply to the president was unanimous: the president could not unilaterally dispatch a special envoy unless he first created a "vacancy" in the diplomatic establishment by removing Monroe.[9] Not surprisingly, the cabinet found good reasons for recommending the recall. Monroe and his allies were "enemies of the whole system of government," and could not safely be entrusted with public office. The protection of government secrets was one important reason. Like virtually all his contemporaries, Monroe was vulnerable to charges of indiscretion in private political conversations. Specific charges against him were supported by intercepted mail, as the charges against Randolph had been. This time, however, it was not the British navy that had done the intercepting. Through the agency of postal officials, the Federalists were now avidly seeking evidence of disloyal acts and attitudes among their opponents. Monroe's intercepted letter showed that he was leaking information to the opposition press. The cabinet found this ample proof of "sinister designs" against the public interest.[10]

Washington accepted the recommendation that Monroe be recalled.[11] Few members of that party remained now in government and none in posts of much importance. In theory, the Federalists' control of sensitive information was now secure. Though there was no overt change in the publicity policy of the executive at this time, the new situation produced significant departures in the way discretion was actually exercised. The change from 1793 to 1796 was striking. Instead of a heterogeneous cabinet in which opposing statesmen sought presidential sanction for taking their views before the public, there was now a highly homogeneous cabinet that not only adopted a common front but felt free to take initiatives without advance presidential approval, because there was no fear of challenge by a colleague. Moreover, the secretaries commonly sought Hamilton's advice on essential matters and confided totally in him without the president's authority.[12]

After Adams became president the situation was aggravated, for Adams and Hamilton disliked and distrusted each other. The new president's command of the situation was attenuated by his habit of taking extended vacations, by the fact that he lacked Washington's awe-inspiring manner and leadership skills, and by a conscious effort on the part of Hamilton and the cabinet to protect the country and the party from what they saw as the president's foibles.

Of course there had been leaks from the cabinet before, but the new situation was different in that covert channels for policy formation and bold initiatives taken without presidential authority became standard practice.[13] Not only were communications made without approval, but the secretaries were increasingly open in avowing that the control of official papers was to be used for partisan ends.

A good example of this opportunism was provided by an incident during the campaign, in which a letter from the French minister to the secretary of state, castigating the administration and voicing the hope that Jefferson would be elected president, was leaked to the opposition press. Indignant Federalists denounced the publishing of this dispatch, and Justice Samuel Chase declared:

> I think the Printer ought to be indicted for a false and base libel on our Government. A free press is the Support of Liberty and a Republican Government, but a licentious press is the bane of freedom, and the peril of Society, and will do more to destroy real liberty than any other Instrument in the Hands of knaves and fools.[14]

At the same time, perceiving the possibility of using the letter against Jefferson, Secretary of War McHenry took active steps to circulate it, along with an anonymous rebuttal he penned in defense of the administration. The source of the original leak, incidentally, has never been established.[15]

The trend toward overtly partisan use of diplomatic papers was reinforced by the Federalists' election victory. The spring and summer of 1797 witnessed an acrimonious exchange of letters between Secretary of State Pickering and Spanish Minister Carlos Martinez de Yrujo, reminiscent of the flap between Randolph and Hammond in 1794. Congress was supplied with the bulk of the correspondence,[16] but after its recess, and while the president was absent from the seat of government, Yrujo took the liberty of writing Pickering an open letter and causing its publication in several papers.[17] The angry Pickering made no protest directly to Yrujo, but instead contemplated legal action against the newspapers. At the same time, he prepared a stern reply, had eighty copies printed up, and circulated them privately to a select audience.[18] Although he cautioned his friends that this document was not to be published until the president or Congress should so order, it found its way into a newspaper all the same. On the president's query, an embarrassed Pickering denied having intended the publication; yet he told the president it had done more good than harm.[19] Later, when Pickering omitted one of Yrujo's letters from an otherwise comprehensive report to Congress, Yrujo protested; Pickering contemptuously rebuffed him and refused to repair the omission.[20] Yrujo was unable to use Hammond's tactic of instigating a congressional call for the missing letter and was left without lawful recourse.

When Pickering told Adams that the publication of his reply to

Yrujo was well designed to persuade Americans that "we are wholly right and our accusers altogether wrong,"[21] the reference was to foreign accusers and "we" ostensibly meant the United States government. The cabinet held precisely the same objective, though, with regard to the domestic opposition, which they regarded as nothing more nor less than the instrument of a foreign power.

Unfortunately for the Republicans, relations with France continued to deteriorate. Adet's efforts to influence the elections or to modify Federalist policy having proved counterproductive, the French government recalled him and sent no replacement. At about the same time they issued new decrees in restraint of American commerce, and, when Washington's special envoy arrived to replace Monroe, they refused to accept his credentials.[22] These events led President Adams, soon after his inauguration, to summon Congress into special session to inform them of what had occurred and to ask their support for an extensive defense buildup to meet the prospect of impending war.

At the same time, much in the spirit of Washington's policy toward Britain, but over the objections of Pickering and Wolcott, Adams resolved to continue the quest for peaceful solutions. On April 14, 1797, he took the cabinet's advice on the course to be followed; one question was whether, assuming a new envoy was to be sent, his instructions ought to be laid before the Senate with his nomination.[23]

Wolcott's reply acknowledged that this had sometimes been done in the past, but, he said, "It does not appear to be in general safe or adviseable to consult the Senate in respect to the organization of Treaties. . . . [A]s the general practice has been otherwise, the question may be considered unembarrassed by precedents."[24] It would have been more precise to say that the question was embarrassed by contradictory precedents. At any rate, Wolcott went on to state his opinion that the Senate's constitutional role was to advise upon ratification of completed treaties. To give them a prior involvement would not only compromise the needed secrecy but also preclude them from exercising a truly independent judgment at the final stage.[25] Pickering concurred, remarking tartly that "any instructions . . . for negotiating a new treaty with France, would reach the Directory sooner than we could send them our minister.''[26] This advice prevailed. When, late in May, the president nominated three special envoys to France—General Charles Cotesworth Pinckney, John Marshall, and Elbridge Gerry—their instructions were not laid before the Senate. That body was told only that the envoys would "negotiate with the French Republic, to dissipate umbrages, to remove prejudices, to rectify errors, and adjust all differences by a treaty between the two Powers.''[27]

As Randolph had not been trusted to draft Jay's instructions, so Pickering was not responsible for the present ones. The secretary of state was on record as opposed to the mission and would likely insist on such a list of ultimata as to make agreement impossible. Thus the president asked John Marshall to frame a more flexible set of guidelines for his own mission.[28] This was different from the earlier precedent in an interesting respect: it was not the Senate opposition or cabinet members of doubtful party affiliation who had to be bypassed in the cause of peace, but leaders of the president's own party who seemed to hope that the talks would fail. The opposition, in contrast, was warm for peace, but under the circumstances this was more of an embarrassment than a help to President Adams. The alignment of forces was like nothing the framers of the Constitution could have anticipated.

The XYZ Affair

Nothing was heard from the envoys until March 1798. In the interim the administration's legislative program met with only limited success. Congress was reluctant to adopt expensive and also provocative measures while negotiations were in progress that might make all unnecessary.

Then word arrived from France that, after all this time, the envoys still had not been officially received. Instead, they reported, they had been visited by unofficial representatives of the French foreign minister. Talleyrand's men had presented a list of outrageous demands: that the Americans apologize for some remarks in President Adams's message to the special session of Congress; that they deliver bribes to French officials as a precondition for negotiating; and that a large, secret loan to France be one term of the agreement. If the envoys did not agree, Talleyrand threatened to unleash upon their government the wrath of the pro-French party in America.

The envoys were not authorized to accept such humiliating terms as these, nor willing to request such authority from their superiors. They had persisted for months in the effort to start serious talks, but finally concluded that Talleyrand would never drop his unreasonable demands. It appeared that the mission was over.

The implications of this news were ominous. The final dispatch, announcing the somber prognosis for the mission, appeared to require that the country be put in a state of readiness for war. It was promptly laid before Congress; other dispatches required deciphering and were held back for the time being.[29] In transcribing these, Pickering honored the envoys' promise to Talleyrand's emissaries that their identities would be kept secret. He assigned them the code names "X," "Y," and "Z," and the dispatches became known to history as the XYZ papers.

On March 13 the president put to his department heads these questions:

> Will it be adviseable to present immediately to Congress the whole of the communications from our ministers in France, with the exception of the names of the persons employed by the minister Talleyrand to exhibit and enforce his requistions for a bribe, under an injunction of secrecy as to that particular?[30]

McHenry advised that:

> (A) full disclosure to Congress, of all the facts, seems to be adviseable and proper. The objections to this course are:
> 1) Danger to the personal safety of the ministers
> 2) It may make an insurmountable bar to any future negotiation
> 3) It may be premature, as circumstances might yet change the designs of the Directory
>
> The first objection is thought to have but a slight foundation, as the French seem to have expected publicity. The second is better founded. But the President, in communicating to Congress, under an injunction of secrecy, the requisites of the French, devolves the responsibility of divulging it on Congress. As to the third, there seems to be no just ground to suppose any favorable change in the Directory as likely.[31]

Despite this gloomy assessment, however, McHenry advised against an immediate declaration of war.

Charles Lee thought it would endanger the envoys if the papers were published before their departure from France was verified. He therefore opposed a communication of the dispatches to Congress at this time and also opposed declaring war for the time being.[32] The written replies of Pickering and Wolcott have been lost. Their views on these questions, as will appear, are amply revealed by other correspondence.

John Adams accepted Attorney General Lee's advice to withhold the papers temporarily.[33] For the other Federalists, however, the political benefits of publishing this information, so damaging to France and to the American friends of France, were a more powerful consideration than the arguments for delay advanced by Lee. The purport of the XYZ papers was already known to party leaders outside the cabinet. As early as March 7, Senator Theodore Sedgwick of Massachusetts rejoiced in the good news: "It will afford a glorious opportunity to destroy faction. Improve it."[34] By March 23 Hamilton was counselling Pickering that:

> [I]t appears to me essential that so much as possibly can, be communicated. Confidence will otherwise be wanting, and criticism will ensue which it will be difficult to repel. The observation is, that Congress are called upon to discharge the most important of all their functions, and that it is too much to expect that they will rely on the influence of the Executive.[35]

The contrast with Hamilton's counsel in the Jay Treaty case should require little comment. Two days later Pickering replied, "As soon as a vessel shall be despatched for France with letters of recall to our envoys, I presume the President will communicate their letters to Congress whether demanded or not."[36] In a separate letter of March 25, Pickering gave Hamilton a full briefing on the contents of the still "secret" papers, remarking that:

> [I]t is really desirable that not Congress only, but the people at large, should know the conduct of the French government towards our envoys, and the abominable corruption of that government, together

with their enormous demands for money. These are so monstrous as to shock every reasonable man when he shall know them. . . .

You will be aware that I communicate these important facts to you *in perfect confidence,* for as you interest yourself so deeply in public affairs, and are so obliging as to communicate your opinions, I thought you should be possessed of facts. I communicate them of myself without the privity of anyone.[37]

Finally, on April 1, Pickering wrote to a subordinate that "I hope and believe, that a full display of facts—of the real character and conduct of the French government—will produce the requisite union and spirit. This display must shortly be made."[38]

As the secretary knew, moves were afoot in Congress to call upon the president for the dispatches. Republicans, unaware of their content, suspected that they were being kept back because they reflected favorably on France and revealed the administration's obstruction of the peace effort. Thus, on March 27 the *Aurora* declared, "We know the reason why Jay's papers were concealed; Mr. Washington was ashamed to let them be seen. The very same reason will be found, sooner or later, to have operated on Mr. Adams."[39] On March 31 the same paper printed a citizens' address to Congress, deploring the secrecy surrounding the mission to France and praying that hostilities be foregone until Congress was "perfectly satisfied that the President has . . . pursued every pacific measure."[40]

Earlier, on March 20, Senate Republican Joseph Anderson of Tennessee had introduced a motion calling for the envoys' instructions and their correspondence.[41] This motion never came to a vote in the Senate, but soon the desires of Pickering and Hamilton became known to certain Federalists in the House. It was John Allen of Connecticut, a Federalist and a hawk, who on March 30 moved:

Resolved, That the President of the United States be requested to communicate to the House the despatches from the Envoys Extraordinary of the United States to the French Republic . . . or such parts thereof as considerations of public safety and interest, in his opinion, may permit.[42]

Allen claimed that his purpose was to refute unfounded insinuations that the administration had not tried to negotiate in good faith.[43] According to one historian, however, "Evidence from the debates and from correspondence with Hamilton indicates that John Allen . . . probably did join the call for papers for the purpose of stirring up the flames of war."[44] Apparently members of the cabinet had connived with Allen to reverse the president's decision to postpone the communication. While informal interbranch cooperation was established practice, the use of leaks by a secretary to subvert presidential policy was not.

There was now bipartisan House support for a call for papers, but the form of the resolution prompted extensive wrangling. Samuel Smith, a Republican from Maryland, wished Allen's proviso ("or such parts thereof . . .") struck out. In his view the president had a right to ask Congress to keep sensitive passages secret, but he had no right to withhold any information from the House.[45] Allen objected:

> There might be parts which it would not be proper to communicate to this House, even confidentially. . . . He wished to leave the President to act according to his discretion. Without some portion of this discretion being allowed him the Government could not proceed.[46]

Many Republicans had never accepted this principle and remained unwilling to do so. Representative Giles retorted that nothing ought to be kept back; he hoped the House would call for all the dispatches and the instructions too. Livingston agreed and moved an amendment to this effect. Recalling, no doubt, his own support for a secrecy proviso in his resolution of 1796, he now explained that even if a qualified call might be proper upon "ordinary occasions," it was not so in the present case, for "they were now called upon to say whether the country should be preserved in peace or go to war."[47]

The force of this argument was not obvious to some. James Bayard of Delaware, for example,

> thought the propriety of this call upon the President was extremely doubtful, and as it regarded the instructions given to our Ministers,

wholly improper. With respect to the communication of the despatches, it was wholly a matter of Executive discretion to judge whether it would be proper to communicate them or not . . . as what was sent here, notwithstanding any vote of secrecy, would not long be kept secret.[48]

It seemed that nothing had been settled by the great debate of 1796, even to the House's own satisfaction. If anything, positions had polarized even further, with Republicans now contending that the president had no discretion whatever and Federalists continuing to argue for unlimited discretion.

Yet a deadlock over legal niceties would prevent the Federalists from bringing the papers before the public. Allen therefore offered to compromise: he would support an unqualified call if it were limited to those matters already known to the French government— that is, to the dispatches but not the envoys' instructions.[49]

Allen's offer threw the House into confusion. To Republicans, this unexpected flexibility was highly suspicious. Perhaps the call for papers was ill-advised after all. Did the Federalists actually wish the papers published or were they perhaps stalling for time? The Republicans now determined to press for an immediate vote on a separate resolution they had introduced on March 27, which would declare the sense of the House that "under existing circumstances it is not expedient for the United States to resort to war against the French republic."[50] Abraham Baldwin of Georgia argued that it was pointless to call for the papers anyway: "[I]f a call is made for the papers, it is well known that he will not be obliged to send them."[51] Albert Gallatin of Pennsylvania agreed that refusal was likely, or at best a transmission of the papers in a "mutilated state." Moreover, he doubted the papers' relevance to the main question before the House. The president had already declared that the mission was terminated, and here his authority was conclusive, but it did not follow that war was expedient, and nothing in the papers could possibly make it so.[52] Livingston joined the chorus too.

[H]e believed the information would not be sent: he supposed this from a former refusal made on the ground of Executive authority.

> He deprecated the decision; but he believed, as precedent would authorize it, it would be made.[53]

Now it was the Republicans who seemed to recognize the Jay Treaty "precedent," and the Federalists who disclaimed reliance on it! As Samuel Sewall of Massachusetts put it,

> It cannot be doubted, that if the legislature was called upon to declare war against any nation, they would have a right to expect that every fact relative to that nation should be laid before them.[54]

Since the president had not asked for a declaration of war and no congressman had formally proposed one, this remark was not precisely a legal argument that Adams would be bound to comply with a call, but more a reassurance that in fact the president would comply. Republicans, by now, had good reason to suspect that their opponents had ulterior motives for supporting the call.[55]

At this point the House adjourned. The next day, Allen announced his readiness to support a resolution covering the instructions as well as the dispatches, provided only that there be affixed a proviso identical to that of Livingston's resolution of 1796: "except such parts of said papers as any existing negotiation may render improper to be disclosed."[56] This, surely, was an offer the Republicans could not refuse—especially when, by the president's own declaration, there were no negotiations ongoing between France and the United States. Yet Representative Nicholas opposed the suggestion as improper, for "it would not be right for any part of the papers to be withheld."[57] Allen reminded the House that his proposal accorded with its precedent, but, instead of insisting on the point, he would avoid further delay and agree to a totally unqualified call. After all,

> he believed the President would be authorized to retain such parts of the papers he may think it improper to communicate; he believed his Constitutional power gave him all the right to do this; and that, therefore, it was immaterial whether the resolution contained any exception, or not.[58]

This move reduced the Republicans to silence, but some Federalists thought Allen had gone too far. Representative Thomas Hartley of Pennsylvania moved that Allen's original, broad proviso be restored; moreover, he "had his doubts whether the House could constitutionally call for the instructions" at all.[59] Robert Goodloe Harper of South Carolina defended Allen's position that an unqualified call would be proper. Under the circumstances the Jay precedent was no obstacle, for:

> the papers now called for were wanted to throw light upon a subject confessedly within the Constitutional powers of the House . . . if the House had a constitutional right to ask for information, they had a right to ask for the whole information, and the President would judge how far he could, with propriety, comply with the call. . . . On a former occasion, when it was moved to modify the resolution calling for papers in the way now proposed, the motion was rejected, because it went to alter the principle contended for; and he believed the same reason would lead to a rejection of the present motion.[60]

And now the House, without record vote, rejected Hartley's motion.[61] Before the final vote on Allen's resolution, two members rose to clarify their understanding of what was at stake. Harrison Gray Otis of Massachusetts, a Federalist stalwart, would vote against the resolution—not because of its unqualified form, and "not from any doubts of the Constitutional right of the House to call for the information," but because the call was unnecessary. The question of war, he thought, was not immediately before the House after all, and "he was not willing to take any share of the responsibility as to the inconveniences and evils which may result from publishing the correspondence in question."[62] Gallatin, for his part, agreed that the information was of no value to the House, but he would not oppose the call, as he thought it presented no danger to the public good.

> It is true . . . that some inconveniences may arise from the despatches being communicated, as it may prevent diplomatic characters from expressing themselves freely in future; but the President of the United States was not afraid of this, as during the last session he had communicated information of this kind, without being applied to for it.

> But if, after having examined the despatches, he is convinced it will be highly injurious to the public welfare, or endanger the safety of our Commissioners, or prevent the happy issue of our negotiation, to communicate the information, he will either give it, or state his reasons for withholding it to the House.[63]

And now, by a vote of sixty-five to twenty-seven, the House adopted Allen's resolution, calling without reserve for the envoys' instructions and their correspondence.[64] This outcome was partly a product of tactical maneuver; yet it was not arrived at without much discussion of the relevant precedents, and it deserves to be considered from a legal as well as a political perspective.

Allen's resolution was like Livingston's in that neither specified the purpose behind the call for papers, but it was different in that it was unqualified. Some members indicated that the latter departure was appropriate because the present call was founded on the House's undoubted power to declare war. Yet no move to so declare was actually pending in the House, nor was it clear why the form of the resolution, as opposed to its very propriety, should depend on such a circumstance.[65] In addition, there were apparently some members who held that the president had no discretion in responding to the call, and others who maintained that he did have discretion regardless of the resolution's form.[66] The differences of opinion were evident in the ranks of both parties.[67]

The final roll call vote was partisan, but made it appear that in a sense there were now three distinct parties in the House. The entire Republican contingent voted aye; it was joined by about twenty Federalists, whom Jefferson called "in truth the Hamilton party."[68] The other twenty-seven Federalists who voted nay were not attuned to the plans of Hamilton and Pickering; probably they hoped that Adams would defy the call as Washington had done. None of these men stated that the form of the call had prompted his opposition. Many had also voted against Livingston's resolution. Indeed, only four individuals who had so voted in 1796 now backed the call for the XYZ papers. Not a single member shifted in the opposite direction.[69]

Viewed as a deliberate institutional decision, the House's performance was an exercise in studied ambiguity, reminiscent of the

Constitutional Convention's performance in shaping Article I, section 5. In both episodes, a complex series of amendments was debated without generating doctrinal consensus; in each case, an extremely simple but highly ambiguous provision was finally resorted to.

If the House's resolution was noncommittal on the extent of presidential discretion, John Adams's response went far toward restoring a semblance of legal clarity. Adams had, after all, disagreed with Washington's response to Livingston's resolution. He was now in a position where his constitutional convictions and the interests of his party both supported compliance with the House's call. There was no need for cabinet consultation this time; the XYZ papers went to Congress the next day. The president's message did not quibble as to form or scope.

> In compliance with the request of the House of Representatives . . . I transmit to both Houses those instructions to and despatches from the envoys . . . omitting only some names and a few expressions descriptive of the persons.
>
> I request that they may be considered in confidence until the members of Congress are fully possessed of their contents and shall have had opportunity to deliberate on the consequences of their publication, after which time I submit them to your wisdom.[70]

Now this message, I submit, can scarcely be regarded otherwise than as a repudiation of Washington's position in the Jay Treaty episode. Washington had invoked a need for secrecy in diplomacy even after talks were completed; he had chastised the House for not stating its purpose and not recognizing the full extent of his discretion; and he had insisted that a casual compliance would "establish a dangerous precedent."[71] Adams tacitly receded from all these points and from the advice given Washington by Wolcott and Pickering at the time, for Wolcott had written "that the House of Representatives has no right to demand papers relating to foreign negotiations either pending or compleated."[72] And Pickering's draft reply to the House had claimed a broad presidential discretion that Adams's present message failed entirely to reaffirm.[73]

Moreover, the factual context offered tenable and traditional grounds for scrupulousness, including the safety of envoys and the need to preserve options for future negotiations. Yet the one thing Adams did to assert his discretion was to excise the names of "X, Y, and Z," together with identity-revealing context.[74] This measure harked back not to the Jay Treaty "precedent" but to the Gouverneur Morris case, where Washington had excised certain names and "harsh expressions" threatening the safety of individuals. In a way Adams's action was more modest still: he protected his envoys not by excising their "harsh expressions" about the French government, but by ordering them home. If publishing these remarks might injure relations with France, he did not take that risk as warranting a withholding on his part, but committed the matter to congressional discretion.

The president's action marked a significant step in legal development, for it pointed toward the restoration of interbranch consensus along the lines of 1794. Congress had a right to call for papers without qualification, but the president also had a right to censor them, certainly for the protection of individuals, perhaps for other "public considerations" as well.

For several days the two houses studied the XYZ papers behind closed doors. Then, on April 5, the Senate ordered five hundred copies of the dispatches printed for use of the members. There is no record of the attendant debate, but some light is shed on this action by surviving correspondence. One Federalist wrote:

> The incessant efforts of the democrats to impeach the integrity of our executive—the misguided zeal of many of our virtuous fellow citizens in favor of France—and the urgent necessity for greater unanimity induced the publication of the despatches. The publication was made by the Senate with a majority of two votes. The democratical party in the House of Representatives was very clamorous for the publication until they became acquainted with the intelligence communicated. From that moment they opposed the publication, and finally they carried a majority against the measure. The Senate finding this to be the case instantly directed the publication. The crisis of our affairs compelled the Senate to overlook all former precedents and to take upon themselves the responsibility of a novel and extraordinary act in diplomatic concerns. The act has produced the most magical effects.[76]

Senator Sedgwick added these observations:

> Mr. Allen was induced, from a conviction of the impossibility of taking any effective measures while the existing temper prevailed, of moving an address for the papers. The President determined as was foreseen he would determine, and the papers were laid before Congress. . . . On the first view the whole faction was overwhelmed with confusion. . . . There were certainly strong objections against publishing the communication & which would have been conclusive, if withholding the publication, could have prevented its publicity. But the substance was known before the order of the Senate for that purpose. The mischief was, therefore, done, and the only question was, whether we should avail ourselves of the opportunity afforded us of acquiring confidence in the Government and Union among the people. The effects as they respect both these objects will, I believe, be considerable.[77]

On April 6 the House likewise ordered twelve hundred copies of the dispatches printed for members' use. Technicalities aside, this was obviously tantamount to a "publication." There was haggling about its propriety and about the number of copies to print. Gallatin made an effort, not very persuasive, to place his party's resistance on principled grounds: "A large majority (of which he was one) were opposed to the publication of these papers, not on the ground of any effect they would produce on the citizens of this country, but from an idea that they ought not to be published before we knew the final issue of our negotiations."[78] The Federalists were not to be deterred.

The question of publishing the instructions was considered separately, partly because of the potential effect on American bargaining options in any future talks. On April 9, the Senate by a vote of sixteen to ten ordered the instructions printed. This time the House, rather than following suit, decided by a narrow margin to let the Senate take exclusive credit for the act.[79]

The House's deference to the Senate here was a new and interesting departure, made possible by the Federalists' control of both houses. When the opposition had controlled the House, no such deference was evident.[80] Yet the protocol now adopted could also be justified by reference to the Senate's privileged role in the diplomatic sphere, especially as far as the envoys' instructions were concerned.

Possibly the Federalists went ahead with the publication because they were convinced that France would not negotiate in any case, but many of them may actually have wished to foreclose the negotiating option by this act. Surely the argument that justified the publication by citing leaks that had already occurred was unpersuasive, for its proponents were the very men responsible for the leaks. Indeed, the Federalists scarcely troubled to conceal the fact that the criteria for this admittedly novel publication included strictly domestic and partisan concerns.[81]

While the XYZ episode has been characterized here as a positive legal development, it by no means represented a detached, impartial effort to stabilize the legal basis of interbranch communications. Nor did it arise out of the sort of conflict the framers had contemplated, between institutions whose occupants were animated by personal ambition to maximize their official prerogatives. Rather, this was a factional struggle in which institutional concerns were decidedly secondary for most participants. Federalist dominance made possible a restoration of interbranch consensus, but it also meant that the impact of such legal agreement on real decisionmaking procedures and real policy outputs might not be at all what proponents of the "rule of law" would expect. Indeed, the apparent success of legalization in this case was followed not by the emergence of a rational and balanced communication system, but by a Federalist effort to bring the entire realm of political discourse, public and private, under heavy-handed legal control.

From Secrecy to Sedition: The Reign of Terror

The publication of the XYZ papers dealt a crushing blow to Republican political fortunes. Their foreign policy was centered on friendship with France, yet the new disclosures showed the French government as corrupt, scornful of America, and, worst of all, convinced that American Republicans were like themselves—not honest patriots but potential tools of manipulation by cynical outside interests. The Federalists zealously exploited the opportunity to drive this message home, hoping to silence all those opposed to a resort to arms against France. Thus Wolcott, who regarded "faction," i.e., Republicanism, as a disease, proclaimed that the publication of the papers was designed to "kill or cure."[82] Pickering likewise looked to "the happiest effects . . . the *coup de grace* to that ill-founded French influence which disgraced our country."[83]

The administration worked tirelessly to circulate the XYZ papers throughout the land. After the initial printing proved insufficient, the House ordered ten thousand copies of the dispatches printed for distribution by the State Department, with the emphasis designated for regions where "the dissemination of information through the medium of newspapers is most obstructed."[84] As Pickering construed this mandate, the target area was not only those districts "where few or no newspapers circulate, but where newspapers of a tendency to mislead, by their falsehoods and misrepresentations, have the freest circulation: for by such the correct 'information' meant by Congress to be disseminated, is 'most obstructed.' "[85] He thus made it his goal to ensure that no chance was lost to bring France's outrageous conduct to the attention of Republican constituencies everywhere.

Public opinion veered sharply against France and Francophiles. The circulation of Republican newspapers plummeted, and their editors were subjected to mounting harassment, including instances of mob violence.[86] The president was deluged with addresses promising public support for all necessary measures, and his warlike replies were widely circulated by the administration.[87] The congressional Republicans, many of whose districts had been saturated with Federalist propaganda, were cowed; a number of them actually deserted the seat of government at mid-session. Federalist legislation, stalled while the XYZ mission was pending and the Republican contingent at full strength, now gained momentum. Congress voted large army and navy expenditures, outlawed trade with French possessions, declined to ask Adams to resume negotiations, and, on July 6, 1798, passed a law abrogating the old Treaty of Alliance with France.[88] Moreover, tough measures to crack down on resident aliens, most of whom were French or Irish and suspect in their politics, as well as measures aimed at citizens of doubtful loyalty, were now brought forward.[89] Resistance to outright war was melting away.

The Republicans were hard pressed to counter the effects of the publicity campaign which their own principles and demands had helped set in motion. Madison was back in Virginia, and only after Congress authorized the publication did Vice-President Jefferson feel free to brief him on developments and share his alarm at the use being made of the XYZ papers.[90] Madison, who had strongly supported the call for papers, thought that publication was designed "more to inflame than to inform" and remarked that Talleyrand's conduct was "scarcely credible," since he must have been aware of the impossibility of secrecy in American politics. Indeed, the envoys' dispatches were so full of "absurdities and improbabilities" that "the injustice seems equal to the temerity of publishing such a libel on the French government."[91] It soon became clear that the XYZ papers could not be effectively explained away. The cause of France was scarcely defensible, and, as Madison began to realize, his party's very survival was in question. The opposition press was a crucial, and a vulnerable, institution.

> It is to be regretted that these papers are so limited in their circulation, as well as that the mixture of indiscretions in some of them should contribute to that effect. It is to be hoped, however, that any arbitrary attacks on the freedom of the press will find virtue enough remaining in the public mind to make them recoil on the wicked authors. No other check to desperate projects seems now to be left. . . .

> The management of foreign relations appears to be the most susceptible of abuse of all the trusts committed to a Government, because they can be concealed or disclosed, or disclosed in such parts at such times as will best suit particular views; and because the body of the people are less capable of judging, and are more under the influence of prejudices, on that branch of their affairs, than of any other. Perhaps it is a universal truth that the loss of liberty at home is to be charged to provisions against danger, real or pretended, from abroad.[92]

In these succinct passages Madison powerfully showed both the shortcomings of the existing system of communications control and the way in which secrecy issues per se were being supplanted by free speech issues as the critical area of concern. Written in May 1798, his last-quoted letter ended on a plaintive note: "I received no paper by last mail but Fenno's [the Federalist mouthpiece]. I hope the bridle is not yet put on the press." Madison's fears were by no means unfounded.

If the Republicans' best hope lay in counter-publicity, they had long been plagued with a dearth of good news fit to print. On June 16, however, the *Aurora* triumphantly announced that a new letter from Talleyrand to Gerry had come into its possession. This letter demanded no bribes or loans; it forcefully recited French grievances against the United States, centering on Jay's Treaty and the accompanying policy shift. Talleyrand affirmed his wish to negotiate, but complained that the hostility of envoys Pinckney and Marshall had interfered; he asked that talks resume between himself and Gerry alone.[93] Benjamin Franklin Bache, editor of the *Aurora,* charged that the administration had suppressed Talleyrand's letter for two weeks, in hopes that war might be declared before it became known. France's alleged truculence was obviously an illusion carefully fostered by Federalist hawks.[94]

If Republicans had reason to regret the lawful congressional disclosure of the XYZ papers, this unauthorized publication of diplomatic correspondence was even more disastrous. Outraged Federalists, ignoring the contents of the leaked dispatch, demanded to know how Bache had obtained a copy and by what authority he had published it. The letter, they declared, had been only two days in the government's possession, and the president himself had not yet seen it. On the floor of Congress Bache was accused of carrying on a "treasonable correspondence" with Talleyrand. Abigail Adams demanded that the hapless editor be "seazed."[95]

Bache swore under oath that his source was domestic, not foreign, and demanded that his accusers produce evidence for their charges of treason, or else retract them.[96] Then it emerged that the government was in possession of a packet addressed to Bache bearing the seal of the French foreign ministry. Boldly, Bache demanded that the packet be returned to him, charging Pickering and Wolcott with theft and denying their right to inspect his mail. Pickering obligingly delivered the unopened packet, and Bache broke the seal in the presence of witnesses. It contained two innocuous pamphlets on English politics written by Bache's friend, the French diplomat Louis Pichon. Bache trumpeted his vindication and demanded apologies for the charges against him; in the process he delivered himself of some harsh expressions on the conduct and motives of the administration.[97]

The effort to place the government on the defensive was a total failure. As Madison had feared, the stigma of disloyalty was silencing many who might otherwise have spoken out for an unbridled press. On June 26, Bache was arrested and charged with the crime, not of printing a secret state paper, but of libeling the government by his attacks on the president and cabinet.[98] Nothing could better highlight the intimate role of leaks in precipitating the great confrontation between government and press that was in the offing.

This was not quite the first attempt to invoke criminal sanctions against the press for publications potentially harmful to the government's foreign policy. However, the history of political libel cases prior to Bache's consisted of just two episodes. Both were abortive prosecutions, begun at the insistence of foreign ambassadors offended by scurrilous press attack.

In 1794 the Washington administration had ordered prosecution of Thomas Greenleaf for libeling British Minister George Hammond in Greenleaf's *New York Journal.* Hammond resented being referred to as "the British Soloman," an "incendiary Jack in Office," a "small creature" who deceived his master about American political realities and his own activities in America.[99] Hammond's demand for legal action was referred to Attorney General Bradford, who advised that the publication was, indeed, *prima facie* libelous. It might be made, "if in point of prudence it be deemed advisable," the subject of criminal action; for domestic law and the law of nations protected a foreign minister against "any malicious publication tending to render him ridiculous or to expose him to public contempt and hatred or to injure him in his profession."[100] Secretary of State Edmund Randolph ordered a prosecution on September 18, 1794, and an indictment was returned on April 7, 1795. A majority of the grand jury thought that Greenleaf had uttered,

> Wickedly, Maliciously and unlawfully . . . a certain Scandalous, Malicious and defamatory Libel . . . in Contempt and open Violation of the Laws of the said United States of America, and the Respect

due to Embassadors and other Public Ministers to the evil example of all others in the like case offending and against the Peace of the United States and their Dignity.[101]

The "laws" offended against were not specified, for there was, in fact, no applicable statute on the books.[102]

Unfortunately the documentary record of Greenleaf's case breaks off with the indictment. The only trace of subsequent events that has come to light is an item from Greenleaf's *Argus* gloating that the prosecution had "ended in mere flatulency."[103] Greenleaf, alas, failed to specify whether the case was dropped for legal or for political reasons, at what stage, or at whose behest—that of the government, the judge, or jury. It can be said, though, that Greenleaf did have two substantial legal points in his favor: a First Amendment argument and an argument that federal crimes must be defined by congressional legislation and could not be prosecuted at common-law. At this stage of history both arguments were highly controversial, but difficult to shrug off at the behest of the unpopular British minister.

The second libel prosecution was that against William Cobbett in 1797 for libeling the Chevalier De Yrujo and the Spanish king. Although Cobbett was an avid Federalist supporter, he was a British citizen. Sometimes his "Peter Porcupine" column was so abusive that the administration was hard pressed to tolerate his continued activity, even if it shared most of his feelings. Not only did Cobbett call Yrujo "a fop, half don and half sans-culotte," but he added for good measure that "The degenerate prince that now sways the Spanish sceptre . . . whom the French have kept on the throne merely as a trophy of their power, or as the butt of their insolence, seems destitute not only of the dignity of a king, but of the common virtues of a man."[104] Attorney General Lee had no difficulty in determining that this publication was libelous, and he expressed no reservations about the prudence of a prosecution. He did give a more substantial legal analysis than the one Bradford had supplied in 1794, which had entirely ignored the issue of press freedom. Lee wrote:

A libel is defined to be a malicious defamation of any person and especially a magistrate made public by either printing writing signs or pictures in order to provoke him to wrath or expose him to public hatred contempt and ridicule [citing Blackstone's *Commentaries*]. . . .

Lord Mansfield has said "that the liberty of the press consists in printing without any previous license subject to the consequence of law," and in this definition I concur with the learned judge. It will then be no infringement of the liberty of the press, to bring a printer before the tribunal of justice to answer for his publications. . . .

It is not usual for nations to take serious notice of publications in one nation containing injurious and defamatory observations upon the other, but it is usual to complain of insults to their embassadors and to require the parties to be brought to punishment. I shall not anticipate the defense which Mr. Cobbett may make, but mean only to say that he should be prosecuted, leaving the event to the proper tribunal.[105]

Now, public opinion was so much behind Cobbett in this case that the grand jury refused to indict, but neither Cobbett's nor Yrujo's troubles were necessarily over.[106]

The flap had begun with Yrujo's public letter to Pickering, printed by both Bache and Cobbett. Though Cobbett had lambasted Yrujo for going public, as well as for the substance of his letter, this did not exonerate Cobbett from complicity as far as Pickering was concerned.[107] In referring Yrujo's libel complaint against Cobbett to the attorney general, Pickering asked Lee to consider whether Bache and Cobbett had not also committed a crime in publishing Yrujo's letter.[108] An affirmative answer would have permitted the Republican Bache to be indicted along with Cobbett and would have established a legal basis for prosecuting insults to American officials as well as those to foreign diplomats, but the attorney general balked at the suggestion.

The Chevalier de Yrujo in sending a translation of his letter to you of the 11 inst. to Benjamin Franklin Bache and William Cobbett and directing it to be printed, deviated from propriety. A foreign minister here is to correspond with the secretary of state on matters which interest his nation, and ought not to be permitted to do it through the press in our country. He has no authority to communicate his sentiments to the people of the United States by publications either in manuscript or print which he shall write and circulate, while resident among us; but his intercourse is to be with the executive of the United States only upon matters that concern his mission or trust. His conduct in this instance I deem a contempt of the government for which he is reprehensible by the president. I cannot discover that this letter is libellous on the government or any public officer, though it may be charged with a degree of indecency and insolence.

The publication of it by Mr. Bache first and Mr. Cobbett afterwards, cannot be considered as criminal unless in the light of a contempt to the government of the United States; for they ought not to have joined the minister in the act. I am of opinion therefore that no prosecution of either of the Editors can be maintained for a libel in this instance; and that no legal prosecution of either of them is adviseable.[109]

Though the attorney general did not explain why it was not "adviseable" to prosecute Bache and Cobbett, he seemed to be suggesting that the unauthorized publication of official correspondence is a punishable "contempt to the government." Yet he cited no authority for this novel proposition, and nothing further was ever heard of it. Even in the heyday of libel trials, no one was ever charged with "contempt" for unauthorized disclosure of state secrets.

There was no want of incentive to develop such a doctrine. Yrujo was not the first foreign diplomat to take his case to the public; Genêt, for one, had done so years before. The administration had responded by seeking his dismissal, not by threatening his associates with legal penalties. Moreover, Randolph and Monroe both published "vindications" after their removals from office, in which executive secrets were laid bare wholesale. Randolph had shed much light on cabinet intrigues, while Monroe was to publish his entire official correspondence as minister to France. Though infuriated by these actions, the administration never took legal measures against either man, nor, so far as is known, even contemplated so doing.[110]

Courts and legislative bodies, it is true, possessed a power to punish "contempts" by individuals who disrupted their proceedings or defied direct orders. Parliament had formerly been known to punish publication of its proceedings as a contempt, but the British practice had changed, and the American Constitution clearly contemplated a more open form of government. Certainly there was no statute or recognized common-law doctrine making leaks of executive secrets a crime.[111]

Several months after the appearance of Monroe's vindication and nearly a year after the attorney general's musings on "contempt to the government," a congressman presented to the House a petition from his constituents,

> stating that they viewed with concern a defect in the laws of the United States, which suffered persons employed by the United States, after they were discharged from office, to print with impunity the secrets of Government, and praying that measures may be adopted to prevent this evil in future.[112]

This proposal, offered to fill a perceived gap in the law, died in committee.[113] That it was limited to former officials, moreover, suggested that there were especially powerful objections, constitutional or prudential, to punishing incumbent officials or printers for similar conduct.

When Bache published Talleyrand's letter to Gerry in June 1798, therefore, this act was not in itself a crime. There was, however, a basis in the Greenleaf and Cobbett cases for lodging libel charges against him, and the state of public opinion had ripened to the point where the administration thought it could, for the first time, successfully indict and convict. The legal basis for the charges was Bache's latest accusations against the government, but his record of provocations was lengthy, and it prominently included his repeated breaches of secrecy from the publication of Jay's Treaty in 1795 to the printing of Talleyrand's letter that led to his arrest.

Bache died of yellow fever prior to his trial. His announced defense strategy would have relied heavily on the absence of a statute making libel a crime.[114] While the government was prepared to proceed on a common-law crime theory, the issue was sticky.[115] Before long the Federalists realized that the new mood in Congress made the problem avoidable. Proposals for a law against sedition had been advanced even before Bache's leak of the Talleyrand letter;

afterwards the idea became irresistible. Bache was arrested on June 26. By July 5 the Senate had passed a bill, introduced June 26, making it a crime to oppose any measures of the government or to publish utterances tending to question official motives or to bring the government into disrepute. This was strong medicine indeed: on reading the Senate bill, Hamilton himself exclaimed, "Let us not establish a tyranny!"[116]

The House toned down the bill in some respects, but could not be persuaded to abandon it. John Allen led off debate by inveighing against the licentiousness into which the press had fallen and singled out Bache as the prime offender.[117] Leaking was not the only irritant that led to enactment of this law, and the law reached a far broader range of "offenses" than that. Indeed, unauthorized disclosure of official secrets was nowhere mentioned in the Sedition Law. Its tendency was simply to outlaw all opposition, and leaking had certainly helped to create the climate in which such a step seemed necessary and proper.[118]

To the Federalist way of thinking security now seemed to require the assertion of total control over political communications, both inside and outside government. The councils of state were already theirs; the remaining targets were the unbridled press, the mails, and the privileged communications of dissident congressmen. The Sedition Law was designed to bring these channels under the maximum possible control. Thus representatives Allen and Harper admitted that Republican congressmen might be subject to prosecution for statements made outside the House and that republication of seditious speeches made on the floor could also be punished. Such innovations, Federalists said, would serve the goal of better informing the people, by winnowing truth from malicious falsehood.[119]

The passage of the Sedition Law on July 10, 1798, by a vote of forty-four to forty-one, inaugurated a period of extraordinary "law enforcement."[120] The story need not be reviewed here in detail.[121] Suffice it to say that the freedoms of speech and press were severely curtailed.[122] Even a congressman was indicted for political statements that he published.[123] In at least one case of prior restraint, efforts were made to prevent booksellers from selling a certain pamphlet whose author was charged with sedition.[124] Men like Gallatin and Jefferson had to reckon with the possibility of deportation or imprisonment.[125] In 1799, a recurrence of armed tax resistance in Pennsylvania led to death sentences for the ringleaders, and the cabinet was chagrinned when President Adams commuted these.[126]

Against this background a remarkable fact emerges: though breaches of secrecy continued to torment those in charge of law enforcement, unauthorized disclosure did not in itself become a criminal act. In sedition trials leaking as such was never the issue. Free speech and press were the issues, though in fact Federalist judges brushed all constitutional arguments aside. While fewer than twenty cases were carried through to final conviction, the trial shut down several presses and put the Republican leadership to great expense and embarrassment.[127] If they were by no means silenced, certainly they were intimidated and hindered in promoting their views.[128] Yet surely an additional law against unauthorized disclosure would have been useful to the government. The failure to enact one begs for explanation.

The point can be dramatized by reviewing the lengthy record of legal proceedings against William Duane. Succeeding as editor of the *Aurora* when Bache died in September 1798, Duane at once became the prime target for Sedition Law enforcement. His allegation that the British had disbursed $800,000 in secret service money in the United States in 1798 prompted a first indictment. Duane offered to substantiate his charge by offering in evidence a letter in which John Adams himself complained of undue British influence in the government. This letter, which Duane had obtained from an official fired for political reasons, was dated 1792, but it was sufficiently embarrassing that the government elected to drop the case rather than allow the letter to be used at trial. Later Duane published the letter anyway, causing a nice political stir. Under the Sedition Law, however, publication of a writing could only be punished if the writing itself was libelous, and it was simply the president's own words that Duane had printed.[129]

In April 1800 Duane was indicted again, this time for libeling the British minister. This charge, too, was legally infirm, since Duane had merely published letters written by the complainant. Moreover, the Sedition Law did not number foreign diplomats among those it was made a crime to libel. The case was never brought to trial.[130]

Duane's greatest coup was his disclosure of a plot afoot in the Senate in February 1800. The disputed-elections bill introduced by James Ross of Pennsylvania would have established a special commission to rule on the credentials of presidential electors; the commission, chosen to assure Federalist control, would meet in secret. This time Duane did not confine himself to publishing bare facts. He stridently denounced the Ross bill as a move to steal the coming election and ranted of a conspiracy to subvert republican institutions. In addition, he stated incorrectly that the bill had already passed and that the committee which drafted it had met secretly without notifying its one Republican member.[131]

The Ross bill was ultimately rejected by moderates in the House, but the Senate determined to punish Duane for his insolence. A committee on privileges was appointed to investigate. Its original mandate was to "find out by what authority he had published the bill," but this was amended so as to specify that not the publication but the misstatements were the objects of concern.[132] Initially, Senator Uriah Tracy of Connecticut had contended that "it was a crime to publish a bill while it was still before the Senate," and that, since Duane had apparently received his information from senators, "it might be necessary to purge some members before the Senate itself acquired a right understanding of its prerogatives." Later, after other members pointed out that the bill had not been under injunction of secrecy, that it had been read with open doors, and that there was no law making such publication a crime, Tracy recanted: "he did not mean to punish for publishing the transaction which took place in the Senate, but to prevent misrepresentation and abuse."[133] Still, Tracy could not join with those who "doubted the power of the Senate to take cognizance of the conduct of members in communicating with their constituents. Will it be said," Tracy demanded, "that the Constitution is an impediment in our way to punish one of our own members, if he should be found guilty of abusing the confidence of his situation? At least we can exercise the power of removing one of our officers if we should convict him of a secret league to transmit intelligence which is officially entrusted to his care."[134]

The committee on privileges duly reported that Duane was guilty of a "high breach of the privileges of the Senate" for his false, malicious, and seditious utterances. The report was approved by a partisan majority, and Duane was summoned to appear before the Senate. After negotiations concerning his right to counsel failed to produce agreement, Duane refused to appear. He was then cited for contempt, and the sergeant at arms was ordered to arrest him.[135] Duane went into hiding, and the Senate's warrant expired when it adjourned seven weeks later. At that point the Senate asked the administration to indict Duane for sedition on account of this publication. An indictment was issued in October 1800, but the case was abandoned after Jefferson's accession to the presidency.[136] The Federalists never had the opportunity to ask Duane who had supplied him with his information and misinformation.[137]

Although Duane's repeated and embarrassing disclosures of official acts and statements were central to the government's real grievance against him, they were unable to indict him for this behavior as such. The attorney general's hint that unauthorized publication might constitute a criminal contempt was not incorporated into the Sedition Law. Even the Senate, whose own "contempt" power was independent of statute, did not feel prepared to censure Duane for publishing the pending bill. They cited him only for "false and malicious utterances" and for his defiance of their subpoena.

The failure to make unauthorized disclosure a crime can scarcely be attributed to inadvertence. Given the political concerns and balance of forces then prevailing, that the Sedition Law was silent on this subject suggests that such a proposal would have encountered resistance from Federalists themselves. One ground of objection stemmed from the government's inability or unwillingness to move directly against officials who leaked information to the press. Foreign ministers, for instance, enjoyed diplomatic immunity. The unfairness of punishing a publisher whose source was immune from prosecution applied to other cases as well. Though there was no immunity strictly speaking, the Federalists were extremely slow to employ penal sanctions against officials and ex-officials for politically motivated acts. In cases ranging from Randolph's indiscreet contacts with France to Senator William Blount's conspiracy with Britain, removal from office had been the sole and sufficient remedy. When it came to leaking information, the fact that the Federalists themselves were far from having clean hands may well have reinforced the sense that an element of judgment or discretion was necessarily involved and that a law proscribing such conduct would be unwise.[138]

The need for such a measure was, to be sure, reduced somewhat by the fact that Federalist control of appointments, removals, and congressional committee selection had largely deprived the Republicans of direct and authorized access to sensitive information. Moreover, the Sedition Law itself provided a partial remedy, since Republican editors who divulged secrets could often be indicted on other pretexts.

Yet none of these arguments is an entirely convincing explanation for the Federalists' failure to adopt an official secrets act. It was, after all, in their power to adopt one and to enforce it as selectively as they wished. They refrained, it is suggested, in recognition that such a law would be unconstitutional. The principles of free speech and free press, as then understood, may have permitted the punishment of malicious falsehoods, but they guaranteed the right to publish "true facts." An accurate copy of an official document or pronouncement may justly be deemed, by definition, a "true fact."[139]

This conclusion is of great theoretical interest, but it cannot be said that it had great impact on the immediate political situation. The principle that made it lawful to print government secrets was small consolation to those without opportunity to sit in government councils. Indeed, the Federalists were by now so confident of their position and so skilled in propaganda that administration policy was quite openly implemented. In this respect things were better than before; it was simply that the opposition was discouraged from speaking out and forbidden to interfere.[140]

Demanding information no longer had much value in the Republicans' fight for survival. To use such a tactic requires a forum in which demands for information can be pressed with some hope of profit. After the disastrous result of the call for the XYZ papers, congressional Republicans had no such expectation. Indeed, they had little to gain from participation in the debates there in general. Another form of struggle would have to serve.

The courts, unfortunately, were not available as honest brokers between the parties, but lent themselves to the Federalist cause with unseemly zeal. Disappointed in his early hopes for judicial nullification of the Sedition Law, Jefferson turned against the doctrine of judicial review. He now developed the theory that state governments had a power to resist the application within their territory of unconstitutional measures, and he secured adoption of resolutions by the states of Kentucky and Virginia that purported to declare the Sedition Law null and void. This strategy created fears for the integrity of the Union, and no other state lent support to the nullification movement.[141]

The only hope was a renewed appeal to the electorate. Yet the voters had rebuffed the Republicans in the 1798 congressional elections.[142] The party leadership now decided to adopt a low profile on foreign policy issues and to take a stand on the issue of repression at home.[143] The Sedition Law and related measures and the broader demand for a free exchange of information and opinion were thus central issues in their campaign. The relevance of secrecy to the Republican effort to justify and legitimize their opposition role was made explicit by Jefferson himself. Though he had deprecated the growth of organized party activity as much as any of the founders, by 1798 Jefferson was arguing that parties were essential to the health of a republic.

> In every free and deliberating society there must, from the nature of man, be opposite parties. . . . Perhaps this party division is necessary to induce each to watch and relate to the people the proceedings of the other.[144]

This ingenious argument marked out for opposition parties a checking role supplementary to that assigned by the framers to the institutional separation of powers. Surely, one could argue, two safeguards were better than one. Yet it was not obvious how an opposition party that lacked an institutional stronghold could succeed in playing this watching and informing role. The thrust of Jefferson's point, therefore, was a plea for electoral support that would restore balance and openness to government, and thus tolerance and a freer play of ideas to politics. In the meantime, it was seemingly up to the Federalists to watch and to inform on each other—a task that, against all expectation, they quickly proceeded to undertake.

The Federalist Schism and the Electoral Remedy

Despite the ascendancy of the Federalists in government and the harsh measures they were using to preserve and extend it, there were forces working in favor of a Republican (and republican) revival. These forces did not reflect any magic in the framers' constitutional design, but they made themselves felt, as they must, through constitutional mechanisms.

The move toward war with France intensified and ripened a latent split within the Federalist party between the hawkish followers of Hamilton and Pickering and the doves loyal to President Adams. The international situation steadily worsened after the XYZ affair, until the United States and France were joined in naval hostilities amounting to undeclared war.[145] Federalists were keenly aware that a formal declaration of war would augment the power of government to repress dissidence at home,[146] but the president was unwilling to ask Congress to declare war. The leak of Talleyrand's letter in June 1798, while it had diverted attention to domestic "law enforcement," also boosted the possibilities for renewed negotiation. The president wished to explore these, but by December, many in Congress grew impatient, and a movement for declaring war grew there without his urging.[147]

It was implicit in the constitutional plan that challenges to presidential leadership might arise in Congress, whose leaders had different constituencies, different career paths, and distinct formal powers from those of the chief executive. After the XYZ affair there were several signs that congressional Federalists had ideas of their own and were not simply passive followers of the president. Important measures, including the Sedition Law, were adopted without presidential request and apparently on Congress's own initiative.[148] Yet this independence was not constitutionally pure, for key legislators were informed, encouraged, and sometimes instigated in their measures by cabinet officers. This was not itself a novelty, of course. What was new was the alignment of department heads (led by Hamilton, a private citizen) on one side and the president on the other side.

After the XYZ affair Hamilton had developed a new program to augment the military and police powers of the government. Looking toward war with France, Hamilton saw the prospect of glory for himself and his country. An American army in league with the British navy could not only repel any French invasion but also liberate Spanish America. Exploratory talks were actually held with Britain, and 1798 witnessed the raising of an army 100,000 strong. The head of this army was General Washington. The second in command, appointed at Washington's insistence and over the president's vehement objection, was Colonel Hamilton.[149]

John Adams, though unaware of many of the intrigues in which Federalists were engaged, was now on notice of a serious challenge to his authority. His personal antipathy toward Hamilton and distrust of Hamilton's ambitions fueled a growing dissatisfaction with the drift toward war—a war that now loomed larger and more dangerous, militarily and politically, than the modest naval conflict the president had originally foreseen. Where previously he had shared the Federalist tendency to regard war as inevitable and to ignore conciliatory hints from France, he now grew receptive to indications that an honorable peace might yet be attained.

As word of American events reached Europe, the French realized that they had miscalculated the strength and the inclinations of the contending American parties and that the United States would not purchase peace on the terms France had demanded. Meanwhile France suffered reverses in Europe, making the prospect of war with the United States costlier than it had been. Talleyrand accordingly followed up his letter to Gerry, disclaiming any desire to offend, with a series of peace feelers culminating in a fairly clear offer to resume negotiations on acceptable terms. These signals trickled back to America between the months of October 1798 and February 1799. To most who learned of them, they were nothing but ploys to gain time and cause division in American councils. The president appeared to his confidants to share this opinion. Though refusing to ask Congress to declare war, he did inform it in December that no acceptable peace overtures had been forthcoming from France. In

January he approved Pickering's warlike report to Congress. He showed no optimism on the prospects for peace.[150]

In February Congress was debating a law giving the president extraordinary powers to retaliate against French subjects, should France implement a recent decree that provided for summary execution of Americans found aboard British fighting ships. It was rumored that France had suspended the decree, and Republicans insisted that the retaliation bill should not be passed until this could be ascertained. Livingston introduced a resolution calling on the president for any information he might have received on the subject.[151] After it emerged in debate that the State Department did in fact possess new information, the resolution passed by a vote of fifty-two to thirty-eight. All those opposed were Federalists, but a dozen Federalists supported the call and thus assured its passage.[152] This roll call, as well as the president's prompt compliance, bespoke the continued vitality of the XYZ precedent, even in a case where disclosure was less helpful to the dominant party's cause.

On the other hand, the disclosure was not especially helpful to the Republicans. Though the president verified the suspension of the French decree, his message pointed out that other decrees still in effect permitted essentially the same harsh treatment of American citizens. His tone gave no hint that the presidential assessment of French intentions had changed.[153]

Three days later, on February 18, the president laid before the Senate an electrifying message: he now possessed "plausible" evidence that France was prepared to negotiate in good faith, and he nominated William Vans Murray as minister plenipotentiary to France on the understanding that Murray would not go there until "direct and unequivocal assurances" were given that he would be properly received.[154]

The Republicans were jubilant; the Federalists were mortified. John Adams had not consulted his cabinet on this decision. The "plausible" letter had been in his hands for some time, but he had concealed from everyone his intention to act upon it.[155] He had broken faith with his party and put faith in the cynical, corrupt, and lying Talleyrand. How could the country properly prepare for war when the president insisted on resuming a pointless negotiation?

As Adams later told it, he had simply done what was needful to keep the peace, for he was persuaded that, if given time to prepare their countermoves, the cabinet would have induced the Senate to reject Murray's nomination. There was stiff Senate resistance all the same. Indeed, to make the mission more acceptable Adams was obliged to appoint two other envoys with Murray, who had seemed to be Talleyrand's choice. Ultimately the nominations of Murray, Chief Justice Ellsworth, and Governor William Davie of North Carolina were grudgingly approved.[156]

The Senate did not ask to see the envoys' instructions, nor were these volunteered. In fact, they were not actually prepared until months later. About eight months elapsed before the mission departed, due in part to a crisis in French politics and in part to stubborn foot-dragging by those in the cabinet who hoped delay would abort the project.[157] In October 1799 the president again took his cabinet and party by surprise, revoking an earlier decision to await news from France and ordering the envoys to depart at once. Jay's mission had demoralized the Republicans; now the Federalists were in utter disarray.[158]

It was not until December 16, 1800, that the results of the mission were laid before the Senate, together with the envoys' journal.[159] The envoys had been unable to effect a comprehensive settlement, but had initialed a "convention" that passed over the most difficult issues and was silent on major American demands. Opposition to ratification might well come from both parties.

Though the Senate met behind closed doors, it neglected to place the convention under injunction of secrecy, and the text was promptly leaked to the public.[160] On December 17, Senator Gouverneur Morris moved the adoption of a standing rule, enjoining secrecy on the members in future proceedings respecting treaties, except as the Senate should otherwise direct. The vote was a tie, which Vice-President Jefferson broke by voting nay. As a Republican paper reported it, Morris's motion had "tended to impeach the conduct of members in the instance of the treaty before them, respecting which there had been no special injunction of secrecy." Those voting "no" ostensibly maintained "that the true principle would be, that in all cases of treaties in which the President recommended secrecy, the injunction should exist until dissolved by the Senate."[161]

On December 18, the Senate called for the envoys' instructions. They were given four days later, and the president requested:

> that these instructions may be considered in strict confidence, and returned to me as soon as the Senate shall have made all the use of them they may judge necessary.[162]

Apparently the president was especially concerned about maintaining the secrecy of these instructions, because further negotiations were likely to occur on the issues still outstanding—and also, perhaps, because there was substance to the charge that the convention before the Senate was inconsistent with the instructions.[163] Some senators might not be above a leak designed to torpedo the convention and preclude further talks.

That same day the Senate adopted a standing rule as follows:

> Resolved, That all confidential communications made by the President of the United States to the Senate, shall be, by the members thereof, kept inviolably secret; and that all treaties which may hereafter be laid before the Senate, shall also be kept secret, until the Senate shall, by their resolution, take off the injunction of secrecy.[164]

By the first part of this rule the Senate seemingly abandoned its hitherto unquestioned prerogative of ordering the disclosure of confidential communications from the president. This was a far more drastic rule than that rejected only five days earlier, which would merely have required secrecy until the Senate should order otherwise. It was contrary to the Senate's practice in the XYZ affair, to the doctrine President Adams had consistently endorsed, and to that endorsed by President-elect Jefferson five days earlier. There is no record of debate or roll call vote for this decision.

The rule was part of a broader drive to lay down settled procedures for treatymaking, which yielded several standing rules adopted that same week. According to one scholar, the expected severity of the pending struggle over the French convention was a stimulus for this burst of activity.[165] Conceivably the president's extreme concern for secrecy in this particular case helped set a conservative tone for the standing rule adopted at the time. Yet Adams himself would never have demanded such a far-reaching, permanent pledge, and if he had, his lame-duck status would have deprived the demand of all force.

It is this circumstance that points to the probable political meaning of the Senate's act. The Federalist majority knew that they would soon be dealing with a Republican president.[166] They were apparently not yet certain which party would control the Senate after March 1801, but they could count on a fairly close division of party strength.[167] They may well have calculated that Jefferson's administration would seek to reduce the Senate's influence and even to strip it of some of its powers by constitutional amendment.[168] The adoption of the new standing rule can be viewed as an effort to blunt these pressures by projecting an accommodating posture toward the new administration—thus laying the groundwork for maximum access to information on the Senate's part. This deferential policy would warrant not only a claim to trustworthiness but also, as *quid pro quo,* an argument that the president had no discretion in responding to Senate calls for papers in its executive capacity. Though Randolph had seemingly conceded this in the Morris episode, subsequent events had left the matter perhaps not free from doubt.

The Senate had long since learned the strategy of waiving one prerogative in order to secure a more valued one. Thus, it had surrendered its early claim to participate in framing envoys' instructions, gaining thereby an unfettered right to reject the resulting treaties. By the same token, the right to demand information was more useful to the Senate than a formal right to publish it—especially when leaking was so difficult to detect and control. Senators must also have been aware of the House's experience with this very matter. The House's first standing order on secrecy, adopted in 1792, was very like the one now adopted by the Senate, and its apparent motive was to ensure presidential cooperation with requests for information. After the House, dominated by the opposition party, liberalized its rule, the president sought new means of ensuring confidentiality and the House's access to papers was reduced. This history could well have prompted Senate Federalists to experiment with a more deferential line. After all, the House had changed its rule; the Senate remained free to do likewise if need arose.[169]

Though the Senate ultimately agreed to a conditional ratification of the convention with France, factional struggle had brought the administration to a point of near collapse. By the end of 1799 the loss of confidence between president and cabinet was so blatant that Adams was forced to act. In the spring of 1800, after the recess of Congress, he demanded McHenry's and Pickering's resignations. Wolcott remained at his post, his secret dealings with Hamilton undiscovered by Adams. The removals, instead of restoring constitutional normalcy to the governmental councils, precipitated a further departure from the norm, as Hamilton, Pickering, and Wolcott resolved to work secretly against the president's reelection. As they saw it, a president nominally of their party but not under their control was less acceptable than a Republican who could be openly attacked.[170]

At Hamilton's request Pickering and Wolcott supplied him with confidential materials designed to dramatize Adams's unfitness for the nation's highest office. Wolcott wrote to Hamilton:

> It is, as I conceive, perfectly proper, and a duty, to make known those defects and errours, which disqualify Mr. Adams for the great trust with which he is now invested; but the publication of particular incidents and conversations, the knowledge of which has resulted from official relations, will, by many good men, be considered as improper. . . . I am clearly of opinion that you ought to publish nothing with your signature, at present.[171]

Hamilton nevertheless chose to incorporate the leaked materials into a signed pamphlet, intended for private circulation among key Federalists. Through the agency of a spy planted by Aaron Burr at the office of Hamilton's printer, the pamphlet immediately got into the newspapers, to the glee of the Republicans and the mortification of all Federalists.[172] Years later Adams was still bitter about the cabinet's betrayal of his foibles. Department heads, he thought, ought to be under an oath of secrecy or at least to act as if they were.[173]

The open split among Federalists set the stage for a sweeping Republican victory in the 1800 elections. Historians differ as to whether the voters were most disgusted by high taxes, foreign policy failures, the spectacle of the Adams-Hamilton feud, or the Federalists' disregard of civil liberties, but clearly the Sedition Law had failed to silence opposition, and in the long run it seems actually to have aided the Republican cause.[174]

This is not to say, surely, that the electoral mechanism provides a sufficient check on governmental interference with the flow of political communication. After all, the 1796 elections, following Washington's refusal to share information with the House, and the 1798 elections, following adoption of the Sedition Law, were both marked by Federalist victories and added momentum to their drive for total control. If Jefferson's victory in 1800 was aided by his emphasis on civil liberties issues, still he might well have failed without indirect help from Talleyrand and from Hamilton. Besides, even if his election were regarded as a rousing endorsement of the Jeffersonian doctrines of tolerance and the rule of law, it could not in itself guarantee that these doctrines would be effectively implemented, for there is more to open govenment than electioneering slogans.

Conclusions

The dramatic events of the Adams years took place in the context of a pervasive trend toward the manipulation of official communications for partisan ends. The major conflicts over control of information did not lend themselves to formulation and solution as secrecy issues in the classic, constitutional sense, for they were conflicts not between governmental institutions but between a governing and an outsider party, or between factions within the governing party that did not coincide with formal institutional boundaries. Moreover, the behavior most often complained of was not unwarranted secrecy, but unwarranted publicity or interference with the communications of another—issues that existing precedents were scarcely designed to deal with.

To a point, policymaking was less secretive than it had been before, and the prerogatives of Congress appeared to receive greater respect from the executive. Thus, despite the Jay Treaty "precedent," the cabinet employed the powers of Congress to effect disclosure of the XYZ papers, and the president willingly acquiesced in the House's call. Yet the results were paradoxical, for the apparent restoration of constitutional balance neither greatly strengthened Congress as an institution nor resolved the major political conflicts of the day. Instead the XYZ episode led to a further deterioration of political checks and balances in a broader sense, while the vitality of the XYZ precedent in mediating serious conflict between future presidents and Congresses remained to be demonstrated.

The framers had looked to the presidency for leadership in difficult times and to Congress for the main check on abuses of presidential power. Though they had calculated on the possibility that a president might err, or might even be a bad man, they had not reckoned with the effects of party on the control system they had designed.

The Sedition Law was a congressional initiative, its enforcement was shaped by the executive branch, and constitutional defenses were dealt with by the courts. On the surface this was interbranch cooperation according to constitutional plan, yet the underlying dynamics obeyed a different law. It was not so much that Congress was manipulated by the executive, as that the powers of both branches, and especially of the presidency, were manipulated by and for the Federalist party—with Hamilton, who held no official post whatever, pulling many of the strings. The checks and balances explicit in the Constitution were scarcely operative, while the vagaries of factional struggle supplied checks of a fortuitous and extralegal nature.

The Republicans, ousted from their bastion in the House of Representatives, had no recourse but to take their case to the people. Their communication lines were unofficial, sometimes covert, and vulnerable to political and legal harassment by a government that recognized few limits on its discretion.

If the record of Washington's second term showed the difficulties that lie in the way of resolving intense partisan and policy disputes by legal means, that of the Adams years brings home the fact that apparent progress in bringing political behavior under legal control may only conceal or even exacerbate the underlying ailments of the body politic. Both the publication of the XYZ papers and the Sedition Law were measures that clarified and even liberalized existing law, but in a deeper sense these measures were products and agents of disorder. The sort of law they represented was not at all what proponents of constitutionalism had seemed to promise. In particular, it is striking that an increasing governmental investment in publicity, a close working relationship between the branches, and an absence of overt conflict about secrecy could coincide with highly repressive relations between government and citizenry.

Victorious Jeffersonians, of course, proclaimed that the elections of 1800 would restore the orthodox "rule of law," yet the significance they attached to the "revolution of 1800" highlighted the equivocal role of presidential campaigns in American politics. Already in those days, the best guarantee of liberty to many Americans lay in the character and vision of the chief executive—a view deliberately encouraged by the cult of Washington and by the increasing focus party leaders placed on attractive candidates rather than specific policy issues.[175] There was a parallel cult centered on the symbolism of the Constitution itself and the impersonal genius it contained; this idea coexisted uneasily with the other, and the relationship between the two was seldom subjected to careful scrutiny.

The emergent function and structure of secrecy issues in political life reflected this ambivalence. By 1800 secrecy had established itself both as a technical problem in public law and as a perennial theme in electoral campaigns. The classic rhetoric on secrecy and openness in government has changed very little since those days. Its manifest function is the adjustment of policymaking procedures; its latent one, the control of office and of policy itself. The significance of the election of 1800 was not that it revolutionized the law or the practice of governmental secrecy, but that it made it possible for the secrecy issue and the broader system of institutional-partisan checks and balances to thrive.

THE FEDERALIST
LEGACY————————————7

The Politics of Constitutional Controls

By the close of the Federalist period the relationships between the separation of powers system and partisan conflict had passed through several distinct phases. At each stage of development events were shaped by a mix of constitutional and extraconstitutional constraints that affected the incidence of secrecy issues, the forum in which they were dealt with and the applicable rules, the outcomes, and the implications.

In the earliest stage, the problems before the system were the establishment of procedural ground rules consistent with the needs of institutional autonomy as well as overall governmental integration and the containment of nascent party conflict. The constitutional framework left each body of government to make rules for its own conduct and left the problem of integration and leadership to informal political techniques which the constitutional system was not well-equipped to regulate. The political context did not give rise to serious difficulties in interbranch relations, and the broad outcome was that in this period each branch controlled its communications in a highly flexible, discretionary manner.

The transition to the second stage illustrated the further play of political forces within the formal structure. The experiment of a bipartisan cabinet had proved unsuccessful, partly for very particular reasons of personality and policy, but partly for structural reasons too. While lonely dissenters have sometimes flourished in Congress or the Supreme Court, the cabinet has not proved a congenial stage for this role. A strong-willed president, confronted with systematically diverging policy approaches, will sooner or later be impelled to opt for a consistent viewpoint rather than vacillate between the two; at this point, the rejected advocate loses his usefulness. If the executive branch seemed destined to be partisan and homogeneous in makeup, the legislature was built for diversity within and between the two houses. Moreover, the staggering of elections and separation of constituencies were highly conducive in the context of a two-party system to the periodic phenomenon of an executive controlled by one party and a legislature partly or wholly controlled by the other. In the Third and Fourth Congresses this possibility was realized, and it gave rise to the classic interbranch confrontations between 1794 and 1796. These conflicts were more legalistic and more subject to the operation of specifically constitutional factors than the party conflicts of earlier or of later phases. Yet the political situation, given the undeveloped state of constitutional doctrine, precluded a solution based on the application of generally recognized norms. The outcome was a victory by fiat for "executive discretion," or, more realistically, for the Federalist party.

Once again a new phase was brought on by electoral vicissitudes and the quirks of individual judgment. After 1796, and especially after 1798, the structural possibility of one-party government was realized, and constitutional checks and balances could not operate as before. In an atmosphere of national security crisis the Federalist leadership seized upon the chance to make its dominance permanent. The notions of executive discretion developed to serve the needs of nationbuilding and of interbranch conflict were now adapted through enlargement of the police power to serve the pursuit of strict control over nongovernmental political activity. Whereas the constitutional issues of the earlier stages related to the separation of powers and the prerogatives of the several branches, now First Amendment issues came to the fore. When the courts proved unwilling to check the government's "law enforcement" program, the Republicans appealed to the people, and were aided in this by the emergence of a split within the Federalist party. The ensuing three-way struggle was resolved through the constitutional mechanisms of removal: first the president removed his department heads; then the voters removed the president. This left the law on secrecy and related issues pretty much where it had been, subject to the continuing vicissitudes of by now familiar forms of rhetorical, institutional, and partisan struggle.

While the Constitution seldom or never supplied strictly outcome-determining legal rules, it supplied a basis both for the elaboration of democratic ideology and for the increasing importance of public opinion. Thus appeals to norms of secrecy and publicity derived from the logic of the Constitution gained an important place in the broader scheme of political restraints on governmental decisionmaking. This rhetorical function of secrecy issues was appropriate to the increasingly central role of the presidency and of presidential elections in American political life.[1] This development was not an explicit part of the framers' program, though many of them may have hoped for something of the sort, but the leaders of the new government increasingly viewed the imperatives of nationbuilding and of an expansive foreign policy as demanding a strong, autonomous presidency. Not only Hamilton but Madison and Jefferson too were conscious of the fragility of the new regime and showed the greatest reluctance to challenge the character, the policies, or the emerging cult of George Washington. His personal popularity, his importance as a symbol of national unity, and the protracted crisis in which the country found itself made such challenges seem irresponsible and self-defeating.

It is hardly surprising that the leaders of a young, modernizing regime, tied economically and culturally to a world caught up in the throes of war and revolution, would look to presidential charisma for support and not always make strict constitutional orthodoxy their highest priority. No one before them had proved that a regime based on the rule of law could survive in such conditions, and surely they were agreed that "the Constitution is not a suicide pact."[2]

Yet the system the Federalists built and passed on to their successors was neither a monarchy nor a dictatorship. It was a pluralistic system based on diverse forms of authority, legitimacy, and participation—though, to be sure, a highly elitist one—and constitutional norms and structures were an integral, functioning part of the system.

On the ideological plane, norms of constitutional stature dictated what could and what could not be said in debate. Secrecy could not be defended on the ground that it helped slow the process of democratization; it could be defended on national security grounds or on those of institutional integrity. The founders accepted secrecy as essential to the performance of functions as diverse as diplomatic negotiations, executive and judicial deliberations, and even, for a time, the legislative work of the Senate. That institutionalized secrecy would bolster the elitist tendencies of the system escaped no one, and it is clear enough that for many this was a good thing. They were also obliged, however, to recognize that the government had to be sufficiently open and responsive to maintain the necessary degree of public acceptance and active support.[3] If the legitimate criteria for secrecy were abused, as they sometimes were, the guilty parties were subject to political attack and ultimate loss of public confidence. Neither officials nor the general public, obviously, typically engaged in a rational balancing of what the long-run public interest required before deciding whether to make particular information available or to keep it secret, whether to demand information or to acquiesce in secrecy for the time being. This does not mean that the process was utterly normless. A long-run trend toward greater publicity and broader participation was stimulated and supported by the rhetorical use made of the people's right to know.

The Constitution was also intermittently but powerfully operative through the mechanism of separated powers. Up to a point the several branches did tend to function as their formal structural attributes and official responsibilities would dictate.[4] The House of Representatives, directly elected, large in size, and excluded from the most sensitive "executive" functions, adopted a relatively open posture. The executive branch, tiny, hierarchically structured, and entrusted with the most sensitive duties, had no direct links with the public and few official ones even with Congress. The Senate was intermediate in size, hybrid in function, and showed some uncertainty as to the identity of its constituency and the appropriate communication posture to adopt. Each body went about its separate business, and each separately confronted the question of publicizing its proceedings or keeping them secret.

When the administration began to develop an agenda for the government as a whole, leaders were beset by crosscutting incentives for cooperation and competition, for sharing and for hoarding information. The resulting behavior was highly complex and not a straightforward product either of an individual's ideological temper or of his institutional affiliation.[5] Cabinet conservatives often found it prudent to advocate the release of sensitive information, sometimes officially, sometimes by informal leaks or even behind the president's back. Congressional liberals not only had secrets of their own, but sometimes supported the executive in withholding information from the country and even from themselves.

The framers had made the right of Congress to obtain information from the executive the key issue for lawful regulation of secrecy—not by express provision but in virtue of the separation of powers system. Secrecy debate was thereby oriented toward this issue, and conflicts that could not be so formulated were hard to deal with in a legalistic or principled way. By the same token, the attempt to deal with an issue according to constitutional criteria did not necessarily facilitate a realistic description of the interests at stake. For example, defenders of Jay's Treaty were obliged to invoke presidential power, even though the mission was a senatorial inspiration.

In the long run Congress was unable to maintain a constant and unrelenting stand for publicity or to prevent the erosion of some of the powers the framers had intended it to wield. Administration supporters usually were loath to assert congressional prerogative to the detriment of party interests, and even the opposition party often behaved as if it would rather capture the presidency than weaken it.[6]

It may be valid from a broad historical perspective to say that the election of 1800 was a victory for constitutionalism and democratic ideology, but it is far from clear that this was actually the decisive issue in the campaign. Jefferson's victory was certainly powerfully aided by other issues, as well as by generous doses of wheeling, dealing, and outright dirty tricks.[7] At any rate, his election gives no grounds for a claim that the electoral mechanism provides a reliable, speedy remedy for abuses of power. It is not only that the Federalists might have won, but that Jefferson's election did not affect the structural weaknesses of the system. The electoral process is far less suitable than that of disciplined constitutional debate within specialized forums for isolating, refining, and resolving procedural questions in a timely and principled manner. The arguments useful for public opinion-molding are likely to be less complex and realistic than those officials, most of them lawyers, might find persuasive. Thus it is difficult to develop in campaign oratory an effective code of official conduct, even if that were a central aim of the leadership. In fact, of course, electoral controls operate in an analytically diffuse but rigidly timed manner, and the salience of any given issue is at the mercy of largely accidental forces. By no means does the early history warrant us in saying that those who commit serious abuses are apt to be discovered and ousted before serious harm can be done to persons, to institutional integrities, and to the fabric of the law. Rather, the checks and balances built into the Constitution seem highly vulnerable to disruption in times of international crisis and especially in situations where Congress and the executive come under the control of the same party.

In the founding period neither party had a monolithic, ideologically determined posture on issues of secrecy and publicity. In fact, party cohesion in congressional votes on secrecy-related issues was often notably weak.[8] Still, if constitutional structures and principles provided the forums, mechanisms, and the language for meaningful debate and coherent regulation, it was party leaders who made the crucial strategic and tactical decisions on what information to demand or withhold, and what grounds to rely upon in accusation or defense. Secrecy would not become an issue unless someone in a position to do so saw fit to make an issue of it. Like institutional considerations, party conflict provided incentives for publicity in some cases and for secrecy in others. Jefferson once suggested that party activity was justified by its role in informing the people,[9] and it is true that party conflict obliged both sides to reach out for public support and to circulate information and propaganda for that end. A united elite might have clung much longer to the old, closed form of politics. Yet it also seems clear that party opposition was the crucial factor in the drift of Washington's administration toward increasingly secretive and unilateral action vis-à-vis Congress in the years 1794 to 1796. The claims of presidential prerogative were repeatedly expanded in order to preserve the Federalists' control over policymaking. When Madison and his allies finally determined to take a stand on the powers of Congress, it was too late. All that remained was to try and capture the presidency.

The central question presented by this history is: why did the constitutional system of checks and balances, and the norms of communication that evolved in the early years, prove so relatively ephemeral in the crises of 1796 and 1798? Why did the system nevertheless emerge relatively intact, ideologically, institutionally, and politically, from those crises?

Several kinds of factors converged to make the situation inauspicious for the development of stable secrecy/publicity norms. The following dimensions of the environment in which secrecy issues develop can be distinguished: the fluid context—the strategic and tactical constraints inherent in the fact that participants have various long- and short-run objectives to consider, and the attitudes, beliefs, and skills that affect the techniques chosen to attain those ends; the rigid structure—the formal roles and channels through which contestants must largely operate; and, finally, the law—established principles and precedents which, though mutable, cannot lightly be set aside, specifying what may and may not be done. These three dimensions are not strictly independent of each other; they interweave in a play of legal/political dynamics that defies reductionistic analysis. It is important, all the same, to draw attention to the special status of normative constraints among the operative factors. It is here that the fulcrum of coherent, intentional regulation should reside. The "facts" can be fast-changing or seen in more than one light; sponsors may be shortsighted or corrupt and seek to manipulate issues for selfish ends; forums may be politically biased and their rules of procedure rigid and unrealistic or sketchy and inefficient. Amidst this chaotic interplay, the logical discipline and universalizing tendencies of normative discourse, if carried on by competent advocates who take the effort at all seriously, supply a helpful buffering and rationalizing force. This effect makes constitutionalism more than a mere window dressing; its possibility is what makes the process of legal development, and its failures, an important subject for study.

In the Federalist period, despite the respect accorded to the rule of law, precedential constraints were especially tenuous. A major reason was the simple immaturity of the norm system after a time of constitutional and ideological upheaval. The flexibility deliberately designed into the Constitution allowed a broad latitude for creative adaptation to an uncertain future and for the coexistence of diverse political creeds in political life. This flexibility was purchased, of course, at the expense of clarity in principle and stability in policy. In the period of nationbuilding, when precedents were intrinsically hard to come by, the temptation was powerful for government to rely on charismatic and traditional forms of authority. This reliance, however, delayed the institutionalization of political life under the new regime. In addition, because of primitive recordkeeping and, perhaps, inexperience, the available precedents were poorly exploited even in full-dress debates.

If the corpus of public law was immature and lacking in depth, the factual context was not conducive to its easy or rapid growth. For the constitutional system suffered a stressful infancy, with challenges ranging from intense class struggle to sectional jealousy to foreign menaces verging on overt warfare. It was, in short, a protracted state of emergency—a situation offering minimal support for constructions of the Constitution, or rulemaking thereunder, that would place rigid limits on governmental power. Emergency, the framers believed, requires discretion, vigor, secrecy, dispatch—in short, executive power.

On top of the difficult foreign and domestic policy questions confronting the government, the development of political parties distorted the structure of governmental interaction in ways that the governing elites were poorly equipped to deal with. Neither their organizational nor their conceptual system was designed with parties in mind. They saw issues as sponsored by individuals, responsible to constituencies and endowed with prerogatives and power resources that were largely defined in terms of official roles. The intricacies of federalism and separated powers were designed, in part, to diffuse and contain the clash of different social interests so that no single one could attain to a stable dominance of the governmental machinery. This design did not anticipate the schism of the elite into two increasingly cohesive groupings that cooperated across institutional boundaries on a wide range of issues. Nor was the system designed to accomodate smoothly a rapidly growing democratic movement, pressing demands for information and access to policymaking that even in quieter and more trustful times it would have been difficult to absorb. In the context of the upheavals in France, this movement was terrifying to conservatives and made the party activities of the opposition seem doubly illegitimate. In taking the administration to task for excessive secrecy, therefore, opposition spokesmen ran the risk of identification as "disorganizers," "Jacobins," and demagogues of the "swinish multitude."

Though the Constitution was designed to maintain a flexible balance between separate institutions, between the values of energy and responsibility, the development of a party system did not facilitate smooth, moderate, or stable adjustments in the operations of government as the needs of the country changed. Instead the workings of the electoral process tended to produce phases of rigid interaction, in which institutions ritualistically confronted one another and reaffirmed factionally dictated positions, punctuated by sudden and sharp alterations of the balance as election results were felt, often a year or more after citizens went to the polls. In these conditions even campaigning and voter behavior that met utopian standards of enlightenment and that focused squarely on secrecy issues could not have guaranteed rational, adaptive responses in governmental decisionmaking. And of course, it is by no means the case that secrecy issues were always a central concern and were explored with great insight and objectivity.

Madison had argued in *The Federalist*[10] that institutional self-interest would drive the separate branches to check each other, so that ambition could be harnessed to the service of liberty, but the emergence of parties greatly undercut the operation of this design. From the beginning, neither house of Congress was able to exert an effective check on the accelerating growth of "executive" power. The cabinet was seldom a force for executive self-restraint, and the courts, strongly Federalist in makeup, had no disposition to question the constitutionality of governmental action so long as their allies remained in power. The upshot was that the electoral system had to bear the brunt of conflict over secrecy, which became an issue of trust in the chief magistrate as much as one of regularity in decisionmaking procedures. Proposals for adjustments in interbranch relations by authoritative techniques such as constitutional amendment, legislation, or adjudication were seldom voiced and never acted upon in the founding period.[11]

Some would view this record as supporting the propositions that secrecy is intrinsically insusceptible to constitutional restraint, that the founders understood as much, and that for theoretical and practical reasons they preferred to leave the matter to official discretion, loosely disciplined by the restraints of a competitive political process. Some might even wish to argue that, for a range of issues far broader than secrecy, constitutional restraints on governmental power are totally beside the point.[12]

The record shows not an inevitable but a highly contingent and partial failure of constitutional controls. After all, the Founding Fathers invested a very substantial effort in constitutional analysis and debate. Many of their efforts were impressive in quality and were designed not for public effect but for decisionmakers' consumption. It was not just one group of "strict constructionists" who found constitutional argumentation meaningful; indeed, Hamilton's briefs on behalf of expansive readings of governmental power were among the most earnest and persuasive of the founders' legal performances.

Rules of procedure, like other kinds of policy, developed in fits and starts and sudden reversals rather than by a smooth, organic, and systematic path. Clearly no simple model of normative regulation can account for all of the decisions made, yet it does not follow that what appeared to be a legal argument on a given day was really "nothing but" a naked power struggle.

Theorists of legal development sometimes speak as if legal systems grow inexorably, as if strife does not disrupt the process but rather feeds it. Thus Von Jhering wrote that "All the law in the world has been obtained by strife."[13] Yet on reflection it seems clear that not every instance of conflict results in the adoption or application of an identifiable rule, much less of a rule consistent with those applied in previous cases.[14] To the extent that legal rule-making proves feasible, this may simply reflect a low level of concern or a high level of consensus about what ought to be done, rather than a system well designed for the resolution of intense conflict. Whereas in stages of high consensus, participants may feel that any stable and reasonable procedure will do, in stages of rapid social change and heated partisan conflict the existing rules of procedure are likely to come under attack or evasion, and new rules will not easily be agreed upon. Rules adopted in such conflictual times are apt to reflect the ambiguities attendant on compromise;

actual practice may, in contrast, reflect the extremism attendant on secret or preemptive unilateral action. In stages of repression the rules can be freely manipulated in accord with the wishes of the dominant group. The resulting system will have some of the attributes of "law" as manifested in other stages, but its real base of authority will rest on fundamentally different grounds. A pluralistic system uses competitive advocacy to maintain belief in the fairness of the rules of the game; a monolithic one may rely solely on coercive enforcement.

The prospects for lawful kinds of conflict resolution, then, appear to depend both on enduring traits of a political system, including cultural and structural features, and on situational factors that make the legal culture more or less vigorous and the institutional control system more or less balanced. The failures of legalization in the Federalist period involved the conjunction of serious destabilizing factors impinging on many different levels of the control system. Yet to an amazing extent the system held. Institutions stood; there were no political executions and relatively few and brief imprisonments. The Constitution became widely revered. The contrast with, say, France was obvious.

The founders were obliged by the logic of their own Revolution, bolstered by earlier English traditions, to own the liberal-republican concepts of popular sovereignty and the rule of law as the fundamental legitimizing principles of their regime.[15] Whatever their private beliefs about the viability of these ideals, public discourse would submit their conduct to discussion and scrutiny in these terms. There was much room for official maneuver in deciding how, when, and by exactly whom this scrutiny should be performed, and that is what the secrecy issue ultimately was about. To call the secrecy issue a legal issue is to claim that the maneuvering was itself somehow disciplined by constitutional arrangements.

We have come to think of the rule of law as virtually synonymous with the workings of the judicial process and to suppose that the law cannot be known or enforced by any other practice. Thus, Charles Black rather casually wrote in the course of praising the Supreme Court's contribution:

[A] Government founded on the theory of limited powers faces and must solve the problem of legitimacy. . . . There are several hopeless

> ways to go about this. . . . First, the determinations of Congress and the President could simply have been made final on all questions affecting their own power. . . . [I]t is not what happened, and I venture to say there is nothing in the history of this country to indicate it ever could have succeeded.[16]

Because the Supreme Court did not in the Federalist era play the role that, according to Black, only an independent, specialized legal tribunal can play, it must be his contention that the rule of law was not operative in the United States before the *Marbury v. Madison* decision in 1803. One way to test this claim is to focus on the special functional merits that Black and others have discerned in the judicial role and to inquire how far these qualities may not inhere in other aspects of the constitutional control system as well. These qualities include detachment (one must not judge his own case); respect for precedent; skill in following precedent and in discerning when it ought not to be followed; and attachment to the long-run interest of the whole people. Thus the strength of the rule of law can be assessed by the extent to which decisions are supported in principled terms, precedents are noted and reconciled or distinguished, and established rules and procedures are respected even when immediate interests might dictate otherwise.[17]

By these criteria there were distinct lacunae in the founders' performance. This should not be surprising; even in a relatively open, modern or modernizing system with a strong legal profession, informal techniques of conflict resolution will often be preferred. Where status hierarchy, voting, or other simple procedures can generate consensus, there may be no incentive to undertake time-consuming and possibly divisive discussions of principle and precedent.[18] Of course a small, closed, and homogeneous leadership group will be especially likely to eschew formalities.[19]

In the founding period neither Congress nor the executive even had an adequate system for collecting and analyzing relevant precedents. The president at least could require written opinions of the department heads and the attorney general. Congress had no mechanism for generating an institutional position save floor debate or referral to an ad hoc committee for report. Given the fairly rapid personnel turnover in both branches, it must be concluded that the government was poorly endowed in terms of memory. Inadequate recordkeeping made it difficult to collect precedents and to document the reasoning behind earlier decisions. Moreover, the legal opinions adopted by policymakers were often one-sided and self-serving. This was especially true of the legal advice that presidents received; and on crucial occasions, opinions and precedents that ran counter to presidential inclination, or that of other powerful leaders, were simply ignored. Even the judiciary appears to have manifested these same weaknesses; in the founding period, its work was distinctive more in subject matter than in intellectual method or political attitude.

Much of this could perhaps be explained away *en masse* by pointing to the intellectual and moral failures of specific persons or to the pervasive effects of class struggle and other corrupting forces, but explanations on those levels fail to do justice to a crucial postulate of constitutionalism: that the genius of a constitutional system is its capacity to perform in a rational and lawful manner even when powerful leaders and social forces are not oriented toward that goal. The framers of the Constitution placed their faith neither in simple moral exhortation, nor in any elite censorial council empowered to enforce a code of public morality upon the officers of government, nor yet in a radical social reform, but in a system of checks and balances ostensibly designed to prevent the worst abuses of power and to strike a long-run balance between competing legitimate values and interests. The rule of law was not, in the founding period at least, a professional shibboleth of the judiciary; it was claimed to be a virtue of the entire political order.[20]

Legalization was surely inhibited by the prevailing atmosphere of crisis, by the fact that secrecy issues were often bound up with the most intensely divisive issues of foreign policy and democratization, and by the fact that there was a valid argument for flexibility in dealing with some of these issues. Nevertheless the founders never abandoned the search for viable constitutional standards of procedure; rather they adhered to the constitutionalist premise that the virtue of the rulers need not and must not be the only safeguard of liberty. Thus it was that President Adams, presented with an opportunity to emulate Washington's handling of the Jay Treaty case, instead yielded up the XYZ papers to Congress and suffered the establishment of what had formerly been deemed an intolerably dangerous precedent.

In light of the novelty of their undertaking and the magnitude of the challenges they faced at home and abroad, the Federalists were impressively successful in the work of building a constitutional order. Not the least of their achievements, and one perhaps too easily taken for granted, was their peaceful surrender of power after the elections of 1800. As shall soon appear, surprisingly few of their legal and administrative arrangements were repudiated by their Jeffersonian successors, and many retain currency today. The substantial quality of the founders' achievement emerges clearly from a summary of the legal precedents that were established in the years covered by this study.

The Early Precedents Summarized

Interbranch Communications: Executive Privilege

Communications from the executive to Congress were the key focus of secrecy conflict in the Federalist period. Such conflict seemed inherent in the constitutional plan; yet, save for the "State of the Union" clause, the framers had not explicitly addressed the question of interbranch communications.

The earliest problem that arose from the congressional perspective was not executive withholding of information but executive efforts to guide the legislative process by submitting reports and proposals. Some elements in Congress sought to curtail communications from the executive in order to preserve the separation of powers, but these efforts were essentially unsuccessful.

In 1790 the president introduced a practice of designating certain messages to Congress as confidential. The ostensible purpose was to preserve secrecy for sensitive military and diplomatic information. Congress respected this policy and initially made no challenge to the new procedures whereby it was implemented. The timing and content of congressional briefings was left to the judgment of the president and his department heads.

Soon Jefferson and Hamilton began maneuvering to ensure an evenhanded flow of information to Congress, and inside the two houses emergent factions and nonaligned members struggled to establish publicity postures appropriate to their institutional and/or partisan concerns.

A new kind of issue arose when Congress sought to call for papers on its own initiative. In the course of a long series of episodes, the cabinet and the two houses began to develop more precise doctrines to regulate their respective roles in the policymaking process. Through a combination of formal and informal techniques, relying increasingly on legalistic and often public dialogue, the government as a whole made significant progress toward synthesizing these various doctrines into a relatively coherent, shared system of norms.

Certain routine reporting requirements had been imposed on the Treasury Department by law in 1789. Hamilton had welcomed and indeed lobbied for the opportunity of influencing legislation through this channel, but the first special investigation by Congress was less to his liking. In 1792 the House of Representatives, after adopting a new standing rule for the strict protection of confidential information, launched an inquiry into the failure of General St. Clair's expedition against the Indians. The cabinet decided upon a course of full cooperation with the House; although, according to Jefferson's diary, they thought the president had a power in principle to withhold information if its release could harm the public interest.

This episode was offered by Attorney General William P. Rogers in 1958 as a precedent for an absolute presidential privilege, even though no papers were withheld and there is no conclusive evidence that the House was even informed of what was said in the cabinet meeting. Raoul Berger, on the other hand, dismissed Jefferson's memorandum as entirely "academic" and nonauthoritative, although the memorandum indicates that the cabinet's position was to be informally communicated to the House and although subsequent events demonstrated that Jefferson's remarks were by no means the doctrinal aberration Berger makes them out to be.[21]

The conventional historical treatments jump directly from the St. Clair episode to the Jay Treaty debate of 1796. Yet the intervening years witnessed the most complex and fateful developments of the period! Late in 1793 the militant Third Congress began to challenge the executive branch's secrecy posture as well as its substantive policies. The House modified its standing rule, now proclaiming its right to disclose confidential communications on its own authority, and began to call for papers omitted from briefings submitted by the executive.

At first the president made no resistance. When the House sought to investigate charges that Hamilton had mishandled public funds, Washington cooperated fully. At one point Hamilton tried to claim that his confidential communications with the president were privileged from disclosure to the House; but the House overrode Hamilton's objection, and when it asked the president to comment on Hamilton's testimony, he found no impropriety in this.

What set the stage for a decisive upheaval in interbranch communications was the outbreak of war in Europe. After Washington issued the Proclamation of Neutrality, it was necessary to enlist congressional and public support in elaborating and enforcing that policy. More information was transmitted to Congress than ever before, some on a public and some on a confidential basis. The House, for its part, successfully called for additional papers, and it exercised in a selective and temperate manner the previously asserted right to disclose information submitted to it in confidence. The Senate, showing a new respect for public opinion and a new independence from the executive branch, finally agreed to hold its legislative proceedings in public and prevailed upon the president to publicize his secret negotiations with Spain.

These measures, too, seem not to have raised much alarm. The president reacted sharply, however, when, in the spring of 1794, the Senate moved to investigate the conduct of Gouverneur Morris, Washington's handpicked ambassador to France. Morris was suspected, and justly so, of contravening the official policy of recognition and friendship for the French Revolution. On this occasion the president departed from his previous policy of complete cooperation; he censored the papers supplied to the Senate, and the Senate made no protest. This episode, passed over in silence and apparently in ignorance in most previous studies of executive privilege, was accompanied by substantial bipartisan discussion involving executive officials, congressional leaders, and even a Supreme Court justice. All consulted were willing to admit that the president had some power to censor papers called for by Congress before submitting them, if he deemed it necessary to protect personal safety or, perhaps, the national honor. The scope and limitations of this power, however, remained to be established.

Early indications were that doctrine would continue to evolve by informal and relatively broad-based discussion, but the departure of Jefferson from the administration, the increasing partisan acrimony and anti-British sentiment in Congress, and the threat of war against a background of the Whiskey Rebellion at home and revolutionary excesses abroad produced a strong conservative and pro-British reaction in the administration's outlook. John Jay was dispatched on a secret mission to London, and anti-British legislation pending in Congress was abandoned at Washington's request. When Jay returned with a commercial treaty in hand, the Senate's consent was obtained in total secrecy. A senator leaked the treaty to the public, but the president signed it despite a storm of protest. The opposition sought to block the funds for the treaty in the House of Representatives. Their resolution calling for the papers connected with the negotiation was preceded by a great constitutional debate. Some Federalists questioned the propriety of the resolution, but it was passed by an overwhelming bipartisan majority. The president, however, refused to comply. He did not rely on his established right to censor the papers for public considerations but claimed instead that the House had no right to any information whatever. The House adopted strong resolutions of protest. Though it ultimately granted the funds needed to implement the treaty, nothing could be further from the truth than the assertion, recently quoted with approval by Chief Justice Warren Burger, that Washington's act was "a refusal the wisdom of which was recognized by the House itself and had never since been doubted."[22] On the contrary, this episode threw the law of secrecy and indeed the whole constitutional system into turmoil and uncertainty.[23]

What has not always been clear in briefer accounts is the extent to which this unsettledness actually represented a step *backward* in the legalization process. We are obliged to apply different standards in judging the quality of the arguments put forward when we realize what a weight of precedent the Federalists were ignoring or misrepresenting, what violence Madison's caution was doing to his own marvelous invention of checks and balances.

By the same token, those who pass too quickly through the early history have often failed to appreciate the full significance of the XYZ episode.[24] What President Adams said and did in that case in 1798 was at odds with Washington's handling of the Jay case in 1796; but it was more than that: it was a return to the moderate ground that had been generally accepted in 1794, and that now seemed to command bipartisan and cross-institutional support once again. This doctrine recognized the right of Congress to call for papers without restriction, but recognized also a presidential power to censor the papers before supplying them—save perhaps where the Senate was acting in its executive capacity, or where a question of impeachment or of declaring war was before Congress. In those cases, the right to know might be absolute. Moreover, the only basis for presidential censorship that was unequivocally exercised and established as valid in the Federalist period was the protection of the safety of individuals. This is hardly the absolute privilege that recent executive spokesmen have purported to discover in the historical record; but neither is it the normless chaos that others have discerned.[25] Beyond this point of established consensus, of course, advocates remained free—memory and imagination permitting—to invoke and reinterpret a range of historic pronouncements and events, whose exact legal status and significance were subject to continued dispute.

Interbranch Communications: Miscellaneous

Executive withholding of information under a claim of right was confined to the special case of diplomatic papers, often designated "confidential" or "private." There were other difficulties, not directly related to the privilege issue, in establishing congressional control of the expenditure of public funds. Between 1793 and 1797 the House pushed vigorously for detailed, itemized appropriations; a standing Ways and Means Committee under Gallatin's leadership took over some planning functions formerly under Treasury control. Even the president's special contingency fund came under scrutiny, but the Republican decline led to a rollback toward a freer executive discretion in the handling of large lump sum appropriations, especially in the military budget.[26]

It must be recognized that the information available to members of Congress depended not simply on the constitutional prerogatives of the legislature, but on informal political relationships as well. Individual members could visit departmental offices in search of information, and there were apparently no clear-cut policies in effect to justify refusal of such requests, even where the information was of a "confidential" nature.[27] Politically motivated leaks from department heads to allies in Congress were another significant information channel.

A question logically distinct from the right of Congress to demand information, but closely related to it in practice, was the right of Congress to publish information supplied by the executive on a confidential basis. This power was asserted in a standing rule of the House and was exercised on several occasions. The executive branch seemed to accept this as a settled prerogative of Congress and even used it to avoid responsibility when reproached by foreign governments for breaches of secrecy.[28] The Senate exercised a similar power in publishing the XYZ papers, but in 1800 it adopted a new rule which seemed to forbid such disclosures. This was probably seen as a *quid pro quo* for Senate insistence on an unqualified right to demand sensitive papers when acting in its executive capacity. Yet by 1812 the rule would be construed as authorizing the Senate to lift its injunction of secrecy by majority vote.[29]

Internal Regulations: The Executive Branch

Internal procedures for regulating the flow of information remained highly informal and flexible, and discretion was sometimes exercised in a blatantly partisan manner. Officials did not violate clear-cut legal norms in disclosing cabinet proceedings or official records to members of Congress, private citizens, newspaper editors, or even foreign diplomats.[30] Although these communications frequently smacked of impropriety and could not be openly acknowledged, the only formal sanction for improper disclosures was removal from office—a technique as likely to produce further breaches of secrecy as to forestall them, since officials removed for political reasons were in the habit of attempting a public vindication of their conduct. A proposal in 1798 to make such breaches of confidence by ex-officials a crime was not adopted by Congress, quite possibly due to constitutional scruple.[31]

Also left unregulated by explicit legal norms was the problem of secrecy between members of the executive branch. In constitutional terms the department heads had no relations with each other, each having a separate area of responsibility and an individual, confidential relationship with the president. This picture was substantially altered by the rise of the cabinet as a collective body and the establishment by some department heads of power bases in Congress and elsewhere that gave them a certain independence from presidential control. In the founding period the resulting conflicts were resolved primarily through electoral politics.

Official publicity efforts were brought to an impressive level by the Adams administration. The mass distribution of the XYZ papers was the most dramatic example, but quieter and more lasting achievements were made in such areas as the publication of the laws of the United States throughout the Union. These functions, subsidized by public funds, were awarded to printers who had suitable political and technical qualifications; proposals for an official government printing establishment were not adopted.[32]

The transition of 1800 produced some interesting developments concerning the disposition of official papers. Outgoing Federalists retained copies of important papers, as Washington had done at his retirement. Pickering wrote that he had doubted the propriety of Jefferson's and Randolph's removals of their papers, but now he appreciated the necessity of placing himself in a position to defend himself against criticism by his successors. It was apparently recognized by most observers that the papers of a retiring official were private property, at least to the extent that he had a right to retain and publish copies.[33] It did not follow that he also had a right to deprive the government of access to the record of earlier administrations. This question was presented in a spectacular way when both the War and Treasury offices were struck by fire at the close of the Federalists' tenure. Apparently, however, neither fire did irreparable damage to important records, and a subsequent congressional investigation produced no support for charges of deliberate arson.

Internal Regulations: Congress

The internal procedures of Congress respecting secrecy and disclosure were also highly flexible and largely unconstrained by written regulations. The publication of journals was, of course, constitutionally required, but traditionally these included only an account of formal motions and record votes and not a transcript of the debates. Moreover, the Senate kept a separate, unpublished journal of its executive proceedings, and any legislative proceedings of either house that occurred behind closed doors could also be kept in a secret journal.[34]

The legislative proceedings of both houses were generally open to the public—in the Senate's case, beginning only in December 1795—but the doors were customarily closed for the reading of confidential messages from the president and for debates on topics such as relations with Algiers or war preparations.[35] When the presidential election of 1800 was thrown into the House on account of a tie in electoral votes between Jefferson and Burr, the balloting was behind closed doors.[36]

The two houses were unwilling to engage official stenographers to report their debates or to defray the costs of private efforts to do this.[37] They were also remiss in providing facilities for reporters who attended the debates. At certain periods these were admitted to the floor, but at other times they were banished to the galleries, where it was difficult to hear accurately. In the House these matters were left to the speaker, and there were repeated charges of partisan discrimination in expelling particular reporters, accused by the speaker of willful misrepresentation of the debates. Republican attempts to censure one Federalist speaker or divest him of his discretion were repeatedly rebuffed.[38] The most dramatic confrontation, though, was the Senate's formal censure of Duane for publishing a "false and malicious" account of its proceedings.[39]

While these policies convey a sense that congressional enthusiasm for publicity was only lukewarm, many of these decisions also reflected a concern for economy, a recognition of the limited public interest in following the debates closely, and annoyance over the crude and insulting, not to say inaccurate, nature of the press coverage members often received.

For the handling of confidential messages the House developed a standard procedure pursuant to its standing rule of December 1793. After the message was read behind closed doors, the papers could, on motion, be referred to a select committee for report on the portions proper to be made public. In at least one case, officials of the executive branch attended such a committee and advised that full disclosure would not be injurious.[40] In the case of the XYZ papers the question of publication was considered in committee of the whole, and the House ultimately deferred to the Senate's discretion.[41] Nothing was done to formalize the criteria for secrecy and disclosure. Although certain factors, such as prejudice to existing or future diplomatic negotiations, were habitually invoked, it would seem that the controlling considerations were often those of domestic politics. The Senate's procedures for disclosure were even less formalized; apparently, even after the standing rule of 1800, a majority could vote to publish at any time.[42]

There is little information available on the extent to which legislators were kept in the dark about the doings of their own colleagues. Undoubtedly informal and private discussions were a frequent occurrence; but when it came to official business, there were no rules authorizing the exclusion of anyone. On the other hand, neither were there rules requiring that committees be bipartisan in makeup, nor did the Federalists accept such a requirement as a matter of grace and comity.[43] We cannot say, however, that committee selection was used by the Federalists for the purposes of secrecy. On one occasion there were accusations of this kind, but they were later admitted to have been without foundation.[44]

A final question related to the sanctions available against a member who disclosed information in violation of an injunction of secrecy. When Senator Stevens T. Mason of Virginia took credit for leaking the text of Jay's Treaty, no action was taken against him. In the Adams years there was an increasing reliance on formal sanctions for sundry political sins. Opposition members of Congress were not entirely immune; yet no one was punished for wrongful disclosure of secret information.[45]

Government and People: Political Crimes and the Right to Know

The years 1798 to 1800 were a time of trial for the United States, in more senses than one. Insofar as the new nation avoided the threat of outright, declared war with France, developed its economic and military strength, improved the machinery for disseminating information, expanded the scope of citizen participation in politics, and finally achieved a peaceful transfer of power from one party to another, it was a time of substantial accomplishment. This record was marred, however, by resort to ugly and repressive measures of partisan warfare, including the use of criminal sanctions to punish criticism of governmental measures and motives.

To our contemporary mind these measures scarcely appear to have been either necessary or proper, and most of the known sedition indictments could not possibly pass muster under modern First Amendment standards.[46] For the purposes of this study, however, the most striking precedential fact is that, for all the Federalists' zeal in discovering and punishing political crimes, the disclosure or publication of government secrets was never made out to be a crime. The reasons for this were developed above at some length; at this point it is useful to add some reflections on the nexus between the secrecy issue and the issue of the right to dissent, as it was perceived in the Federalist period.

A major premise for such analysis would be the favored place which the diffusion of information occupied in the ideology and the real political agenda of the new nation. This was not, in itself, a matter of controversy between the two parties—not, at least, by the time of the Adams administration.[47] The value of publicity was supported by the cultural tradition of the Enlightenment with its emphasis on education as a vehicle of social progress. Perhaps more important, publicity was clearly essential for strengthening the political integration of a large, diverse nation, and marshaling public support for the institutions and programs of the national government, which suffered from a serious lack of visibility in many parts of the country.[48] Although there was widespread reluctance to bring the unpropertied classes into active political participation, the leaders of both parties were strongly impelled to broaden their bases of policy and electoral support. The rapid growth of newspapers and the postal network, of grass roots party organization, and direct popular elections all testify to the increasing investment in publicity. The secular trend toward increasing participation was powerful, and such events as the Jay Treaty and XYZ episodes saw both parties assisting it. If there was to be participation, all could agree, it ought to be *informed* participation; the alternative was the spectacle of the Parisian mob destroying everything gentlemen held sacred.

A second point on which the Founding Fathers initially appeared to agree was that there was, in principle, a distinction between information and misinformation and between liberty and licentiousness in political communication. In 1789, the libertarian Jefferson had written to Madison that the constitutional amendment on freedom of speech might better have been worded as follows:

> The people shall not be deprived or abridged of their right to speak to write or otherwise to publish anything but false facts affecting injuriously the life, liberty, property, or reputation of others or affecting the peace of the confederacy with foreign nations.[49]

It is noteworthy that this formulation would have protected one who published *true facts* potentially disruptive of foreign relations, though not one who falsely charged the government with acting in bad faith. After 1798 Republican spokesmen had a change of heart on the latter point and began to develop a broader concept of First Amendment liberties, which denied that falsity or even malice would justify imposing criminal liability for political speech. At the time this doctrine was highly novel and controversial, whereas the principle of the sovereign people's right to know and to judge the conduct of public servants was already difficult to controvert.

While neither the right to know nor the right to criticize the measures of government was afforded much judicial protection in the founding period, actual penalties for political offenses were relatively mild. Moreover, the development of more liberal doctrine by defenders of the opposition cause was a substantial achievement in itself and laid the basis for the eventual move toward institutionalization of First Amendment freedoms.

Afterword: The Jeffersonian Experience

Every story must end somewhere, and the present narrative has reached a fitting terminus with the "revolution of 1800." The 1800 election is recognized as a critical one that began a new era of American party politics. The event signaled a major realignment of political forces, yet from the perspective of secrecy and related issues the new constellation was essentially a continuation of old themes with "ins" and "outs" exchanging roles. The elections left the Republicans in control of the executive and both houses of Congress; many Federalists were removed from office, and the president led his cabinet and Congress with a firm hand. It was now the Federalists who were poorly positioned to watch over the proceedings of government. The new administration did not find it necessary or proper to resort to measures like the Sedition Law, which expired and was not renewed. Nevertheless, a Federalist campaign broadside of 1803 was able to declare:

> The impenetrable veil of secrecy, which Mr. Jefferson and his friends have thrown over their management of public affairs, partaking much of regal haughtiness, exhibits strong proof of the lordly temper of the present administration, and of the real contempt in which they hold their constituents. . . .

> Thus we see that the present administration conceals from the knowledge of the people their most momentous concerns, and will not suffer them to judge of the propriety of public measures. Without full information of the conduct of our Representatives, we are deprived of the power of rightly exercising one of our most important and valuable privileges; that is of choosing our legislators. If they misbehave we can, and ought to remove them; but if they conceal those measures which most essentially affect our rights, and our property, how can we form a correct judgment of their conduct. The fact itself is full proof that they ought not to be trusted; and neither ought those who sanction such unjustifiable proceedings to be elected.[50]

This document beautifully illustrates the rhetorical and political meaning of secrecy in American politics as of 1800. By that date adherents of both major parties were using secrecy and denunciations of secrecy in highly institutionalized ways. In later years the established patterns apparently continued to hold, and the most prominent episodes concerning presidential secrecy and related matters largely reflected the doctrinal and behavioral predilections observed in the Federalist era. A few salient episodes of the Jeffersonian period in compressed form may indicate the basic continuities of the constitutional history, but also suggest some of the novelties the future held in store.[51]

The Louisiana Purchase

Jefferson's counterparts in Congress supported his foreign policy wholeheartedly at first. In his first inaugural address Jefferson had tried to assume Washington's mantle of president of the whole people. Whatever opinion polls might have revealed, for a time the workings of government seemed to augur success for his effort.

The desire to annex the vast territory of Louisiana, especially if it could be done by peaceful means, was shared by leaders of both parties, including Jefferson, Madison, Burr, and Hamilton. Yet it was necessary to move delicately in seeking to purchase Louisiana from France, because France was reluctant to sell and was asking a price above what many in Congress would have wished to appropriate. There was, in addition, a serious question whether the territory did not in fact belong to Spain—a question which made doubtful the value of the cession to be purchased at such cost from France. Moreover, strict constitutional constructionists—and Jefferson emphatically counted himself as one—had qualms as to the power of the government to acquire territory, since that power was not clearly specified in the Constitution.

The legal difficulties implicit in the situation were resolved mainly by overlooking or suppressing them. The exact extent of the negotiators' powers and the fact that they had exceeded them in certain respects were kept from Congress, and a Federalist move to call for documents respecting Spain's claims to Louisiana was defeated by the Republican majority in the House. As the XYZ episode had already shown, neither party was inclined to adhere dogmatically to the stand it had taken in the Jay Treaty case. As for Jefferson's constitutional scruples on the purchase itself, he was finally persuaded by his advisers to abandon them, on the ground that circumstances would not permit the delay attendant upon adoption of a constitutional amendment. In the end, he determined that "the less we say about constitutional difficulties respecting Louisiana the better." Like the Federalists, then, the Jeffersonians when in command of both Congress and the presidency found it appropriate to make heavy use of the executive capacities to act with vigor, secrecy, and dispatch. Yet because there was no overt interbranch conflict over these actions, in effect the Louisiana purchase stretched the powers of the government as a whole and not simply those of the presidency.[52]

Secret Warmaking

Such was the popularity of territorial expansion that the trend toward informal interbranch cooperation at the expense of constitutional niceties applied to the acquisition of territory by force as well as by purchase. On three separate occasions between January 1811 and February 1813, Congress went behind closed doors to enact secret laws authorizing President Madison to seize parts of Spanish Florida. Though on the last two occasions the United States was at war with Great Britain, it was not at war with Spain and did not wish to be so. For the most part it was the Spanish government and not domestic opposition that was the target of secrecy in this matter. Still, secrecy did lead to anomalous consequences for American soldiers and secret agents who found themselves unable to document the legal authorization for actions they had undertaken behind enemy lines.[53] It also led to the censure of opposition senator Timothy Pickering in January 1812 for reading into the public record a letter concerning the disputed title to Florida, originally sent to the Senate on a confidential basis by Jefferson in 1805. The censure resolution, introduced by Henry Clay, cited Pickering for a breach of the Senate's standing rule of 1800 and specifically relied on the fact that the Senate had never removed its injunction of secrecy—a step which all now agreed the Senate did have a right to take.[54]

Pickering's attempted defense pointed to three circumstances: that others had already referred to the matters discussed in the confidential documents; that no one had objected when Pickering began to read the papers; and that, "as no negotiation was pending, as we had no Minister at any foreign Court, to be affected by the disclosure, there existed no reason for concealment, and I could not consider the papers any longer under the seal of secrecy."[55] These arguments did not impress the Senate, which voted twenty to seven for a strict application of the principle that declassification was a judgment for the Senate as a body to make. Thus the first legislator ever censured for unauthorized disclosures was the very man who, as secretary of state, had been the most zealous enforcer of the Sedition Law and the most scathing critic of leakers in government. The irony of the fact that his motive, like those of his erstwhile victims, was only to question and combat the warlike and legally dubious maneuvers of the incumbent administration is likely to have escaped all concerned.

The War of 1812 was far more controversial than the Louisiana or Florida actions. Indeed, Federalists had opposed the Republicans' policy toward Great Britain for years before war was declared; Jefferson's embargo on trade with that country had proved enforceable in New England only by dint of stern coercive measures. Both Jefferson and Madison in turn were repeatedly accused of misleading Congress and the people concerning French and/or British intentions and acts, in order to trick the country into war. The charges, reminiscent of those raised by Republicans against Federalists in earlier years, were not wholly baseless, for neither Jefferson nor Madison made a clean breast of information that might have undermined the policies he advocated. Madison, it would seem, was by no means a helpless follower of congressional warhawks. According to one biographer:

> As President, during the critical period from March 1809 to June 1812, Madison pursued a course of which the American people had scarcely an inkling. They were totally unaware, as was Congress, that in his first month in office he sent word to the British government that adherence to the Orders in Council would mean war.[56]

John Randolph of Roanoke (Virginia) joined House Federalists in resisting the move toward war; his breaches of secrecy, unlike Pickering's, evoked no punishment. Yet the doves lacked a sufficient numerical strength to pass resolutions demanding further information, and no formal confrontation over secrecy comparable to those of the Washington years would arise. The House declared war behind closed doors, and it was kept secret for fourteen days until the Senate and the president had concurred.[57]

In the Adams years, a similar political configuration had led to a spate of unauthorized disclosures and a systematically repressive governmental response. This pattern was not replicated in connection with the War of 1812. The reasons, which can only be briefly suggested here, are complex and multilayered, involving partisan, doctrinal, and institutional concerns including:

1) A relative dearth of really embarrassing leaks. In general, the Federalists were poorly positioned after 1800 to get their hands on sensitive information. Moreover, in 1812 President Madison managed to place them on the defensive by intercepting and publicizing the private correspondence known as the "Henry papers," which seemed to document pro-British plots by the Federalist "Essex Junto" clique.[58] Yet the Republican party was, to say the least, not thoroughly united behind Madison; with a presidential election in the offing, a hasty resort to repressive measures in hopes of dealing a death blow to the Federalists might have precipitated a split in the Republican party, such as the Federalists had suffered during their own "reign of terror."

2) The Republicans were by now doctrinally committed to a more libertarian stance than the Federalists and so were somewhat more reluctant to move repressively against their critics. They would not have wished to pass draconian laws or prosecute dissidents *en masse,* though by the same token they were not necessarily prepared to repudiate all the broad claims of executive power that Federalist leaders had advanced to justify their actions.[59]

3) Systematic repression of leakers and dissidents could not be carried out without judicial cooperation, and this the Republicans could not under the circumstances hope to obtain. This point is deserving of further elaboration because it brings a new dimension to this study of institutional checks and balances.

The Courts Versus the Presidency

The story of John Marshall's judicial career and his turbulent relationship with the Jeffersonian presidents is a colorful one. Like that of the Jeffersonian foreign policies or the decline of the Federalists after 1800, it is too long to be told here in any depth. However, the temptation is irresistible to at least broach the subject of judicial involvement in secrecy issues, if only to show how closely the results of judicial review adhered to the conceptual frameworks and behavior patterns already established before 1800.

It is seldom remarked that a claim of executive privilege was at issue in *Marbury v. Madison* itself.[60] The case, of course, arose out of the Federalists' eleventh-hour effort to pack the judiciary before the presidency was lost to them. Marbury and his coplaintiffs were justices of the peace appointed by Adams in the final hours of his tenure; though the nominations were confirmed by the Senate, their commissions were never actually delivered. When Marbury filed suit to force delivery by the secretary of state (the officer responsible for such matters), the Supreme Court, consisting entirely of Federalist appointees, was sympathetically inclined. If the plaintiffs could show legal entitlement to their commissions, the political instincts of the justices would be fully in accord with their official duty to repair the wrong. The government's first line of defense was to delay the case by having Congress cancel the Court's forthcoming term; its second was to stymie the litigation by a refusal to give evidence. Clerks of the State Department, when subpoenaed, flatly declined to provide documents or oral testimony and asserted a blanket privilege to conceal everything pertaining to the business of their department.

The Court, according to the official case report, ordered the witnesses to be sworn and to answer all questions to which they could not state a particular, legitimate objection. Ultimately all the plaintiffs' pertinent questions were required to be answered. It emerged that the commissions had in fact been signed and sealed, but the witnesses could not say what had then become of them. Next Attorney General Levi Lincoln, who had been acting secretary of state when the commissions disappeared, was summoned. He, too, informed the Court "that he was not bound, and ought not to answer, as to any facts which came officially to his knowledge while acting as Secretary of State."[61] The plaintiffs' attorney, Charles Lee, admitted that this might be true as to the sensitive foreign affairs functions of the State Department, but he denied that it could apply to the secretary's legal, nondiscretionary duty of sealing and delivering commissions. The Court thereupon determined that

> they had no doubt he ought to answer. There was nothing confidential required to be disclosed. If there had been he was not obliged to answer it . . . but that the fact whether such commissions had been in the office or not, could not be a confidential fact; it is a fact which all the world have a right to know.[62]

Lincoln finally agreed to answer all the plaintiffs' questions save one. He verified that the commissions had been signed and sealed but not delivered, and he asked to be excused from revealing exactly what had been done with them. The Court granted this plea, reasoning that "if they never came to the possession of Mr. Madison, it was immaterial to the present cause what had been done with them by others."[63]

The evidence available sufficed to persuade the Court that Marbury had been wronged, though for technical reasons they found themselves constitutionally precluded from granting him the *mandamus* remedy he sought. Thus a sharp confrontation was avoided, and no definitive ruling emerged on the power of a secretary of state or a president to withhold material information from a judicial proceeding. The Court had acknowledged that some confidential information might be privileged against disclosure, but had reserved to itself a right to evaluate such claims on a case-by-case basis. John Marshall had a healthy respect for executive prerogatives in foreign affairs, having authored in 1799 the doctrine that "the President is the sole organ of the nation in its external relations."[64] However, that power, whatever its limits—and Marshall was later to qualify his dictum substantially[65]—was not implicated in the *Marbury* case. Though the bifurcation of the State Department's functions was a novel legal point, the technique of information management employed by the Court and the executive in this case was very like that resorted to in earlier conflicts between Congress and the executive. In the various investigations of the 1790s the executive had sometimes thought to advance a broad claim of privilege, but, except in the Jay Treaty case, it had always yielded to persistent pressure and supplied Congress with the bulk at least of what it called for. While formalistic arguments based on the separation of powers and distinctions arising from special institutional requirements were typically invoked, the outcomes of interbranch conflict had also depended heavily on the balance of political power. In *Marbury,* be it noted, no overt reference was made by counsel or the Court to the "precedents" of the 1790s, but the Court's *dicta* were not obviously inconsistent with established doctrine. The result fairly reflected prior understandings, as well as the existing balance of political forces. It also left maximum flexibility for dealing with future cases according to their particular factual circumstances.

A conflict pertaining more directly to national security interests arose in 1806 in the case of Samuel Ogden and William Smith, charged under the Neutrality Act of 1794 for participating in Miranda's plot to liberate Venezuela from Spanish rule. When the defendants, claiming to have acted with the government's approval, subpoenaed the secretaries of state, war, and the navy, President Jefferson ordered those officers not to comply. The trial court this time was more compliant than the Supreme Court in *Marbury* had been. Justice Paterson, riding circuit, ruled the officers' testimony immaterial, deeming the accused legally culpable even if their claim of presidential approval was truthful. This stance preserved an air of legality and left the impression that courts might order executive officers to testify in a different case, but that can hardly have comforted the defendants very much. The separation of powers principle, as applied here and in *Marbury,* could lead to a situation where one branch of government treated as criminal or lawless what another may have in fact approved and where the contradiction was not permitted to be openly shown and reconciled. Indeed, when the matter of official support for Miranda was brought before Congress, Republican majorities moved strongly to suppress discussion of it, the Senate going so far as to expunge the affair from its journals. Though the jury voted to acquit Ogden and Smith, it was not on the evidence or the court's instructions, but because the expedition commanded public sympathy. In fact, William Smith was John Adams's son-in-law and held the post of surveyor of the port of New York. The erstwhile complete immunity of officials from the criminal process was clearly a thing of the past.[66]

Another, more famous judicial ruling on executive privilege emerged from the trial of former Vice-President Aaron Burr in 1807. When it fell to Chief Justice Marshall to try the case on circuit, the stage was set for a major political drama. Though Burr and Jefferson were nominally of the same party, they had become mortal political enemies some years before. The true nature of Burr's intrigues remains uncertain, but, to all but Jefferson's close associates, the decision to try Burr for treason and related offenses seemed an overreaction even at the time. Burr even commanded substantial sympathy from leading Federalists, whose hostility to Jefferson overrode their contempt for Hamilton's nemesis. Jefferson tried with slanted evidence to induce Congress to suspend the writ of habeas corpus, fearing judicial obstruction of his moves against the conspirators, but Congress refused to oblige him and the trials proceeded on a normal basis.

Burr's efforts to subpoena ostensibly exculpatory documents in Jefferson's possession precipitated a complex train of events, including several separate rulings by Justice Marshall. At one point he ruled

> that the president of the United States may be . . . required to produce any paper in his possession, is not controverted. . . . The president . . . may have sufficient motives for declining to produce a particular paper . . . to restrain the court from enforcing its production . . . because of the manifest inconvenience of its exposure. The occasion for demanding it ought, in such a case, be very strong . . . before its production could be insisted on.[67]

Marshall plainly intended to reserve the ultimate decision for himself after inspecting the documents *in camera;* he even stated that "I do not think the accused ought to be prohibited from seeing the letter."[68] Yet Jefferson declined to comply fully with the subpoena. One letter he simply withheld without comment; another he yielded up, "excepting such parts as he deemed he ought not permit to be made public."[69] No confrontation ensued, for Burr's counsel was unaware of the first letter's existence and failed to press a demand for the missing portions of the other. The same day Marshall ruled most of the government's evidence inadmissible, making Burr's ultimate acquittal a certainty. The government decided to initiate a new trial in another district and started new commitment proceedings against Burr in Marshall's court. Again Burr subpoenaed the second letter; again the president complied only in part. This time Burr insisted, and Justice Marshall ruled that, without further proof of relevance at least, "he could not think of requiring . . . the exhibition of those parts of the letter which the president was unwilling to disclose." Instead he agreed to allow Burr the benefit of favorable inferences as to what the missing portions might have shown. In addition he indicated that, had the proceeding been a trial rather than a commitment hearing, he would have reached a different result.[70]

For present purposes the key point about this episode is that once again the controversy was in large part resolved by bargaining, procrastination, and indirection rather than simply by an authoritative enforcement of clear and consistent principles. Each of the protagonists got much of what he wanted, but the "law" remained rather unclear. Lawyers continue to debate the precedential significance of Marshall's rulings; but the record does suggest that the power of the courts to compel disclosure of sensitive information, and more importantly, to establish clear and stable criteria for doing so, is subject to the same kinds of limitations as the equivalent power of Congress. The president, at any rate, never accepted Marshall's claim that the courts were final judges of the need for confidentiality, any more than Washington had done vis-à-vis the House in the Jay Treaty case. Rather Jefferson adhered to and even exaggerated the view Madison had taken in 1796—that each branch was final judge of its own prerogatives.[71] Hence disclosures would have to be negotiated by the courts on a case-by-case basis, just as was true for Congress.

A brighter impression of judicial authority emerges from the story of Jefferson's dalliance with the law of seditious libel. Jefferson had, of course, denounced the Sedition Law of 1798, though his criticism always stressed the *federal* government's particular constitutional want of power in the sphere of press regulation. By 1803 he was privately—and successfully—urging action by *state* authorities against Federalist editors who had fallen into license: "a few prosecutions of the most prominent offenders would have a wholesome effect."[72] His second inaugural address in 1805 openly defended these measures, and, by 1806, a *federal* judge he had appointed in Connecticut was prosecuting Federalist publishers and preachers for libeling the president. These prosecutions, in the absence of a federal statute, were ostensibly founded on the common-law. Jefferson did not order the cases started, but initially he endorsed them, and he disavowed the action only in retrospect, after the cases went badly. One defendant offered to prove his charge that Jefferson had tried to seduce a friend's wife; his case had to be dropped. What survived was a test case on the broad concept of federal common-law crimes. This case went to the Supreme Court and resulted in a decision overturning what had been the general understanding of judges who sat in libel cases from 1797 to 1798. Without benefit of oral argument, the Court now held that United States courts might try only crimes defined by the Constitution or acts of Congress. The decision was not, interestingly enough, a mere partisan blow against Jefferson, for by now the Court was composed predominantly of Jeffersonian appointees. In fact, though there was no reported dissent, John Marshall is said to have opposed the decision, while Justice Johnson, a Jefferson appointee, wrote the Court's opinion.[73]

This brief review of the Jeffersonian experience necessarily leaves many questions unanswered. While the motives for some of the actions described remain enigmatic, the account should suffice to show that doctrinal innovations and discontinuities did continue to emerge within judicial, as well as congressional and executive, decisionmaking, but that these could nevertheless be viewed as variations upon a set of constitutionally constrained themes. Each institution of government might vary over time in the vigor of its activity and the strictness of its fidelity to precedent or principle; the system of checks and balances could function accordingly in strikingly diverse ways. That system was no mere pious fraud; it was an imperfect, flexible control system that worked more predictably and more justly in some contexts than in others, yet showed an impressive capacity to restrain and redress abuses in the long run. As had always been true, claims of executive power were most effective where national security could plausibly be invoked, and least effective where opponents of executive policy could command an authoritative organizational base.

In the 1790s and after, conflicts over secrecy were caused less by ideological differences than by considerations of institutional prerogative and political profit. Presidents, along with cabinet members and congressional leaders, had much relevant information to dispose of; each had an impressive weight of legal authority to invoke in struggles for control. The opportunity, the willingness, hence in a competitive context the *imperative* to exercise this authority entailed an imperative to make constitutional arguments in support of publicity and secrecy. While constitutional principles, once announced, were not always rigidly adhered to, there was broad agreement on the relevant practices for contesting secrecy issues, and political realists knew these could not be ignored with impunity—not, at least, so long as organized opposition existed. Thus the political process was disciplined by the law, within fluctuating limits. The constraints of checks and balances fluctuated with shifts in institutional power and authority, but the balance was not symmetrical, for claims asserted on behalf of the presidency were more consistently bold, assertive, and ambitious. Those on behalf of Congress tended to be, at best, compromises demanded by congressional supporters of the incumbent president. The courts, for different reasons, also went to great lengths to avoid open confrontation. The mysteries of judicial decisionmaking are not easily penetrated, but the cases reviewed tend to show that, if in the long run the courts might show some resistance to being used as a partisan weapon *by* the executive, they were most unlikely to lend themselves to use as an offensive weapon *against* it.[74]

By the end of the Jeffersonian era First Amendment doctrine had matured and the party system had mellowed to the point where a repetition of the Federalist "reign of terror" against political critics seemed almost out of the question. The law of secrecy, however, had not found a way to transcend the vicissitudes of shifting electoral returns and political crises. Hence the mechanisms for obliging a reluctant government to release the information necessary for effective criticism were periodically inactive; the spectre of a renewed cycle of opposition, secrecy, leaking, and repression lay dormant but unconquered.

The Lessons of History———————8

There were a number of interesting secrecy episodes in the nineteenth century, which have been collected by historians and/or legal polemicists. No doubt intensive research with primary sources would, as was true for the 1790s, turn up further material of explanatory value. The well-known episodes, by all accounts, appear to have had relatively little impact on the "law of secrecy" as it emerged from the founding period.[1] Nor can they shed much additional light on the particular sore spots of our contemporary constitutional order, insofar as the social, institutional, and international contexts have altered substantially.

Indeed, it would appear that insofar as history is relevant, the founders' experience has at least as much bearing on the modern situation as does anything that came in the later nineteenth and early twentieth centuries. In the intervening years secrecy and freedom of speech were relatively seldom debated, litigated, or treated as controversial and critical issues by politically active men. It is surely no coincidence that the founding period and the Vietnam War era were both, uniquely, times when internal social unrest coincided with a prolonged and divisive crisis in foreign affairs.[2] At most other times either the foreign sphere was relatively calm or a bipartisan consensus on the fundamentals of foreign policy prevailed.

Much of the founding period saw the American state embroiled in cold war tensions with powers of equal or greater strength. By 1800 the Supreme Court had formally recognized the legal status of imperfect or undeclared war, marked perhaps by economic reprisals and occasional naval battles.[3] The judges cannot have been unmindful of this situation during the earlier sedition trials. In later years of the century only the Civil War put comparable pressure on established decisionmaking procedures, the flow of information, and civil liberties. Wartime censorship of military information, introduced in 1812, was renewed at that time, but the controls were weak and with the peace they lapsed again until World Wars I and II.[4] Old patterns then reappeared, as presidents resorted to secret stratagems to outmaneuver isolationist resistance to war preparations and to forestall the rise of radical social opposition to the status quo. In each case, the advent of war made continued, effective opposition impossible, while peace saw a relaxation of most emergency-triggered controls. The abuses that occurred were perceived by most influentials as isolated in time and focus; no overt constitutional crisis ensued.

It was not until the 1960s, in fact, that conditions ripened for a resurgence of the particular sort of crisis the founders had experienced. By now great progress had ostensibly been made in building structural and cultural support for the rule of law. Both congressional oversight and judicial review were securely institutionalized; the executive branch had assumed ever more bureaucratic, and thus ostensibly rulebound, organizational forms; and a much wider, more affluent public had gained the franchise, formal education, and presumably some sympathy for the values of a participant, libertarian political culture. Yet the crisis that appeared when the constitutional system was once more subject to the intense, simultaneous stresses of elite-sponsored radical protest at home and violent conflict abroad was remarkably like that of the Federalist period. In such cases presidents are prone to feel that their programs are essential to avert national disaster, but find it imprudent or impossible to implement these openly and justify them by candid argument. The ensuing scenario followed parallel lines in the founding and recent eras: unilateral, secret initiatives, discovered by dissident elites, led in a seemingly inexorable sequence to credibility gaps, embarrassing leaks of inside information, and increasingly desperate efforts by the administration to silence opposition and restore consensus. The excesses of Vietnam and Watergate, like those of Pickering's "reign of terror," have been widely acknowledged as such; yet, in the absence of meaningful structural reform, what happened at least twice could easily happen again. A happy result seems in no way guaranteed.

The utility of structural reform cannot be demonstrated by the example of a case in which no such reform was attempted; yet neither does the founders' omission to make the experiment argue against its cogency. The record does, I think, show specific weaknesses in the constitutional control system as it was and is. No doubt an intellectually respectable case, if not a politically realistic one, could be made for a major overhaul of the Constitution to redress the balance among the modern executive and the other branches. It seems more appropriate in the present context, however, to highlight some weaknesses in the system of checks and balances that might be redressed without constitutional amendment.

One kind of reform would consist of measures enhancing the institutional capabilities and incentives of Congress as a checking force. Insofar as the congressional tendency to acquiesce passively in presidential foreign policy initiatives arises from the sheer size and diversity of the legislature, it is not clear what remedies would be feasible or even desirable. Historically the system of standing committees grew up in response to these and related problems, but the committee system has not consistently supported congressional prerogatives vis-à-vis the executive, especially in the realm of foreign affairs. Congressional oversight was not highly effective in the Federalist period, even though power was wielded by a mere handful of highly visible characters. The task of Congress is far more difficult today, when the activities of a vast, fragmented bureaucracy are in question. Even the president can oversee the whole to a very limited degree. A reliance on episodic investigations seems ill-suited to the chronic nature of this problem. The search for pertinent structural reform gains further impetus from seemingly permanent changes in the balance of power and allocation of functions between Congress and the president himself.

It was concerns like these, along with the shock value of such events as the Pentagon Papers episode and Watergate, that led to the adoption of such reforms as the War Powers Act of 1973 and the strengthened Freedom of Information Act of 1974.[5] These efforts to address explicit legal prohibitions and requirements to the executive branch have not, unfortunately, always met with whole-hearted acceptance; indeed, in 1980 even these very mild measures are threatened with nullification or repeal. The presidency, at least in the international realm, seems to have largely recovered its imperial momentum; many of the audacious claims of executive power concocted by Richard Nixon's desperate lawyers have already been echoed by his successors.

Insofar as these phenomena reflect widely shared and deeply engrained American perceptions of the international situation, structural reforms are admittedly unlikely to have benevolent and far-reaching effect. Moreover, congressional leaders cannot be expected resolutely to support restraints on the presidency insofar as they themselves may entertain presidential ambitions. Still, it is worth noting that some of the imbalance in the control system reflects a simple want of institutional memory on the part of Congress; its inattention to questions of constitutional prerogative is in some measure attributable to a want of alertness rather than to consciously fixed priorities.

From the outset presidents have been able to rely upon the legal, as well as the political, acumen of cabinet officers in defending and expanding the powers of their office. Attorneys general since Edmund Randolph have functioned less as neutral guardians of legality than as presidential advocates; indeed, to the extent that they have been prepared to adopt a more neutral stance, their advice has tended to be ignored. The cumulative effect has been substantial: today the collected opinions of the attorneys general provide a handy source of self-serving argument for virtually anything a president might wish to do. Congress, meanwhile, has no comparable officer or body of lore available to it. Lacking a specialized advocate endowed with an appropriate mandate, it is poorly equipped to confront the presidency with legal argument, either in the courts or at the bar of public opinion. This situation seems susceptible of an easy remedy: an office of legal counsel to the Congress, endowed with plenary subpoena powers and standing to sue in court, should be established by law.

Whatever the merits of such a proposal, we can be sure that Congress will not always stand up as a body to overreaching by presidents and their advisers. Historically, the second line of defense has been the competitive party system, appealing to the people through the media of mass communication. Such appeals, of course, depend for their efficacy on access to critical information, on the ability and the inclination to make that information public. Neither access, ability, nor inclination can be taken for granted, and it is doubtful whether any of the three can be directly and reliably legislated. It does not follow that legal reform is irrelevant.

Extrapolating a bit from the historical record, I would offer the following propositions, designed to illuminate the questions of when secrecy becomes especially problematic for the system, how the system is likely to respond, and with what results.

1. Secrecy is most likely to become a bone of contention when
    a) the pace of social change is rapid;
    b) established status relations and limits on participation are under fire; and
    c) foreign policy issues are salient and divisive.
2. Even under the above conditions effective challenges to secrecy will require inside sponsorship. The most likely sponsors are elites who
    a) disagree with secret actions or plans, known or suspected;
    b) possess the institutional leverage for demanding information; and
    c) are not inhibited by party loyalty or the felt needs of national security from challenging the leadership.
3. The secrecy issue assumes a constitutional form when
    a) Congress or a court seeks to extract information from a recalcitrant executive;
    b) someone seeks to release information that has been designated secret by the executive; or
    c) the government seeks to punish individuals who challenge official secrecy.
4. A principled resolution of these legal issues depends on
    a) the climate of respect for law and the skills of legal advocates;
    b) the structural mechanisms available for authoritative rule-making; and

c) the situational factors that define the values at stake and constrain the strategies and tactics adopted.

5. The avoidance of legal solutions preserves a kind of flexibility which, for all its pragmatic advantages, may have very serious costs. In particular, the possibility of unsuccessful legal regulation implicit in the above propositions is conducive to a particular scenario of abuses:

a) unilateral and secret foreign policy initiatives by or in the name of the president that run directly counter to congressional and public expectation or desire; then

b) breakdown of information security due to loss of respect for official secrecy criteria and absence of alternatives to leaking as a way of challenging established policy; then

c) harsh repressive measures against officials and private citizens classed as security risks in part because they disclose official secrets or are deemed likely to do so.

Perhaps the gravest legal deficiency of the constitutional control system today is the threat of criminal penalties and prior restraints against unauthorized disclosure of official information. It is commonly held that the Sedition Law of 1798 was a constitutional and political aberration, possible only because of the immaturity of the constitutional system and the unique crisis of the times. Yet in 1917 a broadly worded espionage law and in the 1950s a peacetime sedition law again appeared on the statute books. These laws today permit official intimidation of legitimate political speech and activity that in no way endangers the national security.[6] In the 1970s, Daniel Ellsberg was indicted for xeroxing the Pentagon Papers, and ex-CIA officials were enjoined from publishing any material without advance agency approval.[7] And recently there have been calls for a comprehensive official secrets act, a measure spurned even by those who passed the 1798 Sedition Law.

The laws and judicial doctrines abridging political speech and publication should be not toughened but repealed or overruled. In the present situation, as in the founding era, their impact is not to protect the national interest but to maintain a rigid barrier between the rulers and the ruled, those with and those without a "need to know," those with and those without access to the private, elite channels of influence and information. Of course, no structural arrangement could guarantee that public debate would produce a wise consensus or any consensus at all. Even so, there are cogent grounds for insisting on timely public discussion of the fundamental moral, economic, and political commitments of a society dedicated to constitutional self-government.

NOTES

Chapter 1

1. W. P. Rogers, *Constitutional Law: The Papers of the Executive Branch*, 44 A.B.A. J. 941 (1951), reflects the official position. For concurring views see, e.g., E. S. Corwin, *The President: Office and Powers* (New York University Press 1957), at 182, 211–12; L. Henkin, *Foreign Affairs & the Constitution* (Foundation Press 1972), at 112; and Nixon v. Administrator of General Services, 433 U.S. 425, 510 (1977), dissenting opinion of Burger, C. J.

2. R. Berger, *Executive Privilege: A Constitutional Myth* (Harvard University Press 1974).

3. J. R. Wiggins, *Freedom or Secrecy* (Oxford University Press 1964), Appendix; D. Frohnmayer, *An Essay on Executive Privilege*, printed in Congressional Record, April 30, 1974, at S6603; A.M. Schlesinger, Jr., *The Imperial Presidency* (Houghton Mifflin 1973), at 396, 410.

4. Referred to are the Gouverneur Morris and Hamilton investigations, discussed in ch. 4; Berger missed both. The most comprehensive treatment available is A. Sofaer, *War, Foreign Affairs and Constitutional Power: The Origins* (Ballinger 1976), which has both episodes.

5. Op. cit. n.3, Appendix.

6. For one example of this viewpoint, see B. Cardozo, *The Nature of the Judicial Process* (Yale University Press 1971); see also L. Fuller, *The Morality of Law* (Yale University Press 1964); and n.7.

7. On the realist and skeptical approaches, see C. Black, *The People and the Court*, ch. 6 (Macmillan 1960); R. P. Wolff, ed., *The Rule of Law* (Simon & Schuster 1971); and R. Lefcourt, *Law Against the People* (Random House 1971).

8. My thinking on the relevance of procedural fairness and the stability of the rules draws heavily on the work of John Rawls; see his *A Theory of Justice* (Harvard University Press 1971).

9. United States v. Nixon, 418 U.S. 683 (1974), President's Brief, n.43. All the

papers from this case are printed in L. Friedman, ed., *US V. Nixon* (Chelsea House 1974).

10. The seminal writers are G. Simmel, *The Secret and the Secret Society*, in K. Wolff, ed., *The Sociology of Georg Simmel* (Free Press, 1950); and M. Weber, *Wirtschaft und Gesellschaft*, part 3, ch. 6, in H. Gerth and C. W. Mills, eds., *From Max Weber* (Oxford University Press 1973), at 196, 232-35. See also L. Coser, *Continuities in the Study of Social Conflict* (Free Press 1967); R. Merton, *Social Theory and Social Structure* (Free Press 1957), at 199-202; C. J. Friedrich, *Constitutional Government and Democracy* (Rev. ed. 1950); L. Fuller, *Governmental Secrecy and the Forms of Social Order*, in C. J. Friedrich, ed., *Community* (Nomos II), ch. 15 (Liberal Arts Press 1959); H. Wilensky, *Organizational Intelligence* (Basic Books 1967); R. Lowry, *Toward a Sociology of Secrecy and Security Systems*, 19 Social Problems 1 (1972).

11. Perhaps the best of these treatments are E. Shils, *The Torment of Secrecy* (Free Press 1956); H. D. Lasswell, *National Security and Individual Freedom* (McGraw Hill 1950); C. J. Friedrich, *The Pathology of Politics: Violence, Betrayal, Corruption, Secrecy & Propaganda* (Harper & Row 1972). See also F. Rourke, *Secrecy & Publicity* (Johns Hopkins University Press 1961); D. Wise, *The Politics of Lying* (Random House 1973); S. T. Gabis, *Secrecy in Politics: A Study in Attitudes* (Ph.D. Diss., University of Chicago, Department of Political Science, 1957); W. H. Kraus, *The Democratic Community and the Problem of Publicity*, in Friedrich, ed., op. cit. n.10.

12. The primary sources are seldom indexed, and secrecy events are seldom identifiable as such when an index does exist. Sources, including the *Annals of Congress,* records of the Constitutional Convention, and presidential and cabinet records, were searched page-by-page for substantially the entire period of the study.

Presidential records explored included the published writings of Washington and Adams and the collection of Washington manuscripts in the Library of Congress. Cabinet records included formal opinions submitted to presidents and other correspondence among presidents and department heads, in large part unpublished and available on microfilm at the Library of Congress or National Archives. Some secretaries, such as Jefferson and Hamilton, have left large collections of published papers. The *American State Papers* compilation, series on foreign affairs and finance, was also most useful.

All these records are surprisingly rich in little noticed episodes, but they also contain exasperating gaps. The *Annals of Congress* are demonstrably inaccurate in some particulars and do not cover most of the proceedings that occurred in executive session. The official journal of the House, the Senate's executive journal, and contemporary newspapers supplied additional material and a few corrections; but the House's secret journal has been lost. From one to three or more leading newspapers were covered for every day in periods when important developments were known to have occurred.

The failure of the attorney general's office prior to the 1830s to keep careful records of legal opinions does not speak well of the solemnity accorded to this function. There is no telling how many opinions have been lost. As for judicial matters, the records were kept in many localities and subject to all sorts of damage and careless recordkeeping. Thus, there is no record of the outcome of Greenleaf's prosecution save for his offhand remark in his own newspaper that the case had terminated in "mere flatulency." This comment was found by the desperate method of a day-by-day search through the columns of Greenleaf's paper from the date of the indictment, April 7, 1795, until that of his remark, October 30, 1795, and beyond.

Secondary sources relied upon included sources of historical fact—treatments of diplomatic and of party history, history of the press, biographies, and general history. The published papers of leading figures are of course highly partisan in tone and interpretation; it is surprising how far modern historians continue to identify strongly with one side or another.

The literature of political science and political sociology provided approaches ranging from classical, philosophical studies of secrecy to more empirical treatments of secrecy and security issues in the cold war period. There is also an important body of literature on nationbuilding and the rise of party systems in the founding period, which, while not focused on secrecy issues, provided useful information and theoretical insights. Recourse was also had to some general treatments of organizational communications and of the development of norm systems.

Finally, the strictly legal literature on governmental secrecy was searched to ensure that important episodes or interpretations had not been overlooked.

Time and again I ran across obscure references in one document that became meaningful only when another document was read months later. Some obscurities could not be clarified without engaging in a monumental and probably hopeless investigation; many tantalizing questions therefore had to remain unanswered. Among the most interesting and obscure of my discoveries, I would single out the Hamilton and Morris investigations, ch. 4; the Randolph/Hammond flap, ch. 4; the Innes mission, ch. 4; the Greenleaf libel case, ch. 6; and the material on "contempt," ch. 6.

13. Certain key episodes of the Jeffersonian period are dealt with in ch. 7.

Chapter 2

1. For fuller treatments, see S. T. Gabis, *Secrecy in Politics: A Study in Attitudes* (Ph.D. Diss., University of Chicago, Department of Political Science, 1957); W. H. Kraus, *Democratic Community and the Problem of Publicity*, in C. J. Friedrich, ed., *Community* (Nomos II) (Liberal Arts Press 1959); and H. Arendt, *Lying in Politics*, in *Crises of the Republic* (Harcourt Brace 1972).

2. See Kraus, op. cit. n.1, at 232-38.

3. N. Machiavelli, *The Discourses*, ch. 59, and cf. chs. 34, 44 and 52; *The Prince*, ch. 23 (Modern Library 1950). For a careful interpretation, see Gabis, op. cit. n.1, at 93-118.

4. See Kraus, op. cit. n.1, at 239-52.

5. See J. R. Wiggins, *Freedom or Secrecy* (Oxford University Press 1964), especially chs. 1, 6 and 10; E. G. McPherson, *The Southern States and the Reporting of Senate Debates, 1789-1802,* 12 J. Southern Hist. 223, at 224 (May 1946); J. Goebel, Jr., *History of the Supreme Court of the United States* (Macmillan 1971), Vol. 1 at 45, 302, 329, 378, n.96, 44 n.163; J. Brewer and J. Styles, eds., *An Ungovernable People* (Rutgers University Press 1980), at 141.

6. The eight states mentioned were Delaware, Georgia, Maryland, Massachusetts, North Carolina, New Hampshire, South Carolina, and Virginia. See F. Thorpe, *The Federal and State Constitutions* (7 vols., US GPO 1909); cf. A. Sofaer, *War, Foreign Affairs, and Constitutional Power: The Origins* (Ballinger 1976), at 55 n.212; on the Zenger case, see Wiggins, op. cit. n.5, at 8, 148.

7. See 13 *Journals of the Continental Congress* at 5 (US GPO 1904-37).

8. See Articles of Confederation, Art. IX, printed in M. Farrand, *The Framing of the Constitution* (Yale University Press 1913), at 221; R. Swanstrom, *The Senate, 1787-1801* (US GPO, Sen. Doc. No. 64, 1962), at 238. The four-volume *Secret Journal of Congress* was read in full for this study.

9. See 24 *Journals of the Continental Congress* at 140, 313-15; 25 Id. at 901; Swanstrom, op. cit. n.8, at 238.

10. Rhode Island had a tradition as odd man out, especially where public finance was concerned. See E. J. Ferguson, *The Power of the Purse: A History of American Public Finance, 1776-1790* (University of North Carolina Press 1961), especially at 102f., 126f., 146f., 165, 175, 235f.

11. Id. at 153-54; 1 *Secret Journals of Congress* at 231-53 (Boston 1821); 22 *Journals of the Continental Congress* at 290-300; 23 Id. at 769-70, 791, 812-22, 828-29, 832, 837, 863-69; 24 Id. at 3, 32-36, 43-46; 25 Id. at 845, 848-50; F. Wharton, ed., *Diplomatic Correspondence of the American Revolution* (US GPO 1889), Vol. 5 at 442-43, 657-59, 665-67, Vol. 6 at 184-97; E. C. Burnett, ed., *Letters of Members of the Continental Congress* (Carnegie Institution 1933), Vol 6 at 357-63, 391, 473, 498, 509, 551-68, Vol. 7 at 7-10, 16.

12. See 2 *Secret Journals of Congress* at 580; 3 Id. at 93-95, 451, 464, 527.

13. 3 *Secret Journals of Congress* at 570, 586; 4 Id. at 43-131, 296, 338, 449-54.

14. 1 *Secret Journals of Congress* at 268-70, 273.

15. "It was actually easier for farmers in western Pennsylvania, on the upper Ohio, to send their heaviest produce to Philadelphia by way of New Orleans than directly overland." S.F. Bemis, *Jay's Treaty* (Yale University Press 1962), at 23-24.

16. See generally Bemis, op. cit. n.15, ch. 1.

17. The seminal modern work is of course C. Beard, *An Economic Interpretation of the Constitution of the United States* (Macmillan 1913); see also Ferguson, op. cit. n.10; and other works discussed in L. W. Levy, ed., *Essays on the Making of the Constitution* (Oxford University Press 1969).

18. See M. J. C. Vile, *Constitutionalism and the Separation of Powers* (Oxford University Press 1967); W. B. Gwyn, *The Meaning of the Separation of Powers* (Tulane University Press 1965).

19. J. J. Reardon, *Edmund Randolph* (Macmillan 1974), at 85.

20. *Records of the Federal Convention* (Farrand ed. 4 vols.), Vol. 1 at 9–15 (hereinafter cited as *Records*). Late in July, when deadlock forced an adjournment, the convention voted six to five not to distribute copies of the resolutions already agreed to; see 2 *Records* at 115.

21. 3 *Records* at 86.

22. 2 *Records* at 333n.; 3 *Records* at 28, 73, 368. Not all the public speculations were so anxious in tone; one friendly newspaper remarked that the "profound secrecy hitherto observed by the Convention [we consider] a happy omen, as it demonstrates that the spirit of party on any great and essential point cannot have risen to any height." *New York Daily Advertiser*, Aug. 14, 1787.

23. 2 *Records* at 86. The journals were ultimately published by congressional order in 1818; Madison's more valuable notes did not appear until 1840, after his death. See 3 *Records* at 417-27, 447, 475.

24. 3 *Records* at 368.

25. Reardon, op. cit. n.19, at 99.

26. 3 *Records* at 76.

27. Delaware's representatives were not empowered to agree to any change in the "one state/one vote" principle; see Farrand, op. cit. n.8, at 24. Those of Pennsylvania were empowered only to amend the existing Articles; see B. Schwartz, ed., *The Bill of Rights, A Documentary History* (Chelsea House 1971), Vol. 2 at 603.

28. "Nations can have no secrets," said Tom Paine, "and the secrets of courts, like those of individuals, are always their defects." Quoted in Gabis, op. cit. n.1. at 158. Compare Jefferson's advice to his daughter: "when tempted to do anything in secret, ask yourself if you would do it in public. If you would not, be sure it is wrong." 19 *Writings of Jefferson* at 241.

29. *The Federalist*, No. 64. (Rossiter ed., New American Library 1961).

30. See Letter of June 19, 1813 to Matthew Carr, 13 *Writings of Jefferson* (Lipscomb ed. 1903), at 263.

31. See Article V, para. 4; Article IX, paras. 5 and 6; Article X; Article XI; and Article XIII; printed in op. cit. n.8.

32. Article IX, para. 7.

33. The following account is drawn from 2 *Records* at 156-80, 240-60, 592, 613, 632-35.

34. 2 *Records* at 156.

35. Id. at 166.

36. Previous scholarship appears to have overlooked the fact that the notes kept by Madison give a materially different account of what occurred here from that reported in the official journal of the convention. According to the official journal, Gerry's amendment had two parts; its effect was not only to strike the words, "when acting in a legislative capacity," but to add the words, "except such parts thereof as in their judgment require secrecy." On this account, the adoption of Gerry's amendment on August 10 placed the clause at one stroke in essentially its final form. This would mean that the amendments offered on August 11, on whose terms all accounts are agreed, would lend themselves to a different interpretation from that

espoused in text. Instead of efforts to insert a secrecy provision in a clause that had none at all, they might be viewed as unsuccessful attempts to narrow the existing secrecy provision.

There are compelling reasons for concluding that Madison's account is the correct one. There are many other errors in the official journal; Madison's version in this case is supported by his account of what was said in the debates; by the assumption that Gerry had a consistent position on the issue; and by the fact that James McHenry's notes, like Madison's, indicate that the secrecy proviso was added after the reference to the Senate's legislative capacity had already been removed. (McHenry, however, gives August 11 as the date for both amendments; see 2 *Records* at 256.) Finally, the journal's account would seem to be internally inconsistent, since the amendment it reports as adopted on August 11 would have been utterly superfluous if its account of the August 10 proceedings were accurate.

37. The term "non-legislative" allowed for secrecy also in the case of impeachment trials, which were deemed a "judicial" function.

38. 2 *Records* at 259.

39. Id. at 260.

40. Ibid.

41. Id. at 568.

42. Id. at 613.

43. Id. at 618.

44. Id. at 632, 635.

45. The debates summarized here are reported at 1 *Records* 65–74, 112, 140, 144. The key point appears in the records of debate for June 1. It is intriguing that the several surviving accounts differ in the emphasis given to secrecy. According to Madison, "Mr. Wilson preferred a single magistrate, as giving most energy despatch and responsibility to the Office." 1 *Records* at 65. Rufus King noted the same speech as follows: "Wilson—an executive ought to possess the powers of secrecy, vigour & dispatch—and to be so constituted as to be responsible." Id. at 70. Finally, William Pierce reported that "Mr. Wilson said the great qualities in the several parts of the Executive are vigor and dispatch." Id. at 73. Whether or not Wilson actually mentioned secrecy on that occasion, the litany of "vigor, secrecy and dispatch" was to be many times repeated in the following debates.

46. 1 *Records* at 112.

47. Id. at 140, 144.

48. 2 *Records* at 347.

49. Id. at 158.

50. Id. at 171.

51. 3 *Records* at 252.

52. Compare *The Federalist*, op. cit. n.29, Nos. 47–51. For history of the evolution and refinement of these principles, see, e.g., Corwin, op. cit. n.1, at 177f., 207f.

53. This principle was vigorously, if belatedly, emphasized by Madison in the Jay Treaty debate of 1796; see 5 *Annals of Congress* at 772; and ch. 5.

54. Certainly the constitutional plan for the organization of the executive branch was remarkably sketchy. One principle, however, was clear: executive accountability was to be individual rather than collective. Department heads were subject to impeachment, and Article 2, section 2, empowered the president to secure the individual opinions of those officers in writing, perhaps so that responsibility for specific proposals could be verified. The cabinet, as a collective decisionmaking body, was a later invention, and gradually assumed the conciliar functions that the framers apparently expected the Senate to perform.

55. *The Federalist*, op. cit. n.29, No. 64.

56. Ibid., No. 84.

57. See Ibid., Nos. 23, 69, 70, and 75 for other relevant perspectives on executive power. See also Iredell's remarks at the North Carolina convention, to the effect that the president could be impeached for concealing information from the Senate. J. Elliot, ed., *Debates of the State Conventions* (Lippincott 1881), Vol. 4 at 127.

58. 3 *Records* at 326, 404. He also questioned the ambiguous phrase, "from time to time," noting that the Articles had required monthly publication. Madison replied that it had proved impossible to meet this requirement in practice, and that the people would receive more satisfactory accounts if time were allowed to prepare them properly.

59. Id. at 311.

60. Id. at 169-70.

61. Id. at 233.

62. Schwartz, op. cit. n.27, Vol. 2 at 843.

63. 3 *Records* at 354; 4 Id. at 72-73; Schwartz, op. cit. n.27, Vol. 2 at 969.

64. Schwartz, op. cit. n.27, Vol. 2 at 870.

65. Id. at 902.

66. Id. at 881.

67. Id. at 916.

68. Id. at 1139.

69. Id. at 1061, 1137.

70. See ch. 3, under "The House of Representatives" and "The Senate," on the early publicity postures of the House and Senate.

71. But see ch. 6, under "From Secrecy to Sedition," on the immaturity of First Amendment doctrine in the founding period; and see also L. W. Levy, *Jefferson and Civil Liberties* (Quadrangle 1973). As to voting participation the country had a long way to go: it would seem that no more than one-fourth of the adult white male population actually participated in voting for delegates to the ratifying conventions. See Levy, op. cit. n.17, at 28, 93.

72. While legislators were expressly made immune to "question" by outsiders about their speeches on the floor and given a qualified immunity from arrest during sessions of Congress (see Article 1, section 6), no such privileges were granted to members of the executive branch.

73. See, for example, C. Warren, *The Supreme Court in United States History* (Little Brown 1922) at 215f.; A. T. Mason, *The Supreme Court* (University of Michigan

Press 1962) at 109–110; E. S. Corwin, *Court Over Constitution* (Princeton University Press 1938) at 48–76; and R. Berger, *Congress V. the Supreme Court* (Harvard University Press 1969) at 145–49, 180–216.

74. Marbury v. Madison, 1 Cranch (5 U.S.) 137 (1803).

75. Reference here is primarily to the "political questions" doctrine. For background, see works cited in n.73.

Chapter 3

1. W. Maclay, *Sketches of Debate in the First Senate of the United States* (Burt Franklin 1969), at 24–28, 74.

2. L. D. White, *The Federalists* (Macmillan 1948), at 35.

3. The need for formal regulation was more pressing inside the Treasury Department and the military, each of which had many field officers to supervise and coordinate. See White, op. cit. n.2, chs. 10 & 12. In all the departments, access to the files was apparently readily available to legislators; Id. at 502.

4. Occasionally Vice-President Adams and Chief Justice Jay were consulted as well.

5. At least one significant leak of cabinet opinions occurred in the early days. It involved the essays of Hamilton and Jefferson on the constitutionality of a national bank. See L. D. White, *The Jeffersonians* (Macmillan 1951), at 87.

6. White, op. cit. n.2, at 27, 56–57. See also J. Charles, *The Origins of the American Party System* (Harper & Row 1961), at 53: "Perhaps the most interesting question of those crowded years is how much Washington himself knew and what he really thought about the important policies and events of the 1790's."

7. See, e.g., W. Chambers, *Political Parties in a New Nation* (Oxford University Press 1963), at 32, 39–40; W. Chambers and W. D. Burnham, eds., *The American Party Systems* (Oxford University Press 1967), at 61; White, op. cit. n.2, at 5–6, 56–58, 68–74; Charles, op. cit. n.6, at 12–31; R. Swanstrom, *The Senate, 1787-1801* (US GPO, Sen. Doc. No. 64, 1962), at 232, 269–71.

8. Hamilton was nominated and confirmed on September 11, 1789; see 1 *Annals of Congress* (hereinafter *Annals*) at 80–81. Jefferson was nominated and confirmed on September 26; see 1 *Annals* at 93; he was still en route from France at the time.

9. J. P. Boyd, *Number Seven: Alexander Hamilton's Secret Attempts To Control American Foreign Policy* (Princeton University Press 1964), at xiii–xiv. Boyd's position is somewhat undercut by the fact that Madison too had contacts with Beckwith. See I *Letters and Other Writings of Madison* (Cong. ed. 1865) at 530; I. Brant, *Edmund Randolph: Not Guilty!* 7 William & Mary Q., 3d Ser., at 179 (Apr. 1950).

10. On Beckley's role, see Chambers, op. cit. n.7, at 56; N. E. Cunningham, *The Jeffersonian Republicans* (University of North Carolina Press 1963), at 60–61. Jefferson's personal role in organizing the opposition was apparently minimal; see Chambers, op. cit. n.7, at 57–59 and Charles, op. cit. n.6, at 80–84.

11. 7 *Works of Thomas Jefferson* at 140, quoted in White, op. cit. n.2, at 213.

12. C. M. Thomas, *American Neutrality in 1793* (Columbia University Press 1931), at 7, 33n.

13. Washington employed Gouverneur Morris as his confidential agent on several diplomatic missions. While Morris was technically under Jefferson's authority, his communications with the president were closer. See Boyd, op. cit. n.9, at 14–20, 57–59; and ch. 3, under "The Senate."

14. R. M. Bell, *Party and Faction in American Politics: The House of Representatives, 1789-1801* (Greenwood 1973), at 36–46.

15. A separate, secret journal recorded proceedings behind closed doors; see n.87 below for further discussion.

16. Swanstrom, op. cit. n.7, at 230; E. G. McPherson, *The Southern States and the Reporting of Senate Debates,* 12 J. Southern Hist. 223, 224 (May 1946); B. Schwartz, ed., *The Bill of Rights: A Documentary History* (Chelsea House 1971), Vol. 2 at 981; and ch. 2.

17. E. G. McPherson, *Reports of the Debates of the House of Representatives During the First Congress, 1789-1791,* Quarterly J. of Speech, Feb. 1944, at 64-65; D. H. Stewart, *The Opposition Press of the Federalist Period* (State University of New York Press 1969), ch. 1.

18. 1 *Annals* at 917; McPherson, op. cit. n.17, at 69-70.

19. The other speakers were Tucker, Gerry, Page, Stone, and Madison. For bloc affiliations, see Bell, op. cit. n.14, at 33-35.

20. 3 *Annals* at 252, 297. On the opposition press, see ch. 2, under "The House of Representatives."

21. See 1 *Annals* at 525 (Rep. Benson); cf. Id. at 531 (Rep. Vining) and 555 (Rep. Goodhue).

22. Id. at 506 (Rep. Jackson), 540 (Rep. Page), 557, 597 (Rep. Gerry); cf. the colloquy between Stone and Vining on the relevance of senatorial secrecy, Id. at 590, 594.

23. Rep. Jackson charged that this was a deliberate maneuver; see Id. at 550.

24. White, op. cit. n.2, at 118.

25. In practice, permission to visit departmental offices and inspect the files was apparently routinely granted to senators and representatives and sometimes even to private citizens; see Id. at 502.

26. Swanstrom, op. cit. n.7, at 71; White, op. cit. n.5, at 87–88.

27. See generally Stewart, op. cit. n.17, ch. 1; Chambers, op. cit. n.7, at 41, 57, 60; Swanstrom, op. cit. n.7, at 282; Cunningham, op. cit. n.10, at 13-19.

28. Early on, the name of Jefferson's department was changed from "Foreign Affairs" to "State."

29. 1 *Writings of Jefferson* (Lipscomb ed. 1903), at 292-93; White, op. cit. n.2, at 68-70, 228. One principle for which the opposition now contended was that references should be addressed to the president himself. This was contrary to the spirit of the Treasury Act, though practice had not been entirely consistent; see White, op. cit. n.2, at 74n. The issue would become important where a constitutional basis for refusing information was wanted.

30. 3 *Annals* at 696-722.

31. Swanstrom, op. cit. n.7, at 274-76; White, op. cit. n.2, at 81n.

32. The introduction of this measure was apparently achieved by ruse; see Baldwin's account at 3 *Annals* 703.

33. For background on these issues, see S. F. Bemis, *Jay's Treaty* (Yale University Press 1965).

34. Indeed, the Senate was in recess at the time; see ch. 3, under "The Senate."

35. 2 *Annals* at 1969; Bemis, op. cit. n.33, at 109-19, 257. Actually, Jefferson tendered his report to the House in February 1793, but a committee decided it was "not expedient" to receive the report at that time. See 3 *Annals* at 885, 894; 4 Id. at 392.

36. Bemis, op. cit. n.33, at 140-44.

37. North Carolina and Rhode Island had not yet ratified the Constitution, while New York had been unable to appoint its senators because of local political conflicts. Thus only ten states were represented.

38. 1 *Annals* at 39. This was changed to a weekly publication in March 1792; see 3 *Annals* at 104.

39. Such injunctions appear to have been extremely rare; at least there are few recorded instances where they were used in these years. One involved the debate of February 1792 on a frontier defense bill; see 3 *Annals* 80 for the injunction, and see ch. 3, under "Confidentiality and Executive Privilege," for additional background.

40. 2 *Annals* at 1749; Maclay, op. cit. n.1, at 283.

41. Swanstrom, op. cit. n.7, at 34, 238.

42. *National Gazette*, Dec. 15, 1792, quoted in Id. at 68.

43. J. Goebel, Jr., *History of the Supreme Court of the United States* (Macmillan 1971), Vol. 1 at 444 n.163 (Sen. Wingate); Swanstrom, op. cit. n.7, at 71 (Sen. Read).

44. Swanstrom, op. cit. n.7, at 57.

45. Id. at 243.

46. Maclay, op. cit. n.1, at 4, 9-10, 13, 32, 49-50.

47. 1 *Annals* at 51; 1 *Executive Journal of the Senate* (Washington 1828) (hereinafter *Executive Journal*) at 59; Maclay, op. cit. n.1, at 111-12. For a historical precedent on the right to dissent, see Goebel, op. cit. n.43, Vol. 1 at 329.

48. McPherson's picture of the conflict as essentially sectional seems overstated. Some support for opening the doors came from New York, Rhode Island, and Pennsylvania, while southern senators were about evenly split on the issue. See McPherson, op. cit. n.16, at 232, 234.

49. Of the seven senators sitting in 1791 who had attended the Constitutional Convention, five voted against opening the doors.

50. Swanstrom, op. cit. n.7, at 240-43; 30 *Writings of Washington* (Fitzpatrick ed. 1940), at 363.

51. Maclay, op. cit. n.1, at 201; see also McPherson, op. cit. n. 16, at 228.

52. McPherson, op. cit. n.16, at 229-31; Swanstrom, op. cit. n.7., at 242; Stewart, op. cit. n.17, at 459 n.29.

53. McPherson, op. cit. n.16, at 229-30.

54. 2 *Annals* at 1768.

55. Maclay, op. cit. n.1, at 296.

56. 2 *Annals* at 1768; 3 Id. at 113; McPherson, op. cit. n.16, at 232–34. In 1792, Gunn of Georgia switched to the pro-secrecy side, but this was offset by the opposite shift of Carroll of Maryland, who this time obeyed his instructions to vote for open doors. John Henry once again ignored the instructions and was censured by Maryland's legislature for so doing.

57. Three senators who had opposed publicity in March were able to support this new proposal, but three others switched in the opposite direction, and two publicity supporters were absent.

58. 3 *Annals* at 625–26.

59. Id. at 637–38.

60. While northern senators voted fifteen to two against opening the doors, southerners favored the measure by eight to three. Given the heavily southern cast of the anti-Federalist movement, it is difficult to discriminate clearly between sectional and partisan interpretations of this vote. Compare McPherson, op. cit. n.16, at 223. Foster of Rhode Island, Johnston of North Carolina, and Gunn of Georgia were the chameleons, and Rufus King of New York the most surprising exception to the general pattern. Of course, the Constitution of his state required open legislative doors; thus he knew the effects and advantages of the practice, see ch. 2, n.6. Gunn had already voted in 1792 to admit members of the House to Senate proceedings. See also McPherson, op. cit. at 234–37; 1 *Life and Correspondence of Rufus King* (King ed. 1894), at 377, 539.

61. Swanstrom, op. cit. n.7, at 90–91, 203–4, 233, 235.

62. John Jay served briefly in this capacity before Jefferson assumed his post and Jay became chief justice.

63. Maclay, op. cit. n.1, at 81–83.

64. 1 *Executive Journal* at 19; Swanstrom, op. cit. n.7, at 96–99.

65. 1 *Executive Journal* at 99. Perhaps the precipitating event was the fight over Morris's nomination; see ch. 3, under "The Senate."

66. White, op. cit. n.2, at 128, 342–43.

67. The timing of this mission was something of a slight to Jefferson, whose arrival in New York was expected when Morris was sent off without his consent. See Boyd, op. cit. n.9, at 14–20.

68. One observer, quite possibly a senator, charged that Jefferson, prompted by hostility to the policy views of the Senate majority, had obstructed the giving to the Senate of the supporting information called for. See Letter, Anonymous to Washington, Jan. 20, 1792, Washington Mss., Microfilm, Series 4, Reel 101, Library of Congress.

69. 1 *Executive Journal* at 92–97.

70. Letter, Gouverneur Morris to Washington, April 6, 1792, Washington Mss., op. cit. n.68.

71. Letter, Washington to Morris, "Private," June 21, 1792, Washington Mss., printed in 32 *Writings of George Washington* (Fitzpatrick ed.) at 60.

72. See, e.g., 1 *American State Papers: Foreign Relations* at 390; and see ch. 4, under "The Gouverneur Morris Investigation."

73. April 24, 1790, State Dep't Archives, RG59, Reel M570, National Archives.

74. 1 *Executive Journal* at 65; Swanstrom, op. cit. n.7, at 114.

75. Maclay, op. cit. n.1, at 124; R. Hayden, *The Senate and Treaties, 1789-1817* (Da Capo 1970), at 23 n.4.

76. Great emphasis has been laid on Washington's personality in some accounts of this episode and the overall demise of the conciliar plan; see Swanstrom, op. cit. n.7, at 177; Hayden, op. cit. n.75, at 246. This is indeed a relevant factor, but it may be doubted whether a different president would have found it any more fruitful to consult personally with a Senate composed and disposed as this one was.

77. 1 *Executive Journal* at 55.

78. Hayden, op. cit. n.75, at 9-10, 28, 32, 34-37; 1 *Executive Journal* at 146.

79. Hayden, op. cit. n.75, at 38.

80. 1 *Writings of Jefferson* (Lipscomb ed.) at 294; Boyd, op. cit. n.9, at 21-32.

81. See ch. 3, under "House of Representatives."

82. Hayden, op. cit. n.75, at 5.

83. 1 *Executive Journal* at 59.

84. Hayden, op. cit. n.75, at 46–47.

85. Id. at 51–52.

86. 1 *Annals* at 687.

87. There is no record of a debate or vote on the propriety of a secret House journal. The secret journal itself was lost in the War of 1812. Apparently its contents included certain legislation passed by the House on foreign and military affairs, and transmitted to the Senate without public disclosure. The bills were published when they became law; e.g., H.R. 50A, 50B & 126A, Mar. 1790 and Feb. 1791. Compare ch. 7, under "Afterword."

88. 1 *Annals* at 936.

89. For confidential messages in this period, see 2 *Annals* at 1894, 1967; 3 Id. at 327, 348, 738, 766, 788, 792.

90. 3 *Annals* at 348.

91. By a vote of thirty-four to eighteen; see 3 *Annals* at 354.

92. Id. at 356.

93. Id. at 414.

94. Id. at 492.

95. Not all individuals can be readily classified as to party affiliation in this period. The present conclusions are based on a careful comparison of the slightly different listings in Bell, op. cit. n.14, at Appendix pp. 253-54; and Cunningham, op. cit. n.10, Appendix pp. 267-72. On Giles's role, see White, op. cit. n.2, at 51, 80; Bell, op. cit., at 73 and n.12. Perhaps his strategy flowed from a fear that Hamilton's friends would vote down a congressional investigation. As for Page and Sumter, one can only speculate that they feared a congressional probe would simply be a whitewash.

96. 3 *Annals* at 492.

97. Letter, Knox to Washington, Mar. 30, 1792, Washington Mss., op. cit. n.68.

98. White, op. cit. n.2, at 39–40.

99. 1 *Writings of Jefferson* (Lipscomb ed.) at 303-05.

100. See, e.g., R. Berger, *Executive Privilege* (Harvard University Press 1974), at 167-71; Berger, *Executive Privilege V. Congressional Inquiry*, 12 U.C.L.A. L.Rev. 1044, 1079–84 (1965); and other authorities therein cited.

101. 32 *Writings of Washington* (Fitzpatrick ed.) at 15.

102. Stewart, op. cit. n.17, at 566-67.

103. "They are also the expositions of the documents and information that arise in the administration of Government which this House may require of the Executive Magistrate and which he will communicate as he sees fit. The House may go too far in asking information. He may constitutionally deny such information of facts there deputed as are fit to be communicated and may assist in legislation I always wish for. But I want no opinions from him." 3 *Annals* at 706.

104. See White, op. cit. n.5, at 87; Thomas, op. cit. n.12, at 33n.; Boyd, op. cit. n.9, passim.

105. S. M. Lipset, *The First New Nation* (Doubleday 1967), at 308.

106. The Senate had no policy of bipartisanship in committee appointments; see Swanstrom, op. cit. n.7, at 226–29.

107. Id. at 249; McPherson, op. cit. n.16, at 238.

108. For what it is worth, only eleven of the twenty-nine senators who served in 1789-91 were reelected, and six of those were on record for opening the doors. Swanstrom, op. cit. n.7, at 80; McPherson, op. cit. n.16, at 232, 238.

Chapter 4

1. See R. Swanstrom, *The Senate, 1787-1801* (US GPO, Sen. Doc. No. 64, 1962), at 247.

2. 4 *Annals of Congress* (hereinafter *Annals*) at 33.

3. Id. at 42–43; Bache's *Philadelphia General Advertiser*, Feb. 18, 1794, at 2.

4. See Swanstrom, op. cit. n.1, at 246. The secret inquisitions of the British Star Chamber had left a strong distaste for such proceedings in the minds of many, and the Sixth Amendment specifically required that criminal trials be public.

5. See news item cited in n.3.

6. These were Read of Delaware, recently resigned; Henry of Maryland, who had not yet arrived at the capital; and Robinson of Vermont, whose absence this day is unexplained. Of course it is uncertain that the absentees would have adhered to their previous positions. Henry had been much criticized for defying his state's instructions on this point, while Robinson supported the opposition on many issues at the present session.

7. It is true that some citizens were content to let the Senate debate behind closed doors. On February 8, 1794, Monroe wrote to Madison that, "I found it a subject of complaint as I passed through New Jersey that the doors of the House of Representatives were not shut as those of the Senate were, because the people were already so hostile to Great Britain that it would be difficult to keep them within bounds if encouraged in that licentious spirit by the discussions in Congress." 1 *Writings of Monroe* (Hamilton ed. 1893) at 280. Yet there is no evidence that the Senate really felt pressured to keep its doors shut.

8. 4 *Annals* at 45. The three defectors were Foster of Rhode Island, who, though usually voting with the Federalists, had supported open doors in 1792—but opposed it in 1793; Langdon of New Hampshire, who, like Bradley, had never supported open doors before but became something of an oppositionist in this session; and the freshman Livermore of New Hampshire, who, though later identified as a Federalist, had often voted with the opposition in his earlier career in the lower house. See R. M. Bell, *Party and Faction in American Politics: The House of Representatives, 1789-1801* (Greenwood 1973), at 33, 124, 253–54.

9. 2 *Letters of John Adams* (Adams ed. 1841) at 143; Bache's *Philadelphia General Advertiser*, Feb. 24, 1794, at 3; 1 *Writings of James Monroe* (Hamilton ed. 1893) at 284, Letter of Mar. 3, 1794.

10. 4 *Annals* at 46. A supplementary resolution adopted on February 20 provided that, upon a member's motion to shut the doors, the debate on such would itself be secret. Ibid.

11. 2 *Letters of John Adams* at 144; *Philadelphia General Advertiser*, Mar. 8, 1794, at 3.

12. See E. G. McPherson, *The Southern States and the Reporting of Senate Debates, 1789-1802*, 12 J. Southern Hist. 223, 239–40 (1946). In fact, on March 18, 1794, the Senate, for no apparent reason, ordered "That the Secretary of the Senate pay no further compensation to the printers for the weekly publication of the journals." 1 *Executive Journal of the Senate* (hereinafter *Executive Journal*) at 149. On April 22, however, they resolved that in the future their journals should be printed in the less expensive and more accessible octavo format. 4 *Annals* at 85; see also 6 Id. at 1537. On the enfeeblement of the Senate opposition subsequent to Gallatin's ouster, see Letters of Monroe to Jefferson, 1 *Writings of James Monroe* at 284, 288.

13. Obviously, the hypothesis that the open doors movement was essentially regional in character is equally useless in explaining the final result. Compare McPherson, op. cit. n.12.

14. See 32 *Writings of Washington* (Fitzpatrick ed. 1940) at 419–20.

15. S. F. Bemis, *Jay's Treaty* (Yale University Press 1962), at 201.

16. See C. M. Thomas, *American Neutrality in 1793* (Columbia University Press 1931), at 66; "Helvidius" No. 4, 1 *Letters & Other Writings of Madison* (Cong. ed. 1865) at 643; N. E. Cunningham, *The Jeffersonian Republicans* (University of North Carolina Press 1968), at 58; E. S. Corwin, *The President, Office and Powers* (New York University Press 1957), at 179–81.

17. 1 *Writings of Jefferson* (Lipscomb ed. 1903), at 227, 349; Thomas, op. cit. n.16, at 68; Cunningham, op. cit. n.16, at 55.

18. Thomas, op. cit. n.16, at 68, 236, 238; 1 *Writings of Jefferson* (Ford ed. 1892) at 238, 255–56; 6 Id. at 277, 280, 315, 321, 362, 367, 401; 4 *Works of Hamilton* (Hamilton ed. 1850) at 455–62.

19. 1 *Writings of Jefferson* (Lipscomb ed.) at 384, item of Aug. 6, 1793.

20. L. D. White, *The Federalists* (Macmillan 1948), at 219; Thomas, op. cit. n.16, at 233–35.

21. The correspondence and reports on foreign affairs submitted to Congress prior to December 1793 occupy fifty-two pages in the ASP compilation; the communications of that single month come to 167 pages. It took the House five weeks to read through the December messages; see *Philadelphia General Advertiser,* Mar. 26, 1794, at 2.

22. 1 *Writings of Jefferson* (Lipscomb ed.) at 410.

23. Ibid. See also Thomas, op. cit. n.16, at 243–44; J. J. Reardon, *Edmund Randolph* (Macmillan 1974), at 245.

24. Thomas, op. cit. n.16, at 244.

25. Jefferson to Washington, Dec. 2, 1793, State Dep't Archives, Presidential Correspondence, RG 59, Reel M570, National Archives.

26. *Philadephia General Advertiser,* Dec. 7, 1793, at 2; 4 *Annals* at 137.

27. 4 *Annals* at 251, resolution introduced by William Smith.

28. Hammond to Grenville, No. 2, Feb. 22, 1794, in British Public Records Office (PRO), Series FO5, Vol. 4, Library of Cong.

29. 4 *Annals* at 256.

30. Hammond to Grenville, Nos. 4, 26, 27, 35, and "separate," dated Mar. 7, June 9, June 27, Dec. 1, and Sept. 27, respectively, in PRO, FO5, Vols. 4 and 5, Library of Cong.; see also PRO, FO 115, Vol. 3, items of Mar. 1, Mar. 6, Aug. 8, and Nov. 20; and State Dep't Domestic Letters, Vols. 6 and 7, items of Mar. 3, June 10, June 14, Oct. 7, and Nov. 29, Nat'l Archives. Hammond suspected Randolph of repeatedly leaking secrets without presidential sanction, but the evidence is generally to the contrary. See State Dep't Archives, op. cit. n.25, items of Mar. 26, 29, 30, 31, Apr. 1, May 22, 23; Washington Mss., Series 4, Reel 105, item of Apr. 24, Library of Cong.; and 1 *American State Papers (ASP), Foreign Relations,* at 448.

31. 4 *Annals* at 462, 467. That the House's action was secret at the time may be inferred from *Philadelphia General Advertiser,* Feb. 28, 1794, at 2; cf. Id. at 3.

32. Hammond to Grenville, No. 4, op. cit. n.30.

33. State Dep't Domestic Letters, Vol. 6, at 101, National Archives.

34. See *ASP, Foreign Relations,* Vol. 1 at 327, 461.

35. Thomas, op. cit. n.16, at 243n.; and see n.38.

36. Thomas, op. cit. n.16, at 225, 233–35; Bemis, op. cit. n.15, at 202–3.

37. See R. Ernst, *Rufus King* (University of North Carolina Press 1969), at 188–94; Reardon, op. cit. n.23, at 246–47. The attorney general concluded, without articulating his reasoning, that the case would not support an action against Jay and King. Some observers thought the determination politically motivated; see *Philadelphia General Advertiser,* Dec. 27 and 30, 1793. For Randolph's very different handling of Hammond's libel complaint against Thomas Greenleaf, see ch. 5, under "Domestic Turmoil and Executive Power."

38. Other omissions from the Genêt correspondence were discovered by Congress, and missing documents called for. The episode is not recorded in the *Annals.* Randolph's casual reference in Washington Mss., op. cit. n.30, memo of Feb. 24,

1794 ("Monday afternoon") does not reveal whether the House's call was qualified like that of January 20 or not.

39. *ASP, Foreign Relations,* Vol. 1 at 312, Jan. 16, 1794. For full text, compare No. 38, Id. at 373. This extract was more severely censored than that given to the Senate with the rest of Morris's correspondence. Portions withheld from the Senate were: 1) Para. 2, sentence 2, "although...circumstances"; 2) Para. 3, sentence 5, "iniquitous"; 3) Para. 4, sentence 3, "because...enslaved"; 4) Para. 6, sentence 3; 5) Para. 7, sentence 1. In Para. 7, sentence 7, the second clause was first struck out and then restored.

40. Memo cited n.35.

41. R. Hayden, *The Senate and Treaties, 1789-1817* (Da Capo 1970), at 55-56.

42. Reardon, op. cit. n.23. at 255-57; Bemis, op. cit. n.15, at 197-200. The Spanish viewed the United States as intoxicated with imperial ambition and had their own complaints and fears about American and Indian activities directed against them, not without reason.

43. 4 *Annals* at 143.

44. The items at 4 *Annals* 603, 604, 769 suggest nothing was done. Yet Randolph's memo, discussed below, is to the contrary; and we do know of other House resolutions not reported in the *Annals.* The House kept a secret journal for resolutions taken behind closed doors, some of which are printed in the *Annals* as we have it today.

45. *ASP, Foreign Relations,* Vol. 1 at 454. The transaction is not found in the journals of the Senate.

46. State Dep't Archives, RG 59, Reports of Secretary of State to President and Congress, Vol. 2, at 397. The letter of March 29 to Gov. Shelby, referred to by Randolph in his memo, is printed in ASP, FR, Vol. 1 at 456. It gave no detail on the negotiations but declared that "the executive has been deficient neither in vigilance nor exertions."

47. State Dep't Archives, op. cit. n.25. Innes did not actually arrive until January 1795, a delay exasperating to the Kentuckians. In December 1794 their legislature had resolved once more to instruct their senators "to require information of the steps which have been taken to obtain the navigation of the river Mississippi, and to transmit such information to the executive of this state." Greenleaf's *New York Journal,* Apr. 18, 1795, extra ed., at 1. In additional resolutions they declared their readiness to cooperate with the general government in all necessary steps, peaceful or otherwise, to secure the navigation and British surrender of the western posts. Ibid.

48. Nov. 11, 1794, State Dep't Archives, Domestic Letters, M40 Roll 7.

49. Randolph to Washington, Apr. 20, 1795, State Dep't Archives, op. cit. n.25; and see correspondence printed in *Baltimore Federal Intelligencer,* Apr. 24-27, 1795.

50. 3 *Annals* at 51-53.

51. 4 *Annals* at 21.

52. 4 *Annals* at 149-50.

53. 4 *Annals* at 151.

54. *Philadelphia General Advertiser*, Dec. 30, 1793, at 3; see also Editorial of Dec. 28, Id. at 3; and Letter of "Z," Dec. 31, Id. at 3.

55. 4 *Annals* at 151. While no roll call was recorded, the *General Advertiser* claimed that the resolution passed "with little opposition." Dec. 31, 1793, at 3.

56. This vote is not found in the *Annals,* but see *General Advertiser,* Dec. 31, 1793, at 3.

57. 4 *Annals* at 154.

58. 4 *Annals* at 165.

59. Not in the *Annals*; see *Journal of the House of Representatives*, Feb. 6, 1794, at 57.

60. In fact, only two instances of declassification proceedings in the House are known: that just recited and a case involving a dispatch from Thomas Pinckney in London, partially in cypher, where the committee identified three passages as "of a personal nature" and hence "not necessary to public information." See 4 *Annals* at 564, 684; Reports of House Select Committees, Vol. 1, at 301, National Archives. Not only was disclosure limited in both these cases; its exact scope may well have been negotiated with executive officers who attended committee sessions for the purpose.

61. As early as December 7 a tentative draft of the House's reply to the president's opening message was leaked to the press, to the consternation of the House leadership. *General Advertiser,* Dec. 9, 1793, at 3. Leaks on developments and prospects in foreign affairs were not infrequent, but they tended to consist of terse assessments of governmental attitudes rather than detailed factual disclosures. See, for example, *General Advertiser,* items of Feb. 26 and Mar. 26, 1794.

62. *General Advertiser*, Dec. 31, 1793. That Giles signed the letter suggests he was conscious of no wrongdoing. Yet his letter is dated December 11, five days before the president officially notified the House of the events in question. Perhaps Giles had the information through private channels rather than official ones.

63. *General Advertiser*, Dec. 28, 1793, at 3.

64. 4 *Annals* at 432. "Mr. Hunter" is John Hunter of South Carolina.

65. See C. Warren, *The Supreme Court in United States History* (Little Brown 1922), Vol. 1 at 116; Corwin, op. cit. n.16, at 179 n.29; Act of June 5, 1794, 4 *Annals* at 1461, 1 *Statutes at Large* 381.

66. The episode is noted in Reardon, op. cit. n.23, at 253-54. The only thorough treatment, though still out of context and somewhat misleading, is A. Sofaer, *War, Foreign Affairs, and Constitutional Power: The Origins* (Ballinger 1976), at 83f.; Sofaer, *Executive Privilege*, 75 Colum. L. Rev. 1318 (1975).

67. 4 *Annals* at 34. Genêt had complained to Jefferson about Morris in September 1793; see D. Walther, *Gouverneur Morris, Witness of Two Revolutions* (Funk & Wagnalls 1934), at 255. But Jefferson did not tell the president of it until December 11; see State Dep't Archives, op. cit. n.25. Genêt's successor, Fauchet,

pressed the matter more forcefully and formally demanded Morris's recall some time in February or March; see Walther, op. cit., at 255-57 (20 Germini Year II-April 10, 1794); and Reardon, op. cit. n.23, at 267.

68. 4 *Annals* at 37–38. Some senators were more consistent than others, but on the whole the Senate was sharply divided at this time into two blocs—about fifteen Federalists and thirteen Republicans. On calling for the Morris papers, the Republicans won, thirteen to eleven, with help from the "Federalist" Hawkins of North Carolina (absent: three Federalists, one Republican). On Gallatin's expulsion, they lost, fourteen to twelve (one Federalist absent, Gallatin not voting, Hawkins reverting to the Federalists). On opening the doors for legislative business, the initial vote was fourteen to thirteen against, with one Republican absent. This was not so typical a partisan division as the others. The Federalists King, Potts, and Hawkins voted to open the doors, whereas the Republicans (in this session) Bradley and Langdon voted against it. Then it was Bradley and Langdon who voted to reconsider, bringing Federalists Foster and Livermore with them. King had long supported the open doors drive; see ch. 3, n.60. Potts and Hawkins probably supported it only at the insistence of their state legislatures. Even if party designations are taken with a grain of salt, it is clear that the vote on Gallatin's expulsion was purely partisan, while the open doors issue involved some distinctive political and ideological motives. The call for the Morris papers, finally, was more like the former than the latter.

69. 1 *Works of Fisher Ames* (Ames ed. 1854) at 134; compare 1 *Writings of Monroe* at 288.

70. Washington Mss., op. cit. n.30.

71. Ibid.

72. The letter referred to has not been found.

73. Washington Mss. op. cit. n.30. Today the resolution can be found both in the *Executive Journal of the Senate,* Vol. 1 at 147; and in 4 *Annals* at 37-38.

74. Washington Mss., op. cit. n.30. It is possible that the preceding memo was actually a rough draft of the February 2 memo rather than a separate document.

75. It may be that a belated attempt was made to persuade the Senate to introduce a qualifying clause into its resolution. At least the speculation that negotiations were being held for such purpose accounts as well as any for the curious fact that the resolution, though adopted on January 24, was not at once directed to be transmitted to the president—the normal procedure—and was not in fact delivered until sometime after February 2, as is plain from Randolph's memo of that date. The resolution as transmitted contained no qualification.

76. See ch. 3, under "The Senate." It is unclear whether Randolph thought individual safety the only proper reason for censorship.

77. *General Advertiser,* Mar. 5, 1794, at 3.

78. It seems reasonable, however, to suppose that the "interviews" referred to in Randolph's memo of February 2 are the same as the "conversations" mentioned in that of January 25, which would imply that constitutional issues were under discussion all along.

79. Washington Mss., op. cit. n.30.

80. Bradford did not take office until January 27. Based on internal evidence, his memo was probably written before Randolph's of February 2.

81. Washington Mss., op. cit. n.30.

82. See n.76.

83. Washington Mss., op. cit. n.30, "Wednesday morning." The actual date may have been January 29, or up to three weeks later. Sofaer, op. cit. n.66, at 83n., asserts that Randolph's talks with Wilson and Madison were mandated by the president.

84. The Court had expressly refused to advise the president on certain points of international law which he submitted to them while the Neutrality Proclamation was under consideration, giving as its reason the impropriety of exercising its jurisdiction in the absence of a traditional case or controversy. Thomas, op. cit. n.16, at 456–60.

85. *The Federalist*, No. 51.

86. 4 *Annals* at 56.

87. The complete version is printed in *ASP, FR*, Vol. 1 at 329–412. Unfortunately the editor chose not to indicate which portions had been withheld from the Senate. The censored version is in the Senate Archives; see President's Message to Senate, Feb. 26, 1794, RG 46, National Archives.

88. The exception is Morris's dispatch No. 34, which was not sent to the Senate and is not in the ASP compilation either. The omission appears to have been inadvertent, since the dispatch in question is not obviously super-sensitive. For its text, see J. Sparks, *Life and Correspondence of Gouverneur Morris* (Boston 1832), Vol. 2 at 344–49.

89. This category accounts for three deleted passages, out of a total of forty-three. In a *private* letter to Washington, Morris confessed to having instigated the idea of Genêt's arrest; see *ASP, FR*, Vol. 1 at 397. Morris's private correspondence was not covered by the Senate's call; much of it was, however, of public interest; see Id. at 379f., and Sparks, op. cit. n.88.

90. This category accounts for nine deletions, if one excludes very broad statements like "the courts chicane very much here."

91. This category covers four cases at most.

92. See *ASP, FR*, Vol. 1 at 330.

93. Id. at 332.

94. Id. at 345.

95. Id. at 355.

96. Id. at 360.

97. Id. at 368. Altogether, the combined categories of remarks derogatory to the French (or in one case the Spanish) and gloomy predictions account for as many as seventeen of the forty-three deletions. A few of these could, with some stretching, be viewed as "harsh remarks on the rulers in France," but as the quotes show, the main thrust was different.

98. *ASP, FR*, Vol. 1 at 330.

99. Ibid.

100. Id. at 332.

101. Id. at 333.

102. Id. at 360.

103. Id. at 348.

104. Id. at 367.

105. Id. at 331. Statements betraying royalist sympathy, excluding those counted as possibly deleted to protect informants, number six in all.

106. Ibid.

107. Id. at 346.

108. Id. at 360.

109. This category accounts for four deletions.

110. See, e.g., Id. at 334; but compare Id. at 394.

111. Id. at 394. In the manuscript there is a suspicious gap between this passage and Morris's signature, suggesting that the censor removed something which, in this case, the compiler of the printed version was unable to retrieve from other sources.

112. Id. at 338.

113. On a generous tabulation, they account for no more than sixteen of the forty-three deletions.

114. See Walther, op. cit. n.67, at 238.

115. Id. at 190–91, 211–17.

116. Whether the president knew of or condoned these activities is impossible to establish.

117. Letter of Monroe to Jefferson, 1 *Writings of Monroe* at 283-84.

118. *General Advertiser*, Feb. 26, 1794, at 3; and see n.67.

119. A report of Morris's expected arrival in America in April 1795 prompted one writer to renew the demand for a full investigation of Morris's conduct; see Greenleaf's *Argus*, Apr. 29, 1795; but nothing was done.

120. Another matter left unexplored was that of the sanctions available for dealing with leaks and unauthorized publications. Sometime in the summer or fall of 1794, one of Morris's private letters to Washington did somehow leak out. The dispatch was relatively innocuous (see Sparks, op. cit. n.88, Letter of Mar. 12, 1794); but a note from Randolph to Washington showed the administration's concern. Randolph was unable to trace the leak, and the matter was dropped. See Randolph to Washington, "Saturday," Sept. 6, 1794, State Dep't Archives, op. cit. n.25.

121. *General Advertiser*, Mar. 5, 1794, at 3.

122. Id., Mar. 6 and 7, 1794.

123. 3 *Annals* at 761.

124. 3 *Annals* at 835–40. It is known that the Senate undertook a parallel investigation, but no useful information thereon has been found. See 3 *Annals* at 633; B. Mitchell, *Alexander Hamilton* (Macmillan 1962), Vol. 2 at 248; Swanstrom, op. cit. n.1, at 275.

125. See 3 *Annals* at 1199–1286.

126. 3 *Annals* at 1202, 1216.

127. 3 *Annals* at 1247.

128. Mitchell, op. cit. n.124, at 252.

129. Id. at 260; Cunningham, op. cit. n.16, at 52; 7 *Writings of Jefferson* (Ford ed.) at 216, 220, 228–34.

130. 3 *Annals* at 900.

131. 3 *Annals* at 911, 924, 929, 953, 956, 960, 1202.

132. 3 *Annals* at 955–63.

133. 1 *Writings of Jefferson* (Ford ed.) at 198; 1 *Writings of Jefferson* (Lipscomb ed.) at 337; Reardon, op. cit. n.23, at 213–14.

134. 4 *Annals* at 142, 467. Again the Senate conducted an investigation as well; see Swanstrom, op. cit. n.1, at 275.

135. The statement is in *ASP, Finance*, Vol. 1 at 290–91. This episode, like the Morris investigation, is missing from Attorney General Rogers's 1958 Memorandum on executive privilege and from most other accounts.

136. See White, op. cit. n.20, at 19 on the House's rejection of the claim that department heads have independent authority under the Constitution itself to administer their functions.

137. *ASP, Finance*, Vol. 1 at 291.

138. Id. at 291, 300. Actually, there were three reports or requests for authority by the secretary and one very brief reply by Washington granting approval. Cf. Mitchell, op. cit. n.124, at 273: "years later...Edmund Randolph recounted that Washington at first denied, with passion, having written one of the letters most explicitly endorsing Hamilton's treatment of Dutch loans. However, when this and other permissions from him were produced by Hamilton, he acknowledged them. . . . Madison suggested that Hamilton had avoided exhibiting the President's letters, recognizing that Washington had written or maybe only signed them without close scrutiny."

139. Evident from Randolph's private memo to Washington, Apr. 1794 ("Sunday"), in Washington Mss., op. cit. n.30; *ASP, Finance*, Vol. 1 at 291.

140. Apparently Washington was forewarned of the situation before Hamilton relayed to him the committee's request, through a leak by a member that reached Randolph's ears. See Reardon, op. cit. n.23, at 260; Randolph to Washington, Apr. 1, 1794, State Dep't Archives, op. cit. n.25.

141. *ASP, Finance*, Vol. 1 at 291; 33 *Writings of Washington* (Fitzpatrick ed.) at 18; Reardon, op. cit. n.23, at 261 n.85; 16 *Papers of Hamilton* (Syrett ed.) at 250.

142. The committee noted that in January 1792 the House had called for information to assist it in determining the need for additional revenue; in his reply Hamilton had not discussed the loans or the way they had been applied. The committee apparently did not find the relevance of the loan information sufficiently plain to hold Hamilton culpable for the omission. See *ASP, Finance*, Vol. 1 at 298–99.

143. 4 *Annals* at 532; 2 *Letters & Other Writings of Madison* (Cong. ed.) at 9; White, op. cit. n.20, at 73.

144. Swanstrom op. cit. n.1, at 276; cf. *ASP, Finance*, Vol. 1 at 274.

145. For contrary developments in the Jeffersonian period, see Sofaer, op. cit. n.66, at 177 n. 48, 180.

Chapter 5

1. Secretly, however, General Anthony Wayne was given orders to pursue the hostile Indians under the very guns of the British fortification at Detroit. These orders could have led to an armed engagement with British troops and to a British declaration of war. See A. Sofaer, *War, Foreign Affairs, and Constitutional Power: The Origins* (Ballinger 1976), at 125–27.

2. D. H. Stewart, *The Opposition Press of the Federalist Period* (State University of New York Press 1969), at 169–70; G. D. Luetscher, *Early Political Machinery in the United States* (Philadelphia 1903).

3. *Life and Correspondence of Rufus King* (King ed. 1894), Vol. 1 at 517.

4. King suspected Randolph of having intrigued against Hamilton's appointment; see King, op. cit. n.3, Vol. 1 at 520. Randolph vehemently denied it; see Washington Mss., Series 4, Reel 105, Library of Congress, memo of Apr. 9, 1794. It was probably public outcry after the proposal leaked out that scotched the idea of a Hamilton appointment. See Bache's *Philadelphia General Advertiser*, Mar. 25, 1794, at 3; Id., Apr. 9, 1794, at 2.

5. The argument gained force from the fact that Washington was unwilling to veto any law he deemed constitutional, no matter how strongly he disagreed with it. See L. D. White, *The Federalists* (Macmillan 1948), at 65-66.

6. S. F. Bemis, *Jay's Treaty* (Yale University Press 1962), at 270.

7. R. Hayden, *The Senate and Treaties, 1789-1817* (Da Capo 1970), at 34–39, 54-57, 68.

8. King, op. cit. n.3, Vol. 1 at 521, 523, 562.

9. 1 *Executive Journal of the Senate* (hereinafter *Executive Journal*) at 150.

10. Id. at 151. More precisely, Jay declared that some southern states' insistence on repudiating debts to British creditors (including loyalists) in violation of United States treaty commitments justified the British retention of the western posts. He also thought extreme the southern demand for restitution of slaves carried off and freed by British troops in the war. See 4 *Secret Journals of the Continental Congress* (Boston 1821) at 185.

11. Washington Mss., op. cit. n.4.

12. Cf. White, op. cit. n.5, at 501–2.

13. 1 *Executive Journal* at 151.

14. Id. at 152.

15. Id. at 152-53; *Philadelphia General Advertiser*, May 14, 1794, at 3. Public knowledge of the Senate's debates consisted mainly of rumor and leaked information. Copies of the official legislative journal were made available, but these did

not contain a record of debate, and dissenters were forbidden to enter their views in the journal.

16. Bemis, op. cit. n.6, at 268–72; R. M. Bell, *Party and Faction in American Politics: The House of Representatives, 1789-1801* (Greenwood 1973), at 143–45; R. Swanstrom, *The Senate, 1787-1801* (US GPO, Sen. Doc. No. 64, 1962), at 285.

17. King, op. cit. n.3, Vol. 1 at 523.

18. Bemis, op. cit. n.6, at 289–91; J. J. Reardon, *Edmund Randolph* (Macmillan 1974), at 265. Compare Id. at 251.

19. Reardon, op. cit. n.18, at 286–87.

20. Randolph to Washington, May 6, 1794, Washington Mss., op. cit. n.4.

21. The precedents from Indian negotiations were admittedly less consistent, but these cases were politically and legally quite different. Hayden, op. cit. n.7, at 34–37, 70–71, 78–80, 93.

22. Randolph may, however, have been responsible for alerting the opposition to these developments. Its knowledge is evident from a Letter of Monroe to Jefferson, May 4, 1794, 1 *Writings of Monroe* (Hamilton ed. 1893) at 294. Cf. Randolph's denial of complicity in another leak, in Randolph to Washington, Apr. 19, 1794, op. cit. n.4.

23. Bemis, op. cit. n.6, at 273–77, 291, 299–317, 337–45; Reardon, op. cit. n.18, at 265–66.

24. See Bemis, op. cit. n.6, at 320; Reardon, op. cit. n.18, at 284; Swanstrom, op. cit. n.16, at 273. That Jay's private letters were more candid is evident from Letter of Jay to Hamilton, July 11, 1794, in 4 *Correspondence and Papers of John Jay* (Johnston ed. 1890) at 30: "I think it best that [these facts] should remain unmentioned for the present, and they make no part of my communications to Mr. Randolph, or others. This is not the season for such communications; they may be misinterpreted."

25. See Jay to Grenville, Nov. 22, 1794, in Jay, op. cit. n.24, Vol. 4 at 146. Jay himself was insistent on the need for secrecy; see Jay to Washington, June 23, 1794, Aug. 5, 1794; Jay to Randolph, Sept. 13, 1794; and Jay to Monroe, Feb. 5, 1795; in Id., Vol. 4 at 27, 46, 104, 157–59.

26. *Philadelphia Gazette*, Oct. 20, 1794; *Philadelphia General Advertiser*, Oct. 21 and Dec. 18, 1794.

27. Randolph to Jay, Oct. 20, 1794, in *American State Papers, Foreign Relations* (hereinafter *ASP, FR*) Vol. 1 at 499; see Id. at 484, 499, 500, for other items on this decision. The substance of the dispatch had appeared in *Philadelphia General Advertiser*, Oct. 9, 1794, at 2.

28. Jay to Monroe, Feb. 5, 1795, in Jay, op. cit. n.24, Vol. 4 at 157–59.

29. Reardon, op. cit. n.18, at 286 n.41. The resolution in question is not in the *Annals*.

30. Bemis, op. cit. n.6, at 317, 370. More comical still, in one case the United States government was unable to decipher its own minister's messages, having misplaced the key. See Pickering to Washington, Oct. 2, Oct. 5, 1795, State Dep't Archives, RG59, Reel M570, National Archives.

31. Washington to Jay, Aug. 30, 1794, in Jay, op. cit. n.24, Vol. 4 at 54, docu-

ments American awareness of British secret activities; see also Bemis, op. cit. n.6, at 267n. on the leak of Lord Dorchester's secret warlike speech to the Indians.

32. Hayden, op. cit. n.7, at 94; Swanstrom, op. cit. n.16, at 120-21.

33. Genêt's activities are noted in Reardon, op. cit. n.18, at 255-57; suspected British involvement in the Whiskey Rebellion is noted in Id. at 329-30.

34. An early expression of presidential misgivings is Washington to Randolph, Apr. 11, 1794, State Dep't Archives, op. cit. n.30. For his later views, see 12 *Writings of Washington* (Ford ed. 1889) at 454, 470.

35. It was Randolph, after all, who keynoted the Constitutional Convention by warning against the dangers of excessive democracy. Nevertheless, if Randolph's political views had evolved as later disclosures suggested, his conduct in this affair should not be understood as a product of ideological fervor so much as an attempt to disguise his new true colors and perhaps to protect the loyal opposition by cutting away its revolutionary wing.

36. Madison to Jefferson, Dec. 4, 1794, in Reardon, op. cit. n.18, at 280 n.77. On the immediate impact see N. E. Cunningham, *The Jeffersonian Republicans* (University of North Carolina Press 1968), at 62-65.

37. On the 1794 elections, see R. F. Nichols, *The Invention of the American Political Parties* (Macmillan 1967), at 188-90; Stewart, op. cit. n.2, at 88; W. Chambers, *Political Parties in a New Nation* (Oxford University Press 1963), at 74, 90. That the Republicans won a clear majority is denied, however, by Bell, op. cit. n.16, at 254-56 (compare Third and Fourth Congress tallies); and Cunningham, op. cit. n.36, at 76.

38. Swanstrom, op. cit. n.16, at 288. Actually three of these eleven should be counted as independents.

39. But see items in *Philadelphia General Advertiser*, Sept. 27, 1794, and Bache's successor paper, the *Aurora*, Dec. 30, 1794.

40. *Philadelphia General Advertiser*, Sept. 8, Sept. 18, Oct. 6, 1794; *Aurora*, Nov. 18, 1794; Greenleaf's *New York Journal*, Oct. 18, 1794, Jan. 7, 1795.

41. Quoted and discussed in Bell, op. cit. n.16, at 47, 52.

42. Washington to Jay, Dec. 18, 1794, in Jay, op. cit. n.24, Vol. 4 at 151. Bache had been called upon by Randolph in an effort to discover the source for a certain story. No legal action is known to have been taken against Bache; perhaps his escape provides some support for the claim that leaking information was not regarded as criminal, even if some expressions of opinion were.

43. Randolph to Harrison, State Dep't Domestic Letters, Vol. 7, National Archives. Greenleaf had a record of controversial stands going back many years. In 1788 his press was burned by citizens resentful of his opposition to ratification of the Constitution. The saga of persecution did not end even with his death; in 1798 his widow was forced to sell the business after her assistant was jailed for seditious libel.

44. The allegedly libelous article appeared on September 13, 1794, in Greenleaf's *New York Journal*, at 3. The gist of the "libel" was that British Minister Hammond was a scoundrel and a Jew; that he regarded the United States as an enemy country and persuaded others to do likewise; and that he and Randolph, though seemingly at loggerheads, were actually dissembling in order to impress

their respective superiors. The tone of the piece was contemptuous; a majority of the grand jury thought it designed "to injure, vilify and destroy the Good Name, Fame, Credit and Reputation" of the minister and to "bring him into Great Contempt, Ridicule and Disgrace." Randolph ordered a prosecution on September 18; see Randolph to Harrison, Sept. 18, 1794, and Randolph to Hammond, Sept. 20, 1794, op. cit. n.43. Harrison called on Greenleaf and demanded to know the author of the libel; see Greenleaf's *New York Journal*, Sept. 20, Sept. 24, Oct. 1, 1794; and an indictment issued in due course. Id., Jan. 3 and Apr. 11, 1795; *Aurora*, Jan. 23, 1795. The indictment, dated April 7, 1795, is preserved in the Archives of the judicial branch. Greenleaf, it says, was "in Contempt and open Violation of the Laws. . . and the Respect due to Embassadors and other Public Ministers to the evil example of all others in the like case offending and against the Peace of the United States and their Dignity." The "laws" offended against were not specified; cf. Act of Apr. 30, 1790, Sec. 28, 2 *Annals of Congress* (hereinafter *Annals*) at 2279, punishing physical attacks on ambassadors. The only trace of subsequent proceedings that has come to light is in Greenleaf's *Argus*, Oct. 30, 1795, where it is stated in passing that the prosecution had "ended in mere flatulency, with public contempt for both prosecutor [i.e., Hammond] and attorney [i.e., Harrison]." One would wish for more detail as to whether the case was dropped before or after trial, at whose behest, and why.

45. *Aurora*, Apr. 18, 1795, at 3.

46. Bell, op. cit. n.16, at 53, 145–47.

47. On Jefferson's secretiveness, see G. Wills, *The Founders' Virtues*, New York Review of Books, Nov. 11, 1976, at 24, 26, and references therein cited.

48. Bemis, op. cit. n.6, at 333–36.

49. Id. at 336–45, 354–60, 365–70.

50. Reardon, op. cit. n.18, at 286–87.

51. *Aurora,* Feb. 6 and 10, 1795.

52. Reardon, op. cit. n.18, at 288.

53. Id. at 288–89.

54. Id. at 288.

55. Word reached the United States by January 31, 1795, that a treaty of amity and commerce had been concluded; its leading features were known not long afterwards. See *Aurora*, Jan. 31, Feb. 2 and 10, 1795; *Philadelphia Independent Gazeteer*, Mar. 11, 1795; cf. Boston *Columbian Centinel*, May 30, 1795. For Federalist views, see *Providence, R.I., US Chronicle*, Mar. 26 and July 2, 1795; *Richmond & Manchester Advertiser*, July 2, 1795.

56. See *Philadelphia Independent Gazeteer*, Mar.–June 1795. ("Franklin" was probably Alexander J. Dallas; see Stewart, op. cit. n.2, at 194.) See also *Aurora*, Feb. 10 and Apr. 13, 1795; *Philadelphia Independent Gazeteer*, Mar. 11 and 18, 1795; Boston *Independent Chronicle*, Apr. 23 and May 11, 1795; Greenleaf's *Argus*, May 26, 1795.

57. Greenleaf's *Argus,* May 26, 1795; *Aurora,* Apr. 13, 1795. Cf. *Independent Chronicle*, Apr. 23, 1795; *Philadelphia Independent Gazeteer*, Mar. 11, 1795; Greenleaf's *New York Journal*, Jan. 7, 1795; *Aurora*, Feb. 10, 1795.

58. *Providence, R.I., US Chronicle*, July 2, 1795.

59. *Argus*, Aug. 7, 1795.

60. 4 *Annals* at 855; 1 *Executive Journal* at 178.

61. 1 *Executive Journal* at 179. Hayden, op. cit. n.7, at 75, states that the days between June 8 and June 12 were devoted entirely to a debate over secrecy. No reference is given, nor has any record of such a debate come to light.

62. 1 *Executive Journal* at 183.

63. Hayden, op. cit. n.7, at 81–82.

64. 1 *Executive Journal* at 186. The decisive vote of Gunn of Georgia was apparently secured after Hamilton undertook to secure a personal reward for that gentleman; see King, op. cit. n.3, Vol. 2 at 15.

65. In the final tally the vote was eighteen to nine for lifting the injunction; the nays were cast by Republicans opposing the decision to retain a ban on publication. 1 *Executive Journal* at 190; Hayden, op. cit. n.7, at 89.

66. Hayden, op. cit. n.7, at 90n.2.

67. Ibid.; King, op. cit. n.3, Vol. 2 at 11.

68. Hamilton to Wolcott, June 30, 1795, 18 *Works of Hamilton* (Syrett ed.) at 393; King, op. cit. n.3, Vol. 2 at 115.

69. Reardon, op. cit. n.18, at 296; Stewart, op. cit. n.2, at 198.

70. *Aurora*, July 7, 10, 16, 1795.

71. Article 1, sections 5 and 6 of the Constitution would not bar censure by the Senate, but members of Congress ostensibly would have at least as ample a right of free speech as is granted all citizens by the First Amendment. Thus the Howell censure episode of 1782 was not necessarily in point.

72. The rule adopted in 1800, see ch. 6, under "The Federalist Schism and the Electoral Remedy," was enforced in 1812 by a vote censuring Senator Pickering for reading "confidential" documents while the doors were open; see ch. 7, under "Afterword." But the rule of 1800 is not in force today; see ch. 6, n.169.

73. It is probably no coincidence that fresh praise for Mason reappeared in the opposition press as the Senate reconvened; see *Aurora*, Dec. 12, 1795; *Independent Chronicle*, Dec. 21, 1795.

74. One can only wonder what the Senate would have done, had it been privy to French documents indicating that Mason was paid $2,333 by a French Agent for divulging the treaty. See H. C. Rice, *James Swan: Agent of the French Republic, 1794-1796*, 10 New England Q. 464, 480–81. (1937). Earlier French attempts to learn of the negotiations through Monroe at Paris had not been rewarding, since Jay refused to confide in Monroe without express orders from Philadelphia. See Jay, op. cit. n.24, Vol. 4 at 156-59. In June 1794, with Washington's approval, Randolph showed Fauchet the clause in Jay's instructions that ruled out any commitment to Britain inconsistent with existing undertakings to France; see I. Brant, *Edmund Randolph, Not Guilty!* 7 William & Mary Q., 3d Series, 179, 191 (Apr. 1950). This was not enough to satisfy Fauchet, whose continuing efforts to discover and combat Jay's moves embroiled him in conflicts with the administration much like those in which Genêt had been involved. Fauchet's replacement by Adet in June 1795 was a welcome, if short-lived, relief to the administration; see Reardon, op. cit. n.18, at 293-94. It was Adet who claimed to have bought the

treaty from a senator. The story seems plausible, yet several scholars have dismissed it out of hand. See Swanstrom, op. cit. n.16, at 123n.; J. Charles, *The Origins of the American Party System* (Harper & Row 1956), at 105n.27. For present purposes the truth as to Mason's motives is more or less beside the point. Though unaware of Adet's remarks, the Federalist press was quick enough to impugn Mason's loyalty. Yet even if the publication was beneficial to France, the American people's right to know was also crucially involved. The Senate chose not to punish one who, candidly or not, invoked that principle in his defense.

75. Stewart, op. cit. n.2, at 200–203, 215f.; Charles, op. cit. n.74, at 82, 108–9; Chambers, op. cit. n.37, at 78.

76. *Independent Chronicle*, Aug. 3, 1795; Stewart, op. cit. n.2, at 209.

77. Hamilton, Jay, and King wrote a spirited defense of the treaty; in view of their official status, the contributions of the last two were kept secret. See King, op. cit. n.3, Vol. 2 at 12–13. On Federalist counter-demonstrations, see Id. at 16, 21.

78. Reardon, op. cit. n.18, at 304.

79. White, op. cit. n.5, at 100.

80. See, e.g., *Aurora,* Aug. 15 and 21, 1795; *Argus,* July 4, 1795; *Independent Chronicle*, July 30, 1795.

81. The decision was announced to the cabinet on August 12, and the signing took place August 18, 1795. Reardon, op. cit. n.18, at 309–10.

82. Id. at 301f.

83. Evident from Grenville to Hammond, Nos. 21 and 22, Nov. 20, 1794, in British Public Records Office (PRO), Series FO 115, Library of Congress.

84. Reardon, op. cit. n.18, at 310 n.41.

85. *Aurora*, Aug. 15 and 21, Sept. 22 and 28, 1795; *Independent Chronicle*, Sept. 24 and Dec. 7, 1795; *Argus*, Sept. 8 and 28, 1795; *Richmond & Manchester Advertiser*, Oct. 31, 1795.

86. According to one scholar, the best translation of Fauchet's "precieuses confessions" would be the relatively innocent phrase, "valuable disclosures." Brant, op. cit. n.74, at 193.

87. See Randolph to Washington, Mar. 26, 29, 31, Apr. 1, May 22, Oct. 20, 1794, Feb. 11, July 7, 1795, all in State Dep't Archives, op. cit. n.30; Randolph to Hamilton and Knox, Apr. 24, 1794 and Randolph to Washington, Apr. 9 and 19, 1794, all in Washington Mss., op. cit. n.4; and Randolph to Hammond, March 3, June 10, Oct. 7, 1794, all in State Dep't Domestic Letters, Vol. 7, National Archives.

88. White, op. cit. n.5, at 170.

89. Reardon, op. cit. n.18, at 307f.; Brant, op. cit. n.74; White, op. cit. n.5, at 170-71. A fascinating speculation revolves around Fauchet's identification of certain "flour merchants" as the intended recipients of the funds solicited by Randolph. Many have struggled to make sense of this reference, explaining the merchants' role in Randolph's plans by pointing to the prestige of such persons and their probable contacts with British counterparts; see Reardon, op. cit. at 329-30; Brant, op. cit. at 187, 196. Brant relates that Fauchet had recently gone to

Randolph for a list of persons from whom flour might be purchased for the French army; Id. at 197. Yet the purported power of these merchants to avert a civil war remains mysterious. To my knowledge no student of Randolph's ruin has made reference to Rice's discovery that the French government at about this time was operating a network of agents in the United States whose public activity was procuring supplies for the French army, but who were also engaged in more delicate covert tasks; op. cit. n.74. This suggests that Fauchet's "flour merchants" were in fact French secret agents and that Randolph, apparently without presidential approval, was working with them and had in fact helped Fauchet establish the network. Even if we make the most generous assumptions about Randolph's patriotism, the vagueness of his and Fauchet's memories about these doings is not surprising.

90. Stewart, op. cit. n.2, at 495.

91. Swanstrom, op. cit. n.16, at 133; *Independent Chronicle*, Oct. 29 and Dec. 21, 1795.

92. Anti-treaty stands were taken by governmental bodies in several southern states and by Massachusetts Governor Sam Adams, to mention a few, but the Republicans backed away from claiming that the treaty should be nullified by direct state intervention. See *Independent Chronicle,* Jan. 11 and 18, 1796; *Richmond & Manchester Advertiser*, Apr. 27, 1796.

93. *Aurora*, Aug. 16, 21, Sept. 9, 15, 22, 25, Oct. 22, 1795; *Independent Chronicle*, Aug. 3, Oct. 5, 26, 29, Nov. 16, Dec. 21, 1795.

94. *Independent Chronicle*, Jan. 4, 7, 11, 1796; Stewart, op. cit. n.2, at 223.

95. Articles 10 and 15; for text, see Bemis, op. cit. n.6, at 467, 472-73.

96. See *New Jersey Gazette*, Apr. 12, 1795; *Argus*, Oct. 1, 1796; *Mt. Pleasant & New Jersey Chronicle*, Apr. 16, 1796; *Richmond & Manchester Advertiser*, Apr. 27, 1796; C. G. Bowers, *Jefferson and Hamilton* (Houghton Mifflin 1925), at 295n.3; Swanstrom, op. cit. n.16, at 146; C. Warren, *The Supreme Court in United States History* (Little Brown 1922), Vol. 1 at 162, 166n.; 2 *Life & Correspondence of James Iredell* (McRee ed. 1858) at 435, 441, 474. All these dicta were vehemently pro-Federalist in thrust. After the Senate refused to confirm John Rutledge's appointment as chief justice, probably because of his public opposition to the treaty, it would have been a bold judge indeed who spoke out against it. These grand jury charges did not lead to any actual criminal proceedings, nor were they intended to; see Iredell, op. cit. at 435. However, they helped set a climate in which the prospect of criminal proceedings against opponents of administration policy became increasingly likely.

97. Swanstrom, op. cit. n.16, at 147. Not all the New Jerseyites felt this way; see Monroe to Madison, Feb. 8, 1794, 1 *Writings of Monroe* at 280.

98. Nothing has been uncovered to bolster the contention of some scholars that Madison actually wished the treaty adopted so he could use it as a campaign issue. Compare Bell, op. cit. n.16, at 55-57, 146-47, with Cunningham, op. cit. n.36, at 81-84 and Bowers, op. cit. n.96, at 295.

99. 5 *Annals* at 400, 423-26; Cunningham, op. cit. n.36, at 81.

100. See ch. 4, under "Foreign Crisis and the Politics of Executive Publicity."

101. That talks were in fact still taking place is evident from the fact that in May 1796 the president submitted to the Senate an explanatory article relating to travel and trade between the United States and Canada, which was duly ratified. Hayden, op. cit. n.7, at 91n.; 1 *Executive Journal* at 207.

102. 5 *Annals* at 437 (thirty-seven aye, forty-four nay). Madison blamed his defeat on the cynicism of certain Federalists who shared his legal viewpoint but for tactical reasons did not care to make the resolution less objectionable in form, see 2 *Writings of Madison* (Hunt ed. 1900) at 96. Yet the minority ultimately opposing Livingston's resolution was no greater than that which supported Madison's effort to soften it.

103. He had done so in his capacity as chairman of a House committee that was looking into the plight of impressed seamen—until the Senate revoked his permission; see 5 *Annals* at 628.

104. 5 *Annals* at 426; cf. Id. at 436 (Gallatin).

105. Id. at 628 (Livingston), 444 (Nicholas), 575 (Brent).

106. Id. at 601 (W. Lyman). The Federalists did not deny that in the case of actual impeachment, the House's right to papers would be unqualified; see Id. at 437, 461, 608.

107. Id. at 567 (Bourn).

108. Id. at 435. Rep. Heath went even further, perhaps overstating the case a bit. The call for papers, he avowed, was "founded upon a principle of publicity essentially necessary in this, our Republic, which has never been opposed, that I have either heard or read of, since the first organization or operation of this government." Id. at 448.

109. Id. at 533.

110. Id. at 460 (Harper). William Smith, Id. at 437, also alluded to the censure of David Howell by the old Congress; see ch. 2, under "Intellectual and Political Background"; yet how this could stand as a precedent for executive secrecy under a different Constitution is obscure.

111. 5 *Annals* at 656; cf. Id. at 437 (W. Smith), 460 (Harper).

112. Id. at 452.

113. The latter doctrine was expressly reaffirmed by the Fourth Congress on Dec. 14, 1795; Id. at 141.

114. Rep. Holland attempted to distinguish the powers of the House respecting commercial treaties from its powers respecting treaties of peace and alliance; Id. at 546. His argument had historical roots; as early as 1788 an expounder of the Constitution had contended that, unlike treaties of peace and alliance, commercial ones would require legislative approval, since these were more apt to interfere with existing laws and to impinge directly on the rights of citizens, while less apt to require secrecy. Able constitutional lawyers, including Randolph, continued to hold this view; see Id. at 581; *Aurora*, Aug. 16, 1795; *Independent Chronicle*, Jan. 25, 1796. Yet Rep. Holland attracted no support in the House. The point was lacking in a textual anchor; moreover, if the House's commerce powers could be claimed to give it a voice on commercial treaties, its war powers could with equal logic be invoked for a role in peace treaties as well. Cf. Tracy's remarks on the war power

at 5 *Annals* 608. The Federalists insisted that the treaty was already the law of the land and that the faith of the nation was pledged to carry it out; the House had no right to undo what the president and Senate had done. This was the line Hamilton had taken in his "Camillus" essays; see King, op. cit. n.3, Vol. 2 at 12–13.

115. 5 *Annals* at 628f. On the "precedents," see also Id. at 449 (Swanwick), 565 (Brent), 601 (Lyman), 622 (S. Smith).

116. Id. at 649 (Williams) and 437 (W. Smith).

117. Bell, op. cit. n.16, at 146; Swanstrom, op. cit. n.16, at 141.

118. 5 *Annals* at 759.

119. Bell, op. cit. n.16, at 56, 146.

120. The entire series is in Washington Mss., Series 4, Reel 109, Library of Congress. Hamilton's letters are in his published correspondence.

121. Lee succeeded William Bradford, who died in December 1795.

122. Lee to Washington, Mar. 26, 1796, op. cit. n.120; see also separate memo, probably of Mar. 29, Ibid.

123. Separate memo, dated Mar. 29, Ibid.

124. McHenry to Washington, Mar. 26, 1796, Ibid.

125. Ibid.

126. Wolcott to Washington, Mar. 26, 1796, Ibid.

127. Ibid.

128. Pickering to Washington, probably Mar. 29, 1796, Ibid. Pickering's correction of his language is interesting. Washington's final version read, "all the papers affecting the negotiation."

129. Pickering to Washington, separate memo, Mar. 29, 1796. Ibid. (emphasis in original).

130. Ibid.

131. The Republicans had not dared to rely upon the war powers of Congress as a basis for the resolution, since they were neither eager to declare war nor politically in a position to pass such a measure. The only reference to the war power in the debate was a taunt by the Federalist Tracy; see 5 *Annals* at 608.

132. 20 *Papers of Hamilton* (Syrett ed.) at 68–69.

133. Id. at 81–83 (emphasis in original).

134. Id. at 83.

135. Hamilton to Washington, Mar. 29, 1796, Id. at 87–89. The sequence of ideas has been rearranged to aid clarity of presentation.

136. Ibid.

137. Ibid.

138. Ibid.

139. 5 *Annals* at 759.

140. See ch. 2, under "The Secrecy of the Convention."

141. Washington to Hamilton, Mar. 31, 1796, Washington Mss., op. cit. n. 120; 35 *Writings of Washington* (Fitzpatrick ed. 1940) at 6.

142. 20 *Papers of Hamilton* (Syrett ed.) at 106.

143. Letter of Apr. 19, 1796, 2 *Letters of John Adams* (Adams ed. 1841) at 222. Adams wrote on March 19 that he expected the president to comply; Id. at 212.

144. Iredell, op. cit. n.96, Vol. 2 at 466.

145. Letter of Apr. 18, 1796, 2 *Writings of Madison* (Hunt ed.) at 96; see also Letter to Jefferson, Apr. 4, 1796, Id. at 90.

146. Id. at 90; Cunningham, op. cit. n.36, at 82–83; cf. Bell, op. cit. n.16, at 55.

147. 5 *Annals* at 771.

148. Id. at 772f.

149. Id. at 782–83; Charles, op. cit. n.74, at 110.

150. 5 *Annals* at 969. For Madison's supporting remarks, see Id. at 970.

151. Madison to Jefferson, Apr. 18, 1796, 2 *Writings of Madison* (Hunt ed.) at 95.

152. Madison to Jefferson, Apr. 23, 1796; Id. at 98.

153. A powerful speech by Fisher Ames on this subject was credited by contemporaries as having persuaded some undecided members to support the appropriations. The speech is at 5 *Annals* 1248; on its impact, see Bowers, op. cit. n.96, at 301; Stewart, op. cit. n.2, at 229; Cunningham, op. cit. n.36, at 83–84. A close study of certain key members and their constituency pressures is in Bell, op. cit. n.16, at 147–49; cf. Charles, op. cit. n.74, at 111–15.

154. Hamilton to King, Apr. 15, 1796, 20 *Papers of Hamilton* (Syrett ed.) at 112; Swanstrom, op. cit. n.16, at 143. Hamilton disapproved of this plan; he wrote, "Let us be *right*, because to do right is intrinsically proper, and I verily believe it is the best means of securing final success. Let our adversaries have the whole glory of sacrificing the interests of the nation." 20 *Papers of Hamilton* (Syrett ed.) at 115. Hamilton also lamented the administration's failure to transmit to Congress a certain relevant communication lately received from Britain. See Letters of Apr. 15, 18, 20, Id. at 113n.4, 115, 123, 131.

155. See entry of Mar. 1, 1798, 1 *Writings of Jefferson* (Lipscomb ed. 1903) at 422.

156. 2 *Writings of Madison* (Hunt ed.) at 98, 99, 101.

157. 5 *Annals* at 1280, 1289-91. Muhlenberg was read out of the party for his role in these events; see Charles, op. cit. n.74, at 117; Chambers, op. cit. n.37, at 89. After the defeat of the "highly objectionable" tag, a milder one was proposed that simply declared the treaty "objectionable." This attempt was defeated by a vote of fifty to forty-nine. One absent member later recorded his disposition to vote "no" on the final roll call.

158. Letter to Jefferson, May 1, 1796, 2 *Writings of Madison* (Hunt ed.) at 99; Letter to Monroe, May 14, 1796, Id. at 101.

159. See Bell, op. cit. n.16, at 147–49 for analysis of the defecting Republicans' motives. Bell, however, believes that Madison had always intended to let the treaty pass.

160. One interesting point they contributed was that British and French authorities, far from relying on the supposed power of the president and Senate to make treaties without the House's consent, had given indications of believing that such consent was necessary. *Independent Chronicle*, Apr. 14, 1796. After all, this requirement of legislative assent to treaties was one feature the British and French constitutions had in common. Could it be that the United States was backward in

this respect? Ibid; Norfolk, Va., *American Gazette and General Advertiser*, Apr. 22, 1796.

161. *Independent Chronicle*, Jan. 21, Apr. 11, 25, 1796; *Richmond & Manchester Advertiser*, Apr. 27, 1796.

162. Stewart, op. cit. n.2, at 224–28; Charles, op. cit. n.74, at 117–24.

Chapter 6

1. W. Chambers, *Political Parties in a New Nation* (Oxford University Press 1963), at 113.

2. J. Charles, *The Origins of the American Party System* (Harper & Row 1956), at 89–90, 117; Chambers, op. cit. n.1, at 93, 116.

3. Charles, op. cit. n.2, at 124; Chambers, op. cit. n.1, at 119.

4. See Chambers, op. cit. n.1, at 120–21 for analysis of the elections along these lines.

5. The complexion of both houses was strongly affected by a wave of voluntary retirements, including Madison in the House and many leading Federalists in the Senate. See Chambers, op. cit. n.1, at 132; R. Swanstrom, *The Senate, 1787-1801* (US GPO, Sen. Doc. No. 64, 1962), at 276. See R. M. Bell, *Party and Faction in American Politics: The House of Representatives, 1789-1801* (Greenwood 1973), at 256–57 and Charles, op. cit. n.2, at 94 for two provocatively different tabulations of the election outcome. Charles gives the Republicans a one-vote majority; Bell gives the Federalists an eleven-vote lead in the House.

6. See, e.g., State Dep't Domestic Letters, Vol. 10, entries of Sept. 14, Nov. 10, Dec. 27 and 28, 1797, Jan. 18 and Feb. 9, 1798, National Archives; 6 *Annals* of Congress (hereinafter *Annals)* 1914, 2235, 2320; 7 *Annals* 440, 447, 458. For an instance where the Senate declined to make certain documents public, see 1 *Executive Journal of the Senate* (hereinafter *Executive Journal)* at 222; cf. n.80 for the later publication of these.

7. Monroe had been kept largely in the dark about Jay's negotiations. Indeed, some Federalists were secretly preparing for war with France from the moment Jay's Treaty survived its ordeal in the House. In June 1796 Hamilton was promoting the plan of developing a fleet to be financed by secret loans and to be used ostensibly against Algiers but actually against France. See Charles, op. cit. n.2, at 123.

8. Washington to Pickering, State Dep't Archives, Presidential Correspondence, RG59, Reel M570, National Archives.

9. Pickering to Washington, July 1, 1796, op. cit. n.8.

10. Ibid., entry of July 2, 1796; Charles, op. cit. n.2, at 124 n.78.

11. Washington to Pickering, July 8, 1796, op. cit. n.8.

12. L. D. White, *The Federalists* (Macmillan 1948), at 273f; 1 *Works of John Adams* (Adams ed. 1850) at 520.

13. Charles, op. cit. n.2, at 127; G. Gibbs, *Memoirs of the Administrations of*

Washington and John Adams (the Wolcott Papers) (Van Norden 1846), Vol. 1 at 530; *Life and Correspondence of James McHenry* (Steiner ed. 1907), at 283; State Dep't Domestic Letters, op. cit. n.6, entry of Sept. 14, 1797.

14. Chase to McHenry, Dec. 4, 1796, in McHenry, op. cit. n.13, at 203.

15. Id. at 189–90, 201, 202. Pickering denounced Adet for publishing his letter, but it was Pickering who first went public. See H. J. Ford, *Timothy Pickering*, in S. F. Bemis, ed., *American Secretaries of State and their Diplomacy* (Knopf 1927), Vol. 2 at 200–204.

16. Messages of May 19, June 13, June 22, July 3, 1797, at 7 *Annals* 64, 357, 440; 9 *Annals* 3057, 3082, 3097, 3115, 3127.

17. For text, see 9 *Annals* 3154.

18. Pickering to Yrujo, July 24, 1797, printed at 9 *Annals* 3199. Cf. his earlier protest to Adet, at 6 *Annals* 2768.

19. Pickering Letters of Aug. 26, 30, Sept. 5, 21, Oct. 19, Nov. 10, 1797, State Dep't Domestic Letters, op. cit. n.6; Pickering to McHenry, Oct. 19, 1797, in McHenry, op. cit. n.13, at 269–70.

20. Domestic Letters, op. cit. n.6, entry of Feb. 13, 1798.

21. Ibid., entry of Oct. 19, 1797.

22. Gibbs, op. cit. n.13, Vol. 1 at 502; Ford, op. cit. n.15, at 199f.; Charles op. cit. n.2, at 124.

23. Gibbs, op. cit. n.13, Vol. 1 at 481, 500, 530. Hamilton approved of the plan; see White, op. cit. n.12, at 242f.; Charles, op. cit. n.2, at 125f.

24. Gibbs, op. cit. n.13, Vol. 1 at 516; R. Hayden, *The Senate and Treaties, 1789-1817* (Da Capo 1970), at 38–39, 51–52.

25. Gibbs, op. cit. n.13, Vol. 1 at 516.

26. Swanstrom, op. cit. n.5, at 123.

27. 9 *Annals* at 3096.

28. Ford, op. cit. n.15, at 217; but cf. Charles, op. cit. n.2, at 127.

29. Gibbs, op. cit. n.13, Vol. 2 at 14.

30. 8 *Works of Adams* (Adams ed.) at 568.

31. Id. at 568n.

32. Ibid.

33. 1 *Works of Adams* (Adams ed.) at 518.

34. Charles, op. cit. n.2, at 126.

35. 21 *Papers of Hamilton* (Syrett ed.) at 368.

36. Id. at 378.

37. Id. at 371–73.

38. Domestic Letters, op. cit. n.6, Pickering to Ellicott.

39. *Aurora,* March 27, 1798, at 3.

40. *Aurora*, March 31, 1798, at 2.

41. 7 *Annals* 525; 2 *Life and Correspondence of Rufus King* (King ed. 1894) at 311.

42. 8 *Annals* 1358.

43. Ibid.

44. Bell, op. cit. n.5, at 170; see also M. Dauer, *The Adams Federalists* (Johns

Hopkins University Press 1953), at 141–42; 1 *Works of Adams* (Adams ed.) at 518; 8 *Writings of Jefferson* (Ford ed.) at 397.

45. 8 *Annals* 1358.

46. Ibid.

47. Id. at 1358-59.

48. Id. at 1359-60.

49. Id. at 1360.

50. Id. at 1319.

51. Id. at 1361.

52. Id. at 1363.

53. Id. at 1365.

54. Ibid.; cf. remarks of Rutledge, Ibid.

55. This is not to say that all Federalists were in the know; some who supported the call may have done so out of principle and not because they knew what the papers contained. However, Allen's conduct, in view of his positions on other issues, must have put the opposition on alert. See Bell, op. cit. n.5, at 170; *Aurora*, Apr. 7 and 13, 1798; and see nn. 69 and 152.

56. 8 *Annals* 1368.

57. Ibid.

58. Id. at 1368-69.

59. Id. at 1369.

60. Ibid.

61. Ibid.

62. Id. at 1370.

63. Id. at 1371.

64. Ibid.

65. Compare Id. at 1359 (Livingston), 1365 (Sewall), and 1369 (Harper) with Id. at 1370 (Otis). Livingston offered the war power argument as a reason for striking the secrecy proviso; yet later he seemingly conceded that the president had a residual power to withhold all the same; Id. at 1365. Sewall said the war power would give the House a right "to demand every fact"; yet he voted against the call for papers. Harper said it was the war power that made *any* call proper in the present case.

66. Compare remarks of Smith, Giles, Livingston, Baldwin, Gallatin, Livingston, and Nicholas, Id. at 1358, 1359, 1361, 1363, 1365, 1368, 1371.

67. Id. at 1365 (Sewall, though he voted against the call); 1368 (Allen); 1369 (Harper).

68. 8 *Writings of Jefferson* (Ford ed.) at 397.

69. Those who voted no were almost silent in the debate, while those in favor contended for their various specific approaches. The remarks of Sewall, 8 *Annals* 1365, and Otis, Id. at 1370, did not address themselves to formal details. Only Hartley, Id. at 1369, can be charged on this record with having felt strongly on the point of a qualified versus an unqualified call; yet Hartley had voted against Livingston's 1796 resolution even though it was qualified.

Based on Bell's table of party affiliation, op. cit. n.5, at 255–57, and on a comparison of the roll calls at 5 *Annals* 759 and 8 *Annals* 1371, it appears that twenty-one Federalists and twenty-seven Republicans were present for the votes on both the 1796 and the present call for papers. (One member, N. Freeman, had switched parties in the meantime, see Bell at 173, 255-57. He opposed Livingston's resolution but supported the XYZ call. The William Smith of Charleston, see Bell at 257, who voted in 1796 was no longer in the House in April 1798; it was William Smith of Pinckney who participated on the latter occasion.)

All twenty-seven Republicans supported both calls for papers. Fifteen Federalists opposed both calls. Three—Dent of Maryland, Parker of Virginia, and Grove of North Carolina—supported both calls, possibly out of constitutional conviction. Three Federalists who had opposed Livingston's resolution now supported the XYZ call: Wadsworth of Massachusetts, Harper of South Carolina, and Williams of New York. A fourth changeling, Freeman of Massachusetts, was no longer a Federalist. In the cases of Williams and Wadsworth, at least, there are fair grounds for asserting that legalistic reasoning was not the basis for the shift. See Bell at 154, 170; Harper's speech at 8 *Annals* 1369; personal communication from Bell to myself; and n.152.

70. 8 *Annals* at 1374.

71. For Washington's message, see ch. 5, under "Defiance and Legal Impasse."

72. See ch. 5, under "Defiance and Legal Impasse."

73. Ibid. Pickering's draft message stated flatly: "The Resolution of the House now before me, contains a demand for *all* the papers with respect to *past* negotiations. . . while it exhibits no reason, no object, by which I may judge of the propriety of a compliance: and therefore I cannot comply, without establishing a dangerous precedent." Washington Mss., Series 4, Reel 109, Library of Congress. Adams could have said the same.

74. Evident from comparison of the printed, censored version, 9 *Annals* 3322–67, with the original, Dispatches from Foreign Ministers, France, M34, Roll 8 National Archives.

75. Gibbs, op. cit. n.13, Vol. 2 at 39; Pickering to Hamilton, 21 *Papers of Hamilton* (Syrett ed.) at 378.

76. Troup to King, in King, op. cit. n.41, Vol. 2 at 328. The Senate's action is reported, without roll call, at 7 *Annals* 525, 535-36.

77. King, op. cit. n.41, Vol. 2 at 312–13.

78. 8 *Annals* 1377–79. The vote is not officially reported, but was given by Jefferson as seventy-five to twenty-four; 8 *Writings of Jefferson* (Ford ed.) 397; and by the *Aurora* as seventy-five to twenty-three; Apr. 6, 1798.

79. 8 *Annals* 1384, 1393. On the greater sensitivity of the instructions, see Id. at 1359 (Bayard), 1360 (Allen), 1369 (Hartley); cf. Id. at 1393 (Nicholas). It may be that the House thought the instructions were, even more than the dispatches, for the Senate to dispose of, but this was not made explicit. See A. Sofaer, *War, Foreign Affairs, and Constitutional Power: The Origins* (Ballinger 1976), at 254, 358 n.602 for later precedents.

80. A supporting example is the publishing of Pinckney's instructions; see Ford, op. cit. n.15, at 205-6; and see n.6. A possible counter-example would be the actions of the two houses in response to Kentucky's demands for information; see ch. 4, under "Foreign Crisis and the Politics of Executive Publicity." It is uncertain,

however, what action the House actually took in that case or at what time they may have acted.

81. Of the three House and two Senate votes on publishing the dispatches and the instructions, a roll call is available only for the Senate's sixteen to ten decision to print the instructions. This vote involved a "strange bedfellows" alignment— Yea: twelve Federalists and four Republicans; Nay: five Federalists and five Republicans—that was predictable neither from party status nor from the usual constitutional rhetoric. Compare, e.g., the roll calls at ch. 3, under "Confidentiality and Executive Privilege," ch. 4, under "The Opening of the Senate's Doors," ch. 5, under "Defiance and Legal Impasse," and ch. 6, under "The XYZ Affair."

82. 21 *Papers of Hamilton* (Syrett ed.) at 397; for the impact, see Gibbs, op. cit. n.13, Vol. 2 at 44-45.

83. Domestic Letters, op. cit. n.6, Letter to Ellicott.

84. 8 *Annals* 1973.

85. Domestic Letters, op. cit. n.6, entry of Aug. 2, 1798. The record of Pickering's correspondence between July 24 and September 7 is replete with reference to this subject, to the virtual exclusion of other business.

86. D. H. Stewart, *The Opposition Press of the Federalist Period* (State University of New York Press 1969), at 293f., 313, 515, 611; *Aurora*, Apr. 7, 13 and 14, 1798; J. M. Smith, *Freedom's Fetters* (Cornell University Press 1956), at 192-93; C. G. Bowers, *Jefferson and Hamilton* (Houghton Mifflin 1925), at 366-76.

87. Domestic Letters, op. cit. n.6, entries of Aug. 18 and Sept. 7, 1798; Stewart, op. cit. n.86, at 298; Charles, op. cit. n.2, at 127 n.88.

88. 8 *Annals* 2083-86, 2127.

89. On the congressional scene, see Bell, op. cit. n.5, at 165-75; N. E. Cunningham, *The Jeffersonian Republicans* (University of North Carolina Press 1963), at 126. The alien laws had little to do with secrecy issues, though in one curious episode Pickering did use a threat of deportation thereunder to induce a French ex-consul to surrender the key to his cypher. See Domestic Letters, op. cit. n.6, entries of Apr. 12, May 30, June 5 and 18, 1799.

90. Letters of Apr. 5 and 6, 8 *Writings of Jefferson* (Ford ed.) 397, 401. Jefferson had not always been so circumspect; his letters became more reticent after the disastrous leak of his letter to Mazzei. See Cunningham, op. cit. n.89, at 118f.

91. Letters to Jefferson, Apr. 2, 22, 29, 1798, 2 *Letters and Other Writings of Madison* (Cong. ed.) at 131-34, 137-38.

92. Letters of May 5, 13, Id. at 139-40.

93. Printed at 9 *Annals* 3425. Talleyrand also reproached the United States government for doing nothing to suppress the torrent of abuse against France in the American press. To this the envoys replied,

Among those principles deemed sacred in America; among those sacred rights considered as forming the bulwark of liberty, which the Government contemplates with awful reverence, and would approach only with the most cautious circumspection, there is no one of which the importance is more deeply impressed on the public mind than the liberty of the press. . . .However desirable those measures might be which might correct without enslaving the press, they have never yet been devised in America. No regulations exist which enable the Government to suppress whatever calumnies and invectives any individual may choose to offer to the public eye; or to punish such calumnies and invectives, otherwise than by a legal prosecution in courts which are alike open to all who consider themselves as injured. Without doubt this abuse of a valuable privilege is a matter of peculiar regret when it is extended to the Government of a foreign nation. . . .It is a calamity incident to the nature of liberty, and which can produce no serious evil to France.

This spendid defense of a free press, printed at 9 *Annals* 3449, formed an ironic contrast to the legislative program set afoot by the publication of Talleyrand's letter.

Gerry actually tried to hold separate talks with Talleyrand after his associates departed; see 9 *Annals* at 3484, 3519. For this, he suffered strenuous criticism; see Domestic Letters, op. cit. n.6, entries of Sept. 4 and 21, 1798 (Pickering); Gibbs, op. cit. n.13, Vol. 2 at 33–37, 124–60 (Wolcott); *Life and Correspondence of Iredell* (McRee ed. 1855), Vol. 2 at 531. In January 1799, Pickering drafted a report to Congress on French relations which took Gerry sternly to task. Adams deleted this language, but Pickering privately circulated the unexpurgated version. Gibbs, Vol. 2 at 180; 37 *Writings of Washington* (Fitzpatrick ed.) at 126; 8 *Works of Adams* (Adams ed.) at 621f.; Ford, op. cit. n.15, at 230.

94. *Aurora*, June 16, 1798.

95. 8 *Annals* 1972; Smith, op. cit. n.86, at 193.

96. *Aurora,* June 19 and 21, 1798. Bache's source has never been identified. His biographer says it was probably Jefferson, but supplies no supporting argument, nor does he show that the vice-president had access to dispatches before they were given to the Senate. B. Faÿ, *Two Franklins* (Little Brown 1933), at 347-48.

97. The whole story appears in *Aurora*, June 21-25, 1798; see also Greenleaf's *New York Journal*, June 22, 23 and 27, 1798; Boston *Independent Chronicle*, June 25-28, 1798. A patriotic American traveler, entrusted with the packet, saw fit to turn it in and to publicize the fact. Other, similar packets were addressed to Randolph, Monroe, Baldwin, Genêt, and perhaps Jefferson, all targets of cabinet surveillance. Gibbs, op. cit. n.13, Vol. 2 at 68; Smith op. cit. n.86, at 193–95.

No opinion from this period on the legality of mail seizures has come to light. Certainly there was no law to authorize it, but the practice was not entirely novel. The old Congress had authorized mail searches by resolutions of September 17, 1785 and October 23, 1786; see 1 *Secret Journals of Congress, 1781-1787* at 266, 270. Apparently by mid-1798 the practice was again commonplace; see Charles, op. cit. n.2, at 124n.; Faÿ, op. cit. n.96, at 319; Bowers, op. cit. n.86, at 373; Cunningham, op. cit. n.89, at 138–39; Smith, op. cit. n.86, at 164n.; Stewart, op. cit. n.86, at 464. It is open to conjecture whether Pickering surrendered the packet to Bache unopened because he recognized that the law was not with him, or whether he simply calculated that Bache would be obliged to make the contents public voluntarily.

98. The indictment itself seems to be lost. According to all reports, Bache was charged with libeling the president and cabinet in "sundry publications and republications." See Smith, op. cit. n.86, at 189–203; J. C. Miller, *Crisis in Freedom: The Alien and Sedition Acts* (Little Brown 1951), at 63–65; Stewart, op. cit. n.86, at 305–6.

99. See also ch. 5, under "Domestic Turmoil and Executive Power."

100. Correspondence of the Attorneys General, entry of Sept. 17, 1794, National Archives.

101. Randolph to Harrison, Domestic Letters, op. cit. n.6, Vol. 7, entry of Sept. 18, 1794; United States v. Greenleaf, RG21, District Courts of the United States, Apr. 7, 1795, National Archives.

102. But cf. Act of Apr. 30, 1790, Sec. 2 *Annals* 2279, Punishing physical assaults on foreign ministers.

103. Greenleaf's *Argus*, Oct. 30, 1795.

104. *Porcupine's Gazette*, July 14, 15, and 19, 1797.

105. Op. cit. n.100, entry of July 27, 1797.

106. For more on Cobbett, see G. Hildreth, *History of the United States* (Harper & Cross 1880), Vol. 5 at 164–73; F. Wharton, *State Trials of the United States in the Administrations of Washington and John Adams* (Carey & Hart 1849), at 23–24, 322f.; Miller, op. cit. n.98, at 66n.; Ford, op. cit. n.15, at 221–26. Republicans hardly leapt to the defense of Cobbett's constitutional rights; see Boston *Independent Chronicle*, July 27, 1797.

107. One writer defended Yrujo on the ground that he was entitled to reply publicly to Pickering's published charges against him; Cobbett retorted that the government was within its rights to publish its accusations against Spain, but that Yrujo's reply was nevertheless a "crime": "Every man has a right to instruct, advise and correct his own family. . . but, if an impertinent stranger. . . should interfere, audaciously oppose his advice to that of the father, and moreover, contradict and calumniate him, . . . would not such an insolent scoundrel deserve to be kicked into the street?" *Porcupine's Gazette*, July 19, 1797.

108. Domestic Letters, op. cit. n.6, entry of July 24, 1797.

109. Op. cit. n.100, separate memo of July 27, 1797.

110. On Randolph's vindication, see J. J. Reardon, *Edmund Randolph* (Macmillan 1974) at 316, 318, 321-22, 332-34. On the Monroe episode, see Ford, op. cit. n.15, at 227; Hildreth, op. cit. n.106, at 98–102; Gibbs, op. cit. n.13, Vol. 2 at 9, 12, 55; Boston *Independent Chronicle*, Jan. 4-8 and Jan. 29–Feb. 1, 1798; Stewart, op. cit. n.86, at 284; McHenry, op. cit. n.13, at 298; Iredell, op. cit. n.93, Vol. 2 at 516.

111. On the British and colonial precedents, see J. R. Wiggins, *Freedom or Secrecy* (Oxford University Press 1964), at 3–10.

112. 8 *Annals* 1312; 3 *Journal of the House of Representatives* 239; *Aurora*, Mar. 31, 1798. The *Annals* wrongly identify Kittera as from New Jersey.

113. Careful search has failed to uncover any trace of a committee report. The referral to committee had passed by only a thirty-nine to thirty-seven vote in the first place. The proposal was pretty clearly a slap at Monroe, and perhaps the

Federalists were content to make the gesture of introducing it and then let the matter lie.

114. *Aurora*, June 27, 1798. He was also prepared to argue that the prosecution infringed the liberty of the press.

115. The government had not been consistent over the years on the existence of common-law or nonstatutory crimes. In 1793 in Henfield's case, the administration had insisted that a prosecution could be founded directly on the president's Proclamation of Neutrality without the need for supporting legislation. Henfield was indicted for enlisting aboard a French privateer and taking up arms against Great Britain, "in violation of treaties and the supreme law of the land." The judges upheld the charge, but the jury acquitted. Wharton, op. cit. n.106, at 199. In 1794, Justice Iredell charged a grand jury that even the Proclamation was not legally crucial, as a duty of citizens to respect their country's neutrality arose directly from the law of nations and the common-law. Iredell, op. cit. n.93, Vol. 2 at 423, 467.

On the other hand, in 1794 the attorney general had ruled that rioting in front of a foreign consul's home was no crime, because the act of 1790, strictly construed, protected only higher ranking officials against such injury. Op. cit. n.100, entries of Feb. 20 and July 2, 1794. Moreover, in his opinion on Cobbett's libel case, the attorney general had noted with approval the Supreme Court's 1796 decision that "the judicial power of the United States" was confined to cases where jurisdiction was explicitly vested in the courts by statute. Curiously, he drew the conclusion that the Supreme Court would not have original jurisdiction over the present case, but failed to consider the possibility that the circuit court would not have jurisdiction either.

By 1798 several justices of the Supreme Court had had occasion to rule directly on the existence of federal common-law crimes, and their opinions were not unanimous. Wharton, op. cit. n.106, at 38, 44. At least two other common-law libel prosecutions were started at roughly the same time as Bache's; both produced convictions. Smith, op. cit. n.86, at 181–82; Miller, op. cit. n.98, at 65–66; Domestic Letters, op. cit. n.6, entries of June 28 and July 7, 1798. Yet the issue was not authoritatively settled until 1812; see ch. 7, under "Afterword"; and the continuing uncertainty about it was plainly a major factor in the passage of the Sedition Law; see Miller, op. cit., at 66; Stewart, op. cit. n.86, at 467.

116. A milder bill had been introduced in the House as early as June 4 (see 8 *Annals* 1868), but this was laid aside in favor of the Senate's bill after the events recited. The Senate vote on final passage was eighteen to six, one Federalist voting no; see 7 *Annals* 599. For more on the legislative history, see Smith, op. cit. n.86, at 100-143; Miller, op. cit. n.98, at 67-70. For the attitudes of Hamilton and other leaders, see Miller, op. cit., at 71-73, 182; Smith, op. cit., at 109, 151-53, 181; Gibbs, op. cit. n.13, Vol. 2 at 78; M. Smelser, *George Washington and the Alien & Sedition Acts*, 59 Am. Hist. Rev. 322 (Jan. 1954).

117. 8 *Annals* 2093f.

118. Another provocation was Dr. George Logan's self-appointed peace mission, which prompted the Logan Act of 1799, still in force today. Smith, op.

cit. n.86, at 58, 101-7. Miller, op. cit. n.98, at 63-64, stresses the influence of Bache's leak on enactment of the Sedition Law.

119. See remarks at 8 *Annals* 2093-2100 (Allen), 2103f. (Harper); Smith, op. cit. n.86, at 118-25; Miller, op. cit. n.98, at 59.

This theory was not new. As Gouverneur Morris had reminded Washington years before, Pitt in England had used a fifth-column theory to outlaw his opposition in wartime. In May 1797, a grand jury in Virginia returned on its own initiative a presentment, marking "as a real evil the circular letters of several members of the late Congress, and particularly. . . Samuel J. Cabell, endeavouring at a time of real public danger to disseminate unfounded calumnies against the happy government of the United States, and thereby to separate the people therefrom, and to increase or produce a foreign influence ruinous to the peace, happiness, and independence of these United States." Although no further action was taken, this presentment and the court's tacit acceptance thereof touched off a violent storm of Republican criticism. Federalists were defiant; Governor Davie of North Carolina retorted that "surely the greatest evil with which we were threatened at the present alarming crisis, was the disorganizing effect of the correspondence of certain members of Congress, the baneful influence of which is visible in every part of the Southern States." Iredell, op. cit. n.93, Vol. 2 at 510-15; Smith, op. cit. n.86, at 183. On another occasion Pickering proposed to prosecute John Clopton, a Virginia representative running for reelection, for an alleged libel of the president in a private letter that found its way into a newspaper. Clopton lost his seat to John Marshall and the idea of court action was dropped; see Smith, op. cit., at 183.

120. 8 *Annals* 2171. According to Bell's table of party affiliation, op. cit. n.5 at 256-57, the ayes included forty-three Federalists and one Republican, Tillinghast of Rhode Island; the nays included thirty-eight Republicans and three Federalists—Bullock of Massachusetts and Dent and Matthews of Maryland. Note that Tillinghast was also the lone "Republican" to oppose the call for the XYZ papers, while Dent and Matthews both supported that measure. The party status of these three being highly doubtful—see also Bell at 166—there can be little hesitation in identifying this vote as a strictly partisan one.

121. Wharton, op. cit. n.106, is richly documented. Good modern treatments are Smith, op. cit. n.86; and Miller, op. cit. n.98. See also Bowers, op. cit. n.86; and L. W. Levy, *Jefferson and Civil Liberties* (Quadrangle 1963) for briefer treatments. For the Federalist side of the story, see Gibbs, op. cit. n.13; and Hildreth, op. cit. n.106.

122. In addition to sedition trials, I would cite the violation of mail privacy, see n.97 above; the threat of deportation against journalists of foreign extraction, see Smith, op. cit. n.86, at 174, 181-82; Domestic Letters, op. cit. n.6, entries of July 7, 1798, Jan. 1 and May 22, 1799; Bowers, op. cit. n.86, at 405; interferences with reporting of the debates in Congress, see ch. 7, n.38, and episodes of personal violence which, if not demonstrably instigated or condoned by the government, were not convincingly condemned either; see Bowers, op. cit., at 368-71, 383-84.

123. Matthew Lyon of Vermont was an early and notorious victim of the Sedition Law, having been a target of unsuccessful Federalist efforts to expel him from the

House. Reelected while in prison, he resumed his seat in the Sixth Congress. Smith, op. cit. n.86, at 229; Wharton, op. cit. n.106, at 333; Stewart, op. cit. n.86, at 471.

124. Smith, op. cit. n.86, at 342. A court action was inconsistent with the First Amendment even under the narrow Federalist view of that provision; the technique employed here was informal.

125. For talk of deporting Gallatin under the Alien Law, see Smith, op. cit. n.86, at 26. For talk of indicting Jefferson for sedition, see Miller, op. cit. n.98, at 133. Perhaps the Republicans' fears were a bit exaggerated, but so were those of the Federalists. See, e.g., Bowers, op. cit. n.86, at 368-71.

126. Wolcott blamed the rebellion on seditious publications, and Pickering deplored the president's leniency. See Gibbs, op. cit. n.13, Vol. 2 at 305, 361.

127. Smith, op. cit. n.86, at 185; Wharton, op. cit. n.106, passim; Bowers, op. cit. n.86, at 404. Some of the defense efforts are recounted in Gibbs, op. cit. n.13, Vol. 2 at 293; Smith, op. cit., at 344; Cunningham, op. cit. n.89, at 169-72; Stewart, op. cit. n.86, at 10 n.26.

128. Indeed, the Republican press was apparently stronger in 1800 than it had been in 1796. Miller, op. cit. n.98, at 221-22; Chambers, op. cit. n.1, at 150-51.

129. Smith, op. cit. n.86, at 282-88; Miller, op. cit. n.98, at 196. The official was Tench Coxe, who had passed information to the opposition while serving at the Treasury, but did not surface until Duane's indictment. See L. K. Caldwell, *The Administrative Theories of Hamilton & Jefferson* (Russell & Russell 1964), at 91; Gibbs, op. cit. n.13, Vol. 2 at 55; White, op. cit. n.12, at 288; Stewart, op. cit. n.86, at 269-70, 485, 546; *Aurora*, Oct. 6, 1800.

130. Smith, op. cit. n.86, at 301 n.75; *Aurora*, May 13, 1800. The Briton's letters had come to light through the arrest and search of a suspected horse thief who turned out to be a courier. The arresting officer had enjoyed reading the letters and made them available to Duane; legal proceedings against the officer foundered on the argument that his search was a lawful act. That the publication was not culpable went without saying. See 8 *Works of Adams* (Adams ed.) at 668; Wharton, op. cit. n.106, at 682-83.

131. Smith op. cit. n.86, at 288f.; Bowers, op. cit. n.86, at 397; Swanstrom, op. cit. n.5, at 304-5; Stewart, op. cit. n.86, at 482; *Aurora*, Apr. 4, 1800.

132. 10 *Annals* at 53, 62, 63, 68; Smith, op. cit. n.86, at 300; Bowers, op. cit. n.86, at 442-43.

133. 10 *Annals* at 87; Smith, op. cit. n.86, at 290-92.

134. 10 *Annals* at 86; cf. Id. at 68, 69, 84, 88. By "officers" Tracy meant not senators but clerks and the like.

135. Id. at 109-112, 121-25; Smith, op. cit. n.86, at 295-98; Miller, op. cit. n.98, at 199-201; Swanstrom, op. cit. n.5, at 217-22, 306-8. Curiously, it appears that this outcome was accomplished only because Jefferson broke a crucial tie by voting against Duane and for the privileges of the Senate! *Aurora*, Mar. 27, 1800; Miller, op. cit., at 201. It is difficult to say whether this was done out of reverence for the Senate or with an eye to his presidential campaign. Soon after, Jefferson had another chance to break a tie vote involving Duane, and this time he voted to require the Senate to accept and read a petition on behalf of that gentleman; see 10

Annals at 180; *Aurora,* May 13, 1800; Smith, op. cit., at 300. These actions well illustrate the extraordinary subtleties of Jefferson's thought.

136. 10 *Annals* at 183–84; Smith, op. cit. n.86, at 301–5; Miller, op. cit. n.98, at 201. Duane was able to continue publishing the *Aurora* at this time, and there is some question as to how serious were the Senate's efforts to apprehend him; see ops. cit. n.135.

137. Several likely suspects denied having supplied Duane with information. The Senate showed no inclination to dispute these denials or to pursue the matter further. See 10 *Annals* at 92 (Pinckney); Id. at 88 (Bloodworth); Smith, op. cit. n.86, at 288; Swanstrom, op. cit. n.5, at 302, 306.

138. Executive officers might conceivably be immune while in office, but surely are not so upon removal. The limited immunity of legislators under Article 1, section 6 would not bar punishment by the legislature itself—see ch. 7, under "Afterword" —nor did it prevent the prosecution of Matthew Lyon for sedition, n.123 above. In connection with a debate in the House on the possibility of impeaching Sen. Blount, Gallatin had made these observations:

> An argument had been adduced in favor of impeachment of a Senator, from that body having free access to the Executive records. This assertion was not correct; as he recollected a case in which the Senate applied to the President for certain papers, which, if they had free access to his record, they would not have had occasion to have requested. He also recollected that the request was only granted in part. He believed indeed that some Senators, as well as some members of the House, might, by special favor of the Secretary of State, have access to this record, but he believed it might be refused to the members of either House.

7 *Annals* at 415, July 6, 1797. These remarks represent the clearest instance discovered of allusion to the Gouverneur Morris episode as a precedent. The claim that the State Department did not generally permit legislators to inspect its records seems dubious; cf. ch. 5, under "Jay's Mission," and n.171.

139. The right to prove truth as a defense had been espoused by liberal American thinkers as early as the Zenger case in 1735 and was by now generally accepted. It proved of little use in the sedition trials, where the truth of *opinions* could not be established to judicial satisfaction. See Levy, op. cit. n.121, at 47–51.

140. So far had the Federalist attitude changed that by 1798 Steven Higginson, noting the need of a "popular" form of government for "constant and convincing displays of the wisdom and rectitude of public measures," actually proposed that the government engage two or three full-time publicists to bring its case to the people. This proposal was way ahead of its time. Gibbs, op. cit. n.13, Vol. 2 at 178.

141. For Jefferson on judicial review, see Miller, op. cit. n.98, at 139; C. Warren, *Supreme Court in United States History* (Little Brown 1922), Vol. 1 at 82, 215f. On nullification, see Miller, op. cit., at 166–77; Bowers, op. cit. n.86, at 407–10; Cunningham, op. cit. n.89, at 126f.

142. The effect of the Sedition Law on the 1798 elections is disputed. Compare

Chambers, op. cit. n.1, at 141–42; Dauer, op. cit. n.44, at 233; and Cunningham, op. cit. n.89, at 133 with Wharton, op. cit. n.106, at 26; and Miller, op. cit. n.98, at 178.

143. Charles, op. cit. n.2, at 138; Chambers, op. cit. n.1, at 143.

144. Chambers, op. cit. n.1, at 149; Cunningham, op. cit. n.89, at 142.

145. A. De Conde, *The Quasi-War* (Scribner's 1966). The Supreme Court recognized the legal status of undeclared or imperfect war in Bas v. Tingy, 4 Dall. (4 U.S.) 37 (1800).

146. Gibbs, op. cit. n.13, Vol. 2 at 170 (Wolcott to Adams); Id. at 51 (Ames to Wolcott); 70 (Higginson to Wolcott); and 109 (Cabot to Wolcott); Bowers, op. cit. n.86, at 438.

147. Gibbs, op. cit. n.13, Vol. 2 at 210; Bowers, op. cit. n.86, at 429–30.

148. See, e.g., Miller, op. cit. n.98, at 71; cf. Smith, op. cit. n.86, at 152, 181; see Bell, op. cit. n.5, at 165–77, for a very complex analysis of issue-oriented voting blocs in the Fifth Congress.

149. Gibbs, op. cit. n.13, Vol. 2 at 50, 224; Charles, op. cit. n.2, at 59–62, 133–34. The intrigues included various Carribean and Latin American operations in concert with England; see Charles, op. cit., at 134; Bowers, op. cit. n.86, at 427; 8 *Works of Adams* (Adams ed.) at 635n.

150. 9 *Annals* at 2420; 1 *Works of Adams* (Adams ed.) at 535f.; 8 Id. at 621–23; Gibbs, op. cit. n.13, Vol. 2 at 180; Ford, op. cit. n.15, at 230.

151. 9 *Annals* at 2907–14. In form the resolution, like that calling for the XYZ papers, was a "request" without qualification.

152. 9 *Annals* at 2915. A more detailed breakdown yields some interesting points. The fifty-two members supporting this call included forty Republicans and twelve Federalists. Of those twelve, some were old friends of publicity and some were new converts. Grove of North Carolina had supported Livingston's resolution and the XYZ call as well; so had Parker of Virginia. Both, however, had voted for the Sedition Law. Seven other Federalists, mostly from the South, had come over to the side of publicity during the XYZ episode and adhered to that position now. These included, notably, Harper of South Carolina, who had vehemently opposed Livingston's resolution, but found a principled basis for distinguishing the XYZ call; Allen of Connecticut, who continued to support publicity, though many had impugned his motives for doing so in the XYZ case; and Matthews of Maryland, who had voted against the Sedition Law as well. (The others in this group of seven were Baer of Maryland, Bayard of Delaware, Chapman of Pennsylvania, and Thomas Pinckney of South Carolina. A tenth Federalist supporting this call, Spaight of North Carolina, had missed the XYZ vote. Finally, two Federalists who had opposed the XYZ call now came over to the pro-publicity side. These were Bullock of Massachusetts and Schureman of New Jersey. Bullock was another of the three Federalists who voted against the Sedition Law; see Bell, op. cit. n.5, at 166. In all, about one-fourth of the House Federalists were now prepared to support calls for papers even when there was no obvious political advantage in so doing.

The thirty-eight members voting against the present call included one pseudo-

Republican, Tillinghast of Rhode Island, who had opposed the XYZ call and voted for the Sedition Law; see Bell, op. cit., at 166. The thirty-seven Federalists so voting included eleven old hands who had opposed both Livingston's resolution and the XYZ call; a twelfth who had opposed Livingston's resolution and missed the XYZ vote; and seven newer members, not present in 1796, who had opposed the XYZ call. Another eight Federalists had not participated in either of the earlier votes. All twenty-seven of these men, therefore, had consistently negative stands on congressional calls for papers.

Ten other Federalists were more complex in their conduct. Eight of them had supported the XYZ call; their opposition to the present call suggests that their votes in 1798 had been motivated by expediency only. The same inference applies to Williams of New York, who had opposed Livingston's resolution, supported the XYZ call, and now reverted to the conservative side. The most mysterious case of all is Dent of Maryland, who had supported Livingston's resolution and the XYZ call and even voted against the Sedition Law. Why Dent should have opposed the present call for papers is beyond my imagination to explain.

153. 9 *Annals* at 2917. The retaliation bill passed by a vote of 56-30; see Id. at 3052.

154. 1 *Executive Journal* at 313.

155. Pickering and Wolcott claimed to have had no forewarning, yet Pickering had been asked by Adams to draft a treaty proposal on the supposition that France might send an envoy. See Gibbs, op. cit. n.13, Vol. 2 at 187. Talleyrand's letter had reached the president on January 31; see 1 *Works of Adams* (Adams ed.) at 542. It was sent to Congress February 18 and became public only the following summer when Citizen Pichon secured its publication in a Virginia newspaper—a proceeding which apparently led to no legal action against the publisher. On the leak, see Id. at 541n.; 9 Id. at 247; Gibbs, op. cit., Vol. 2 at 249.

156. See 1 *Executive Journal* at 317-18, 326-27; Iredell, op. cit. n.93, Vol. 2 at 513, 531; Wharton, op. cit. n.106, at 38-39; Gibbs, op. cit. n.13, Vol. 2 at 204, 223; Swanstrom, op. cit. n.5, at 110, 126, 300; Dauer, op. cit. n.44, at 238.

157. Gibbs, op. cit. n.13, Vol. 2 at 251, 263f.; 1 *Works of Adams* (Adams ed.) at 550f.

158. Gibbs, op. cit. n.13, Vol. 2 at 267-68, 277-80; Charles, op. cit. n.2, at 62-64.

159. 1 *Executive Journal* at 359.

160. Gibbs, op. cit. n.13, Vol. 2 at 458.

161. Smith's *National Intelligencer*, Dec. 19, 1800 (not in *Executive Journal*).

162. 1 *Executive Journal* at 361, 383. A treaty with Prussia was submitted to the Senate on December 6, 1799, only ten days before the French Convention; in that case the president made no secrecy request. Later the Senate asked for the negotiator's instructions, and these were supplied, again without any special request for secrecy. Id. at 326, 339-40.

163. Hayden, op. cit. n.24, at 115-18, 125 n.1, states flatly that the convention was inconsistent with the envoys' instructions.

164. 1 *Executive Journal* at 361.

165. Hayden, op. cit. n.24, at 126; Swanstrom, op. cit. n.5, at 191-92.

166. Credible projections of the election results were circulating by December 11; see Letter of Gouverneur Morris in A. Morris ed., *Diary & Letters of Gouverneur Morris* (Scribner's 1888), Vol. 2 at 396.

167. In a letter of January 26, Morris wrote that the party alignment would apparently be fifteen to fifteen, with two "feeble members upon whom no dependence can be placed"; Id. at 402. The actual lineup proved to be eighteen Republicans and fourteen Federalists; Chambers, op. cit. n.1, at 182.

168. See Swanstrom, op. cit. n.5, at 312, for indications that Jefferson entertained such ideas.

169. The Senate did in fact reassert its independence in 1826; see 2 *Register of Debates in Congress* at 142-46; cf. ch. 7, under "Afterword."

170. Bowers, op. cit. n.86, at 456; Chambers, op. cit. n.1, at 148; White, op. cit. n.12, at 250-52.

171. Gibbs, op. cit. n.13, Vol. 2 at 416; cf. Id. at 376, 397, 421 and 430. Hamilton also proposed to obtain State Department records through the good offices of congressional allies, but there was doubt among the plotters as to whether congressmen in fact had access. That recent cabinet officers were uncertain about the applicable rule suggests that actual practice was extremely informal. See Gibbs, op. cit., at 447-48, 456-57; cf. n.138.

172. Id. at 429; Smith, op. cit. n.86, at 405 n.61; Stewart, op. cit. n.86, at 481. Thomas Cooper, himself a recent victim of the Sedition Law, demanded that Hamilton be prosecuted for libeling the president, but Adams did not choose to take such drastic action. *Aurora*, Dec. 31, 1800; D. Malone, *Threatened Prosecution of Hamilton under Sedition Act,* 29 Am. Hist. Rev. 76 (Oct. 1923).

173. Gibbs, op. cit. n.13, Vol. 2 at 209-14, 426.

174. Compare Miller, op. cit. n.98, at 134, 230; Smith, op. cit. n.86, at 431-32; Charles, op. cit. n.2, at 135f.; Stewart, op. cit. n.86, at 486; Cunningham, op. cit. n.89, at 219-28, 249-57; Chambers, op. cit. n.1, at 141, 150-60.

175. For full discussion, see Cunningham, op. cit. n.89, at 249f.; W. Chambers and W. D. Burnham, eds., *The American Party Systems: Stages of Political Development* (Oxford University Press 1967), chs. 1, 3 and 10; Charles, op. cit. n.2, at 137f.; Chambers, op. cit. n.1, ch.1 and passim; Bell, op. cit. n.5, ch. 1, ch. 3 at 53f., ch. 6 at 146 and ch. 7.

Chapter 7

1. See N. E. Cunningham, *The Jeffersonian Republicans* (Greenwood 1973), at 249; W. Chambers & W. D. Burnham, eds., *The American Party Systems: Stages of Political Development* (Oxford University Press 1967), chs. 1, 3 and 10; J. Charles, *Origins of the American Party System* (Harper & Row 1961), at 137f.; W. Chambers, *Political Parties in a New Nation* (Oxford University Press 1963).

Some interesting remarks on the dysfunctionalities of the electoral cycle are offered by Wheeler, in F. Greenstein and N. Polsby, eds., *Governmental Institutions and Processes* (Addison Wesley 1975), ch. 1 at 6.

Young argues that the constitutional structure left the presidency at the mercy of congressional and cabinet factions, until the party system gave presidents their own popular constituency; see J. S. Young, *The Washington Community 1800-1823* (Harcourt Brace 1966). On the other hand, the rules of the game gave him plenary power to instruct, select, and remove department heads. The important restraints on the realization of this control came less from the formal legislative, impeachment, and appointing powers of Congress than from the practical needs of specific presidents to work amicably with specific other influentials in or out of Congress. In the Federalist period, except for the closing years of Adams's term, these constraints were not a very important inhibition on presidential freedom of action.

2. Mr. Justice Goldberg, in Kennedy v. Mendoza-Martinez, 372 U.S. 144 (1962).

3. Compare the insights of modern writers, such as G. Simmel, *The Secret and the Secret Society*, in K. Wolff, ed., *The Sociology of Georg Simmel*, part 4 (Free Press 1950); M. Weber, *Wirtschaft und Gesellschaft*, part 3, ch. 6, in H. Gerth and C. W. Mills, eds., *From Max Weber* (Oxford University Press 1973), ch. 8 at 232–35; R. Merton, *Social Theory and Social Structure* (Free Press 1957), at 199–202; H. Wilensky, *Organizational Intelligence* (Basic Books 1967); Lon Fuller, *Governmental Secrecy and the Forms of Social Order*, in C. Friedrich, ed., *Community* (Nomos II), ch. 15 (Liberal Arts Press 1959); C. Friedrich, *Constitutional Government and Democracy* (Rev. ed. 1950); M. Halperin, *Bureaucratic Politics and Foreign Policy* (Brookings 1974), chs. 9 and 10.

4. For structural perspectives, see J. March, *Handbook of Organizations* (Rand McNally 1965), ch. 18 at 785; Weber, op. cit. n.3; Wilensky, op. cit. n.3; F. Rourke, *Secrecy & Publicity* (Johns Hopkins University Press 1961); L. Pye, *Politics, Personality & Nation Building* (Yale University Press 1962), at 27; N. Polsby, *The Institutionalization of the United States House of Representatives*, 62 Amer. Rol. Sci. Rev. 144 (1968).

5. For theoretical statements, compare Wilensky, op. cit. n.3, at 128-29, 138-39; M. Goldschmidt, *Publicity, Privacy, and Secrecy*, 7 Western Pol. Q. 401, 403 (1954); R. Dahl and C. Lindblom, *Politics, Economics and Welfare* (Harper 1953), at 260-61; Simmel, op. cit. n.3, at 336n.; J. Habermas, *Legitimation Crisis* (Beacon 1975), at 11-12; Greenstein and Polsby, op. cit. n.1, ch. 3 at 234.

6. Anthony King, in Greenstein and Polsby, op. cit. n.1, at 234, remarks that "No one has explored to what extent congressmen and senators adopt. . . a posture . . . as defenders of Congress's prerogatives per se against executive encroachments. This possibility has never been systematically investigated."

7. For good general treatments, see Chambers, op. cit. n.1, at 150f.; Cunningham, op. cit. n.1, at 144f.; C. G. Bowers, *Jefferson and Hamilton* (Houghton Mifflin 1925), at 445f.

8. Reference should be made to a finding of Lowi that party cohesion tends to be strongest on "procedural" issues; see Chambers and Burnham, op. cit. n.1, at 270. If secrecy issues, such as resolutions calling for papers are "procedural," our data do not support this generalization. Some secrecy-related votes followed

strict party lines, but more often than not at least one party would split on such issues; see ch. 6, nn. 81 and 152.

9. See ch. 6, under "From Secrecy to Sedition." For perspectives on the role of party in the Federalist period, see Chambers and Burnham, op. cit. n.1; Cunningham, op. cit. n.1; R. M. Bell, *Party and Faction in American Politics: The House of Representatives, 1789-1801* (Greenwood 1973).

10. *The Federalist,* No. 51.

11. For proposed amendments, see ch. 2, under "Ambiguities and Demands for Change"; ch. 5, under "Jay's Treaty." For legislative proposals, see ch. 5 under "Livingston's Resolution"; ch. 6, under "From Secrecy to Sedition." I have found just two occasions when adjudication was mentioned as a possibility in the Federalist years. Several representatives referred to it in the 1789 House debate on the president's power to remove department heads. There was no specific objection raised, but neither was the idea taken up. See R. Berger, *Congress V. The Supreme Court* (Harvard University Press 1969), at 145-49. Hamilton suggested to Washington that the constitutionality of Jay's Treaty might be adjudicated if Congress so desired; again, the suggestion was simply ignored. See ch. 5, under "Defiance and Legal Impasse." Cf. ch. 4, n.84 on the Supreme Court's refusal to provide advisory opinions on points of international law at the time of the Neutrality Proclamation. For theoretical remarks on the importance of having a final arbiter in a control system, see March, op. cit. n.4, at 905; L. L. Whyte, *Hierarchical Structures* (Elsevier 1969), at 225.

12. A. M. Schlesinger, Jr., *The Imperial Presidency* (Houghton Mifflin 1973); R. Dahl, *A Preface to Democratic Theory* (University of Chicago Press 1956); and for radical views, see R. Lefcourt, ed., *Law Against the People* (Random House 1971); M. Cain and A. Hunt, *Marx and Engels on Law* (Academic Press 1979).

13. In Kocourek & Wigmore, eds., *Formative Influence of Legal Development,* Evolution of Law series, Vol. 3 (Little Brown 1918), ch. 17 at 440.

14. The contrary proposition seems implicit in many treatments. See, e.g., L. Coser, *The Functions of Social Conflict* (Free Press 1956), at 123f.; L. Coser, *Continuities in the Study of Social Conflict* (Free Press 1967); Kocourek and Wigmore, op. cit. n.13; Simmel, op. cit. n.3, at 365; Weber, op. cit. n.3; Polsby, op. cit. n.4; N. Polsby, *Legislatures,* in Greenstein and Polsby, op. cit. n.1; Chambers, op. cit. n.1, at 15, 36, 124; Sullivan, Pressman, and Arterton, *Explorations in Convention Decision Making* (W. H. Freeman 1976), at 38-39; Wilensky, op. cit. n.3, at 39; T. Parsons, *An Outline of the Social System,* in Parsons et al., *Theories of Society* (Free Press 1965), at 40, 41, 45, 55-59, 68-72, 75.

15. For an interesting treatment on perceptions of the rule of law in eighteenth century England, see J. Brewer and J. Styles, eds., *An Ungovernable People* (Rutgers University Press 1980), Introduction and ch. 4.

16. C. Black, *The People and the Court* (Macmillan 1960), at 47-48.

17. Id. at 49-50; see also L. Fuller, *The Morality of Law* (Yale University Press 1954), at 39f.

18. For a suggestive theoretical treatment of differential decisionmaking costs, see T. Sowell, *Knowledge and Decisions* (Basic Books 1980), ch. 2. The lines be-

tween purely ad hoc decisions, decisions involving informal rules or precedents, and those involving formal rules or precedents may not always be clear in practice. One key indicator of institutionalization of a rule or precedent, surely, is its reduction to written form, a practice thought by some theorists to be increasingly common as systems "modernize." Kocourek and Wigmore, op. cit. n.13, chs. 23 and 25. As for the effect of institutionalization, the argument would seem to be that it makes the rule or precedent less ambiguous and more resistant to change, but the claim deserves careful empirical study.

19. The importance of class barriers and class conflict in understanding secrecy behavior has been noted by Habermas, op. cit. n.5, at 116, 123, 132-34; J. Habermas, *A Theory of Communicative Competence,* 13 Inquiry 360 (1970); B. Nelson, *Community,* in Friedrich, ed., op. cit. n.3; Simmel, op. cit. n.3; Coser, *Continuities,* op. cit. n.14; H. Nieburg, *Culture Storm* (St. Martin's 1973); and S. M. Lipset, *The First New Nation* (Doubleday 1967). Lipset seems to imply that procedural regularity is an elitist value and that active public participation in politics is thus inimical to the rule of law; op. cit. at 308. Surely this is not invariably so, but it is likely to be true when public opinion is poorly socialized in liberal ideology, polarized on important substantive policy questions, and when governing institutions are "arenas" mirroring the lines of social cleavage, rather than "transformative" agencies run by a cohesive and autonomous leadership group. For this last distinction, see Polsby, op. cit. n.4.

20. According to Habermas, op. cit. n.5, at 111-12, a separated powers system is conducive to compromise, not to discursive conflict resolution. This may imply a movement away from formal rulemaking.

21. R. Berger, *Executive Privilege: A Constitutional Myth* (Harvard University Press 1974), at 167.

22. Nixon v. Administrator of General Services, 433 U.S. 425, 510 (1977) (Burger, C. J., dissenting). The remark is quoted from a dictum of Justice Sutherland in 1936, the inspiration for which is not known. Thus folly perpetuates itself.

23. Compare R. Swanstrom, *The Senate, 1787-1801* (US GPO, Sen. Doc. No. 64, 1962), at 142; L. Henkin, *Foreign Affairs and the Constitution* (Foundation Press 1972), at 161; D. Frohnmayer, *An Essay on Executive Privilege,* Cong. Rec., Apr. 30, 1974, at S6603; J. R. Wiggins, *Freedom or Secrecy* (Oxford University Press 1964), at 258-59; Berger, op. cit. n.21, at 178-79.

24. See W. P. Rogers, *Constitutional Law: The Papers of the Executive Branch,* 44 Amer. Bar Ass'n. J. 941 (1958); Berger, op. cit. n.21.

25. See discussion at ch. 4, under "The Gouverneur Morris Investigation," ch. 4, under "Conclusions," and ch. 6, under "The XYZ Affair." Compare Wiggins, op. cit. n.23; Frohnmayer, op. cit. n.23; Henkin, op. cit. n.23; Schlesinger op. cit. n.12, at 55, 91, 377; J. W. Howard, *Constitutional Limitation & American Foreign Policy,* in G. Dietze, ed., *Essays on the American Constitution* (Prentice-Hall 1964).

26. On "private" correspondence, see A. Sofaer, *War, Foreign Affairs, and Constitutional Power: The Origins* (Ballinger 1976), at 93, 177-82, 236-37, 248-49; on appropriations control, see L. D. White, *The Federalists* (Macmillan 1948),

at 326-34, 342-43; and see 6 *Annals of Congress* (hereinafter *Annals*) at 1668, 2027, 2040f., 2163f., 2224f., 2292f., 2321f., 2341f., 2355f. for relevant incidents. The Senate had no standing committees as yet; see Swanstrom, op. cit. n.23, at 226n. For a new reporting requirement imposed on the Treasury as late as 1800, see G. Gibbs, *Memoirs of the Administrations of Washington and John Adams* (Van Norden 1846),Vol. 2 at 341.

27. See ch. 6, n. 171; White, op. cit. n.26 at 501.

28. 6 *Annals* at 1914f., 2235, 2320; 7 Id. at 440, 447, 458; State Dep't Domestic Letters, Vol. 10, National Archives, entries of Sept. 14, Nov. 18, Dec. 28, 1797; Randolph's remarks at ch. 4, under "Foreign Crisis and the Politics of Executive Publicity"; and McHenry's at ch. 6, under "The XYZ Affair."

29. See ch. 6, under "The Federalist Schism and the Electoral Remedy," and ch. 7, under "Afterword."

30. See ch. 3, under "The Executive Branch," ch. 5, under "Jay's Mission," and under "Jay's Treaty," for some choice instances of leaking and indiscretion.

31. See ch. 6, under "From Secrecy to Sedition."

32. Domestic Letters, op. cit. n.28, entries of Feb. 3, Mar. 23, Apr. 4 and 16, 1799; Gibbs, op. cit. n.26, Vol. 2 at 344; White, op. cit. n.26, at 506.

33. White, op. cit. n.26, at 501; Gibbs, op. cit. n.26, Vol. 2 at 461-62. The right was subject perhaps to exception in cases where state secrets were involved; Id. at 480. In 1841 a federal court held that Washington's papers were private property and the copyright belonged to his estate; Folsom v. Marsh, 9 Fed. Cas. 342 (No. 4901), 2 Story 100 (C.C.D. Mass. 1841). No question of executive privilege, of congressional power to regulate the disposition of official papers, or of the people's right to know was before the court. Indeed, Judge Story felt that to recognize the copyright was to provide an important incentive for publication—the profit motive.

34. For secret House proceedings, see ch. 3, under "confidentiality and Executive Privilege," ch. 4, under "Foreign Crisis and the Politics of Executive Publicity" and "The Amendment of the House's Standing Order"; on the Senate Journals, see ch. 3, under "The Senate." In January, 1797, a proposal to establish a third Senate journal for secret legislative proceedings was rejected; 6 *Annals* at 1537.

35. 6 *Annals* at 1895; 7 Id. at 238-39, 332-33, 377, 408, 466; for examples from later years, see Sofaer, op. cit. n.26, at 305, 319, 324; 5 I. Brant, *James Madison* (Bobbs Merrill 1956), at 427, 431, 474.

36. Bowers, op. cit. n.7, at 502; 10 *Annals* at 1009.

37. Official stenographers were first proposed by Gerry in 1792; see E. G. McPherson, *Reporting the Debates of Congress,* 1942 Quarterly J. of Speech 141, 142-43, (Apr. 1942); D. H. Stewart, *The Opposition Press of the Federalist Period* (State University of New York Press 1969), at 459-60; White, op. cit. n.22, at 499-500. Members' concern over inaccurate reporting was incessant; indeed, errors were made inevitable by the poor facilities available to reporters; see *Aurora,* Dec. 12, 1795, Feb. 2 and 23, 1796. The refusal to appoint official reporters was repeatedly reaffirmed; see 6 *Annals* at 1590, 1597, 1608, 1607-11; Id. at 671, 687; 10 Id. at 797-816.

38. See 7 *Annals* 38; Swanstrom, op. cit. n.23, at 250-51; and E. G. McPherson, *The Southern States and the Reporting of Senate Debates, 1789-1802,* 12 J. Southern Hist. 223, 239-40 (May 1946) for material on the Senate's policy. Duane was expelled from the House in 1797; see G. Hildreth, *History of the United States* (Harper & Cross 1880), Vol. 5 at 411; Bache, likewise in February 1798; see *Aurora,* Feb. 14 and Mar. 27, 1798; J. M. Smith, *Freedom's Fetters* (Cornell University Press 1956), at 190 (episode misdated); and Samuel Harrison Smith in 1801; see Hildreth, op. cit. See also 8 *Annals* 1294 for a fleeting reference to the Duane expulsion; 7 Id. at 1036, 1044, 1068, 8 Id. at 1283-95 for the aftermath of the Bache expulsion; and 10 Id. at 1036-41 for the Smith affair.

39. See ch. 6, under "From Secrecy to Sedition."

40. See 7 *Annals* at 458 (Blount impeachment inquiry). For another instance of executive guidance on congressional secrecy, see Domestic Letters, op. cit. n.28, entry of Dec. 28, 1797.

41. See ch. 6, under "The XYZ Affair."

42. See ch. 7, under "Afterword."

43. All-Federalist committees were common in the Senate in view of a principle that opponents of a measure should not be assigned to work on it. Swanstrom, op. cit. n.23, at 22-29.

44. Duane charged that Charles Pinckney had been excluded from deliberations on the Ross elections bill of 1800, but Pinckney admitted this was untrue. In view of the practice noted in n.43, one wonders how Pinkney had come to be a member of the committee in the first place.

45. See ch. 6, under "From Secrecy to Sedition," and ch. 7, under "Afterword."

46. See generally F. Wharton, *State Trials of the United States in the Administrations of Washington and John Adams* (Carey & Hart 1849); Smith, op. cit. n.38; and J. C. Miller, *Crisis in Freedom: The Alien and Sedition Acts* (Little Brown 1951); for a view more sympathetic to the Federalists, see Gibbs, op. cit. n. 26, Vol. 2 at 73f. One of the more flagrantly silly trials was that of Jedediah Peck, whose crime was to circulate (not to author) a petition declaring the Sedition Law unconstitutional and urging its repeal. See Smith, op. cit., at 393; Bowers, op. cit. n.7, at 402. See also New York Times Co. v. Sullivan, 376 U.S. 254 (1964).

47. The attitude of the Senate in the early years bespoke a different set of priorities; see ch. 3, under "The Senate." It is interesting that John Adams received such a large share of the blame for this, in light of his open and candid conduct of the presidency for most of his term. The liberalization in Adams's attitude highlights the powerful democratizing forces at work in the 1790s.

48. This remained true and bedeviling to the government even at a later period, as is stressed by Young, op. cit. n.1. For a study of the integrative role of publicity before the Revolution, see R. Merritt, *Symbols of American Community 1735-1775* (Yale University Press 1966).

49. L. Levy, *Jefferson and Civil Liberties* (Quadrangle 1963), at 49.

50. N. E. Cunningham, *The Making of the American Party System, 1789-1809* (Prentice-Hall 1965), at 160.

51. Since the research for this time period has relied mainly on secondary sources, the interpretations offered must be taken with an extra grain of salt.

52. Sofaer, op. cit. n.26, at 177, 196-97 and notes; Schlesinger, op. cit. n.12, at 35; S. T. Gabis, *Secrecy in Politics: A Study in Attitudes* (Ph.D. Diss., University of Chicago, Department of Political Science, 1957).

53. Sofaer, op. cit. n.26, at 189, 238, 305f., 319, 324f., 330f.

54. Id. at 246-47 and notes; 22 *Annals* at 65-83; cf. 2 *Register of Debates in Congress* at 142-46 (Feb. 1826).

55. 22 *Annals* at 76.

56. Brant, op. cit. n.35, Vol. 5 at 481.

57. On Jefferson's policies, see Sofaer, op. cit. n.26, at 196f.; Levy, op. cit. n.49, chs. 5 and 6. On 1812, see Sofaer, op. cit., at 236-37, 279-90; Brant, op. cit. n.35, Vol. 5 at 474-81 and passim; and R. Rutland, *Madison's Alternatives* (Lippincott 1975); but see Young, op. cit. n.1, for a "weak presidency" interpretation.

58. For one leak episode, see Rutland, op. cit. n.57, at 79; for the Henry papers episode, see Id. at 134f.

59. None of the Federalists showed any constitutional scruples about the political crimes program, though with hindsight many recognized it was a political mistake. On the other hand, each of the main protagonists was capable of drawing a line somewhere. See Smith, op. cit. n.38, at 145 (Adams); ch. 6, under "From Secrecy to Sedition" (Pickering and Hamilton); and ch. 6, n. 116.

On the Jeffersonians' conduct, see Levy, op. cit. n.49. L. D. White, *The Jeffersonians* (Macmillan 1951), at 95, maintains that they resurrected the Jay precedent; Henkin, op. cit. n.23, at 112, claims that later executive secrecy practices went even beyond the Jay doctrine. Other writers see doctrine and practice as ambiguous and consistent over time; see ops. cit. n.25. For a few minor clarifications and departures of the Jeffersonian era, see Sofaer, op. cit. n.26, at 177 n.48, 180 (unqualified calls addressed to State Dep't); Id. at 254, 358 n.602 (distinction between instructions and correspondence).

60. Marbury v. Madison, 1 Cranch (5 U.S.) 137 (1803).

61. 1 Cranch (5 U.S.) at 143; and see C. Warren, *The Supreme Court in United States History* (Little Brown 1922), Vol. 1 at 232-42; P. Freund, *Foreword on Executive Privilege,* 88 Harvard L. Rev. 1, 21-23 (1974).

62. 1 Cranch (5 U.S.) at 144-45.

63. Id. at 145.

64. 10 *Annals* at 613.

65. Little v. Barreme, 2 Cranch (6 U.S.) 170 (1804).

66. Sofaer, op. cit. n. 26, at 189, 203n.; Brant, op. cit. n.35, Vol. 4 at 323-39; A. Beveridge, *Life of John Marshall* (Houghton Mifflin 1919), Vol. 3 at 436 n.1.

67. Berger, op. cit. n.21, at 190.

68. Id. at 191.

69. Ibid.

70. Compare Id. at 187-91; Sofaer, op. cit. n.26, at 193-95; Warren, op. cit. n.61, Vol. 1 at 301-11; Freund, op. cit. n.61, at 24-31.

71. Warren, op. cit. n.61, Vol. 1 at 266.

72. Levy, op. cit. n.49, at 59.

73. Id. at 66 n.73; see United States v. Hudson & Goodwin, 7 Cranch (11 U.S) 32 (1812).

74. The leading cases are: on congressional power to compel information, Nixon v. Administrator of General Services, 433 U.S. 425 (1977); Senate Select Committee v. Nixon, 498 F.2d 725 (D.C. Cir. 1973); on executive privilege in judicial proceedings, United States v. Nixon, 418 U.S. 683 (1974); and for additional pronouncements on executive secrecy in diverse contexts, Totten v. United States, 92 U.S. 105 (1876); United States v. Curtiss-Wright Corp., 299 U.S. 304 (1936); Civil Aeronautics Bd. v. Waterman S.S. Co., 333 U.S. 103 (1948); New York Times Co. v. United States, 403 U.S. 713 (1971); United States v. Snepp, 62 L.Ed. 2d 704 (1980).

Chapter 8

1. None of the standard accounts—W. P. Rogers, *Constitutional Law: The Papers of the Executive Branch,* 44 Amer. Bar Ass'n J. 941 (1958); J. R. Wiggins, *Freedom or Secrecy* (Oxford University Press 1964); D. Frohnmayer, *An Essay on Executive Privilege,* Cong. Rec., Apr. 30, 1974, at S6603; L. Henkin, *Foreign Affairs and the Constitution* (Foundation Press 1972); A. M. Schlesinger, Jr., *The Imperial Presidency* (Houghton Mifflin 1973); A. Sofaer, *War, Foreign Affairs, and Constitutional Power: The Origins* (Ballinger 1976); R. Berger, *Executive Privilege: A Constitutional Myth* (Harvard University Press 1974)—makes out any major discontinuities in legal development after 1800. Either they argue that what had already been established was reaffirmed and extended, or that the uncertainty surrounding the subject was increased.

2. On the centrality of foreign policy issues in the Federalist period, see P. Goodman and W. D. Burnham, chapters in W. Chambers and W. D. Burnham, eds., *The American Party Systems: Stages of Political Development* (Oxford University Press 1967); J. Charles, *Origins of the American Party System* (Harper and Row 1961).

3. Bas v. Tingy, 4 Dall. (4 U.S.) 37 (1800).

4. See Wiggins, op. cit. n.1; and Schlesinger, op. cit. n.1 for details.

5. War Powers Resolution, Public Law 93-148, 93d Cong., House Joint Res. 542, Nov. 7, 1973, 87 *Statutes at Large* 555-60; Freedom of Information Act, 5 U.S.C. sec. 552, as amended by Public Law 93-502, 88 *Statutes at Large* 1561-64. Additional legislative proposals designed to strengthen constitutional restraints are discussed in M. Halperin and D. Hoffman, *Top Secret* (New Republic Books 1977).

6. See 18 U.S.C. secs. 792f., 2381f., 9371; 22 U.S.C. secs. 601f.; 42 U.S.C. secs. 2256f.; 50 U.S.C. secs. 781f. for the most important provisions.

7. See United States v. Russo and Ellsberg, No. 9373-WMB-CD (C.D. Cal. 1972); United States v. Snepp, 62 L. Ed. 2d 704 (1980); United States v. Marchetti, 466 F.2d 1309 (4th Cir. 1972). The constitutional arguments against these sorts of proceedings are elaborated in Halperin and Hoffman, op. cit. n.5, Appendices A and B; M. Halperin and D. Hoffman, *Freedom VS. National Security* (Chelsea House 1977).

BIBLIOGRAPHY

Primary Sources

Manuscript and Microfilm Sources

British Public Records Office Collection, Library of Congress: Series FO5, Vols. 4 and 5; Series FO115, Vol. 3(Mss.).

Congressional Archives, National Archives: President's Message to Senate, Feb. 26, 1794, RG46 (Mss.); Reports of House Select Committees, RG233, Vol. 1 (Bound).

Miscellaneous, National Archives: Correspondence of the Attorneys General, RG60 (Microfilm); Records of the United States District Courts, RG21 (Mss.).

State Department Archives, RG59, National Archives: Domestic Letters (Microfilm M40); Dispatches from Foreign Ministers—France (Microfilm M34); Presidential Correspondence (Microfilm M570); Reports of Secretaries of State to President and Congress, Vol. 2 (Bound).

Washington Mss., Library of Congress: Series 4, Reels 101, 105 and 109 (Microfilm).

Records of Official Proceedings (Chronological)

Journals of the Continental Congress (Washington 1904-1937).

Secret Journals of the Continental Congress, 1785-1788 (Boston 1821).

Diplomatic Correspondence of the American Revolution (Wharton ed. 1889).

Records of the Federal Convention (Farrand ed. 1911).

Debates in the Several State Conventions on the Adoption of the Federal Constitution (Elliot ed. 1836).

The Federal and State Constitutions (Thorpe ed. 1909).

Annals of Congress, 1789-1824 (Washington 1834).
Register of Debates in Congress, 1825-37 (Washington 1825-1837).
Journal of the House of Representatives (official) (Philadelphia 1826).
Executive Journal of the Senate (official) (Washington 1828).
Legislative Journal of the Senate (official) (Philadelphia 1820).
American State Papers (Gales & Seaton 1832): *Finance,* Vol. 1; *Foreign Relations,*
    Vols. 1 and 2; *Miscellaneous,* Vol. 1.

Court Decisions

Bas v. Tingy, 4 Dall. (4 U.S.) 37 (1800).
Civil Aeronautics Bd. v. Waterman S.S. Corp., 333 U.S. 103 (1948).
Environmental Protection Agency v. Mink, 410 U.S. 73 (1973).
Folsom v. Marsh, 9 Fed. Cas. 342 (No. 4901), 2 Story 100 (C.C.D. Mass. 1841).
Kennedy v. Mendoza-Martinez, 372 U.S. 144 (1962).
Knopf v. Colby, 509 F. 2d 1362 (4th Cir. 1975).
Little v. Barreme, 2 Cranch (6 U.S.) 170 (1804).
Marbury v. Madison, 1 Cranch (5 U.S.) 137 (1803).
New York Times Co. v. Sullivan, 376 U.S. 254 (1964).
New York Times Co. v. United States, 403 U.S. 713 (1971).
Nixon v. Administrator of General Services, 433 U.S. 425 (1977).
Nixon v. Sirica, 487 F.2d 700 (D.C. Cir. 1973).
Senate Select Committee v. Nixon, 498 F.2d 725 (D.C. Cir. 1973).
Snepp v. United States, 62 L.Ed. 2d 704 (1980).
Totten v. United States, 92 U.S. 105 (1876).
United States v. Burr, 25 Fed. Cas. 30, 55, 187 (C.C.D. Va. 1807).
United States v. Curtiss-Wright Export Corp., 399 U.S. 304 (1936).
United States v. Hudson & Goodwin, 7 Cranch (11 U.S.) 32 (1812).
United States v. Marchetti, 466 F.2d 1309 (4th Cir. 1972).
United States v. Nixon, 418 U.S. 683 (1974).
United States v. Reynolds, 345 U.S. 1 (1953).
United States v. Russo & Ellsberg, No. 9373-WMB-CD (C.D. Cal. 1972).
United States v. Smith, 27 Fed. Cas. 1192 (No. 16, 342) (C.C.D. N.Y. 1806).

Published Papers and Correspondence

Letters of John Adams (Adams ed. 1841).
Works of John Adams (Adams ed. 1850).
Writings of John Adams (Ford ed. 1913).
Works of Fisher Ames (Ames ed. 1854).
Papers of Alexander Hamilton (Syrett ed. 1962-1979).
Works of Alexander Hamilton (Lodge ed. 1904).
Works of Alexander Hamilton (Hamilton ed. 1850).
Life and Correspondence of James Iredell (McRee ed. 1858).
Correspondence and Papers of John Jay (Johnston ed. 1890).
Writings of Thomas Jefferson (Ford ed. 1892).

Writings of Thomas Jefferson (Lipscomb ed. 1903).
Life and Correspondence of Rufus King (King ed. 1894).
Letters and Other Writings of James Madison (Cong. ed. 1865).
Writings of James Madison (Hunt ed. 1900).
Life and Correspondence of James McHenry (Steiner ed. 1907).
Writings of James Monroe (Hamilton ed. 1893).
Diary and Letters of Gouverneur Morris (Morris ed. 1888).
Life and Correspondence of Gouverneur Morris (Sparks ed. 1832).
Writings of George Washington (Fitzpatrick ed. 1940).
Writings of George Washington (Ford ed. 1889).
Memoirs of the Administrations of Washington and John Adams (Wolcott papers)
        (Gibbs ed. 1846).
Letters of Members of the Continental Congress (Burnett ed. 1933).
The Federalist (Rossiter ed. 1961).

Newspapers

Baltimore Federal Intelligencer & Daily Gazette.
(Boston) *Columbian Centinel.*
Boston Gazette.
(Boston) *Independent Chronicle.*
Mt. Pleasant & New Jersey Chronicle.
New London Bee.
(New York) *Argus* (Thomas Greenleaf).
New York Journal & Patriotic Register (Thomas Greenleaf).
Norfolk, Va., American Gazette & General Advertiser.
(Philadelphia) *Aurora* (Benjamin Franklin Bache/ William Duane).
Philadelphia Gazette.
(Philadelphia) *Gazette of the United States.*
Philadelphia General Advertiser (Benjamin Franklin Bache).
Philadelphia Independent Gazeteer.
(Philadelphia) *Porcupine's Gazette* (William Cobbett).
(Philadelphia) *National Gazette.*
Providence, R.I., US Chronicle.
Richmond Va. & Manchester Advertiser.
(Washington, D.C.) *National Intelligencer.*

Secondary Sources

Books

Arendt, H. *Crises of the Republic* (Harcourt Brace 1972).
Bell, R. M. *Party and Faction in American Politics: The House of Representatives,
        1789-1801* (Greenwood 1973).

Bemis, S. F. *Jay's Treaty* (Yale University Press 1962).

Bemis, S. F., ed. *American Secretaries of State and their Diplomacy* (Knopf 1927).

Berger, R. *Congress V. the Supreme Court* (Harvard University Press 1969).

Berger, R. *Executive Privilege: A Constitutional Myth* (Harvard University Press 1974).

Beveridge, A. *Life of John Marshall* (Houghton Mifflin 1919).

Black, C. *The People and the Court* (Macmillan 1960).

Bowers, C. G. *Jefferson and Hamilton* (Houghton Mifflin 1925).

Bowman, A. *The Struggle for Neutrality* (University of Tennessee Press 1974).

Boyd, J. P. *Number Seven: Alexander Hamilton's Secret Attempts to Control American Foreign Policy* (Princeton University Press 1964).

Brant, I. *James Madison* (Bobbs Merrill 1956).

Brewer, J. and J. Styles. *An Ungovernable People* (Rutgers University Press 1980).

Brigham, J. *Constitutional Language* (Greenwood 1978).

Cain, M. and A. Hunt, *Marx and Engels on Law* (Academic Press 1979).

Caldwell, L. K. *The Administrative Theories of Hamilton and Jefferson* (Russell & Russell 1964).

Cardozo, B. *The Nature of the Judicial Process* (Yale University Press 1971).

Chambers, W. *Political Parties in a New Nation* (Oxford University Press 1963).

Chambers, W. and W. D. Burnham, eds. *The American Party Systems* (Oxford 1967).

Charles, J. *The Origins of the American Party System* (Harper & Row 1961).

Clegg, S. *Power, Rule and Domination* (Routledge & Kegan Paul 1975).

Clegg, S. *The Theory of Power and Organization* (Routledge & Kegan Paul 1979).

Corwin, E. *Court Over Constitution* (Princeton University Press 1938).

Corwin, E. *The President: Office and Powers* (New York University Press 1957).

Coser, L. *Continuities in the Study of Social Conflict* (Free Press 1967).

Coser, L. *The Functions of Social Conflict* (Free Press 1956).

Cunningham, N. E. *The Jeffersonian Republicans* (University of North Carolina Press 1963).

Cunningham, N. E. *The Making of the American Party System, 1789-1809* (Prentice-Hall 1965).

Dahl, R. *A Preface to Democratic Theory* (University of Chicago Press 1956).

Dahl, R. and C. Lindblom. *Politics, Economics, and Welfare* (Harper 1953).

Dauer, M. *The Adams Federalists* (Johns Hopkins University Press 1953).

De Conde, A. *The Quasi-War* (Scribner's 1966).

Dietze, G., ed. *Essays on the American Constitution* (Prentice-Hall 1964).

Dorsen, N. and S. Gillers. *None of Your Business* (Viking 1974).

Ernst, R. *Rufus King* (University of North Carolina Press 1969).

Evan, W. *The Sociology of Law* (Free Press 1980).

Farrand, M. *The Framing of the Constitution* (Yale University Press 1913).

Faÿ, B. *Two Franklins* (Little Brown 1933).

Ferguson, E. J. *The Power of the Purse* (University of North Carolina Press 1961).

Franck, T. and E. Weisband. *Secrecy and Foreign Policy* (Oxford University Press 1974).

Friedman, L., ed. *United States V. Nixon* (Chelsea House 1974).

Friedrich, C. *Constitutional Government and Democracy* (Rev. ed. 1950).
Friedrich, C. *Constitutional Reason of State* (Brown University Press 1957).
Friedrich, C. *The Pathology of Politics: Violence, Betrayal, Corruption, Secrecy & Propaganda* (Harper & Row 1972).
Friedrich, C., ed. *Community* (Nomos 2) (Liberal Arts Press 1959).
Fuller, L. *The Morality of Law* (Yale University Press 1964).
Gabis, S. T. *Secrecy in Politics: A Study in Attitudes* (Ph.D. Dissertation, University of Chicago, Department of Political Science, 1957).
Gerth, H. and C. W. Mills, eds. *From Max Weber* (Oxford University Press 1973).
Goebel, J. *History of the Supreme Court of the United States*, Vol. 1 (Macmillan 1971).
Greenstein, F. and N. Polsby, eds. *Governmental Institutions and Processes* (Addison Wesley 1975).
Gwyn, W. *The Meaning of the Separation of Powers* (Tulane University Press 1965).
Habermas, J. *Legitimation Crisis* (Beacon 1975).
Halperin, M. *Bureaucratic Politics and Foreign Policy* (Brookings 1974).
Halperin, M. and D. N. Hoffman. *Freedom VS. National Security* (Chelsea House 1977).
Halperin, M. and D. N. Hoffman. *Top Secret* (New Republic Books 1977).
Hayden, R. *The Senate and Treaties, 1789-1817* (Da Capo 1970).
Henkin, L. *Foreign Affairs and the Constitution* (Foundation 1972).
Hildreth, R. *History of the United States* (Harper & Cross 1880).
Hinds, A. *Precedents of the House of Representatives* (US GPO 1907).
Kocourek, A. and J. Wigmore, eds. *Formative Influence of Legal Development* (Little Brown 1918).
Lasswell, H. *National Security and Individual Freedom* (McGraw Hill 1950).
Lefcourt, R., ed. *Law Against the People* (Vintage 1971).
Levy, L. W. *Jefferson and Civil Liberties* (Quadrangle 1973).
Levy, L. W., ed. *Essays on the Making of the Constitution* (Oxford University Press 1969).
Lipset, S. *The First New Nation* (Doubleday 1967).
Luetscher, G. *Early Political Machinery in the United States* (Philadelphia 1903).
Maclay, W. *Sketches of Debate in the First Senate of the United States* (Burt Franklin 1969).
March, J. *Handbook of Organizations* (Rand McNally 1965).
Mason, A. *The Supreme Court* (University of Michigan Press 1962).
Merritt, R. *Symbols of American Community 1735-1775* (Yale University Press 1966).
Merton, R. *Social Theory and Social Structure* (Free Press 1957).
Miller, J. C. *Crisis in Freedom: The Alien and Sedition Acts* (Little Brown 1951).
Mitchell, B. *Alexander Hamilton* (Macmillan 1962).
Mott, F. *American Journalism* (Macmillan 1962).
Nichols, R. *The Invention of the American Political Parties* (Macmillan 1967).
Nieburg, H. *Culture Storm* (St. Martin's 1973).
Nieburg, H. *Nuclear Secrecy and Foreign Policy* (Public Affairs 1964).
Parsons, T. et. al. *Theories of Society* (Free Press 1965).

Pennock, J. and J. Chapman, eds. *Constitutionalism* (Nomos 20) (New York University Press 1979).

Pye, L. *Politics, Personality and Nation Building* (Yale University Press 1962).

Rawls, J. *A Theory of Justice* (Harvard University Press 1971).

Reardon, J. J. *Edmund Randolph* (Macmillan 1974).

Rourke, F. *Secrecy & Publicity* (John Hopkins University Press 1961).

Rutland, R. *Madison's Alternatives* (Lippincott 1975).

Scheingold, S. *The Politics of Rights* (Yale University Press 1974).

Schwartz, B., ed. *The Bill of Rights: A Documentary History* (Chelsea House 1971).

Shils, E. *The Torment of Secrecy* (Free Press 1956).

Smith, J. M. *Freedom's Fetters* (Cornell University Press 1956).

Sofaer, A. *War, Foreign Affairs and Constitutional Power: The Origins* (Ballinger 1976).

Sowell, T. *Knowledge and Decisions* (Basic Books 1980).

Stewart, D. *The Opposition Press of the Federalist Period* (State University of New York Press 1969).

Sullivan, D., J. Pressman and C. Arterton, *Explorations in Convention Decision Making* (W. H. Freeman 1976).

Swanstrom, R. *The Senate, 1787-1801* (US GPO, Senate Doc. No. 64, 1962).

Thomas, C. M. *American Neutrality in 1793* (Columbia University Press 1931).

Thompson, J. and S. Padover. *Secret Diplomacy 1500-1815* (F. Ungar 1963).

Tugwell, R. *The Compromising of the Constitution: Early Departures* (Notre Dame University Press).

Vile, M. J. C. *Constitutionalism and the Separation of Powers* (Clarendon 1967).

Walther, D. *Gouverneur Morris, Witness of Two Revolutions* (Funk & Wagnall's 1934).

Warren, C. *The Supreme Court in United States History* (Little Brown 1922).

Wharton, F. *State Trials of the United States in the Administrations of Washington and John Adams* (Cary & Hart 1849).

White, L. D. *The Federalists* (Macmillan 1948).

White, L. D. *The Jeffersonians* (Macmillan 1951).

Whyte, L. L. *Hierarchical Structures* (Elsevier 1969).

Wiggins, J. R. *Freedom or Secrecy* (Oxford University Press 1964).

Wilensky, H. *Organizational Intelligence* (Basic Books 1967).

Wise, D. *The Politics of Lying* (Random House 1973).

Wolff, K., ed. *The Sociology of Georg Simmel* (Free Press 1950).

Wolff, R. P., ed. *The Rule of Law* (Simon & Schuster 1971).

Young, J. S. *The Washington Community, 1800-1828* (Harcourt Brace 1966).

Articles

Berger, R. *Executive Privilege v. Congressional Inquiry,* 12 U.C.L.A. Law Rev. 1044 (1965).

Bishop, J. *The Executive's Right of Privacy: An Unresolved Constitutional Question*, 66 Yale Law J. 477 (1957).

Brant, I. *Edmund Randolph: Not Guilty!* 7 William & Mary Q., 3d Ser. (Apr. 1950).

Collins, P. *The Power of Congressional Committees of Investigation To Obtain Information From the Executive Branch*, 39 Georgetown Law J. 563 (1951).

Coser, L. *Dysfunctions of Military Secrecy*, 11 Social Problems 13 (1963).

Freund, P. *Foreword on Executive Privilege*, 88 Harvard Law Rev. 1 (1974).

Frohnmayer, D. *An Essay on Executive Privilege*, Cong. Rec., Apr. 30, 1974, at S6603.

Goldschmidt, M. *Publicity, Privacy, and Secrecy*, 7 Western Pol. Q. 401 (1954).

Habermas, J. *A Theory of Communicative Competence*, 13 Inquiry 360 (1970).

Kramer, R. and H. Marcuse. *Executive Privilege—A Study of the Period 1953-1960*, 29 George Washington Law Rev. 623, 827 (1961).

Landis, J. *Constitutional Limitations on the Congressional Power of Investigation*, 40 Harvard Law Rev. 153 (1926).

Lowry, R. *Toward A Sociology of Secrecy and Security Systems*, 19 Social Problems 1 (1972).

McPherson, E. G. *Reporting the Debates of Congress*, 1942 Quarterly J. of Speech 141 (1942).

McPherson, E. G. *Reports of the Debates of the House of Representatives During the First Congress, 1789-1791*, 1944 Quarterly J. of Speech 64 (1944).

McPherson, E. G. *The Southern States and the Reporting of Senate Debates*, 12 J. Southern Hist. 223 (1946).

Malone, D. *Threatened Prosecution of Hamilton Under Sedition Act*, 29 Amer. Hist. Rev. 76 (1923).

Mitchell, J. *Government Secrecy in Theory and Practice*, 58 Columbia Law Rev. 199 (1958).

Parry, C. *Legislatures and Secrecy*, 67 Harvard Law Rev. 737 (1954).

Philos, C. *The Public's Right To Know and the Public Interest*, 19 Federal Bar J. 41 (1959).

Polsby, N. *The Institutionalization of the United States House of Representatives*, 62 Amer. Pol. Sci. Rev. 144 (1968).

Potts, C. *Power of Legislative Bodies to Punish for Contempt*, 74 U. Pa. Law Rev. 691 (1926).

Rice, H. C. *James Swan: Agent of the French Republic, 1794-96*, 10 New England Q. 464 (1937).

Rogers, W. P. *Constitutional Law: The Papers of the Executive Branch*, 44 Amer. Bar Ass'n J. 941 (1958).

Ruebhausen, O. and O. Brim. *Privacy and Behavioral Research*, 65 Columbia Law Rev. 1184 (1965).

Schwartz, B. *Executive Privilege and Congressional Investigatory Power*, 47 California Law Rev. 3 (1959).

Smelser, M. *George Washington and the Alien & Sedition Acts*, 59 Amer. Hist. Rev. 322 (1954).

Sofaer, A. *Executive Privilege*, 75 Columbia Law Rev. 1318 (1975).

Sofaer, A. *The Presidency, War, and Foreign Affairs: Practice Under the Framers*, 40 Law & Cont. Problems 12 (1976).

Sofaer, A. *Review of Berger's "Executive Privilege"*, 88 Harvard Law Rev. 281 (1974).

United States v. Nixon (Symposium), 22 U.C.L.A. Law Rev. 4 (1974).

Wiggins, J. R. *Government Operations and the Public's Right to Know*, 19 Federal Bar J. 62 (1959).

Wills, G. *The Founders' Virtues*, New York Rev. of Books, Nov. 11, 1976.

Wofford, H. *The Blinding Light: The Uses of History in Constitutional Interpretation*, 31 U. Chicago Law Rev. 502 (1964).

Wolkinson, H. *Demands of Congressional Committees for Executive Papers*, 10 Federal Bar J. 103 (1949).

Younger, I. *Congressional Investigation and Executive Secrecy: A Study in the Separation of Powers*, 20 U. Pittsburgh Law Rev. 755 (1959).

INDEX

Carroll, Charles, 275 n56

Censorship, 5, 9, 117, 127, 143, 236-38, 253, 258. *See also* Executive privilege

Censure, congressional: of administrators, 120; of journalists, 208, 241; of legislators, 15, 147, 241-42, 247, 290n71. *See also* Immunity

Central Intelligence Agency, 262

Chapman, John, 307 n152

Chase, Samuel, 182

Checks and balances: in constitutional design, 19, 33, 39, 233; and courts, 249; and international crisis, 226; and Jay's mission, 134; and Madison's conduct, 110, 143, 237; and one-party rule, 219-20, 222; assessment, 227, 255-56, 259. *See also* Separation of powers

Civil War, 258

Class. *See* Conflict, class; Elitist politics

Clay, Henry, 247

Clopton, John, 304n119

Cobbet, William, 201-4, 303n115

Coit, Joshua, 155

Colonial period, 13-14

Commander-in-chief clause, 32

Commerce, regulation of, 33, 54, 100, 146; embargoes, 103, 131, 248

Confidential communications: declassification by Congress, 16, 94-95, 100-104, 125-26, 156, 179, 192, 215, 236, 239, 241-42, 247, 281 n60; and French convention, 215; and Morris investigation, 111, 116, 127; origin of practice, 69-70; and pending

negotiations, 91, 96, 126-27; and XYZ affair, 188, 193; assessment, 234, 236, 238. *See also* House of Representatives; Injunctions of secrecy; Senate

Conflict: class, 12-13, 17-19, 46, 77, 177, 179, 228, 233, 243, 312n19; domestic, 7, 16, 115, 129, 168, 196; international, 7, 10, 13, 32, 84, 88-89, 115, 129, 168, 174, 211, 222, 226, 228, 233, 257 (*see also* War); and legalization, 230-31; sectional, 14, 16, 17-19, 22, 29, 46, 58, 81, 87, 96, 104, 172, 179, 228, 248, 274n48, 275n60, 286n10. *See also* Checks and balances; Elitist politics; Parties; Separation of powers

Congress: Confederation (old Congress), 14-16, 24, 37, 134, 155, 301n97; Continental, 14; United States, 4, 9-10, 24-29, 55; First Congress, 6, 37-38, 44, 47-48, 54, 72, 79; Second Congress, 53, 72, 76, 118, 120; Third Congress, 72, 91, 118, 121, 125, 222, 235; Fourth Congress, 140, 222, 293n113; special sessions, 34-35, 89-90, 144, 183-84. *See also* Calls for information; House of Representatives; Investigations; Recess of Congress; Senate; *specific powers and functions*

Constitutional Convention, 19-33, 154, 158, 165, 168, 170, 193, 269n23, 274n49, 288n35. *See also* Framers of the Constitution

Constitutions: of the states, 14, 32, 37; of the United States,

Gouverneur Morris and, 112, 126, 236; and Great Britain, 89, 131; and Jay's Treaty, 137, 179; and Louisiana purchase, 246; message to Congress by, 64; peace overtures by, 199, 213-14; and Republican party, 149-50, 173, 198, 208, 248; revolution in, 229, 231; and Spain, 201; trade with, 54; treaty with, 54, 115, 197; war with, 197, 211-13, 242; and XYZ affair, 183-84, 186-87, 194, 196

Franking privilege, 49-50

Freedom of Information Act, 259

Freeman, Nathaniel, 298 n69

Freneau's *National Gazette*, 52

Fries' rebellion, 206

Gallatin, Albert, 85-86, 117, 133, 189, 191, 195, 205, 238, 282 n68, 293 n104, 298 n66, 306 n138

Genêt, Edmond, 90-91, 94-96, 106, 111, 115, 132, 140-41, 149, 203, 281 n67, 301 n97

George III, 13

Gerry, Elbridge, 27-29, 38, 184, 199, 204, 212, 273 n19, 273 n22, 300 n93

Giles, William, 72, 102, 119-20, 188, 298 n66

Goodhue, Benjamin, 273 n21

Grand Inquest. *See* Impeachment; Investigations; Oversight function of Congress

Great Britain: and France, 89-90, 144, 213; and Hamilton, 46-47, 89, 135-36, 144, 174, 212; negotiations with, 46-47, 55, 91-92, 104, 131, 134-35, 145; peace of 1783 with, 16-17; publicity in, 13, 204, 231; and Randolph, 148, 150; and Republican party, 132, 140, 173, 201, 237; secret agents of, 46-47, 150, 206, 208; trade with, 54; and War of 1812, 247-48

Greenleaf, Thomas, 141, 200-201, 204

Greenleaf's *Argus*, 201

Greenleaf's *New York Journal*, 200

Grenville, Lord William, 136, 144, 148

Grove, William, 298 n69, 307 n152

Gunn, James, 275 n56, 275 n60, 290 n64

Habeas Corpus, 253

Hamilton, Alexander: and Adams, 181, 192, 211-12, 217-19; and Burr, 252; early activities, 44-47, 52-55, 63, 68, 78, 80-81; and the founding, 14, 15, 18, 21, 34, 36-37; and Hamilton investigations, 118-24, 126-27; and Jay's mission, 132-33, 135-37, 147, 150, 174, 291 n77, 293 n114; and Livingston's resolution, 158, 161-65, 167-69, 171, 295 n145; and Louisiana, 246; and Morris investigation, 105, 108; and Neutrality, 89-91, 93, 95; resignation from cabinet, 142; and St. Clair episode, 70, 72-76; and Sedition law, 205; and Washington, 45-46, 78, 123, 133, 139, 142, 158, 212; and Whiskey rebellion, 139-40; and XYZ affair, 186-88, 192; assessment, 142-44, 223, 230, 234-35

About the Author

DANIEL N. HOFFMAN is Assistant Professor of Political Science at the University of Vermont in Burlington. He is the coauthor (with Morton H. Halperin) of *Top Secret* and *Freedom VS. National Security*.